Murray Brothers

Qaulity Helm & Fighting Chairs

-  **Fighting Chairs**
- **Fishing Chairs**
- **Helm Chairs**
- **Rocket Launchers**
- **Hi-Lo Tables**
- **Casual Furniture**

FACTORY
1306 53rd Street
West Palm Beach, Florida 33407
407-845-1366 • Fax 407-844-4355

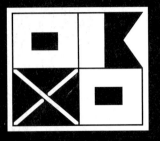

TOM FEXAS DESIGN ADVANTAGES

- **Higher Speeds/Longer Range**
- **Wider Beam/More Living Space**
- **More Stability/Easy Handling**
- **Best Materials/Finest Quality**
- **Customizing is our Speciality!**

	MIKELSON 72	MIKELSON 78
LOA	72' 06"	77' 01"
BEAM	20' 06"	20' 06"
FUEL	3000 gal.	3000 gal
POWER	MTU 1150 hp.	MTU 1150 hp.

MANUFACTURED IN SAN DIEGO

MIKELSON 50

LOA	50' 05"
BEAM	16' 08"
FUEL	1000 gal.
POWER	435/600 hp.

MIKELSON 60

LOA	59' 01"
BEAM	17' 02"
FUEL	1000 gal.
POWER	750/820 hp.

MIKELSON/YACHTS

SEE US AT THE MIAMI BOAT SHOW!
MARRIOT SLIP #303

Mikelson Yachts, Inc. MAIN OFFICE 2330 Shelter Island Drive #202, San Diego, CA 92106 • 619/222-5007 • FAX 619/223-1194
EAST COAST Mikelson Yacht Sales of Florida, Inc. P.O. Box 70; Indian Rocks Beach, FL 34635 • 813/596-2941 • FAX 813/596-2813

1996
EDITION

The McKnew/Parker
Consumer's Guide to

SPORTFISHING
BOATS

28'–82'

1975–Current

From the Editors of the POWERBOAT GUIDE
Ed McKnew & Mark Parker

International Marine
Camden, Maine

PUBLISHED BY
International Marine
A Division of The McGraw-Hill Companies
Camden, Maine 04843
1-800-822-8158

COMPILED BY
American Marine Publishing, Inc.
P.O. Box 30577
Palm Beach Gardens, FL 33420
1-800-832-0038

FOR ADVERTISING INFORMATION
Contact Ben Wofford, Director of Advertising
407-624-8100 • Fax 407-627-6636

ISBN 0-07-045496-5

Printed and bound in the United States of America.

Table of Contents

Introduction . . . .*xix*

About the Authors . . . .*xx*

Acknowledgments . . . .*xxi*

How to Use This Book . . . .*xxiii*

Frequently Asked Questions . . . .*xxv*

Useful Terms . . . .*xxxi*

Directory of Yacht Brokers & Dealers 1

Directory of Marine Surveyors 13

Albemarle 30 Express 23

Albemarle 32 Flybridge 23

Albemarle 32 Express 24

Albin 28 Tournament 24

Albin 32 Sportfisher 25

Atlantic 34 Sportsman 25

Bertram 28 Flybridge Cruiser 27

Bertram 28 Sportfisherman 27

Bertram 28 Bahia Mar 28

Bertram 28 Moppie 28

Bertram 30 Flybridge Cruiser 29

Bertram 30 Moppie 30

Bertram 31 Flybridge Cruiser 31

Bertram 31 Sportfisherman 31

Bertram 31 Bahia Mar 32

Bertram 33 Flybridge Cruiser 32

Bertram 33 Sportfisherman 33

Bertram 35 Convertible 33

Bertram 37 Convertible 34

Bertram 38 Convertible 34

Bertram 38 III Convertible 35

Bcrtram 38 Special 35

Bertram 42 Convertible 36

Bertram 43 Convertible 37

Bertram 43 Moppie 38

Bertram 46 Convertible (Early) 39

Contents, cont.

Bertram 46 Convertible 40
Bertram 46 Moppie 42
Bertram 50 Convertible 44
Bertram 54 Convertible 45
Bertram 58 Convertible 46
Bertram 60 Convertible 46
Bertram 72 Convertible 47
Bimini 29 Sportfisherman 47
Black Watch 30 Sportfisherman 48
Black Watch 30 Flybridge 48
Black Watch 36 Flybridge 49
Blackfin 29 Combi 51
Blackfin 29 Flybridge 51
Blackfin 31 Combi 52
Blackfin 32 Sportfisherman 52
Blackfin 32 Combi 53
Blackfin 33 Sportfisherman 53
Blackfin 33 Flybridge 54
Blackfin 33 Combi 54
Blackfin 38 Combi 55
Blackfin 38 Convertible 56
Boston Whaler 31 Sportfisherman 57
Brendan 28 Sportfisherman 57
Cabo 31 Express 59
Cabo 35 Flybridge 59
Cabo 35 Express 60
Californian 35 Convertible 60
Californian 38 Convertible 61
Californian 42 Convertible 61
Californian 48 Convertible 62
Carolina Classic 28 62
Chase 38 Sportfisherman 63
Cheoy Lee 48 Sport Yacht 63
Cheoy Lee 50 Sport Yacht 64
Cheoy Lee 58 Sport Yacht 64

Contents, cont.

Cheoy Lee 66 Sport Yacht 65
Cheoy Lee 70 Sportfisherman 65
Chris Craft 30 Tournament Sportfisherman 66
Chris Craft 315 Sport Sedan 66
Chris Craft 360 Sport Sedan 67
Chris Craft 382/392 Commander 68
Chris Craft 422 Sport Sedan 69
Chris Craft 45 Commander 70
Chris Craft 482 Convertible 70
Contender 35 71
Cruisers 3210 Sea Devil 71
Davis 44 Sportfisherman 72
Davis 44 Express 72
Davis 47 Sportfisherman 73
Davis 61 Sportfisherman 74
Dawson 33 Express 74
Dawson 38 Sportfisherman 75
Delta 36 Sportfisherman 76
Delta 38 Sportfisherman 76
Donzi F-33 78
Donzi 65 Sportfisherman 78
Dorado 30 79
Duffy 35 Sport Cruiser 80
Duffy 42 Sport Cruiser 80
Dyer 29 81
Egg Harbor 33 Sedan 83
Egg Harbor 33 Convertible 84
Egg Harbor 34/35 Golden Egg 85
Egg Harbor 36 Sedan 86
Egg Harbor 37 Convertible 87
Egg Harbor 38 Golden Egg 88
Egg Harbor 40 Sedan 89
Egg Harbor 41 Sportfisherman 90
Egg Harbor 42 Golden Egg 91
Egg Harbor 43 Sportfisherman 92

Contents, cont.

Egg Harbor 46 Sedan 93
Egg Harbor 48 Sportfisherman 94
Egg Harbor 54 Golden Egg 95
Egg Harbor 58 Golden Egg 96
Egg Harbor 60 Convertible 97
Fountain 27/29 Center Console 98
Fountain 27/29 SF Cruiser 99
Fountain 8.8M/31 Center Console 100
Fountain 31/32 SF Cruiser 101
Gamefisherman 34 102
Gamefisherman 40 102
Garlington 44 103
Grady-White 280/300 Marlin 103
Hatteras 32 Flybridge & Express SF 105
Hatteras 36 Convertible (Early) 106
Hatteras 36 Convertible 106
Hatteras 36 Sedan Cruiser 107
Hatteras 36 Sportfisherman 107
Hatteras 37 Convertible 108
Hatteras 38 Convertible 108
Hatteras 39 Convertible 109
Hatteras 39 Sport Exp. 110
Hatteras 41 Convertible 111
Hatteras 42 Convertible 111
Hatteras 43 Convertible (Early) 112
Hatteras 43 Convertible 113
Hatteras 45 Convertible (Early) 113
Hatteras 45 Convertible 114
Hatteras 46 Convertible (Early) 115
Hatteras 46 Convertible 116
Hatteras 48 Convertible 116
Hatteras 50 Convertible (Early) 118
Hatteras 50 Convertible (Current) 118
Hatteras 52 Convertible 120
Hatteras 53 Convertible 121

Contents, cont.

Hatteras 54 Convertible 122
Hatteras 55 Convertible 123
Hatteras 58 Convertible 124
Hatteras 60 Convertible 125
Hatteras 65 Convertible 126
Hatteras 82 Convertible 126
Henriques 28 Express Fisherman 128
Henriques 35 Main Coaster 129
Henriques 38 Sportfisherman 130
Henriques 38 El Bravo 130
Henriques 44 Sportfisherman 131
Hydra-Sports 2800 Sportfisherman 131
Hydra-Sports 3300 Sportfisherman 132
Innovator 31 132
Intrepid 30 Open 133
Intrepid 31 Walkaround 133
Intrepid 33 Cuddy 134
Intrepid 38 Evolution 134
Island Gypsy 32 Fisherman 135
Jefferson FS 35 136
Jersey 36 Convertible 136
Jersey 40 Dawn Convertible 137
Jersey Devil 44 Sportfisherman 137
Jersey 42/44 Convertible SF 138
Jersey 47 Convertible 138
Jupiter 31 Center Console 139
Luhrs Tournament 290 (Early) 141
Luhrs Tournament 290 141
Luhrs Tournament 290 Open 142
Luhrs Alura 30 142
Luhrs Tournament 300 143
Luhrs Tournament 320 143
Luhrs Tournament 320 Open 144
Luhrs 340 Sportfisherman 144
Luhrs Tournament 342 145

Contents, cont.

Luhrs Alura 35 145
Luhrs Tournament 350 146
Luhrs Tournament 380 146
Luhrs Tournament 380 Open 147
Luhrs Tournament 400 147
Mako 282 Center Console 148
Mako 286 Inboard 148
Mako 263/293 Walkaround 149
Mako 295 Dual Console 149
Marlin 350 Sportfisherman 150
Mediterranean 38 Convertible 152
Mediterranean 54 Convertible 152
Mikelson 48 Sedan & 50 Sportfisher 153
Mikelson 60 Sportfisher 154
Mikelson 72 Sportfisher 154
Nauset 35 Sport Cruiser 155
North Coast 31 Sportfisherman .155
Ocean 29 Super Sport 156
Ocean 32 Super Sport 156
Ocean 35 Super Sport 157
Ocean 35 Sport Cruiser & Sportfisherman 158
Ocean 38 Super Sport (Early) 159
Ocean 38 Super Sport 159
Ocean 40 Super Sport 160
Ocean 42 Super Sport (Early) 160
Ocean 42 Super Sport 161
Ocean 44 Super Sport 161
Ocean 46 Super Sport 162
Ocean 48 Super Sport (1986-90) 162
Ocean 48 Super Sport (1991-94) 163
Ocean 48 Super Sport (Current) 163
Ocean 50 Super Sport 164
Ocean 53 Super Sport 164
Ocean 55 Super Sport 166
Ocean 58 Super Sport 166

Contents, cont.

Ocean 63 Super Sport 167

Ocean 66 Super Sport 167

Ocean Master 31 Center Console 168

Orca 36 170

Pace 36 Sportfisherman 170

Pace 40 Sportfisherman 171

Pace 48 Sportfisherman 171

Pacemaker 30 Sportfisherman 172

Pacemaker 34 Convertible 172

Pacemaker 36 Sportfisherman 173

Pacemaker 37 Sportfisherman 173

Pacemaker 38 Sportfisherman 174

Pacemaker 40 Sportfisherman 175

Pacemaker 48 Sportfisherman 177

Pacifica 36 Sportfisherman 179

Pacifica 44 Sportfisherman 179

Phoenix 29 Convertible 181

Phoenix 29 SF Convertible 181

Phoenix 33/34 Convertible 182

Phoenix 33/34 Tournament 182

Phoenix 37/38 Convertible 183

Phoenix 38 Convertible 183

Post 42 Sportfisherman 185

Post 43 Sportfisherman (Early) 185

Post 43 Sportfisherman 186

Post 44 Sportfisherman 186

Post 46 Sportfisherman 188

Post 50 Sportfisherman 189

Precision 2800 189

Pro-Line 2950 Mid-Cabin Walkaround 190

Pursuit 2800 Open 190

Pursuit 2855 Express 192

Pursuit 3000 Express 192

Pursuit 3250 Express 193

Radovich 34 Sportfisherman 193

Contents, cont.

Rampage 28 Sportsman 195
Rampage 31 Sportfisherman 195
Rampage 33 Sportfisherman 196
Rampage 36 Sportfisherman 196
Rampage 40 Sportfisherman 197
Riviera 33 Convertible 197
Riviera 36 Convertible 198
Riviera 39 Convertible 198
Riviera 42 Convertible 199
Riviera 48 Convertible 199
Ronin 38 Convertible 200
Ronin 48 Convertible 200
Rybo Runner 30 Center Console 201
Sea Ray 310 Amberjack 201
Sea Ray 310 Sport Bridge 202
Sea Ray 390 Sedan Sportfisherman 202
Sea Ray 440 Convertible 203
Shamrock 31 Grand Slam 203
Silverton 37 Convertible 205
Silverton 41 Convertible 205
Southern Cross 44 Sportfisherman .206
Southern Cross 52 Sportfisherman .206
Stamas 288 Liberty 207
Stamas 290 Express 207
Stamas 290 Tarpon 208
Stamas 310 Express 208
Stamas 32 Sport Sedan & Sportfisherman 209
Stamas 360 Express 210
Stratos 3300 Center Console 210
Strike 29 Sportfisherman 211
Striker 34 Canyon Runner 213
Striker 37 Canyon Runner 213
Striker 41 Sportfisherman 214
Striker 44 Sportfisherman 214
Striker 50 Sportfisherman 215

Contents, cont.

Striker 54 Sportfisherman 215
Striker 58/60 Sportfisherman 216
Striker 62 Sportfisherman 216
Striker 70 Sportfisherman 217
Tiara 2900 Open 219
Tiara 3100 Open (Early) 219
Tiara 3100 Open 220
Tiara 3100 Convertible 220
Tiara 3300 Flybridge 221
Tiara 3300 Open 221
Tiara 3600 Open 222
Tiara 3600 Convertible 222
Tiara 3700 Open 223
Tiara 4300 Convertible 223
Tiara 4300 Open 224
Tollycraft 34 Sport Sedan 224
Tollycraft 37 Convertible 225
Tollycraft 40 Sport Sedan 226
Topaz 29 Sportfisherman 227
Topaz 32 Sportfisherman 227
Topaz 32 Royale 228
Topaz 36 Sportfisherman 228
Topaz 37 Sportfisherman 229
Topaz 38 Flybridge SF 229
Topaz 39 Royale 230
Trojan 36 Convertible 230
Trojan 12 Meter Convertible 231
Uniflite 28 Salty Dog 231
Uniflite 32 Sport Sedan 232
Uniflite 34 Sport Sedan 232
Uniflite 36 Sport Sedan 234
Uniflite 38 Convertible 234
Uniflite 42 Convertible 235
Uniflite 48 Convertible 235
Viking 35 Convertible 237

Contents, cont.

Viking 35 Sportfisherman 238
Viking 38 Convertible 238
Viking 40 Sedan 239
Viking 41 Convertible 240
Viking 43 Convertible 241
Viking 43 Express/Open Fisherman 242
Viking 45 Convertible 243
Viking 46 Convertible 244
Viking 47 Convertible 244
Viking 48 Convertible 245
Viking 50 Convertible 246
Viking 53 Convertible 248
Viking 57 Convertible 250
Viking 58 Convertible 250
Viking 68 Convertible 252
Wellcraft 2800 Coastal 252
Wellcraft 2900 Sport Bridge 253
Wellcraft 3200 Coastal 253
Wellcraft 3300 Coastal 254
Wellcraft 3300 Sport Bridge 254

About These Prices 256
Prices 257

Introduction

This book is written to help buyers sort through the hundreds of different production sportfishing boats, 28 to 82 feet in length, currently available on the nation's new and used markets. Over three hundred popular models are reviewed in these pages—center consoles and cuddys, express fishermen and convertibles, inboards and outboards, and even a couple of jackshaft designs—a wide cross section of sportfishing boats ranging in price from the affordable to the truly opulent. For each, we have included complete factory specifications together with floorplan options, real-world performance data, production history, engine choices and production updates. Throughout, the authors' opinions are freely expressed. Advertising hype notwithstanding, some boats are simply better than others and those that stand out at either extreme are occasionally noted. No attempt has been made to maliciously abuse a particular model, however, and the comments represent nothing more or less than the opinions of the authors. Needless to say, the services of experienced marine professionals are strongly recommended in the sale or purchase of any boat.

The prices quoted in this book reflect the market conditions projected by our staff for 1996. Those wishing to establish a consistent pattern for depreciation will be disappointed: we know of no such schedule. Rather, we have evaluated each model on its own merits and assigned values based on our own research and experience. While we are aware of the prices other appraisal guides assign to various models, we are often in disagreement with those values and believe that our estimates are more reflective of actual resale values. **It is very important to review the section, ABOUT THESE PRICES, on page 256 before referencing the assigned values.** And remember, no matter what the various price guides (including ours) might say, the fact remains that the only real value of a boat is what someone is willing to pay for it on a given day.

The CONSUMER'S GUIDE TO SPORTFISHING BOATS, 28' TO 82', is one of several annual marine publications written by Ed McKnew and Mark Parker. The series is a spin-off of the hugely successful POWERBOAT GUIDE, a marine industry reference compiled annually for the exclusive use of yacht brokers, dealers, lenders and marine surveyors.

We sincerely hope you will find the information in this book to be useful, and we welcome any comments you might care to offer regarding the content or the character of this publication. ❏

About the Authors

 Ed McKnew has been involved in the marine industry since the mid 1970s, first as a yacht broker and later as the owner of several brokerage operations in Michigan and Texas. He holds a business degree from Oakland University in Rochester, Michigan, and worked for several years in the trucking industry before becoming a yacht broker in 1976. Ed currently lives and works in Palm Beach Gardens, Florida, where he and his partner own and operate American Marine Publishing. When he's not writing about boats, Ed spends his spare time pursuing his long-standing interest in the American Civil War.

 Mark Parker has been a boating enthusiast since before he can remember. A graduate of Southwest Texas State University with a degree in marketing, Mark held a USCG Masters license and has captained several large sportfishing boats. He is a native of Texas and worked as a broker in both Texas and Florida for twelve years. He and Ed McKnew began researching the original POWERBOAT GUIDE in 1987, and he has co-edited the project since then. He currently works full time with American Marine Publishing. Mark and his wife, Sherri, reside in Palm Beach Gardens, Florida.

Acknowledgments

We wish to thank the following individuals for their generous support. These are the people who were there to lend assistance in the beginning. Without their help this series of books would never have been published.

Floyd Appling, Jr.

Bill Burgstiner

Steve & Delores Brown

Top & Sandy Cornell

George & Helene Gereke

Edward & Betty Groth

Freddy & Patti Hamlin

How to Use This Book

For the most part, the contents of this book are straightforward and easily understood. Before launching into the pages, however, we strongly suggest that you take a few moments and review the following points. Failure to do so is likely to result in some confusion and misunderstanding.

Factory Specifications

The specifications listed for each model are self-explanatory, although the following factors are noted:

1) *Clearance* refers to bridge clearance, or the height above the waterline to the highest point on the boat. Note that this is often a highly ambiguous piece of information since the manufacturer may or may not include such things as an arch, hardtop, or mast. Use this figure with caution.

2) *Weight* is a factory-provided specification that may or may not be accurate. Manufacturers differ in the way they compute this figure. For the most part, it refers to a dry boat with no gear.

3) *Designer* refers to the designer of the hull only.

4) *NA* means that the information is not available.

Performance Data

Whenever possible, performance figures have been obtained from the manufacturer or a reliable dealer or broker. When such information was unavailable, the authors have relied upon their own research together with actual hands-on experience. The speeds are estimates and (in most cases) based on boats with average loads of fuel, water, options and gear.

All speeds are reported in knots. Readers in the Great Lakes or inland waterways may convert knots to miles-per-hour by multiplying a given figure by 1.14.

Cruising Speeds, Outboard Engines

On average, we calculate the cruising speed of an outboard engine at about 4,000 rpm, or 1,200–1,500 rpm off a motor's top rpm rating.

Cruising Speeds, Gas Engines

Unless otherwise noted, the cruising speed for gas-powered inboard (or stern drive) boats is calculated at 3,000–3,200 rpm.

Cruising Speeds, Diesel Engines

The cruising speeds for diesel-powered boats are calculated as follows:

1) Detroit (2-stroke) Diesels—about 200–250 rpm off the top rpm rating.

2) Other (4-stroke) Diesels—about 350–400 rpm off the manufacturer's maximum rpm rating.

Floorplans

When there are two or more floorplans, the most recent layout comes last.

Pricing Information

Used-boat prices have been compiled from 1975, the base year for our calculations. Boats whose production runs were previous to that year are noted in the Price Schedule with four asterisks (****).

In the Price Schedule, six asterisks (******) indicate that we have insufficient data to render a value for a particular year.

While diesel engines nearly always add significant value to a boat, there are some cases where the differences in the type or horsepower of diesel engines installed in a particular model will seriously affect the average resale value. Those cases in which we believe the diesel options do indeed affect the value of an individual boat have been noted in the Price Schedule.

The Retail High is the average selling price of a clean, well-equipped and well-maintained boat with low-to-moderate engine hours. Boats with an exceptional equipment list or those with unusually low hours will usually sell at a figure higher than the published Retail High.

The Retail Low is the average selling price of a boat with below-average maintenance, poor equipment, high-time engines, or excessive wear. High-time boats in poor condition will generally sell for less than the published Retail Low.

Used boats located in the following markets are generally valued at 10–15% higher than published prices:
1) Great Lakes
2) Pacific Northwest
3) Inland Rivers & Lakes

The prices presented in this book reflect our best estimates of used-boat prices for the model year 1996. They are intended for general use only and are not meant to represent exact market values.

Frequently Asked Questions

In an effort to clear away some of the confusion regarding the purchase of a new or used sportfishing boat, we have listed below some of the more common questions asked by potential buyers. The answers presented to these questions are our own and we welcome responses from others who hold differing views. For the most part, however, we believe the information presented here will address several important issues confronting buyers of boats listed in this publication.

I hear a lot of brokers talking about deep-V hulls. Should I be looking for this in my next boat?

The majority of manufacturers of over-30-foot designs build their boats on modified-V hulls because it provides owners with the best combination of performance, stability, and economy. Other builders specialize in fishing boats with deep-V hulls. It's true that deep-V designs offer superior rough water performance, but at a cost. They tend to roll more at trolling speeds (especially in a beam sea), and they're more sensitive to the added weight of a tower. They also require more power to get up on plane although there's no serious penalty in cruising economy once they're up and running.

Aside from their excellent head-sea capabilities, deep-V hulls generally track much better than modified-V designs of similar length and displacement. A Bertram 46, for example, will require a lot less steering effort in a quartering or following sea than an Ocean 46 or Egg Harbor 54 — boats with relatively flat bottoms. Although less stable at slow speeds, the deep-V is a more stable design at cruising speeds. While a deep-V hull involves some compromise in larger boats (over 30 feet), they are almost the standard in outboard fishing boats.

I've been looking at a boat with prop pockets. What are the advantages and disadvantages of this type of hull?

Prop pockets are used to reduce shaft angles which often results in improved fuel economy and engine efficiency at cruising speeds. Manufacturers like Sea Ray and Phoenix have used them for years. Because prop pockets also reduce draft, a secondary benefit is the ability to operate with less fear of grounding in shallow waters.

One criticism we've often heard of boats with prop pockets is that they don't back down very well since they lack the "bite" that a more exposed propeller can get. Most experienced captains agree that backing a boat with prop pockets—whether "backing down" on a fish or maneuvering in a marina—takes a little more finesse than with a conventional hull.

Are diesel engines worth the extra cost?

Yes. Range is often a factor in sportfishing boats and diesels can deliver up to 50%

more range than a similar gas-powered boat. If diesels are not in the budget, make sure that the speed and range capabilities of a prospective boat are sufficient for the type of running you will be doing.

In a family or express cruiser, the choice between gas and diesel isn't always so clear, but more and more builders are installing diesels in their models under 35 feet. Diesels are becoming more affordable, too, as new technology allows manufacturers to reduce both the size and weight of diesel engines while increasing their performance. At least with sportfishing boats, the resale value of a diesel-powered model will usually go a long way toward justifying the added up-front expense.

I know that engine hours are important but what constitutes a lot of hours on a particular set of motors?

This is always a hard question to answer, so we'll just offer up some general guidelines. When it comes to gas engines (inboards and I/Os), most brokers figure that motors with over 1,000 hours are probably tired. With turbocharged diesels 3,500 hours is a lot of running time, and with naturally aspirated diesels it's not uncommon to pile up 5,000 hours before an overhaul is required. The tragedy is that many of today's ultra-high-performance diesels never see 2,000 hours before an overhaul. Sometimes this is a manufacturer problem, but premature marine diesel death usually results from improper owner care and maintenance. Lack of use and poor exercise habits may be the number-one killer. Humidity (moisture) on cylinder components can be avoided with regular running and engine heaters. Diesel engines should be run under a load whenever possible. If your mechanical surveyor suggests new oil, fuel, or water hoses, do it. Trying to save money here can be expensive.

That said, it's important to note that there are far too many variables to make any buying decisions based upon engine hours alone. It's imperative to have the diesels in a used boat surveyed just as you have the boat itself professionally examined before reaching a final decision. It's not quite so critical with gas engines since they cost far less to rebuild than diesels; however it's always worth the small expense of having a compression test done on gas engines just to see what you're getting into.

Determining the actual hours on an engine (or a set of engines) can be difficult. There are generally hour meters (that often aren't working) installed in boats over 25 feet, but they're not always found in smaller gas-powered boats and outboard models. Even if you have access to all the service records, we strongly suggest that you rely on an expert to evaluate the engines in any boat you have a serious interest in owning.

How can I spot a boat that's been fished hard?

Many owners of expensive sportfishermen employ full-time captains to maintain their vessel to new-boat standards. Generally, how a boat has been maintained will determine what kind of service to expect more than the number of hours she's been fished. It's obvious that a five-year-old Davis 47 with a tuna tower, outriggers, and a full electronics package sitting in Palm Beach with 1,500 hours on the meters has been fished—the question is whether she's been well maintained during her lifetime.

Can I rely on the boat tests that I read in the national magazines?

Yes, they're usually accurate as far as they go. For example, the performance figures—speeds at various rpm's, fuel burn data, etc.—are quite reliable although it's always wise to keep in mind that these are new boats with light loads and plenty of factory preparation. Don't look for a lot of hard-hitting criticism in these tests, however, because most boating publications (including this one) depend upon boat manufacturers for a major part of their advertising revenues.

We've read a lot of boat tests over the years. In our opinion, the best and most comprehensive are conducted by *Boating* magazine. *Sea* and *Sport Fishing* also have some excellent reviews.

Are freshwater boats really worth more?

Sure, no question about it. Salt water is hard on a boat, especially the gelcoat, electronics, paint, metalwork, and engine room components. And while nearly all diesel-powered boats have closed cooling systems, the same is not always true of gas engines. In a saltwater environment it's wise to look for a boat with a closed cooling system since it usually lengthens engine life considerably.

Another reason freshwater boats often bring a premium price has to do with the fact that they generally have fewer engine hours. The boating season in most freshwater regions is shorter than many of the largest saltwater boating areas. Furthermore, the majority of freshwater vessels spend their winters out of the water—many in a protected environment with reduced exposure to the corrosive effects of sun, wind and rain.

As you might imagine, a well-maintained saltwater vessel is probably a better investment than a poorly maintained freshwater boat. One final factor that equalizes the values between the two is equipment. Especially with fishing boats, an East Coast saltwater boat is often outfitted with better equipment and more elaborate electronics.

Should I avoid a boat if the manufacturer has gone out of business or is currently undergoing hard times?

Emphatically, no. There are plenty of good used boats on the market from manufacturers who couldn't survive the poor economy of the past several years. The parts you will need from time to time are always available from catalog outlets or suppliers. Engine parts, of course, are easily secured from a number of sources. Generally speaking, there are no components used in a production model that cannot be replaced (or repaired) by a good service yard.

Note that many of the most popular models on today's brokerage market have been built by companies now out of business.

Why do I see so few Asian-built sport-fishing boats?

While Asian builders have secured a significant share of today's motor yacht market (and near-domination of the market for trawlers), their products have enjoyed very limited success with the hard-core sport-fishing market. Aside from Ronin, Mikelson and Pace, there are very few Taiwanese imports taken seriously among tournament-level anglers on either coast. There's probably a good deal of pro-American sentiment and pride at work here but it's a situation that's not likely to change anytime soon.

Outboard brackets are becoming more and more common. What are the pros and cons?

The benefits of an outboard bracket are increased cockpit space, reduced engine noise, and the ability to trim the boat even farther, thus reducing wetted surface and increasing speed.

The drawbacks inherent in a boat with outboard brackets are reduced fishability (it's harder to get a rod tip out around the motors) and shifted weight distribution. The farther aft the weight load, the harder it is to keep the hull up on plane at slower speeds.

For resale, should I only consider a brand of boat with big-name market recognition?

There is no question that certain popular brands have consistently higher resale values. There are, however, many designs from small or regional builders that are highly sought after by knowledgeable boaters. Often, the market for these models is tighter and generally less saturated than the high production designs—a factor that often works to a seller's advantage.

Why is 27-foot boat with twin 200-hp outboards faster than the same boat with 200-hp inboard engines?

Simple. You can trim outboard engines to gain maximum prop efficiency for speed and conditions. Inboards have fixed shaft angles regardless of speed or sea conditions. Trimming outboards lifts the hull farther out of the water, reducing the wetted surface and drag considerably.

Also, two-stroke outboards are designed for cruising at a higher percentage of maximum rated rpm than the four-stroke gas inboard, and the outboard's horsepower-to-weight ratio is better. It should be said that in rough-water conditions inboard models are generally better designs, as the centralized weight of the engines allows the boat to stay on plane and handle better at much lower speeds than outboard designs.

I'm considering the purchase of a 40' convertible. I've heard several times that I want a fast boat, one that's capable of running 30 knots wide open. How important is that in a fishing boat?

It's nice to have a fast boat—the less time it takes you to get there, the more time you have to fish. Speed is especially important in tournament-level boats where it's often necessary to travel long distances in order to drop a line.

In fact, however, the top speed isn't anywhere near as important as the ability to attain a fast *cruising* speed. (Running wide open for long periods shortens engine life considerably.) A 40-foot boat capable of cruising at 27 knots is considered fast by the standards of most knowledgeable skippers. For a smaller boat with outboards, 40 knots is a fast cruising speed. While a fast boat is nice (and often a measure of efficiency), sea conditions often equalize the speed of the fleet.

I've heard some horror stories about boats with blistered bottoms. Should I reject a boat with blisters or is there a way to address the problem?

Blisters can almost always be repaired although the process can require a fair amount of time and expense. With that in mind, it is rare indeed to see a blistering problem so severe that it actually affects the integrity of the hull.

While some boats tend to re-blister again and again, most bottoms properly dried and protected should remain blister-free for five years or longer.

Are there any significant differences between a West Coast fishing boat and an East Coast model?

The differences are relatively minor. West Coast anglers do a lot of their fishing off the bow, so it's common to see their boats with wider sidedecks and more elaborate pulpits. Too, since the weather is often cooler, many West Coast boats have the helm all the way forward on the bridge—just behind the windscreen—to enjoy some protection from the wind and to better see the foredeck fishing action. Traditional East Coast boats have the helm aft on the bridge so the captain can see the action in the cockpit and handle the boat accordingly.

How important is a lower helm?

That depends upon your location. A lower helm is a great convenience (a luxury, actually) when you're getting an early start on a chilly morning. For visibility (and to avoid seasickness), however, most skippers prefer the bridge station for heavy-weather running. On the other hand, aside from the added expense (which can be considerable), a lower helm takes up room in the salon that would otherwise be devoted to living space. Too, a lower helm requires a front windshield—something a lot of yacht designers and builders have eliminated in their newer models.

Note that a lower helm in Florida (or along the Gulf Coast) is sometimes a hindrance to a boat's resale value since it's often viewed as a useless feature on a fishing boat in a warm climate.

Why would I want a tower on my next boat?

Towers are designed for spotting bait, feeding or traveling gamefish, birds, rip and weed lines, and other changing surface conditions. They are also handy for working through reefs or other underwater obstructions. Many people buy boats with towers because they look good and towers are a lot of fun to ride in.

Consideration should also be given to the fact that towers require substantial maintenance. Proper care in a saltwater environment requires a weekly wash and chamois, periodic waxing, and repairs. Towers also add weight and windage and raise the boat's center of gravity—a design factor of more significance for a flybridge boat than for a low-profile express model.

How much does it cost to fish-rig a new boat or a cruise-equipped used model?

Obviously, this depends on the size of the boat but there are some general guidelines. A full tower for a mid-size flybridge convertible will run between $20,000 and $28,000 including options and accessories. A smaller tower for a 33' express model will run around $12,000–$18,000. A half tower (or hardtop) on the aforementioned convertible will run somewhere between $10,000 and $15,000, and about $6,000–$10,000 for the express. A full-size tuna chair will cost from $5,500 to $8,000. A smaller (marlin) chair should run $4,000–$6,000. Outriggers sell for $2,000–$4,000 depending on length, brand, and number of spreaders.

Electronics are expensive and, given the rapidly changing state of the technology, they will be dated in 4–5 years. Theoretically, the only required piece of electronics needed for serious fishing is a video depth recorder. It's common, however, for fully-equipped fishing boats to be fitted out with more and better electronics than comparably sized cruising boats.

If I decide to buy a used boat, should I use a broker?

If you have plenty of time on your hands you could locate a good boat at a fair price without a broker. Unless you find a boat for sale by the owner, you end up working with a broker anyway — the listing agent.

When choosing a broker consider that you are about to spend a large amount of money. Do your homework and end up with an agent who you feel has your long-term interests at heart. You're not paying for his time and expertise until you purchase a boat through him. Keeping many brokers in competition against one another often results in no one giving you the time and attention that you'll require. ❏

Useful Terms

Abaft—behind

Athwartships—at a right angle to the boat's length

Bulkhead—an upright partition separating compartments in a boat

Bulwark—a raised portion of the deck designed to serve as a barrier

Chine—the point at which the hullsides and the bottom of the boat come together

cid—referring to the cubic inch displacement of an engine, i.e., 454-cid gas engine

Coaming—vertical surface surrounding the cockpit

Cuddy—generally refers to the cabin of a small boat

Deadrise—the angle from the bottom of the hull (not the keel) to the chine

Deep-V Hull—a planing hull form with at least 17° of deadrise at the transom and a fairly constant "V" bottom shape from stem to stern.

Displacement Hull—a hull designed to go through the water and not capable of planing speed

Forefoot—the underwater shape of the hull at the bow

Freeboard—the height of the sides of the hull above the waterline

gph—gallons per hour (of fuel consumption)

Gunwale (also gunnel)— *the upper edge of* the sheerline

Hull Speed—the maximum practical speed of a displacement hull. To calculate, take the square root of the LWL (waterline hull length) and multiply by 1.34.

Knot—one nautical mile per hour. To convert knots to statute mph, multiply by 1.14.

Modified-V Hull—a planing hull form with less than 17° of transom deadrise

Nautical Mile—measurement used in salt water. A nautical mile is 6,076 feet.

Planing Speed—the point at which an accelerating hull rises onto the top of the water. To calculate a hull's planing speed, multiply the square root of the waterline length by 2.

Semi-Displacement Hull—a hull designed to operate economically at low speeds while still able to attain efficient planing speed performance

Sheerline—the fore-and-aft line along the top edge of the hull

Sole—a nautical term for floor

Statute Mile—measurement used in fresh water. A statute mile equals 5,280 feet.

Tender—refers to (a) a dinghy, or (b) lack of stability

Directory of Yacht Brokers & Dealers

(Sorted Alphabetically by State)

ALABAMA

A&M Yacht Sales
5004 Dauphin Island Pkwy.
Mobile, AL 36605
334-471-6949; Fax 334-479-4625
Hatteras, Viking, Bertram

KV Yacht Brokerage
27844 Canal Rd., Sportsman's Marina
Orange Beach, AL 36561
205-981-9600; Fax 205-981-9602

Marine Brokerage Service
201 Blount Ave.
Guntersville, AL 35976
205-582-8529; Fax 205-582-1656

The Marine Group
Orange Beach Marina, PO Box 650
Orange Beach, AL 36561
205-981-9200; Fax 205-981-9137

ARIZONA

Action Marine
1366 W. Broadway
Mesa, AZ 85210
602-964-6463; Fax 602-969-3026
Luhrs, Mainship

CALIFORNIA

Ballena Bay Yacht Brokers
1150 Ballena Blvd., #121
Alameda, CA 94501
510-865-8601; Fax 510-865-5560
Krogen

Bayside Yacht Sales
164 Marina Drive
Long Beach, CA 90803
310-430-3131; Fax 310-493-4333
DeFever, Krogen

Bill Gorman Yachts
1070 Marina Village Pkwy., #100
Alameda, CA 94501
510-865-6151; Fax 510-865-1220

Cays Boat Sales
509 Grand Caribe Isle
Coronado, CA 92118
619-424-4024; Fax 619-575-7716

Cays Boat Sales
2384 Shelter Island Dr.
San Diego, CA 92106
619-523-3666; Fax 619-523-3670

City Yachts
10 Marina Blvd., San Francisco CA 94123
415-567-8880; Fax 415-567-6725
West Bay

Darlene Hubbard Yacht Broker
1715 Strand Way
Coronado, CA 92118
800-435-3188; Fax 619-435-3189

Fleming Yachts
510 - 31st Street, #H
Newport Beach, CA 92663
714-723-4225; Fax 714-723-4093
Fleming

Fraser Yachts
2353 Shelter Island Dr.
San Diego, CA 92106
619-225-0588; Fax 619-225-1325

Fraser Yachts
3471 Via Lido
Newport Beach, CA 92663
714-673-5252; Fax 714-673-8795

Fraser Yachts
320 Harbor Dr.
Sausalito, CA 94965
415-332-5311; Fax 415-332-7036

Lager Yacht Brokerage Corp.
400 Harbor Dr. #C
Sausalito, CA 94965
415-332-9500, Fax 415-332-9503

Lemest Yacht Sales
24703 Dana Drive
Dana Point, CA 92629
714-496-4933; Fax 714-240-2398

Newmark's Yacht & Ship Brokers
210 Whalers Walk
San Pedro, CA 90731
310-833-0887; Fax 310-833-0979

Newport Boats
1880 Newport Blvd.
Costa Mesa, CA 92627
714-642-8870; Fax 714-642-9824
Maxum

Newport Yacht Brokers
Box 5741, 400 S. Bayfront
Newport Beach, CA, 92662
714-723-1200; Fax 714-723-1201

Newport Yacht Sales
13555 Fiji Way
Marina del Rey, CA 90292
310-301-0020; Fax 310-821-8755

Newport Yacht Sales
3404 Via Oporto, #203
Newport Beach, CA 92663
714-675-1800; Fax 714-675-9533

Norcal Yachts
1070 Marina Village Pkwy., #103
Alameda, CA 94501
510-814-8560; Fax 510-814-8563

Oceanic Yacht Sales
308 Harbor Dr.
Sausalito, CA 94965
415-331-0533; Fax 415-331-1642
Grand Banks

Offshore Yachts
3412 Via Oporto, Suite 203
Newport Beach, CA, 92663
714-673-5401; Fax 714-673-1220

Passage Yachts
1220 Brickyard Cove Rd.
Point Richmond, CA 94801
510-236-2633; Fax 510-234-0118
Beneteau, Tiara

1

Yacht Broker & Dealer Directory

Peter Crane Yacht Sales
6 Harbor Way, Suite 106
Santa Barbara, CA 93109
805-963-8000; Fax 805-966-0722

Price & Bell Yacht Brokers
3005 Peninsula Rd.
Channel Islands Harbor, CA 93035
805-984-8550; Fax 805-984-8552

R.D. Snyder Yachts
1231 Shafter St.
San Diego, CA 92106
619-224-2464; Fax 619-224-7396

Richard Boland Yacht Sales
1070 Marina Village Pkwy., #107
Alameda, CA 94501
510-521-6213; Fax 510-521-0118
Viking, Ocean, Riviera

San Diego Yacht Sales
2525 Shelter Island Dr.
San Diego, CA 92106
619-523-1000; Fax 619-221-0308
Hylas

Seaward Yacht Sales
101 Shipyard Way, Suite K
Newport Beach, CA 92663-4447
714-673-5950; Fax 714-673-1058
Vitech, Nordic, Tayana

Southshore Yacht Sales
997 G Street
Chula Vista, CA 91910
619-427-3357; Fax 619-427-6549

Southwestern Yacht Sales
1500 Quivira Way
San Diego, CA 92109
619-224-4102; Fax 619-224-7874
Beneteau, Sabreline

Summit Marine Boat Centers
1700 Verne Roberts Circle
Antioch, CA 94509
510-777-9300
Bayliner

Superior Yacht Sales
Pier 40, South Beach Harbor
San Francisco, CA 94117
415-543-2650; Fax 415-543-2677
Vitesse

Superior Yacht Sales
29 Embarcadero Cove
Oakland, CA 94606
510-534-9492; Fax 510-534-9495
Vitesse

The Crow's Nest
2515 Shelter Island Dr.
San Diego, CA 92106
619-222-1122; Fax 619-222-3851
Bertram, Hatteras, Tiara

The Crow's Nest
2801 W. Coast Hwy., #260
Newport Beach, CA 92663
714-574-7600; Fax 714-574-7610
Bertram, Hatteras, Tiara

Tocci Yachts
3 Marina Plaza
Antioch, CA 94509
510-706-0292; Fax 510-706-0281
Carri Craft, Holiday Mansion

Trident Yacht Sales
43 Embarcadero Cove
Oakland, CA 94606
510-261-2792; Fax 510-261-2794

Warner Boat Sales
4695 Admiralty Way
Marina del Rey, CA 90292
310-822-0688; Fax 310-822-6411
Mediterranean

Wescal Yachts
16400 Pacific Coast Hwy., #106
Huntington Beach, CA 92649
310-592-4547; Fax 310-592-2960

Yachtline International
3810 W. Channel Islands Blvd. #l
Oxnard, CA 93035-4001
805-985-8643; Fax 805-985-3889
Ocean Alexander

Yamaha Marina Del Rey
13555 Fiji Way
Marina del Rey, CA 90292
310-823-8964; Fax 310-821-0569
Tiara, Wellcraft

CONNECTICUT

Boats Incorporated
133 East Main Street
Niantic, CT 06357
203-739-6251; Fax 203-739-3394
Grady White, Albemarle, Boston Whaler, Parker

Boatworks Yacht Sales
Dauntless Shipyard, Box 668
Essex, CT 06426
203-767-3013; Fax 203-767-7178
Sabreline, Grand Banks

Boatworks Yacht Sales
95 Rowayton Ave.
Rowayton, CT 06853
203-866-0882; Fax 203-853-4910
Sabreline, Grand Banks

Chan Moser Yachts
123 Downs Ave.
Stamford, CT 06902
203-324-4479; Fax 203-348-4540

Coastal Marine
143 River Rd., Box 228
Cos Cob, CT 06807
203-661-5765; Fax 203-661-6040
Albin

Eastland Yachts
33 Pratt St.
Essex, CT 06426
203-767-8224; Fax 203-767-9094

Jensen Yacht Sales
142 Ferry Rd.
Old Saybrook, CT 06475
203-395-1200; Fax 203-395-1465
Carver, Holiday Mansion

North East Yachts
54 Riverview St.
Portland, CT 06480
203-342-1988; Fax 203-342-4132
Blackfin, Bertram

Northrop & Johnson of Essex
P.O. Box 190
Essex, CT 06426
203-767-0149 ; Fax 203-767-0878

Norwalk Cove Marina
Beach Road
East Norwalk, CT 06855
203-838-2326; 800-243-2744 ; Fax 203-838-9258
Hatteras, Azimut

Norwest Marine
130 Water St.
South Norwalk, CT 06854
203-853-2822
Luhrs, Regulator, Wahoo!

Portland Boat Works
1 Grove St.
Portland, CT 06480
203-342-1085; Fax 203-342-0544
Post, Tiara

Yacht Broker & Dealer Directory

Rex Marine Center
144 Water St.
South Norwalk, CT 06854
203-866-5555; Fax 203-866-2518
Stamas, Formula, Island Packet

Sail Westbrook
PO Box 1179
Westbrook, CT 06498
203-399-5515; Fax 203-399-8076

FLORIDA

Alliance Marine
2608 N. Ocean Blvd.
Pompano Beach, FL 33062
305-941-5000; Fax 305-782-4911
Legacy

American Trading Industries
500 SE 17th St., #220
Ft. Lauderdale, FL 33316
305-522-4254; Fax 305-522-4435

Ameriship Corporation
3285 SW 11th Ave.
Ft. Lauderdale, FL 33315
305-463-7957; Fax 305-463-3342
Exporter, Contender

Atlantic Pacific Cruising Yachts
2244 SE 17th St.
Ft. Lauderdale, FL 33316
305-463-7651; Fax 305-779-3316
Vagabond, Ultimate

Atlantic Yacht & Ship
850 NE 3rd St., #210
Dania, FL 33004-3402
305-921-1500; Fax 305-921-1518

Bassett Boat Co.
700 NE 79th Street
Miami, FL 33138
305-758-5786
Sea Ray

Boger Yacht Sales
2305 Beach Blvd
Jacksonville Beach, FL 32250
904-247-7966; Fax 904-247-7972

Bradford International Yacht Sales
3151 State Road 84
Ft. Lauderdale, FL 33312
305-791-2600; Fax 305-791-2655

Bruce A. Bales Yacht Sales
1635 S. Miami Rd., #2
Ft. Lauderdale, FL 33316
305-522-3760; Fax 305-522-4364

Cape Yacht Brokerage
800 Scallop Dr.
Port Canaveral, FL 32920
407-799-4724; Fax 407-799-0096
Beachcat

Catamaran Sales
1650 SE 17th St., #207
Ft. Lauderdale, FL 33316
305-462-6506; Fax 305-462-6104
Euphoric, Privilege

Charles Morgan Associates
200 Second Ave. S.
St. Petersburg, FL 33701
813-894-7027; Fax 813-894-8983

Coast Marine
230 Eglin Parkway SE
Ft. Walton Beach, FL 32548
904-244-3333; Fax 904-243-2433
Wellcraft, Excell, Cruisers

Coastal Yacht Sales
300 S. Duncan Ave., Ste. 189
Clearwater, FL 34615
813-593-7900; Fax 813-449-9743
Ocean

Complete Yacht Services
3599 E. Indian River Dr.
Vero Beach, FL 32963
407-231-2111; Fax 407-231-4465
Grand Banks, Sabreline

Custom Brokerage Yacht Sales
11422 SW 87th Terrace
Miami, FL 33173
305-598-9875; Fax 305-598-2239

Dave Pyles Yacht Sales
2596 SW 23rd Terrace
Ft. Lauderdale, FL 33312
305-583-8104; Fax 305-797-7669

Daytona Marina & Boatworks
645 S. Beach St.
Daytona Beach, FL 32114
904-253-6266; Fax 904-253-8174

East-West Yachts
10 Avenue A, Ft. Pierce Yacht Center
Ft. Pierce, FL 34950
407-466-1240; Fax 407-466-1242
Brokerage

East-West Yachts
800 N. Flagler Dr.
West Palm Beach, FL 33401
407-655-2323; Fax 407-655-2310
Brokerage

Eastern Yacht Sales
1177 Avenue C
Riviera Beach, FL 33404-6943
407-844-1100; Fax 407-844-8946
Freedom, Beneteau, Tollycraft, Whaler, J Boats, Catalina

Edgewater Yacht Sales
PO Box 34227
Pensacola, FL 32507
904-492-2588; Fax 904-492-3334

Fairline Marine
201 SE 15th Terrace, #210
Deerfield Beach, FL 33441
305-481-3569; Fax 305-481-2433
Fairline (Squadron and Phantom)

First Marine Group
1495 Old Griffin Rd.
Dania, FL 33004
305-923-4800; Fax 305-923-3139
Apache, Baha

Fish Tale Marina
7225 Estero Blvd.
Ft. Myers Beach, FL 33931
813-463-4448; Fax 813-765-1419
Blackfin, Grady White, Fountain

Florida Yacht Charters & Sale
1290 Fifth Street at Miami Beach Marina
Miami Beach, FL 33139
305-532-8600; Fax 305-672-2039
Albin, Hunter

Fraser Yachts
2230 SE 17th St.
Ft. Lauderdale, FL 33316
305-463-0600; Fax 305-763-1053
Benetti, Christensen, Vitech, Custom

Gilman Yacht Sales
1212-A U.S. Hwy 1
North Palm Beach, FL 33408
407-626-1790; Fax 407-626-5870

Grand Lagoon Yacht Brokers
3706 Thomas Dr.
Panama City Beach, FL 32408
904-233-4747; Fax 904-233-4741

Yacht Broker & Dealer Directory

Great American Marine
11620 Cleveland Ave.
Ft. Myers, FL 33901
813-277-9919
Donzi, Excel

H&H Yacht Sales
450 Basin St.
Daytona Beach, FL 32114
904-255-0744; Fax 904-253-8842
Brokerage Services

Hal Jones & Co.
1900 SE 15th St.
Ft. Lauderdale, FL 33316
305-527-1778; Fax 305-523-5153
Grand Banks

Hatteras of Lauderdale
401 SW 1st Ave.
Ft. Lauderdale, FL 33301
305-462-5557; Fax 305-462-0029
Hatteras, Tiara

Helms • Kelly • MacMahon Int'l Yachting
1650 SE 17th St., Suite 101
Ft. Lauderdale, FL 33316
305-525-1441; Fax 305-525-1110
Brokerage Services

Herb Phillips Yacht Sales
1535 SE 17th St., #117B
Ft. Lauderdale, FL 33316
305-523-8600; Fax 305-523-8609
Striker

HMY Yacht Sales
850 NE 3rd. St.
Dania, FL 33004
305-926-0400; Fax 305-921-2543
Post, Hines-Farley, Viking, Cabo

HMY Yacht Sales
2401 PGA Blvd., Suite 190
Palm Beach Gardens, FL 33410
407-775-6000; Fax 407-775-6006
Post, Cabo

Kenyon Power Boats
19400 U.S. 19 North
Clearwater, FL 34624
813-539-7444; Fax 813-531-7098
Bayliner, Maxum, SeaCat, Starcraft

Lazzara Int'l Yacht Brokerage
5300 W. Tyson Ave.
Tampa, FL 33611
813-835-5300; Fax 813-835-0964
Brokerage

Luxury Yacht Corp.
1900 SE 15th Street
Ft. Lauderdale, FL 33316
305-764-3388; Fax 305-763-8852
Mainship, Vantare, Mikelson

Merrill-Stevens Yacht Sales
1270 NW 11th St.
Miami, FL 33125
305-858-5911; Fax 305-858-5919

Merritt Yacht Brokers
2040 SE 17th St
Ft. Lauderdale, FL 33316
305-761-1300; 800-446-6695; Fax 305-463-8617

Naples Boat Mart
829 Airport Road North
Naples, FL 33963
813-643-2292; Fax 813-643-6197
Luhrs, Regal

Naples Yacht Brokerage
774 12th Ave. South
Naples, FL 33940
941-434-8338; Fax 941-434-6848

New Wave Marine Center
13255 Biscayne Blvd. NE
North Miami, FL 33181
305-892-2628; Fax 305-892-0444
Regal, Century

Offshore Yacht & Ship Brokers
404 Riberia St.
St. Augustine, FL 32084
904-829-9224; Fax 904-825-4292

OKB Marine
3427 S. Orange Ave.
Orlando, FL 32806
407-859-2628; Fax 407-856-0512
Hydrasports, Glastron

Ortega Yacht Sales
3420 Lake Shore Blvd.
Jacksonville, FL 32210
904-388-5547; Fax 904-384-8400
Sabreline

Oviatt Marine
850 NE 3rd St., Suite 201
Dania, FL 33004
305-925-0065; Fax 305-925-8822
DeFever

Palm Beach Yacht Brokerage
226 Royal Palm Beach
Palm Beach, FL 33480
407-835-8393; Fax 407-835-4214

Palm Beach Yacht Club
800 N. Flagler Dr.
West Palm Beach, FL 33401
407-655-2323; Fax 407-655-2310

Power Yacht Sales International
PO Box 654101
Miami, FL 33265-4101
305-661-2095; Fax 305-661-3518

Prestige Yachts
600 Barracks St., Suite 102
Pensacola, FL 32501
904-432-6838; Fax 904-432-8999
Tiara, Silverton

Reel Deal Yachts
2550 S. Bayshore Dr.
Coconut Grove, FL 33133
305-859-8200; Fax 305-854-8044
Donzi, Mako, Blackfin, Luhrs, Egg Harbor, Mainship

Rhodes Yacht Brokers
2901 NE 28th Court
Lighthouse Point, FL 33064
305-941-2404; Fax 305-941-2507

Richard Bertram, Inc.
3660 NW 21st Street
Miami, FL 33142
305-633-9761; Fax 305-634-9071
Bertram, Ocean Alexander

Richard Bertram, Inc.
801 Seabreeze Blvd.
Ft. Lauderdale, FL 33316
305-467-8405; Fax 305-763-2675
Bertram, Ocean Alexander

Richard Bertram, Inc.
2 Fishing Village Dr.
Key Largo, FL 33037
305-367-3267; Fax 305-367-2128
Bertram, Ocean Alexander

Richard Bertram, Inc.
2385 PGA Blvd.
Palm Beach Gardens, FL 33410
407-625-1045
Bertram, Ocean Alexander

Royal Yacht & Ship Brokers
3859 Central Ave.
St. Petersburg, FL 33713
813-327-0900; Fax 813-327-7797

Rybovich-Spencer Group
4200 N. Dixie
West Palm Beach, FL 33407
407-844-4331; Fax 407-844-8393

Yacht Broker & Dealer Directory

Shear Yacht Sales
2401 PGA Blvd., Suite 182
Palm Beach Gardens, FL 33410
407-624-2112; Fax 407-624-1877
Island Gypsy, Novatec, Iollycraft

Singer Island Yacht Sales
11440 U.S. Highway 1
Palm Beach Gardens, FL 33408
407-622-0355; Fax 407-622-0339

South Florida Marine Yacht Brokerage
4800 N. Federal Hwy., Suite 113B
Boca Raton, FL 33431
407-750-5155; Fax 407-750-8533

Stella Marine
2385 PGA Blvd.
Palm Beach Gardens, FL 33410
407-624-9950; Fax 407-624-9949
Carver, Pursuit, Albemarle, Pro-Line

Stella Marine
250 SW Monterey
Stuart, FL 34994
407-287-1101; Fax 407-287-8445
Carver, Pursuit, Albemarle, Pro-Line

Striker Yacht Corporation
1535 SE 17th St., #117B
Ft. Lauderdale, FL 33316
305-523-8600; Fax 305-523-8609
Striker

Stuart Yacht
450 SW Salerno Rd.
Stuart, FL 34997
407-283-1947; Fax 407-286-9800

Sunny Isles Boat Sales
3450 N. Federal Hwy.
Lighthouse Point, FL 33064
305-784-1501; Fax 305-784-1960
Chaparral, Silverton

Sunshine Yacht Sales
20533 Biscayne Blvd., Suite 4-156
North Miami Beach, FL 33180
305-949-2248; Fax 305-944-7173

Taber Yacht Sales
Pirates Cove Marine,
PO Box 1687
Port Salerno, FL 34992
407-288-7466; Fax 407-288-7476

The Allied Marine Group
401 SW 1st Ave.
Ft. Lauderdale, FL 33301
305-462-5527; Fax 305-462-0029
Hatteras, Tiara

The Boatworks
6921 - 14th Street West (U.S. 41)
Bradenton, FL 34207
813-756-1896; Fax 813-753-9426
Bayliner, Wellcraft, Mako, Blackfin, Century

The Marine Group of Palm Beach
2401 PGA Blvd., Suite 164
Palm Beach Gardens, FL 33410
407-627-9500; Fax 407-627-9503

United Derecktor Gunnell
901 SE 17th St., #205
Ft. Lauderdale, FL 33316
305-524-4616; Fax 305-524-4621

Universal Yacht
1645 SE 3rd Ct., Suite 214
Deerfield Beach, FL 33441-4465
305-420-0229; Fax 305-420-0117

Walker's Yacht Sales
1006 N. Barfield Dr.
Marco Island, FL 33937
813-642-6764; Fax 813-642-0476
Luhrs, Formula, Pursuit, Tiara

Walker's Yacht Sales
895 - 10th St. South
Naples, FL 33940
813-262-6500; Fax 813-262-6693
Luhrs, Formula, Pursuit, Tiara

Walsh Yachts
1900 S.E. 15th Street
Ft. Lauderdale, FL 33316
305-525-7447; Fax 305-525-7451
Ferretti

Wayne Roman Yachts
155 E. Blue Heron Blvd.
Riviera Beach, FL 33404
407-844-5000; Fax 407-844-0124

West Florida Yachts
4880 - 37th St. South
St. Petersburg, FL 33711
813-864-0310; Fax 813-867-6860

Woods & Oviatt
Pier 66 Marina, 2301 SE 17th St.
Ft. Lauderdale, FL 33316
305-463-5606; Fax 305-522-5156
Brokerage Services

Yacht Brokerage USA
125 Basin St. at Halifax Harbor Marina
Daytona Beach, FL 32114
904-253-9353; Fax 904-253-0401

Yacht Perfection
1133 Bal Harbor Blvd., #1141
Punta Gorda, FL 33950
813-637-8111; Fax 813-637-9918

Yacht Sales International
300 Alton Rd.
Miami Beach, FL 33139
305-534-3226; Fax 305-534-2924
Ocean

Yachtmasters
290 Coconut Ave.
Sarasota, FL 34236
813-366-3722; Fax 813-365-8411
Brokerage

ZK Yacht
850 NE 3rd Street, Ste. 209
Dania, FL 33004
305-923-7441; Fax 305-923-7477
Brokerage Services

GEORGIA

Robert P. Minis, Inc.
102 McIntosh Dr.
Savannah, GA 31406
912-354-6589; Fax 912-354-6589
Brokerage Services

ILLINOIS

Class Sea Yachts
207 N. Hager
Barrington, IL 60010
708-382-2100; Fax 708-381-1265
Post

Harborside Marina
27425 South Will Rd.
Wilmington, IL 60481
815-476-2254
Bluewater, Nordic Tugs, Cruisers

Larsen Marine Service
1663 N. Elston Ave.
Chicago, IL 60614
312-993-7711; Fax 312-772-0891
Tiara

INDIANA

H&M Yacht Brokerage
1 Newport Dr.
Michigan City, IN 46360
219-879-7152

Yacht Broker & Dealer Directory

Kentuckiana Yacht Sales
700 East Market St.
Jeffersonville, IN 47131
812-282-7579; Fax 812-282-8020
Jefferson, Gibson, Mainship

IOWA

Anderson Marine at Dubuque Marina
Eagle Point Ext.
Dubuque, IA 52001
319-582-3653; Fax 319-582-0941
Bayliner, Wellcraft

River Bend Yacht Sales
2363 W. Dale Ct.
Bettendorf, IA 52722-2147
319-355-2726; Fax 319-355-0938
Brokerage Services

LOUISIANA

Competition Marine
2233 Lafayette Ave.
Harvey, LA 70059
504-366-8021
Stamas

Mayer Yacht Services
PO Box 840060
New Orleans, LA 70184
504-945-2268; Fax 504-942-2708
Brokerage Services

MAINE

Casco Bay Yacht Exchange
239 US Rt. 1
Freeport, ME 04032
207-865-4016; Fax 207-865-0759
Brokerage Services

Hinckley Yacht Brokerage
Box 699, Shore Rd.
Southwest Harbor, ME 04679
207-244-5531; Fax 207-244-9833
Hinckley

North Star Yacht Sales
DiMillo's Marina, Long Wharf
Portland, ME 04101
207-879-7678; Fax 207-879-1471

The Yacht Connection
14 Ocean Street
South Portland, ME 04106
207-799-3600; Fax 207-767-5937
Brokerage Services

MARYLAND

Anchor Yacht Basin
1048 Turkey Point Rd.
Edgewater, MD 21037
410-269-6674; Fax 410-798-6782
Phoenix, Dawson

Arnold C. Gay Yacht Sales
"C" Street, PO Box 538
Solomons, MD 20688
410-326-2011; Fax 410-326-2012
Brokerage

Burr Yacht Sales
1106 Turkey Point Rd
Edgewater, MD 21037
410-798-5900; Fax 410-798-5911
Fleming, Bertram

Cherry Yachts
2830 Solomons Island Rd.
Edgewater, MD 21037
410-266-3801; Fax 410-266-3805

Gemini Marine Group
326 1st Street, #32
Annapolis, MD 21403
800-525-5105; Fax 410-267-6127

Jackson Marine Sales
PO Box 483, Hances Point
North East, MD 21901
410-287-9400; Fax 410-287-9034
Onset, Mercury & OMC

Martin Bird & Associates
326 First Street
Annapolis, MD 21403
410-268-1086; Fax 410-268-0942

Nautilus Yacht Sales
Skipjack Cove Yachting Resort
PO Box 56
Georgetown, MD 21930
410-275-1100, 800-654-BOAT;
Fax 410-275-1133
Brokerage Services

Oxford Yacht Agency
317 S. Morris St.
Oxford, MD 21654
410-226-5454; Fax 410-226-5244
Grand Banks

Reynolds Yacht Sales
PO Box 147
Georgetown, MD 21930
410-648-5347; Fax 410-648-5263
Brokerage Services

Riverside Marine
11051 Pulaski Hwy
White Marsh, MD 21162-1813
410-686-1500
Bayliner

Solomons Yacht Brokerage
PO Box 380, 255 "A" Street, Town Center
Marina
Solomons, MD 20688
410-326-6748; Fax 410-326-2149
Brokerage Services

Tidewater Yacht Sales
64A Old South River Rd.
Edgewater, MD 21037
410-224-3100; Fax 410-224-6919
Bayliner, Fountain

Warehouse Creek Yacht Sales
301 Pier One Rd.
Stevensville, MD 21666
410-643-7878; Fax 410-643-7877
Cruisers

William Magness Yachts
301 Pier One Rd., #103
Stevensville, MD 21666
410-643-8434; Fax 410-643-8437
Brokerage Services

Yacht-Net Ltd.
1000 West St.
Annapolis, MD 21401
410-263-0993; 800-822-9303;
Fax 410-267-7967
Brokerage Services

MASSACHUSETTS

Alden Yachts, Power & Sail
Allen Harbor Marine
335 Lower County Rd.
Harwich Port, MA 02646
508-432-0353; Fax 508-432-0487
Pursuit, Tiara

Boston Yacht Sales
275 River St.
North Weymouth, MA 02191
617-331-2400; Fax 617-331-8215
Hatteras, Viking, Sabreline, Brokerage

Brewer Yacht Sales
14 Union Street
Plymouth, MA 02360
508-746-4500
Grand Banks

Yacht Broker & Dealer Directory

Burr Bros. Boats
309 Front St.
Marion, MA 02738
508-748-0911; Fax 508-748-1557
Boston Whaler, Sun Fish/Laser, Avon, Dyer

Buzzards Bay Yacht Sales
PO Box 369
Westport Point, MA 02791
508-636-4010; Fax 508-636-5929
Brokerage Services

Cataumet Boats
Route 28A
Bourne, MA 02532
508-563-7102; Fax 508-563-5157
Grady White, Albemarle, Brendan

Dudley Yacht Sales
42 Fiddler's Cove Marina
North Falmouth, MA 02556
508-564-4100; Fax 508-564-4129
Brokerage Services

Gary Voller's Yacht Sales
Barnstable Marine Freezer Rd.
Barnstable, MA 02630
508-362-3626; Fax 508-362-8011
Brokerage

Gifford Marine Co.
676 Dartmouth St.
South Dartmouth, MA 02748
508-996-8288; Fax 508-997-9705
Grady White, Tiara

Green Harbor Marina
PO Box 338, Dyke Rd., Rt. 139
Green Harbor, MA 02041
617-837-1181
Rampage

Hyannis Marina
21 Arlington St.
Hyannis, MA 02601
508-775-5662; Fax 508-775-0851
Sea Ray, Formula

Hyannis Yacht Sales
157 Pleasant St.
Hyannis, MA 02601
508-790-2628; Fax 508-790-0996
Cabo, Ocean, Luhrs, Regulator

Nauset Marine
Box 357, Route 6A
Orleans, MA 02653
508-255-0777; Fax 508-255-0373
Nauset

Northrop & Johnson
43 Water St.
Beverly, MA 01915
508-921-6600; Fax 508-921-6691
Brokerage Services

Thomas Marine
R-24 Ericsson St.
Dorchester, MA 02122
617-288-1000; Fax 617-282-5728
Sea Ray

Wells Yachts
91 Front St.
Marblehead, MA 01945
617-631-3003; Fax 617-639-2503
Tiara, Pursuit, Catalina, J-Boats

MICHIGAN

Barrett Boat Works
821 W. Savidge St.
Spring Lake, MI 49456
616-842-1202; Fax 616-842-5735
Brokerage Services

Bay Harbor Marina
5309 E. Wilder Rd.
Bay City, MI 48707
517-684-5010
Silverton, Pro-Line, Cruisers

Colony Marine
6509 M-29 Hwy., Box 388
Algonac, MI 48001
810-794-4932; Fax 810-794-2147
Sea Ray

Eldean Boat Sales, Ltd.
2223 South Shore Dr.
Macatawa, MI 49434
616-335-5843; Fax 616-335-5848
Grand Banks, Bertram, Ocean

Harbor Boat Shop, The
13240 West Bayshore Dr.
Traverse City, MI
49684
616-922-3020; Fax 616-922-3003

Irish Boat Shop
PO Box 259
Harbor Springs, MI, 49740
616-526-6226; Fax 616-526-5565
Boston Whaler, Sea Ray

Irish Boat Shop
1300 Stover Rd.
Charlevoix, MI 49720
616-547-9967; Fax 616-547-4129

Jefferson Beach Marina
24400 E. Jefferson
St. Clair Shores, MI 48080
810-778-7600; Fax 810-778-4766
Viking Yachts, Sunseeker, Fountain,
Formula, Maxum, Bayliner Yachts
Brokerage Services

John B. Slaven, Inc.
Box 864, 31300 N. River Rd.
Mt. Clemens, MI
810-463-0000; Fax 810-463-4317
Brokerage

McMachen Marine
30099 South River Rd.
Mt. Clemens, MI 48045
810-469-0223; Fax 810-469-1646
Tiara, Sea Ray, Tollycraft
Brokerage Services

Onekama Marine
Portage Lake
Onekama, MI 49675
616-889-4218; Fax 616-889-3398
Silverton, Larson, Cruisers

Pier 33
3000 - 28th St. SW
Grand Rapids, MI 49418
616-538-3314
Pro-Line, Brokerage Services

Superbrokers of Traverse City
12719 SW Bayshore Dr., #9
Traverse City, MI 49684
616-922-3002; Fax 616-922-3013
Brokerage Services

Toledo Beach Marina
11840 Toledo Beach Rd.
LaSalle, MI 48145
313-847-3823; Fax 313-243-3815
Hatteras, Silverton, Pro-Line

MINNESOTA

Harris Yacht Sales
6351 St. Croix Trail N., #141
Stillwater, MN 55082-6973
612-439-2000; Fax 612-439-3859
Brokerage Services

Owens Yacht Sales
371 Canal Park Dr.
Duluth, MN 55802
800-879-2684; Fax 218-722-4730
Worldwide Charters, Brokerage

Yacht Broker & Dealer Directory

NEW HAMPSHIRE

Marine USA
5 Route 101A, #8
Amherst, NH 03031
603-673-0024
Bayliner

Northeast Yachts
2456 Lafayette Rd.
Portsmouth, NH 03801
603-433-3222; Fax 603-431-2817
Brokerage Services

NEW JERSEY

Bob Massey Yacht Sales
1668 Beaver Dam Rd.
Pt. Pleasant, NJ 08742
908-295-3700; Fax 908-892-0649
Jefferson, Onset

Clarks Landing Marina
PO Box 2182
Ocean City, NJ 08226-8182
609-898-9889; Fax 609-390-1260
Luhrs, Pursuit, Blackfin, Bertram
Brokerage Services

Clarks Landing Marina
847 Arnold Ave.
Pt. Pleasant, NJ 08742
908-899-5559; Fax 908-899-5572
Luhrs, Pursuit, Pro-Line, Bertram

Comstock Yacht Sales
704 Princeton Ave
Brick Town, NJ 08724
908-899-2500; Fax 908-892-3763
Post, Silverton, Regulator, Tiara

Integrity Marine
9401 Amherst Ave.
Margate City, NJ 08402
800-435-2337; Fax 609-487-1716
Post

Seaport Yacht Sales
94 East Water St.
Toms River, NJ 08753
908-286-2100
Tollycraft

South Jersey Marine Brokers
602 Green Ave.
Brielle, NJ 08730
908-223-2200; Fax 908-223-0211
Viking, Cabo, Ocean

Sportside Marine
1627 "F" Street
South Belmar, NJ 07719
908-280-2111; Fax 908-280-1011
Brokerage

Total Marine
411 Great Bay Blvd.
Tuckerton, NJ 08087
609-294-0480
Phoenix, Powerplay

NEW YORK

Bruce Tait & Assoc. Yacht Sales
Waterfront Marina, Bay Street
Sag Harbor, NY 11963
516-725-4222; Fax 516-725-9886

City Island Yacht Sales
673 City Island Ave.
City Island, NY 10464
718-885-2300; Fax 718-885-2385

Fred Chall Marine
1160 Merrick Rd.
Copaigue, NY 11726
516-842-7777; Fax 516-842-7998
Hatteras, Wellcraft

Fred Chall Marine
124 Woodcleft Ave.
Freeport, NY 11520
516-546-8960; Fax 516-546-8888
Hatteras

McMichael Yacht Brokers
447 E. Boston Post Rd.
Mamaroneck, NY 10543
914-381-5900; Fax 914-381-5060
Nauticat, J-Boats

Orange Boat Sales
51-57 Route 9W
New Windsor, NY 12553
914-565-8530; Fax 914-565-2706
Baja, Thompson, Regal, Rinker, Bayliner,
Pro-Line, Maxum

Owasco Marine
377 Owasco Rd.
Auburn, NY 13021
315-253-0693; Fax 315-253-2104
Celebrity, Glastron, Crestliner

Rowe Boats International
1 Coastland Dr.
Plattsburgh, NY 12901
518-563-1400; Fax 518-563-1400
Marine Trader Intl., Catalina/Capri, Dyer

Rowland Boats & Motors
1598 North Highway
Southampton, NY 11968
516-283-3444; Fax 516-283-3489
Carolina Classic, Regulator, Wahoo,
Carolina Skiff, Sailfish

Security Marine Yacht & Boat Sales
1 World's Fair Marina
Flushing Meadows, NY 11368
718-478-7600; Fax 718-533-8530
Brokerage

Star Island Yacht Club
PO Box 2180
Montauk, NY 11954
516-668-5052; Fax 516-668-5503
Tiara, Shamrock, Phoenix

Star Island Yacht Club
116 Woodcleft Ave.
Freeport, NY 11520
516-623-6256; Fax 516-868-7332
Tiara, Shamrock, Phoenix

Surfside 3 Marina
846 S. Wellwood Ave.
Lindenhurst, LI NY 11757
516-957-5900; Fax 516-957-8099
Carver, Sea Ray

Van Schaick Island Marina
South Delaware Ave.
Cohoes, NY 12047
518-237-2681; Fax 518-233-8355
Carver, Trojan, Mainship

WhiteWater Marine
5500 Sunrise Highway
Sayville, NY 11782
516-589-2502; Fax 516-567-4855
Parker, Maxum, Stingray

Woodcleft Marine
195 Woodcleft Ave.
Freeport, NY 11520
516-868-1730
CrownLine

NORTH CAROLINA

70 West Marina
Highway 70
Morehead City, NC 28557
919-726-5171; Fax 919-726-9993
Tiara, Jersey, Albemarle

Yacht Broker & Dealer Directory

Baker Marine
6 Marina St.
Wrightsville Beach, NC 28480
910-256-8300; Fax 910-256-9542
Grand Banks, Hatteras, Tiara

Beaufort Yacht Sales
328 Front St.
Beaufort, NC 28516
919-728-3155; Fax 919-728-6715
Viking, Freedom, Valient

Causeway Marina
300 Morehead Ave., Box 2366
Atlantic Beach, NC 28512
919-726-6977; Fax 919-726-7089
Stamas

Harbourside Yachts
PO Drawer 896
Wrightsville Beach, NC 28480
910-350-0660; Fax 910-350-0506
Carver, Blackfin, Luhrs, Trojan

McCotters Marina
Route 7, Box 221
Washington, NC 27889
919-975-2174

Pages Creek Marina
7000 Market St.
Wilmington, NC 28405
910-799-7179; Fax 910-799-1096
Mako

Quay & Associates
PO Box 397
Atlantic Beach, NC 28512
919-247-2280; Fax 919-247-1194

The Boat Rack
7865 Spinnaker Bay Dr.
Sherrills Ford, NC 28673
704-478-2118; Fax 704-478-2628
Silverton

OHIO

Allcraft Marine
4505 Kellogg Avenue
Cincinnati, OH 45226
513-533-8800
Silverton

Coastal Marine & Yacht Sales
1805 W. Lakeshore Dr.
Port Clinton, OH 43452
419-732-2150; Fax 419-732-8820
Tollycraft, Wellcraft, Ocean

Island Yacht Sales
4236 E. Moore's Dock Rd.
Port Clinton, OH 43452
419-797-9003; Fax 419-797-6846

Lake & Bay Yacht Sales
PO Box 237
Marblehead, OH 43440
419-798-8511; Fax 419-798-8511
Egg Harbor, Phoenix

Lakeside Marine
1000 N. Erie Beach Rd.
Lakeside, OH 43440
419-798-4406; Fax 419-798-4089
Tiara, Pursuit

North Shore Boat Brokerage
1787 Merwin
Cleveland, OH 44113
216-241-2237

Progressive Marine Consultants
7130-C Harbor Rd.
Lakeside, OH 43440
419-732-8191; Fax 419-734-9679
Blackfin

Progressive Marine Consultants
111 East Shoreline Dr.
Sandusky, OH 44870
419-627-1177; Fax 419-627-0406
Brokerage Services

The Flerlage Marine Company
2233 Eastern Ave.
Cincinnati, OH 45202
513-221-2233; Fax 513-872-5287
Sea Ray, Harbor Master

Treasure Cove Marina
2555 NE Catawba
Port Clinton, OH 43452
419-797-4492; Fax 419-797-6450
Sea Ray

Treasure Cove Marina
5782 Heisley Rd.
Mentor, OH 44060
216-942-2544
Sea Ray

OKLAHOMA

Cedar Port Marina
Hwy. 28, Box 546
Disney, OK 74340
800-435-8250; Fax 918-435-8390
Silverton, Maxum, Powerquest

Yacht Links
Applegate Cove Marina
HC61, Box 308
Sallisaw, OK 74955
918-775-4522; Fax 918-775-4538
Brokerage Services

OREGON

Compass Point Yachts
1521 N. Jantzen Ave.
Portland, OR 97217
503-286-7070; Fax 503-286-7077
Silverton, Ocean Alexander

Northwest Boat Center
719 N. Marine Dr.
Portland, OR 97217
503-289-9338

Oregon Yacht Sales
2305 NW 133rd Place
Portland, OR 97229
503-285-5586; 503-799-5028
Fax 503-690-0824
Tollycraft, Tiara, Queenship, Symbol, Ocean,
Fountain

RHODE ISLAND

Alden Yacht Brokerage
1909 Alden Landing
Portsmouth, RI 02871
401-683-4285; Fax 401-683-3668
Alden Yachts, Power & Sail

Black Watch Brokerage
One Little Harbor Landing
Portsmouth, RI 02871
401-683-5777; Fax 401-683-5620
Brokerage Services

Brewer's Yacht Sales
222 Narragansett Blvd.
Portsmouth, RI 02871
401-683-3977; Fax 401-683-0696

Eastern Yacht Sales
One Lagoon Rd.
Portsmouth, RI 02871
401-683-2200; Fax 401-683-0961
Brokerage Services

Eastern Yacht Sales of RI
One Masthead Dr.
Warwick, RI 02886
401-885-2400; Fax 401-885-2457
Tollycraft, Catalina, Beneteau

Yacht Broker & Dealer Directory

Island Gypsy Yacht Sales, Ltd.
138 Wharf Rd.
Warwick, RI 02889
401-737-2233; Fax 401-737-2207
Island Gypsy

Newport Yacht Services
PO Box 149
Newport, RI 02840
401-846-7720; Fax 401-846-6850

Northrop & Johnson
19 Brown & Howard Wharf
Newport, RI 02840-3471
401-848-5500; Fax 401-848-0120

Standish Boat Yard
1697 Main Road
Tiverton, RI 02878
401-624-4075; Fax 401-624-3438
Cape Dory, Albin

The Point Boat Co.
360 Gooseberry Rd.
Wakefield, RI 02880
401-789-7189; Fax 401-783-5350
Albin

Twin City Marine
600 High St.
Central Falls, RI 02863
401-723-6100
Four Winns, Cruisers, Quest

SOUTH CAROLINA

American Yacht Sales
1880 Andell Buffs Blvd.
Johns Island, SC 29455
803-768-9660; Fax 803-768-7300
Luhrs, Mainship, Albemarle, Shamrock, Cobia

Berry-Boger Yacht Sales
Box 36, Harbour Place, #101
N. Myrtle Beach, SC 29597
803-249-6167; Fax 803-249-0105
Wellcraft, Gibson

DYB Charters & Yacht Sales
14 New Orleans Rd., Suite 14
Hilton Head, SC 29928
803-785-4740; Fax 803-785-4827
Catalina, Gamefisherman

Hilton Head Yachts, Ltd.
PO Box 22488
Hilton Head Island, SC 29925
803-686-6860; Fax 803-681-5093

Sea Ray of Charleston
4415 Sea Ray Dr.
North Charleston, SC 29405
803-747-1889
Sea Ray

Wilkins Boat & Yacht Co.
1 Harbour Place
N. Myrtle Beach, SC 29582
803-249-6032; Fax 803-249-6523
Sonic

TENNESSEE

Erwin Marine Sales
1940 Hixson Marina Rd.
Hixson, TN 37343
615-843-0232; Fax 615-843-0233
Sea Ray, Harbor Master, Marinette, Formula

Fox Road Marina, LLC
1100 Fox Rd.
Knoxville, TN 37922
615-966-9422; Fax 615-966-9475
Holiday Mansion

Hatteras of Nashville
341 Hill Ave.
Nashville, TN 37210
615-254-9107
Hatteras

Jim Bennett Yacht Sales
Route 4, Box 532
Iuka, TN 38852
601-423-9999; Fax 601-423-3339
Bluewater, Carver

Leader Marine
722 E. College St.
Dickson, TN 37055
615-446-3422; Fax 615-446-9819
Cruisers

Loret Marine
PO Box 556
Harrison, TN 37341
615-344-8331; Fax 615-344-6275
Carver, Monterey, Four Winns

Peer Gynt Enterprises
6421 Fairest Dr.
Harrison, TN 37341
615-344-5628; Fax 615-344-0960
Brokerage

Phil's Marine Sales
4935 Highway 58, Suite C
Chattanooga, TN 37416
615-892-0058; Fax 615-894-3281

VIP Yachts
11211 Crown Point Dr.
Knoxville, TN 37922
615-693-3039; Fax 615-675-2144
Bluewater

TEXAS

Boats Unlimited
1900 Shipyard Dr.
Seabrook, TX 77586
713-334-2559
Brokerage Services

Coastal Yacht Brokers
715 Holiday Dr. North
Galveston, TX 77550
409-763-3474; Fax 713-488-8782

Fox Yacht Sales
Box 772, Island Moorings Marina
Port Aransas, TX 78373
512-749-4870; Fax 512-749-4859
Bertram, Blackfin
Brokerage Services

Houston Yacht Sales
585 Bradford Ave., Suite B
Kemah, TX 77565
713-334-7094; Fax 713-334-4936
Hatteras, Marlin, Ocean

Jay Bettis & Company
2509 NASA Road 1
Seabrook, TX 77586
713-474-4101; Fax 713-532-1305
DeFever, Shamrock, Mainship

Ron's Yacht Brokerage
1101 Shipyard Dr., Box 621
Seabrook, TX 77586
713-474-5444; Fax 713-474-7024

Sea Lake Yachts
1500 FM 2094, Box 1611
Kemah, TX 77565
713-334-1993; Fax 713-334-4795
Brokerage Services

Vega Yacht Sales
4106 NASA Road 1
Seabrook, TX 77586
713-326-5588; Fax 713-532-1275
Brokerage Services

Weaver & Cameron
2511B NASA Rd. 1, Suite 200
Seabrook, TX 77586
713-326-1111; Fax 713-532-3075
Brokerage Services

Yacht Broker & Dealer Directory

VIRGINIA

Atlantic Yacht Brokers
932 Laskin St., Suite 200
Virginia Beach, VA 23451
804-428-9000; Fax 804-491-8632
Ocean Yachts, Cabo

Bluewater Yacht Sales
25 Marina Rd.
Hampton, VA 23669
804-723-0793; Fax 804-723-3320
Hatteras, Viking

Casey Marine
1021 W. Mercury Blvd.
Hampton, VA 23666
804-591-1500; Fax 804-826-5557
Pro-Line, Baja, Robolo, Maxum, Luhrs

Coastal Yacht Sales
Rt. 1210
Gloucester Point, VA 23062
804-642-3732; Fax 804-642-4966
Brokerage Services

Commonwealth Yachts
PO Box 1070
Gloucester Point, VA 23062
804-642-2156; Fax 804-642-4766
Brokerage Services

Dominion Yacht Brokers
2100 Marina Shores Rd.
Virginia Beach, VA 23455
804-481-0533; Fax 804-481-0056
Brokerage Services

Dozier's Dockyard
PO Box 388
Deltaville, VA 23043
804-776-6711; Fax 804-776-6998

Norton's Yacht Sales
PO Box 220, Route 636
Deltaville, VA 23043
804-776-9211; Fax 804-776-9044
Luhrs, Hunter, Silverton

Tidewater Yacht Sales
10A Crawford Parkway
Norfolk, VA 23704
804-393-6200; Fax 804-397-1193
Baylincr, Fountain

Virginia Yacht Brokers
424 E. Queen St.
Hampton, VA 23669
804-722-3500; Fax 804-722-7909
Brokerage Services

WASHINGTON

AAA Yacht Finders
2415 "T" Ave., Suite 3
Anacortes, WA 98221
360-299-2628; 800-704-2628
Fax 360-293-3246
Brokerage Services

Alliance Yacht Sales
2130 Westlake Ave. North
Seattle, WA 98109
206-283-8111; Fax 206-283-4200
Offshore

Bayside Yacht & Ship Sales
1724 #2 W. Marine View Dr.
Everett, WA 98201
206-258-2790

Bellingham Yacht Sales
1801 Roeder Ave.
Bellingham, WA 98225
800-671-4244; Fax 360-671-0992
Sabreline (Motoryachts 34'-49')

Breakwater Marina
5603 Waterfront Dr.
Tacoma, WA 98407
206-752-6663; Fax 206-752-8291
Hershine

Elliott Bay Yachting Center
2601 West Marina Pl., #D
Seattle, WA 98199
206-285-9563; Fax 206-281-7636
Brokerage Services

Fraser Yachts
1500 Westlake Ave. N.
Seattle, WA 98109
206-282-4943; Fax 206-285-4956
Brokerage Services

Gig Harbor Yacht Sales
Box 528, 3119 Harborview Dr.
Gig Harbor, WA 98335
206-851-2674; Fax 206-858-2674

Intrepid Yacht Sales
2144 Westlake Ave. North
Seattle, WA 98109
206-282-0211; Fax 206-281-8250
Grand Banks, Eastbay

Intrepid Yacht Sales
1015 Thomas Glenn Dr., #1
Bellingham, WA 98225
360-676-1248; Fax 360-676-9059
Grand Banks, Eastbay

Lake Union Yacht Sales
3245 Fairview Ave. E. #103
Seattle, WA 98102
206-323-3505; Fax 206-323-4751
Island Gypsy, Catalina
Brokerage Services

Marina Yacht Sales
1500 Westlake Ave. N., Suite 8
Seattle, WA 98109
206-298-9900; Fax 206-270-9045
Brokerage Services

Murray Wasson Marine Sales
4224 Marine View Dr.
Tacoma, WA 98422
206-927-9036; Fax 206-927-9034
Albin

Nordic Northwest Yacht Brokerage
2046 Westlake
Seattle, WA 98109
206-282-8847; Fax 206-282-5951
Nordic Tugs

Olympic Boat Centers
16340 Aurora Ave. North
Seattle, WA 98113
206-363-5562
Bayliner

Olympic Boat Centers
13200 Bel-Red Rd.
Bellevue, WA 98005
206-454-9929
Bayliner

Olympic Boat Centers
10 East Allison St.
Seattle, WA 98102
206-322-3880
Bayliner

Olympic Boat Centers
6610 - 16th St. East
Fife, WA 98424
206-922-0303
Bayliner

Olympic Boat Centers
6790 Martin Way
Olympia, WA 98506
206-491-1679
Bayliner

Pacific Boatland
11704 Hwy. 99
Vancouver, WA 98686
206-573-0621
Cruisers

Yacht Broker & Dealer Directory

Picks Cove Marine Center
1940 East D Street
Tacoma, WA 98421
206-572-3625
Symbol

San Juan Yacht Sales
PO Box 69
Anacortes, WA 98221
360-293-4117; Fax 360-293-6683
Symbol

Skipper Cress Yacht Sales
1019 Q Ave., Suite B
Anacortes, WA 98221
800-996-9991; Fax 360-293-7874
Nordic Tugs

Sundance Yacht Sales
1001 NE Boat St.
Seattle, WA 98103
206-633-2850
Carver

Yarrow Bay Yacht Sales
5207 Lake Washington Blvd. NE
Kirkland, WA 98033
206-822-6066
Cruisers

WISCONSIN

Bay Marine of Sturgeon Bay
PO Box 229
Sturgeon Bay, WI 54235
414-743-6526
Cruisers

Cal Marine
1024 Bay Shore Dr.
Sister Bay, WI 54234
414-854-4521; Fax 414-854-5137
Tiara, Silverton, Powerquest, Pursuit

Emerald Yacht Ship Mid America
1933 S. First St.
Milwaukee, WI 53204
414-671-1110; Fax 414-671-1211
Brokerage Services, New Construction

Fox River Marina
P.O. Box 1006
Oshkosh, WI 54902
414-235-2340
Wellcraft, Cruisers

Lakeside Marina
902 Taft Ave.
Oshkosh, WI 54901
414-231-4321; Fax 414-231-0004
Bayliner, Carver, Chaparral, Larson

Professional Yacht Sales
451 S. Second St.
Prescott, WI 54021
715-262-5762; Fax 715-262-5658
Mainship, Holiday Mansion

Shipyard Marine
164 South Shore Dr.
Washington Island, WI 54246
414-847-2533
Albemarle, Navigator

Skipper Buds
N 10 W 24850 Silvernail Rd
Pewaukee, WI 53072
414-544-1200
Hatteras, Sea Ray, Chris Craft

Sturgeon Bay Yacht Harbor
306 Nautical Drive
Sturgeon Bay, WI 54235
414-743-3311; Fax 414-743-4298
Ocean/Alexander, Thunderbird/Formula

Tinus Marine
307 Forest St.
Oconomowoc, WI 53069
414-567-7533; Fax 414-567-8677
Fountain

Marine Surveyor Directory

PROFESSIONAL SURVEYOR ASSOCIATIONS

ABYC . . . . .AMERICAN BOAT & YACHT COUNCIL
ASA . . . . .AMERICAN SOCIETY OF APPRAISORS
AIMS . . . . .AMERICAN INSTITUTE OF MARINE SURVEYORS
NAMI . . . . .NATIONAL ASSOCIATION OF MARINE INVESTIGATORS
NAMS . . . . .NATIONAL ASSOCIATION OF MARINE SURVEYORS
NFPA . . . . .NATIONAL FIRE PROTECTION ASSOCIATION
SAMS . . . . .SOCIETY OF ACCREDITED MARINE SURVEYORS
SNAME . . . . . . .SOCIETY OF NAVAL ARCHITECTS & MARINE ENGINEERS

ALABAMA

Michael Schiehl
M.J. Schiehl
PO Box 1990
Orange Beach, AL 36561-1990
334-981-6611; Fax 334-981-2611
NAMS

Donald Smith
Port City Marine Services
3263 Demetroplis Rd., Ste. 8C
Mobile, AL 36693
334-661-5426; Fax 334-460-9898
SAMS (AMS), ABYC

CALIFORNIA

Hans Andersen
Anderson Int'l. Marine Surveyors
433 North H St., Ste. G
Lompoc, CA 93436
805-737-3770; Fax 805-737-3773
SAMS (AMS)

Clark Barthol, CMS
Clark Barthol Marine Surveyors
27 Buccaneer St.
Marina del Rey, CA 90292
310-823-3350; Fax 310-827-7883
NAMS, ABYC

Thomas Bell
Thomas Bell & Associates
1323 Berkeley Street, #A
Santa Monica, CA 90404-2503

310-306-1895
SAMS (AMS), ABYC, NAMI, ASA

Roby Bessent
Pacific Marine Surveyors
PO Box 3111
Long Beach, CA 90803
310-434-5711; Fax 310-434-5711
NAMS, ABYC

Christopher Bishop
James E. Dillon & Assoc.
175 Filbert St., Ste. #201
Oakland, CA 94607
510-452-2866; Fax 510-452-2875
NAMS

John Bonner
John Bonner & Assoc.
131 Steuart St., Ste. #650
San Francisco, CA 94105
415-495-0778; Fax 415-495-6120
NAMS

Robert Bornholdt
Marine Surveyor
1310 Rosecrans
San Diego, CA 92106
619-224-2944

Archibald Campbell
Campbell's Marine Survey
340 Countryside Drive
Santa Rosa, CA 95401
707-542-8812; Fax 707-542-8812
SAMS (AMS), ABYC, ASME, SNAME

Carl Colditz
Giannotti Marine Services
1631 Spinnaker Dr., #204
Ventura, CA 93001
805-658-8836; Fax 805-658-8953
NAMS

William Engstrom
Marine Surveyor
1251 W. Sepulveda Blvd., #160
Torrance, CA 90502
310-534-4345; Fax 310-534-4345
NAMS

James Enzensperger
Pacific Cargo Inspection Bureau
1490 - 66th Street
Oakland, CA 94608-1014
510-420-1386; Fax 510-420-0660
NAMS

John Flachsenhar, Jr.
Marine Surveyor
1067 Shafter St.
San Diego, CA 92106
619-223-8167
NAMS

William Hansen
Fireman's Fund Insurance Co.
PO Box 3136
San Francisco, CA 94119
415-541-4434; Fax 415-541-4441
NAMS

Marine Surveyor Directory

Marvin Henderson
Marvin Henderson Marine Surveyors
2727 Shelter Island Dr., #C
San Diego, CA 92106
619-224-3164; Fax 619-588-7607
NAMS, ABYC, NFPA, SNAME

Richard Jacobson
J.A. Jacobson & Assoc.
1324 N. Avalon Blvd.
Wilmington, CA 90744
310-834-4553

Bill Jewell
American Marine Consultants
5055 N. Harbor Dr., Ste. D
San Diego, CA 92106
619-223-7380
ASNE, ABYC

Douglas Johnstone
Admiralty Marine Surveyors
920 N. Avalon Blvd.
Wilmington, CA 90744
310-835-7139; Fax 310-835-9161
NAMS

Chris Kieffer
Marine Surveyor
1310 Rosecrans St., #K
San Diego, CA 92106
619-224-2944

Jack Mackinnon
Marine Surveyor
PO Box 335
San Lorenzo, CA 94580-0335
510-276-4351; Fax 510-276-9237
SAMS (AMS), ABYC

Douglas Malin
Malin Marine Surveyors
5942 Edinger Ave., #113
Huntington Beach, CA 92649
714-897-6769; Fax 714-897-6769
SAMS (AMS), ABYC, NFPA

Albert Milani, CMS
Ocean Marine Consultants, Inc.
664 Santana Rd.
Novato, CA 94945
415-892-4385; Fax 415-892-4385
NAMS, SNAME

Don Parish
Marine Surveyor
4140 Oceanside Blvd., #159-320
Oceanside, CA 92056
619-721-9410
ABYC

Kent Parker
Marine Surveyor
PO Box 2604
San Rafael, CA 94912
415-457-5312

Gerald Poliskey
G.A. Poliskey & Associates
5014 Esmond Ave.
Richmond, CA 94805
510-236-1793; Fax 510-236-1797
SAMS (AMS), NAMS, SNAME, ABYC,
NFPA

Capt. Joseph W. Rogers
Rogers & Assoc., Certified Marine Surveyors
400 Dolores St., #A - Yacht Harbor
Santa Cruz, CA 95062
408-475-4468; Fax 408-475-4468
NAMS, ASA

Todd Schwede
Todd Schwede & Associates
2390 Shelter Island Dr., #220
San Diego, CA 92106
619-226-1895; Fax 619-223-8942
SAMS (AMS), NAMI, ABYC

Rod Whitfield
R.J. Whitfield & Associates, Inc.
7011 Bridgeport Circle
Stockton, CA 95207-2357
209-956-8488; Fax 209-956-8490
SAMS (AMS), NAMI, ABYC

Stanley Wild
Stan Wild & Associates
1912 Stanford St.
Alameda, CA 94501
510-521-8527; Fax 510-521-8196
NAMS

Donald Young
Donru Marine Surveyors & Adjusters
32 Cannery Row
Monterey, CA 93940
408-372-8604; Fax 408-373-2294
SAMS (AMS), ABYC

CANADA

Timothy McGivney
Aegis Marine Surveyors, Ltd.
745 Clark Dr.
Vancouver, B.C., Canada V5L 3J3
604-251-2210; Fax 604-254-0515
NAMS, ABYC, SNAME

Barry Smith
Barry D. Smith & Company

#9-323 Governors Ct.
New Westminster, B.C., Canada V3L 5S6
604-522-2877
NAMS

CONNECTICUT

Robert Hughes
Marine Surveyor
88 Eastwood Rd.
Groton, CT 06340
203-446-9473

Art Kelsey
Marine Surveyors Bureau
23 Riverside Dr., #B1
Clinton, CT 06413
203-399-9309; Fax 203-399-4996
NAMS, ABYC, NFPA

James Taylor
Taylor Yacht Surveys
#5 The Laurels
Enfield, CT 06082
203-749-7400

FLORIDA

Mel Allen
Allen's Boat Surveying & Consulting
638 North U.S. Hwy 1, Suite 207
Tequesta, FL 33469-2397
407-747-2433; Fax 407-745-3245
SAMS (AMS), ABYC, NFPA

William Ballard
Ballard & Assoc., Inc.
18845 SW 93rd Ave.
Miami, FL 33157
305-252-8008; Fax 305-255-4681
SAMS (AMS)

Dennis Brown
Marine Surveyor
414 Sandpiper Dr.
Satellite Beach, FL 32937
407-779-9750
ABYC, NFPA

Pete Brown
Marine Surveyor
11340 - 7th St., East
St. Petersburg, FL 33706-3038
813-367-2489
NAMS

C.H. Brown, Jr.
Marine Surveyor
2925 Lake Pineloch Blvd.
Orlando, FL 32806
407-843-8138

Marine Surveyor Directory

Brett Carlson
Carlson Marine Surveyors & Adjusters
1002 NE 105th St.
Miami Shores, FL 33138
305-891-0445; Fax 305-891-8446
SAMS (AMS)

Clyde Carter
Darling & Co., Marine Surveyors
PO Box 8703
Longboat Key, FL 34228
813-922-5341
SAMS (SA), ABYC, NFPA

Charles Corder
Chapman School of Seamanship
4343 SE St. Lucie Blvd.
Stuart, FL 34997
407-283-8130; Fax 407-283-2019
SAMS (AMS)

Ric Corley
Capt. Tom Corley & Son Marine Surveyors
1701 Grant Avenue
Panama City, FL 32401
904-784-9939; Fax 904-233-4982
SAMS (AMS), ABYC, NFPA, NAMS, NAMI

Jerome Cramer
Slakoff, Cramer & Associates
1524 S. Andrews Ave., Suite 215
Ft. Lauderdale, FL 33316
305-525-7930; Fax 305-525-7947
SAMS (AMS)

Tom Drennan
Continental Marine Consultants, Inc.
618 North US Hwy #1, Suite 301
North Palm Beach, FL 33408
407-844-6111; Fax 407-844-7152
NAMS

Capt. Larry C. Dukehart
Marine Surveyor & Consultant
PO Box 1172
Islamorada, FL 33036-1172
305-664-9452; Fax 305-664-9453
SAMS (AMS), ABYC, NFPA, NAMI

Tom Fexas
Tom Fexas Yacht Design, Inc.
333 Tressler Dr., Suite B
Stuart, FL 33497
407-287-6558; Fax 407-287-6810
NAMS

Dean Greger
Coastal Marine Surveyors
23 Winston Dr.
Belleair, FL 34616
813-581-0914
ABYC

William King
Atlantic Marine Survey
6201 SE Monticello Terrace
Hobe Sound, FL 33455-7383
407-545-0011; Fax 407-545-1025
SAMS (AMS), ABYC

Drew Kwederas
Global Adventure Marine Associates
4120 NE 26th Ave.
Ft. Lauderdale, FL 33308
305-566-4800; Fax 305-566-4802
ABYC, NFPA, SNAME, ASNE, NACE

Veronica Lawson
Veronica M. Lawson & Associates
PO Box 1201
Naples, FL 33939
813-434-6960; Fax 813-649-1374
NAMS, SNAME, ABYC, NFPA

Capt. F. Michael McGhee
Black Pearl Marine Specialities, Inc.
6695 NW 25th Terrace
Ft. Lauderdale, FL 33309
305-970-8305; Fax 305-970-8303
ABYC, NFPA, ASA, AIMS

Marty Merolla
Marty Merolla Certified Marine Surveyor, Inc.
4300 SE St. Lucie Blvd., #128
Stuart, FL 34997
407-286-4880; Fax 407-221-9408
NAMS

Downing Nightingale, Jr.
North Florida Marine Services, Inc.
3360 Lakeshore Blvd.
Jacksonville, FL 32210
904-384-4356; Fax 904-384-4356
SAMS (AMS), AMS

Allen Perry
Ocean Adventures, Inc.
453 Spinnaker Dr.
Naples, FL 33940
813-261-5466
SAMS (SA), ABYC, NAMS

Henry Pickersgill
Henry W. Pickersgill & Co., Inc.
26231 MTN Lake Rd.
Brooksville, FL 34602
800-348-8105; Fax 904-754-1789
NAMS

Thomas Price
Price Marine Services, Inc.
9418 S.E. Sharon St.
Hobe Sound, FL 33455-6833
407-546-0928; Fax 407-546-1503
SAMS (AMS), ABYC, NFPA

John Reeve
Reeve Marine Associates, Inc.
P.O.Box 4202
Tequesta, FL 33469
407-747-5493
SAMS (SA), ABYC

Mark Rhodes
Rhodes Marine Surveyors
4701 N. Federal Hwy., Ste 340, Box C-8
Lighthouse Point, FL 33064-6563
305-946-6779; Fax 305-783-0057
SAMS (AMS), ABYC, NFPA

Mike Rhodes
Rhodes Marine Surveyors
4701 N. Federal Hwy., Ste 340, Box C-8
Lighthouse Point, FL 33064-6563
305-946-6779; Fax 305-783-0057
SAMS (AMS), ABYC, NFPA

Edward Rowe
Ed Rowe & Associates
1821 SW 22nd Ave.
Ft. Lauderdale, FL 33312
305-792-6062; Fax 305-792-8404
SAMS (AMS), ABYC

Robert Russo
Jacksonville Towing and Salvage Corp.
2268 Mayport Rd., #118
Atlantic Beach, FL 32250
904-249-0309; Fax 904-247-3366
SAMS (SA)

James Sanislo
C&J Marine Surveyors
4163 Frances Dr.
Delray Beach, FL 33445
407-495-4920; Fax 407-495-8701
SAMS (AMS)

Norman Schreiber II
PO Box 350247
Ft. Lauderdale, FL 33335
305-537-1423; Fax 305-761-9087
NAMS, SNAME, ABYC, NFPA

James Shafer
Harbor Marine Services
979 Sultan Dr.
Port St. Lucie, FL 34953
407-340-5570; Fax 407-340-5570
SAMS (SA), ABYC, NAMI

Ronald Silvera
R.E. Silvera & Associates
1904 SW 86th Ave.
North Lauderdale, FL 33068
305-720-8660
SAMS (AMS), SNAME, ABYC, ASA

Marine Surveyor Directory

Eugene Sipe, Jr.
Nautical Services Technologies
424 Production Blvd., #70
Naples, FL 33942-4723
941-434-7445; Fax 941-947-5175
SAMS (AMS)

Ed Stanton
Rhodes Marine Surveyors
4701 N. Federal Hwy., Ste 340, Box C-8
Lighthouse Point, FL 33064-6563
305-946-6779; Fax 305-783-0057
SAMS (AMS), ABYC, NFPA

Mickey Strocchi
Strocchi & Company
PO Box 16541
Jacksonville, FL 32245-6541
904-398-1862; Fax 904-398-1868
SAMS (AMS)

Donald Walwer
D&G Marine, Inc.
58 Ocean Blvd.
Naples, FL 33942
813-643-0028; Fax 813-643-0028
SAMS (AMS)

Ted Willandt
Marine Network
4211 Harbour Island Dr.
Jacksonville FL 32225
904-641-3334
SAMS (AMS), ABYC, NAMI

Dick Williamson
Professional Marine Surveys, Inc.
7491-C5 N. Federal Hwy, #232
Boca Raton, FL 33487
407-272-1053
SAMS (AMS), ABYC, NFPA

GEORGIA

Ronald Collins
Marine Surveyor
26 North End Dr.
Brunswick, GA 31525
912-262-0448

HAWAII

Dennis D. Smith
Marine Surveyors & Consultants, Inc.
677 Ala Moana Blvd., Ste. 812
Honolulu, HI 96813
808-545-1333
SAMS (AMS)

Alfred Gallant, Jr.
Marine Surveyor
47-457 Aiai Place
Kaneohe, HI 96744

IOWA

Michael Baxter
U.S. Inland Marine Surveying
1599 Vail Ave.
Muscatine, IA 52761
319-263-6235
NAMS

ILLINOIS

Lee . H Asbridge
Marine Surveyor
440 N. McClurg Ct., #313
Chicago, IL 60611
312-527-1774; Fax 312-464-9640
SAMS (AMS), ABYC, NFPA

Chris Kelly
Professional Yacht Services
733 Sheridan Rd.
Winthrop Harbor, IL 60096
800-535-0072; Fax 708-872-0073
SAMS (SA), ABYC, NFPA, NAMI

James Singer
Marine Surveyor
1854 York Lane
Highland Park, IL 60035
708-831-9157; Fax 708-831-9155
SAMS (AMS), ABYC, NAMI

INDIANA

Chris McNamara
McNamara Marine Surveys, Inc
702 Domke Dr.
Valparaiso, IN 46383-7816

KENTUCKY

Jim Hill, CMS
Marine Surveyor
187 Dogwood Hills Club Rd.
Gilbertsville, KY 42044
800-967-6646

Gregory Weeter
Riverlands Marine Surveyors
935 Riverside Dr.
Louisville, KY 40207
502-897-9900; Fax 502-897-9910
NAMS, ABYC

LOUISIANA

Stanhope Hopkins
Stanhope Hopkins Surveyors
PO Box 15141
New Orleans, LA 70175-5141
504-895-2667

Larry Strouse
Bachrach Wood, Peters & Assoc., Inc.
PO Box 7415
Metairie, LA 70010-7415
504-454-0001; Fax 504-454-3257
NAMS

Albert Westerman
Albert B. Westerman & Co.
2800 Sells St.
Metairie, LA 70003-3543
504-888-8865; Fax 504-455-7960
NAMS, SNAME, ABYC

MAINE

Carl Beal
Casco Marine Consultants, Inc.
5 Ledgeview Ln., RFD Five
Brunswick, ME 04011
207-729-6711; Fax 207-729-6547
SAMS (AMS)

Malcolm Harriman
Marine Surveyor
8 Country Club Rd.
Manchester, ME 04351
207-622-2049
SAMS (AMS)

Malcolm Harriman
Marine Surveyor
PO Box 5151
Elsworth, ME 04605
207-667-1157
SAMS (AMS)

MARYLAND

Thomas Brittain
Marine Surveyor
8809 Thomas Lea Terr.
Gaithersburg, MD 20879
301-948-0015
NAMS, ABYC, SSCD

Peter Hartoft
Hartoft Marine Survey, Ltd.
PO Box 3188, 310 Giddings Ave.
Annapolis, MD 21403
410-263-3609
ABYC, NAMS, MTAM

Marine Surveyor Directory

Frederick Hecklinger
Frederick E. Hecklinger, Inc.
17 Hull Ave.
Annapolis, MD 21403
410-268-3018
NAMS

Michael Kaufman
Kaufman Design, Inc.
PO Box 4219
Annapolis, MD 21403
410-263-8900; Fax 410-263-3459
NAMS

Woodrow Loller
Woodrow W. Loller, Inc.
204 Washington Ave.
Chestertown, MD 21620
410-778-5357; Fax 410-778-5357
NAMS, ABYC

Catherine C. McLaughlin
Marine Surveyor
29142 Belchester Rd.
Kennedyville, MD 21645
410-348-5188; Fax 410-348-5657
SAMS (AMS), ABYC, NFPA, NAMI, ASA

Capt. Michael Phil Heuman, Jr.
Heuman & Assoc.
3707 Paca Avenue
Abingdon, MD 21009
800-794-8258; 800-458-8258; Fax 410-538-6498
NFPA, ABYC, ASA

Michael L. Previti
Previti Marine Surveyor & Consultant Inc.
PO Box 1210
Solomons, MD 20688
410-326-0826; 800-823-0866; Fax 410-326-0826
ABYC

Richard Stimson
R.M. Stimson & Associates
7074 Bembe Beach Rd., #102
Annapolis, MD 21403
410-268-0080; 800-278-4676; Fax 410-268-0080
NAMS, ABYC

Capt. Wright
KIS Marine
5830 Hudson Wharf Rd.
Cambridge, MD 21613
410-228-1448
SAMS (SA)

MASSACHUSETTS

Donald B. Pray
Donald B. Pray Associates
PO Box 66
South Weymouth, MA 02190
617-335-3033; 800-454-7729
Fax 617-331-0607
SAMS (AMS), ABYC, NFPA

Edwin Boice
Robert N. Kershaw, Inc.
25 Garden Park
Braintree, MA 02184
617-843-4550; 800-537-742
 Fax 617-849-6653
NAMS, SAMS (AMS)

J. Raymond Gaffey
Robert N. Kershaw, Inc.
25 Garden Park
Braintree, MA 02184
617-843-4550; 800-537-7429
Fax 617-849-6653

Robert Kershaw
Robert N. Kershaw, Inc.
25 Garden Park
Braintree, MA 02184
617-843-4550; 800-537-7429
Fax 617-849-6653
NAMS, SAMS (AMS)

Christopher Leahy
Leahy Associates
PO Box 6313
North Plymouth, MA 02362
508-746-5971; Fax 508-279-0130
SAMS (SA), ABYC, NFPA, NAMI

Joseph Lombardi
Manchester Yacht Survey
PO Box 1576
Manchester, MA 01944
800-253-7458; Fax 508-526-8390
SAMS (AMS), ABYC, SNAME

Capt. Norman LeBlanc
Yacht Surveyor
23 Congress St.
Salem, MA 01970
508-744-8289; Fax 508-741-4365
SAMS (AMS)

Allen Perry
Ocean Adventures, Inc.
419 Sippewissett Rd.
Falmouth, MA 02540
508-540-5395; Fax 508-540-0560
SAMS (SA), ABYC, NAMS

Norman Schreiber II
Transtech - Marine Division
140 Wendward Way
Hyannis, MA 02601
508-775-0183
SNAME, ABYC, NFPA

Ronald Tarr
Harris Associates
9 Rocky Neck Ave.
Gloucester, MA 01930
508-281-6600; Fax 508-281-2460
SAMS (AMS), ABYC

Donald Walwer
D&G Marine, Inc.
PO Box 635
North Eastham, MA 02651
508-255-2406; Fax 508-255-2406
SAMS (AMS)

MICHIGAN

Jim Cukrowicz
Personal Marine Services
52671 CR 388
Grand Junction, MI 49056
616-434-6396; Fax 616-637-4040
SAMS (AMS)

Capt. A. John Lobbezoo
Great Lakes Marine Surveyors, Inc.
PO Box 466, 16100 Highland Dr.
Spring Lake, MI 49456-0466
616-842-9400; Fax 616-842-9401
SAMS (AMS), ABYC, NFPA

Robert McCarthy, Jr.
Robert McCarthy, Marine Surveyor
30060 South River Rd.
Mt. Clemens, MI 48045
313-468-8390

Terry Purdie
Marine Surveyors Company
25025 Jefferson Ave.
St. Clair Shores, MI 48080
313-773-8859

MINNESOTA

A. William Fredell
Marine Surveyor
408 Quarry Lane
Stillwater, MN 55082
612-439-5795
SAMS (AMS)

Marine Surveyor Directory

Paul Liedl
Croix Marine Consultants
531 Mariner Dr.
Bayport, MN 55003
612-439-7748
SAMS (SA), ABYC

John Rantala, Jr.
Rantala Marine Surveys & Services
1671 - 10th Ave, #2
Newport, MN 55055
612-458-5842
SAMS (AMS), ABYC

MISSISSIPPI

Edna Rae Andre
Rush Andre Marine Surveyor & Consultant
414 McGuire Circle
Gulfport, MS 39507
601-863-5962; Fax 601-865-9776
SAMS (SA), ABYC, NFPA, NAMI

Robert Payne
Marine Management, Inc.
PO Box 1803
Ocean Springs, MS 39564
601-872-2846; Fax 601-872-2846
NAMS, ABYC

MISSOURI

Jim Hill, CMS
Marine Surveyor
3653 Boston Farm Rd.
St. Louis, MO 63044
800-967-6646

Peter Merrill
Merrill Marine Services
12231 Manchester Rd.
St. Louis, MO 63131
314-822-8002; Fax 314-822-1232
NAMS

William Wolter
Cairo Marine Service
209 S. Broadway, #161
Cape Girardeau, MO 63701
618-734-4370

NEW HAMPSHIRE

Capt. David A. Page
Marine Surveyor/Adjuster
2456 LaFayette Rd.
Portsmouth, NH 03801
603-433-1568; Fax 603-427-0876
SAMS (AMS), ABYC, NAMI, NFPA

Donald B. Pray
Donald B. Pray Associates
PO Box 340
Madison, NH 03849
603-367-8208; 800-454-7729
SAMS (AMS), ABYC, NFPA

NEW JERSEY

Charles Batten
Argo Marine Surveys
895 Briarcliff Drive
Toms River, NJ 08753

William Campbell
W.J. Campbell, Marine Surveyor
9 Gate Rd.
Tabernacle, NJ 08088
609-268-7476; Fax 609-268-2421
NAMS, SNAME

Frank Christiansen
Frank Christiansen Associates
280 Highway 35
Red Bank, NJ 07701-5900
908-530-7700; Fax 908-530-4716
NAMS

Capt. Rob Cozen
Certified Marine Surveyor
108 Ridge Rd.
Cherry Hill, NJ 08002
609-429-5508
USSA, ABYC, NAMI, SNAME

John Klose
Bayview Associates
PO Box 368
Barnegat Light, NJ 08006
609-494-7450
SAMS (AMS)

David Talbot
Talbot Marine Survey, Inc.
404 Maxon Ave.
Pt. Pleasant, NJ 08742

NEW YORK

Capt. Shawn Bartnett
Bartnett Marine Services, Inc.
52 Ontario St.
Honeoye Falls (Rochester), NY 14472
716-624-1380; Fax 716-624-4168
NAMS, ABYC, NFPA, SNAME, NAMI

Richard Belt
Marine Surveyors Bureau

2055 Merrick Rd., #386
Merrick, NY 11566
516-683-1199; Fax 914-684-9870
NAMS, ABYC, NFPA

Ward Bury
Marine Surveyor
PO Box 2247
Liverpool, NY 13089
315-461-8627; Fax 315-461-8627
SAMS (AMS), ABYC, NFPA

Rocco Citeno
Long Island Marine Surveyor, Inc.
PO Box 542
Sayville, NY 11782
516-589-6154; Fax 516-589-6154
ABYC, NFPA

Donald Cunningham
McGroder Marine Surveyors
Box 405, 228 Central Ave.
Silver Creek (Buffalo), NY 14136
716-934-7848; Fax 716-934-7849
NAMS, ABYC, NFPA

Capt. Jim Dias
Marine Surveyors Bureau
215 Central Ave.
White Plains, NY 10606
800-426-2825; Fax 914-684-9870
NAMS, SAMS (AMS), ABYC, NFPA

John Fitzgibbon
McGroder Marine Surveyors
Box 405, 228 Central Ave.
Silver Creek (Buffalo), NY 14136
716-934-7848; Fax 716-934-7849
NAMS, ABYC, NFPA

William Foster
Marine Surveyor
185 Harrison Place
Staten Island, NY 10310
718-816-0588; Fax 718-816-0588
SAMS (SA), ABYC, NFPA, NAMI

Joseph Gaigal
Suffolk Marine Surveying
RFD 1, Box 174G
St. James, NY 11780
516-584-6297; Fax 516-584-2265
SAMS (AMS), ABYC, NFPA, NAMI,SNAME

James Gambino
Marine Surveyor
66 Browns Blvd.
Ronkonkoma, NY 11779
516-588-5308; 800-381-1779
SAMS (SA), ABYC, NFPA, NAMI

Marine Surveyor Directory

Chris Garvey
Garvey & Scott Marine
15 Trail Rd.
Hampton Bays, NY 11946
516-723-3510; Fax 516-723-3510
SAMS (AMS), ABYC

Walter Lawrence
Lawrence Marine Services
PO Box 219
Alton, NY 14413
315-483-6680; Fax 315-483-6734
SAMS (SA)

William Matthews
Admiralty Marine Surveyors & Adjusters
PO Box 183
Westhampton, NY 11977-0183
516-288-3263; Fax 516-288-0253
NAMS, SNAME, ABYC

Daniel Merin
Daniel Merin, Marine Surveyor
PO Box 128
Chatham, NY 12037
518-392-2518; Fax 518-392-6287
SAMS (SA), ABYC

Capt. H.L. Olsen
Olsen Marine Surveyors Co.
PO Box 283
Port Jefferson, NY 11777
516-928-0711; Fax 516-928-0193
SNAME

William Reilly
Marine Surveyor
249 City Island Ave.
City Island, NY 10464
718-829-2365; 718-885-1617; Fax 718-829-2365
SAMS (AMS), SNAME

Paul Robinson
Marifax Marine Services
21 Swanview Dr.
Patchogue, NY 11772
516-654-3300; Fax 516-654-3300
SAMS (AMS), ABYC

Roy Scott Garvey & Scott Marine Surveyors
32 Colony Rd.
Port Jefferson Station, NY 11776
516-476-1010; Fax 516-331-8552
SAMS (AMS), ABYC

Kenneth Weinbrecht
Ocean Bay Marine Services
PO Box 668
Yaphank, NY 11980
516-924-4362; Fax 516-924-4381
SAMS (AMS), ABYC, NFPA, NAMI

NORTH CAROLINA

Rob Eberle
Eberle Marine Surveys
PO Box 124
New Bern, NC 28560
919-633-4280; Fax 919-635-1912
SAMS (AMS), ABYC

Carl Foxworth
Industrial Marine Claims, Inc.
9805 White Cascade Dr.
Charlotte, NC 28269
704-536-7511; Fax 803-651-7425
SAMS (AMS), ABYC, NAMI, NFPA

James C. Harper
James C. Harper & Associates
PO Box 494
Wrightsville Beach, NC 28480
919-452-0768
NAMS, SNAME

OHIO

Glen Kreis
Marine Surveyor
10558 Ridgevale Dr.
Cincinnati, OH 45240
513-851-5878

OKLAHOMA

Thomas Benton
Accredited Marine Surveyor
RR 3, Box 178-5
Cleveland, OK 74020
918-243-7689; Fax 918-243-7235
SAMS (AMS), NAMI, ABYC, NFPA

OREGON

Steven Cox
Marine Surveyors Northwest
7776 SW Barnard Dr.
Beaverton, OR 97007
503-641-4604

PENNSYLVANIA

Einar Groething
Technical Maritime Services
204 N. Benjamin Dr.
West Chester, PA 19382-1946
610-436-5110; Fax 610-436-5119
NAMS, M.E.

William Major
Bristol Yacht Services, Inc.
110 Mill St.
Bristol, PA 19007
215-788-0870; Fax 215-788-0790
SAMS (AMS), ABYC

RHODE ISLAND

Robert Daigle, SA
Marine Surveyor
141 Plain Road
North Kingstown, RI 02852
401-295-8061
SAMS (SA)

Richard Learned
Learned & Associates
84 Gateway Rd.
North Kingstown, RI 02852
401-294-9232; Fax 401-294-9710
ASA, ABYC, NAMI

Donald B. Pray
Donald B. Pray Associates
PO Box 1224
Newport, RI 02840
401-423-2774; 800-454-7729
Fax 401-423-0934
SAMS (AMS), ABYC, NFPA

Jon Stolte
Marine Surveyors Bureau
580 Thames St., #255
Newport, RI 02840
401-596-0101; Fax 203-399-4996
NAMS, ABYC, NFPA

SOUTH CAROLINA

Carl Foxworth
Industrial Marine Claims, Inc.
515 Creekside Dr.
Murrells Inlet, SC 29576
803-651-2800; Fax 803-651-7425
SAMS (AMS), ABYC, NAMI, NFPA

TENNESSEE

James Robbins
Marine Surveyor
1793 The Lane Road
Cookeville, TN, 38506-8756
615-537-6743, 615-537-6719
SAMS (AMS)

Marine Surveyor Directory

Rudolf H. Roemer
World Class Marine Services
3515 St. Elmo Ave.
Chattanooga, TN 37409
615-267-8557; Fax 615-267-8452
NAMS, SNAME

TEXAS

Bobby Brown
Blue Water Surveyors, Inc.
5009 Marcus Dr.
Flower Mound, TX 75028
214-355-1389; Fax 214-355-1758
SAMS (SA), ABYC

Peter Davidson
Able Seaman Marine Surveyors
320 S. Chaparral St.
Corpus Christi, TX 78401
512-884-7245; Fax 512-882-6631
SAMS (AMS), ABYC, NFPA, NAMI

James Merritt
Tangent Development Co.
1715 Harlequin Run
Austin, TX 78758
512-266-9248; Fax 512-835-8938
SAMS (AMS), ABYC, NAMI, SNAME, USSA

John B. Oliveros
Marine Surveyor
127 Marlin St.
Galveston, TX 77550
409-763-3123
NAMS, ABYC

Dale Vandermolen
C & V Marine Surveyors
PO Box 31174
Corpus Christi, TX 78463
512-855-3801
NAMS

VERMONT

William Talbott
Marine Surveyor
RD Box 2450
N. Ferrisburg, VT 05473
802-425-2973
NAMS

VIRGINIA

Bill Coker
Entre Nous Marine Services
PO Box 1865
Hampton, VA 23669
804-723-2883; Fax 804-867-7206
ABYC, NFPA, SAMS (SA)

L. Wayne Hudgins
Wolftrap Marine Surveying
Route 666
Hallieford, VA 23068
804-725-3410
SAMS (SA), ABYC

Stephen Knox
Knox Marine Consultants
355 Crawford St., #601
Portsmouth, VA 23704-2823
804-393-9788; Fax 804-393-9789
NAMS

Danny Reynolds
Aetna Casualty and Surety
5040 Corporate Woods Dr.
Virginia Beach, VA 23462
804-671-2757; Fax 804-671-2791
NAMS

George Zahn, Jr.
Ware River Associates
5604 Roanes Wharf Rd.
Gloucester, VA 23061
804-693-4329; Fax 804-693-4329
SAMS (AMS), SNAME, ABYC, NFPA

WASHINGTON

Matthew Harris
Reisner, McEwen & Harris
1333 Lincoln St., #323
Bellingham, WA 98226
360-647-6966; Fax 360-733-9022
NAMS, SAMS (AMS), ABYC

Capt. David L. Jackson
Marine Surveyors & Consultants
909 3rd St.
Anacortes, WA 98221
206-293-4528; Fax 206-293-0366
NAMS

John Marples
Marples Marine Services
4530 Se Firmont Dr.
Port Orchard, WA 98366
206-871-5634
NAMS

Jay McEwen
Reisner, McEwen & Assoc., Inc.
2500 Westlake Ave. North, #D
Seattle, WA 98109
206-285-8194; Fax 206-285-8196
NAMS, ABYC, ASA

Steve Nelson
Marine Surveyor
PO Box 1356
Friday Harbor, WA 98250-1356
206-392-1670

Ronald Reisner
Reisner, McEwen & Assoc., Inc.
2500 Westlake Ave. North, #D
Seattle, WA 98109
206-285-8194; Fax 206-285-8196
NAMS, SAMS (AMS)

WISCONSIN

Chris Kelly
Professional Yacht Services
2132 - 89th Street, #1
Kenosha, WI 53143
800-535-0072; Fax 708-872-0073
SAMS (SA), ABYC, NFPA, NAMI

Edward Montgomery
Northern Marine Survey Co.
1014 John Avenue
Superior, WI 54880
715-394-6848
ABYC

1996
EDITION

The McKnew/Parker
Consumer's Guide to

SPORTFISHING
BOATS

28'–82'

1975–Current

ALBEMARLE 30 EXPRESS

SPECIFICATIONS

Length ....29'9"	Waste ....15 gals.
Beam ....11'0"	Clearance ....NA
Draft ....NA	Hull Type.................Deep-V
Weight ....13,500#	Deadrise Aft....................22°
Fuel ....300 gals.	Designer ....Albemarle
Water ....30 gals.	Production 1995–Current

The Albemarle 30 Express is a tournament-level sportfisherman with the kind of drop-dead sex appeal one normally associates with a custom-built boat. Newest in the line of well-regarded Albemarle designs, the 30 Express is heavily built on a solid fiberglass, deep-V hull with plenty of beam and a well-flared bow. Albemarle boats have long known for their superb ride and excellent handling qualities, but the huge cockpit—one of the largest to be found in a boat this size—comes as a surprise. Here, an angler will find such amenities as split tackle centers, a circulating transom livewell and excellent storage. The helm console is on the centerline, and the entire helm deck can be hydraulically raised for access to the engines. Below, the upscale cabin is arranged with V-berths forward (the backrests swing up to become single berths) along with a head (with a stall shower!), a spacious galley area and good headroom. Twin 300-hp Cat diesels will cruise the 30 Express at 28–29 knots and reach a top speed of 34 knots. ❏

ALBEMARLE 32 FLYBRIDGE

SPECIFICATIONS

Length ....32'2"	Fuel ....309 gals.
Beam ....10'11"	Cockpit ....85 sq. ft.
Draft ....3'0"	Hull Type.................Deep-V
Weight ....18,000#	Deadrise Aft....................18°
Clearance ....NA	Designer ....Albemarle
Water ....49 gals.	Production 1988–Current

From a distance, the Albemarle 32 has the bold and aggressive profile of a larger boat. Those who have been aboard the smaller Albemarle 27 will not be surprised with the quality engineering built into the 32 Flybridge. Her deep-V hull (18° transom deadrise) is solid fiberglass and reinforced on the bottom with a grid stringer system. The unobstructed cockpit is set up for serious fishing and includes two fish boxes under the sole. Inside, there's a real salon with room for a sofa and chairs—very unusual in just a 32-foot fishing boat. A double berth is fitted in the stateroom of early models (V-berths are now standard), and a stall shower is located in the head. Attractively decorated and featuring plenty of teak cabinetry and trim, this is a surprisingly spacious interior. Standard (but less popular) 454-cid gas engines will cruise the Albemarle 32 Flybridge at 22 knots and reach 32 knots top. Optional 300-hp Cummins diesels will cruise at a fast 27 knots and deliver 31–32 knots wide open. ❏

See Page 257 for Pricing Information

See Page 257 for Pricing Information

ALBEMARLE 32 EXPRESS

SPECIFICATIONS

Length	32'2"	Fuel	320 gals.
Beam	10'11"	Cockpit	NA
Draft	3'0"	Hull Type	Deep-V
Weight	13,500#	Deadrise Aft	18°
Clearance	NA	Designer	Albemarle
Water	50 gals.	Production	1990–Current

Sharing the same all-glass deep-V hull as the original 32 Flybridge, the Albemarle 32 Express is a dedicated offshore sportfisherman with a well-arranged and efficient cockpit layout to go with her basic, no-frills cabin accommodations. Albemarle has a history of building no-nonsense fishing boats, and the 32 Express is a very substantial platform indeed. Aside from her good looks and solid construction, she's loaded with practical features. The cockpit is large and completely unobstructed—no protruding cleats or hatches anywhere. The raised helm provides excellent visibility, and the side decks are wide enough to allow safe passage forward. There are two large in-deck fish boxes with macerator pumps and washdowns under the gunwales. For engine access, the entire bridgedeck can be hydraulically raised at the flick of a switch. If the belowdecks accommodations are limited, they're tastefully finished and include berths for four and a stand-up head. Cat or Cummins 300-hp diesels will cruise the Albemarle 32 Express at a fast 27–28 knots and reach 32 knots top. ❏

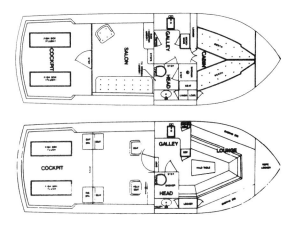

ALBIN 28 TOURNAMENT EXPRESS

SPECIFICATIONS

Length w/Pulpit	29'11"	Water	36 gals.
Hull Length	28'4"	Fuel, std	132 gals.
Beam	9'9"	Fuel, opt	192 gals.
Draft, I/Os	1'10"	Hull Type	Modified-V
Draft, Inboard	3'2"	Deadrise Aft	16°
Weight	7,500#	Production	1993–Current

The Albin 28 is a practical coastal fisherman with a large cockpit, wide side decks, and a roomy interior with accommodations for four. A traditional-looking boat with her Downeast styling, her balsa-cored hull boasts a prop-protecting skeg for increased tracking and stability. A centerline engine box completely dominates the cockpit (standard power is a single V-drive inboard), but there's still plenty of working space for anglers. An optional molded hardtop with sliding side windows makes the helm a semi-enclosed area. Inside, the look is straightforward and basic—white gel-coated bulkheads, snap-out carpeting, and a few pieces of teak trim. A quarter berth extends beneath the bridgedeck, and the cabin headroom is adequate thanks to the raised foredeck. Additional features include a side-dumping exhaust, stainless steel radar arch, and a transom livewell. The engine box in the center of the cockpit provides easy engine access. Note that a bow thruster is a popular option. A single V-drive 280-hp GM diesel will cruise the Albin 28 at an efficient 18–19 knots with a top speed of about 22 knots. ❏

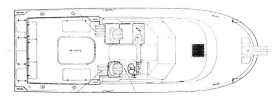

See Page 257 for Pricing Information   **See Page 257 for Pricing Information**

ALBIN 32 SPORTFISHER

SPECIFICATIONS

Length	32'4"	Fuel	280 gals.
Beam	12'3"	Cockpit	92 sq. ft.
Draft	3'10"	Hull Type	Modified-V
Weight	13,500#	Deadrise Aft	14°
Clearance	8'10"	Designer	T. Compton
Water	96 gals.	Production	1989–Current

The 32 Sportfisher represented a departure from Albin's trawler-boat heritage when she came out in 1989—an attempt to crack the sport fishing market with a practical and fuel-efficient trunk cabin express cruiser. Built on a modified-V hull with a full-length keel and moderate deadrise aft, the Albin 32 features a large fishing cockpit with livewell, bait rigging center, transom door, seawater washdown, and lockable rod storage as standard. The side decks are wide, and high bulwarks provide secure footing in rough seas. Below, the U-shaped dinette in the standard floorplan will sleep two, and a unique mid-cabin fitted beneath the bridgedeck has a double berth and a single berth to port. An optional layout introduced in 1994 has three staterooms with the galley aft. Headroom is excellent thanks to the raised foredeck, and hatches in the cockpit sole provide good access to the engine and V-drive unit. With the standard single 300-hp Cummins diesel, she'll cruise around 18 knots with an outstanding 700 miles-plus range. Note that a bow thruster is standard with single-screw installations. ❑

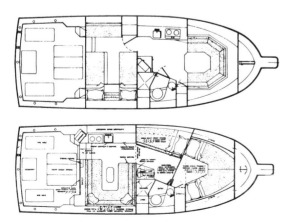

See Page 257 for Pricing Information

ATLANTIC 34 SPORTSMAN

SPECIFICATIONS

Length	34'0"	Fuel	300 gals.
Beam	12'0"	Cockpit	NA
Draft	3'0"	Hull Type	Modified-V
Weight	13,500#	Deadrise Aft	16°
Clearance	8'0"	Designer	J. Scopinich
Water	40 gals.	Production	1988–92

Until the 34 Sportsman came along, Atlantic Yachts had been known primarily for their line of trawler-style cruisers and motor yachts. It came as a surprise, then, to see their first new design in years fall into the sportfisherman category. A popular model with good handling qualities, she was built on a solid fiberglass hull with a modified-V bottom and generous flare at the bow. Her large bi-level cockpit was offered in several deck configurations for use as an express cruiser or sportfisherman. A centerline hatch on the bridgedeck provides decent access to the motors. Below, the cabin accommodations are laid out in the conventional manner with V-berths forward, an enclosed head with shower, small galley, and a dinette seating area. Standard gas 454-cid engines cruise the Sportsman at 25 knots and reach a top speed of 31–32 knots. Optional 300-hp GM 8.2 diesels cruise around 27 knots and reach 31 knots top. A total of 77 Atlantic 34s were built before production ended in 1992. ❑

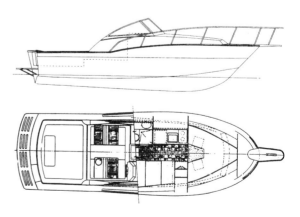

See Page 258 for Pricing Information

THE NEW BERTRAM 46
DESIGNED WITH THE MOST POWERFUL COMPUTER OF ALL:
THE MIND OF THE BOAT ENTHUSIAST.

You might call it "higher technology."

It's the ability to instinctively know, from the sound of an engine or the feel of a helm, exactly how to balance a boat, refine her, and perfect her.

It's a quality you'll only find in boatbuilders who have spent their 35 years on the water, instead of behind the desk. Boatbuilders as obsessive and enthusiastic about their boats as the people who buy them.

This is what's behind the totally new Bertram 46.

Strong, rugged, and seaworthy, she's every inch a Bertram. But in every way, this boat improves upon a predecessor most people thought was already nearly perfect.

Her new, even smoother-riding hull lets her go faster, farther, and accelerate quicker, without a single extra horsepower.

Her ingenious mid-galley design keeps the chef out of the salon, but not out of the fun.

And although she's a 46 in the slip, she feels like a 60 below. With a stylish, airy, all-new interior finished in light maple; two state-rooms, two heads, a roomy dinette; even a standard washer/dryer.

After carefully listening to hundreds of other Bertram enthusiasts, we have incorporated just about everything on their collective wish list - a list of new features and refinements that could go on and on.

As our president and most ardent boat enthusiast says, "You have to see and feel the new 46 to truly understand how special she really is."

So naturally, we invite you to visit a Bertram dealer soon and see the boat destined to be one of the world's top sportfishermen. Call 305-633-8011, or fax 305-635-1388.

We believe that once your mind processes the data, you'll find greatness to be an inescapable conclusion.

BERTRAM
The Dynasty Continues.

BERTRAM 28 FLYBRIDGE CRUISER

SPECIFICATIONS

Length	28'6"	Fuel	165/185/240 gals.
Beam	11'0"	Cockpit	85 sq. ft.
Draft	2'8"	Hull Type	Deep-V
Weight	12,060#	Deadrise Aft	23°
Clearance	9'4"	Designer	D. Napier
Water	54 gals.	Production	1971–94

With over 2,800 built, the 28 FB Cruiser is the best-selling Bertram ever. Designed along the lines of the classic Bertram 31, the 28 quickly established her reputation as a durable offshore fisherman and high-quality family cruiser. An excellent sea boat, she's built on a deep-V hull with a steep 23° of transom deadrise. Her cabin layout includes berths for four with a dinette, an efficient galley, and a stand-up head. The mica interior was dropped in 1983 and replaced with a contemporary light oak woodwork. Updates in 1990 included a rearranged interior with a more open floorplan and an enlarged flybridge. An optional teak interior became available in 1991. Superior workmanship and constant engineering updates and refinements have kept her in the forefront of small fishing boat designs. Twin 228/230-hp gas engines (21 knots cruise/30 knots top) were standard until 1986, when they were replaced with the current 260-hp MerCruisers (23 cruise/32 top). Updates in 1992 include optional 230-hp Volvo diesels (27 knots cruise). Fuel increases came in 1980 and 1986. ❏

BERTRAM 28 SPORT FISHERMAN

SPECIFICATIONS

Length	28'6"	Fuel	185 gals.
Beam	11'0"	Cockpit	85 sq. ft.
Draft	2'8"	Hull Type	Deep-V
Weight	11,320#	Deadrise Aft	23°
Clearance	9'4"	Designer	D. Napier
Water	27 gals.	Production	1971–83

The Bertram 28 Sport Fisherman has the same deep-V hull and superstructure profile of her sistership, the 28 Flybridge Cruiser, but with an open deckhouse (no salon bulkhead) for improved fishability. A galley and dinette were optional (although most were so equipped), and the head is fitted below the forward berths in the cabin. Simple and easy to clean, this type of basic open-air deck layout is ideal in a sportfishing day boat. Few changes were made to the 28 SF during her long production run, and while she never attained the level of popularity enjoyed by the more versatile Flybridge Cruiser, used models are still valued today by knowledgeable anglers. From the standpoint of construction and design, few production fishing boats in this size range can match the performance of the Bertram 28s in bad weather. Indeed, her seakeeping qualities are phenomenal for such a small flybridge boat. Note the unique grabrails which serve to divide the cockpit from spectators. Most were powered with 230-hp MerCruiser engines for a cruising speed of around 20–21 knots and a top speed of 30. ❏

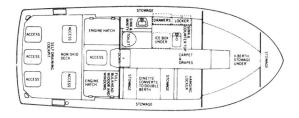

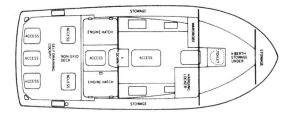

See Page 258 for Pricing Information

See Page 258 for Pricing Information

BERTRAM 28 BAHIA MAR

SPECIFICATIONS

Length	28'6"	Fuel	185/240 gals.
Beam	11'0"	Cockpit	85 sq. ft.
Draft	2'8"	Hull Type	Deep-V
Weight	11,700#	Deadrise Aft	23°
Clearance	7'10"	Designer	D. Napier
Water	48 gals.	Production	1985–92

The Bertram 28 Bahia Mar shares the same hull as the Bertram 28 FBC and SF models. Easily recognized in a crowd, her low-profile deckhouse and wraparound windshield reflect a distinctive European styling influence. The Bahia Mar is a superb sea boat, and her deep-V hull and low center of gravity result in superior offshore performance and handling characteristics. Equally at home as an offshore fisherman or pocket cruiser, she features a large, unobstructed cockpit with low freeboard and a basic (but well-finished) cabin layout offering overnight accommodations for two. Visibility from the helm position is good, and sightlines are excellent in all directions. The original raised engine boxes were eliminated in the 1986 models in favor of a flush deck; either way, service access to the motors is good. An impressive performer, standard 260-hp MerCruiser gas engines will cruise the 28 Bahia Mar around 23 knots and reach a top speed of 32–33 knots. Twin 230-hp Volvo diesels (28 knots cruise) became optional in 1992. The fuel capacity was increased in 1986 to 240 gallons. ❑

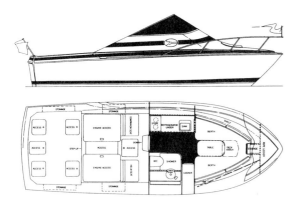

See Page 258 for Pricing Information

BERTRAM 28 MOPPIE

SPECIFICATIONS

Length	28'6"	Fuel	234 gals.
Beam	11'0"	Cockpit	85 sq. ft.
Draft	2'7"	Hull Type	Deep-V
Weight	10,400#	Deadrise Aft	23°
Clearance	7'1"	Designer	D. Napier
Water	27 gals.	Production	1987–94

The latest in a long string of Bertram 28-footers, the Moppie is a very stylish inboard runabout with the quality engineering expected of a Bertram product. Her sleek profile is attractively accented with painted windshield frame and bowrails, and the Moppie has the modern sportboat "look" popular with many of today's performance-boat buyers. She's built on the standard Bertram 28 deep-V hull with solid fiberglass construction and a steep 23° of transom deadrise. Aside from her superb handling characteristics, the Moppie's primary attraction is her expansive and versatile bi-level cockpit layout. The lower level has a generous 85 sq. ft. of fishing space with plenty of room for a fighting chair. In a practical design application, the galley is concealed in molded lockers abaft the helm and companion seats in the cockpit. The cabin accommodations are basic with a head and V-berths. A good performer with standard 260-hp MerCruiser gas engines, the 28 Moppie will cruise around 24 knots and reach 31–32 knots top. Optional 230-hp Volvo diesels cruise at 28 knots. ❑

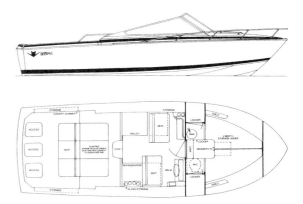

See Page 258 for Pricing Information

28

SPECIFICATIONS

Length	30'7"	Fuel	220 gals.
Beam	11'4"	Cockpit	101 sq. ft.
Draft	3'0"	Hull Type	Deep-V
Weight	16,500#	Deadrise Aft	18.5°
Clearance	8'5"	Designer	D. Napier
Water	61 gals.	Production	1984–85

Bertram rarely misfires when it comes to new model introductions, so it's notable when one of their designs fails to catch on with the public. Such was the case with the Bertram 30 Flybridge Cruiser—a boat that some (including a lot of industry professionals) thought destined to replace the classic Bertram 31 in the hearts of serious anglers. She's exactly the same length as the Bertram 31, but with slightly smaller cockpit dimensions, less transom deadrise (18.5° vs. 23°), improved trolling stability, and a notably dryer ride. The improvements carried into the interior as well, where the Bertram 30's stylish oak-paneled accommodations provide luxuries undreamed of in the old Bertram 31. Lasting only two years in production, the Bertram 30 Flybridge Cruiser proved too expensive for the market, and she was withdrawn in 1985. With standard MerCruiser 340-hp gas engines, she'll cruise at 22 knots and reach a top speed of about 30 knots. Note that the equally short-lived Bertram 30 Express Cruiser (1984–85) is the same boat without the flybridge. ❏

See Page 258 for Pricing Information

Sport Cruiser

Sportfish

SPECIFICATIONS

Length	30'6"	Fuel	275 gals.
Beam	11'3"	Cockpit	50 sq. ft.
Draft	2'11"	Hull Type	Deep-V
Weight	12,500#	Deadrise Aft	18.5°
Clearance	NA	Designer	Bertram
Water	40 gals.	Production	1994–Current

Designed to appeal to cruisers as well as anglers, the Bertram 30 Moppie is a good-looking inboard express with a sleek profile to go with her rugged construction. Employing the hull from the Bertram 30 FBC (1984–85), the Moppie's clean lines offer plenty of sex appeal without the integral swim platform and molded pulpit common in other modern express boats. Three deck plans make her adaptable to fishing, cruising, or daytime activities. The standard layout has a helm seat and a wide-open bridge; the Sport Cruiser features a large L-shaped settee opposite the helm; and the Sportfish version comes with a companion seat, bait prep center, washdowns and rod holders. The interior is the same for all three versions with a double berth forward, a small galley, dinette, and a stand-up head with shower. Access to the motors (which are below the bridgedeck) is very good. Standard 454-cid gas engines will cruise the Moppie at 23 knots and reach 31 top. Optional 291 Cummins (or 300-hp Cats) will cruise at 27 knots (31 top), and 340-hp Cats will cruise about 30 knots and reach 33 wide open. ❏

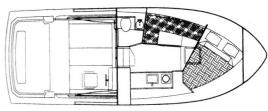

Standard Deck Layout

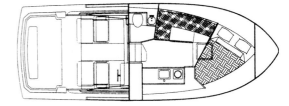

Optional Sportfish Layout

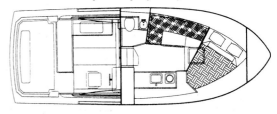

Optional Sport Cruiser Layout

See Page 258 for Pricing Information

BERTRAM 31 FLYBRIDGE CRUISER

SPECIFICATIONS

Length	30'7"	Fuel	170/222 gals.
Beam	11'2"	Cockpit	110 sq. ft.
Draft	3'1"	Hull Type	Deep-V
Weight	10,600#	Deadrise Aft	23°
Clearance	11'0"	Designer	Ray Hunt
Water	18 gals.	Production	1961–83

Nothing in powerboating has equaled the continued worldwide popularity of the original deep-V boat—the Bertram 31. One of several Bertram 31 models, nearly 2,000 Flybridge Cruisers were built over the years, and used models are continually in demand regardless of age or condition. Unquestionably, the chief attribute of any Bertram 31 is her legendary deep-V hull design. In addition to her superb seakeeping characteristics (and a sometimes wet ride), the 31 FBC has a large fishing cockpit and comfortable (if Spartan) cabin accommodations with berths for four. Regular production ended in 1983, but 23 "Silver Anniversary" models were built in 1986 with oak interiors and custom hull striping. Twin 330-hp MerCruiser gas engines have powered the majority of the Bertram 31s, with several GM, Cat, or Cummins diesels offered as options. The Mercruisers cruise around 23 knots with a top speed of 32+ knots. Diesel-powered 31 FBCs have less speed and horsepower but greatly improved range (300+ miles). Note that the fuel capacity increased in 1972 from 170 to 222 gallons. ❏

See Page 258 for Pricing Information

BERTRAM 31 SPORT FISHERMAN

SPECIFICATIONS

Length	30'7"	Fuel	170/222 gals.
Beam	11'2"	Cockpit	110 sq. ft.
Draft	3'1"	Hull Type	Deep-V
Weight	10,600#	Deadrise Aft	23°
Clearance	11'0"	Designer	Ray Hunt
Water	18 gals.	Production	1961–82

The Bertram 31 Sport Fisherman is the quintessential American fishing machine—a genuine classic that gave birth to the deep-V hull design and (not incidentally) to the Bertram company as well. This is one of the few small boats that can compete in bluewater tournament events without being at all out of place. Performance in head and following seas is outstanding, and her open cabin layout and ease of maintenance quickly earned the 31 SF a loyal and dedicated following among serious anglers and charter boat operators. Over 500 changes were made in the Bertram 31 during her long production run (mainly cosmetic or hardware-related), but the only significant design modification consisted of widening the hull chines in the early days. Standard 330-hp MerCruiser gas engines will cruise around 23 knots and reach a top speed of 33 knots. Many diesel options were offered over the years. The fuel capacity was increased in 1972 from the original 170 gallons to 222 gallons. A stable and highly maneuverable sportfisherman, used Bertram 31s are always in demand despite her well-known reputation for being a wet ride. ❏

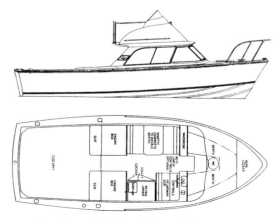

See Page 258 for Pricing Information

BERTRAM 31 BAHIA MAR

SPECIFICATIONS

Length	30'7"	Fuel	222 gals.
Beam	11'2"	Cockpit	147 sq. ft.
Draft	2'9"	Hull Type	Deep-V
Weight	9,400#	Deadrise Aft	23°
Clearance	8'3"	Designer	Ray Hunt
Water	18 gals.	Production	1966–81

Built on the legendary Bertram 31 deep-V hull with a steep 23° of deadrise at the transom, the 31 Bahia Mar is an open sport-cruiser design with a large fishing cockpit and basic interior accommodations for two. Bahia Mars have attracted a remarkable following among serious anglers who have come to appreciate her numerous fishing attributes. The 31 Bahia Mar is a stable fishing platform and ranks with the best modern designs when it comes to overall fishability. Her completely open cockpit arrangement puts the helm close to the action, and the cockpit itself is much larger than in most other sportfishermen of her size. Visibility from the helm is another feature fisherman have come to admire—sightlines are excellent in all directions. The Bahia Mar is considered a superb all-round utility boat, and many have seen years of operation in charter and dive-boat fleets. Engine boxes provide easy access to the motors. Standard 330-hp gas engines cruise around 23 knots and reach about 33 knots top. Several diesel options were offered over the years. ❏

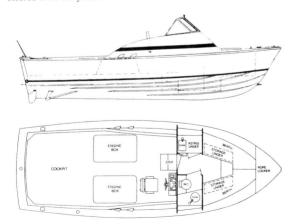

See Page 258 for Pricing Information

BERTRAM 33 FLYBRIDGE CRUISER

SPECIFICATIONS

Length	33'0"	Fuel, Gas	250/315 gals.
Beam	12'6"	Fuel, Dsl.	255 gals.
Draft	3'0"	Cockpit	72 sq. ft.
Weight	22,800#	Hull Type	Deep-V
Clearance	12'6"	Deadrise Aft	17°
Fresh Water	70 gals.	Production	1977–92

The Bertram 33 FB Cruiser is a particularly flexible boat that can provide adequate service as a weekend fisherman while still offering excellent cruising accommodations. Combined with her deep-V hull, the 33 FBC's high deckhouse makes for a tender boat offshore. She was originally offered with a single-stateroom layout until a more popular two-stateroom interior became standard in 1980. In 1981 a new tournament flybridge was added, and in 1984 a teak interior decor replaced the woodgrain mica cabinetry. The Bertram 33 II version (introduced in 1988) has a restyled flybridge and an oak interior. Changes in 1990 included a revised layout with a stall shower in the head. In 1992, a varnished maple interior became standard (teak was optional). Twin 454-cid gas engines will cruise the Bertram 33 around 19 knots. Optional 260-hp Cats cruise at 22 knots, and the newer 320-hp Cats cruise at 25–26 knots (30 knots top). Note that the fuel capacity was increased for the gas models in 1980, although late diesel-powered 33s were still fitted with a 255-gallon tank. ❏

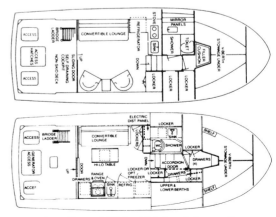

See Page 258 for Pricing Information

32

BERTRAM 33 SPORT FISHERMAN

SPECIFICATIONS

Length ....33'0"	Fuel, Gas........250/310 gals.
Beam.............................12'6"	Fuel, Dsl. ....250 gals.
Draft ....3'0"	Cockpit..................116 sq. ft.
Weight ....22,400#	Hull Type................Deep-V
Clearance ....11'6"	Deadrise Aft ....17°
Water ....70 gals.	Production 1979–92

The Bertram 33 SF is a big boat for her size with good styling, superior construction, and proven offshore performance. Built on the same hull as the 33 FB Cruiser, she has a larger cockpit than her sistership but no salon. Her aggressive low-profile lines, spacious flybridge, and top-quality engineering have made the 33 a favorite with deep-water fishermen. The interior accommodations were enlarged and rearranged in 1986 by moving the cabin bulkhead aft a few inches and replacing the dinette with a settee. The loss in cockpit space (122 to 116 sq. ft.) is negligible. A light oak interior was added in 1985, and the flybridge was restyled in 1988. Engines are located under raised boxes in the cockpit for easy access. Twin 330-hp gas engines were standard (20 knots cruise/29 knots top), and optional 260-hp 3208T Cat diesels were optional (23 knots cruise/27 knots top). Optional 320-hp Cats (1992 only) cruise at 27 knots and reach 31 knots top. Note that the fuel capacity for gas models was increased to 310 gallons in 1980. ❏

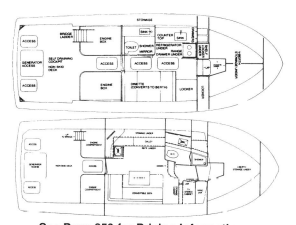

See Page 259 for Pricing Information

BERTRAM 35 CONVERTIBLE

SPECIFICATIONS

Length ....35'4"	Fuel................285/273 gals.
Beam.............................13'3"	Cockpit ....92 sq. ft.
Draft ....3'2"	Hull Type................Deep-V
Weight ....22,500#	Deadrise Aft...................19°
Clearance ....12'6"	Designer..............D. Napier
Water ....50/75 gals.	Production 1970–86

Few boats can rival the 15-year production run enjoyed by the Bertram 35 Convertible. For many, thirty-five feet is the ideal size for an offshore convertible short of going into serious debt. The Bertram 35's interior layout is well-suited for family cruising, although she's most at home as a fishing boat where her large cockpit, precise handling, and enviable seakeeping qualities are most appreciated. In 1981 a Mk II model came out with an updated tournament-style flybridge, and in 1984 a teak interior replaced the original woodgrain mica decor. Note that the vinyl cockpit sole of early models was replaced in 1982 with fiberglass—a notable improvement. Twin 350-hp Crusader gas engines were standard (19–20 knots cruise/28 top) during her production run, with 215-hp Cummins (around 18 knots cruise/22 knots top) or 300-hp Cat (23 knots cruise/27 knots top) diesels available as options. With the 300-hp Cats (1981–85 models), the Bertram 35 becomes a much improved performer. A popular boat, used models are always in demand. ❏

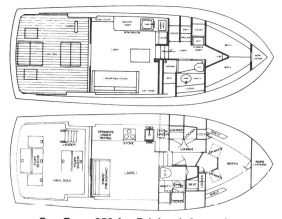

See Page 259 for Pricing Information

BERTRAM 37 CONVERTIBLE

SPECIFICATIONS

Length	37'9"	Fuel	473 gals.
Beam	13'3"	Cockpit	93 sq. ft.
Draft	3'9"	Hull Type	Deep-V
Weight	32,410#	Deadrise Aft	18°
Clearance	12'11"	Designer	D. Napier
Water	100 gals.	Production	1986–Current

Beautifully styled and designed for the rigors of tournament-level fishing and serious offshore cruising, the 37 Convertible has been a very popular boat for Bertram. She's built on a deep-V hull (cored from the waterline up) using modern unidirectional fabrics and carbon fiber composites throughout. Below, her upscale two-stateroom layout includes overhead rod storage in the salon, over/under bunks in the (very) small guest cabin, a walkaround island berth forward, and light oak cabinetry and woodwork throughout. Note that maple woodwork became standard beginning in 1993. Considered by many to be among the best in her class, the Bertram 37 receives high marks for her superb handling and exceptional performance. A fast boat, 450-hp 6V92s will cruise at 27 knots (31 knots top), and the more recent 550-hp 6V92s will cruise at 30 knots and reach 34+ knots wide open. Cat 375-hp diesels will cruise the Bertram 37 at 22–23 knots (27 knots top), and 435-hp 6V71s (1986–88 only) cruise at 24–25 knots. Resale values are excellent. ❑

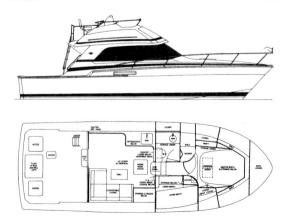

See Page 259 for Pricing Information

BERTRAM 38 CONVERTIBLE

SPECIFICATIONS

Length	37'8"	Fuel	350 gals.
Beam	14'5"	Cockpit	109 sq. ft.
Draft	3'6"	Hull Type	Deep-V
Weight	26,000#	Deadrise Aft	22°
Clearance	NA	Designer	Ray Hunt
Water	100 gals.	Production	1970–76

The Bertram 38 Convertible was the second of three 38-foot Bertram models built over the years, the first being a Hunt-designed flybridge cruiser produced for the family market back in the early 1960s. In the case of the 38 Convertible, the emphasis was on fishability, pure and simple. Her deep-V hull was designed along the lines of the original Bertram 31, and her extra-wide beam provides the stability often missing in an early deep-V designs. Long out of production but still popular with budget-minded anglers, her large and uncluttered fishing cockpit and practical cabin accommodations continue to have wide appeal in spite of her age. The interior is efficiently arranged with the galley up, V-berths in the forward stateroom, and over/under berths in the guest cabin. By any standard, the woodgrain mica interior of the Bertram 38 is plain, but clean-up is easy. Twin 325-hp gas engines were standard (18 knots cruise/27 knots top), however most of the Bertram 38 Convertibles were delivered with the GM 8V53 or Cummins V903 diesels and cruise around 17–18 knots. ❑

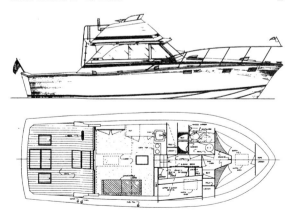

See Page 259 for Pricing Information

BERTRAM 38 III CONVERTIBLE

SPECIFICATIONS

Length	38'5"	Fuel	395 gals.
Beam	13'3"	Cockpit	100 sq. ft.
Draft	4'2"	Hull Type	Deep-V
Weight	30,400#	Deadrise Aft	17°
Clearance	13'0"	Designer	D. Napier
Water	100 gals.	Production	1978–86

The Bertram 38 III is an entirely different boat from the earlier Bertram 38 Convertible (1970–76). She has a more graceful profile, less beam, a shallower "V" bottom—from 22° of transom deadrise to a more moderate 17°—and generally improved handling characteristics. Aimed at the sportfishing market, the 38 III's large cockpit and tournament-style flybridge make her well suited for serious bluewater events. Inside, her two-stateroom layout is efficient and well organized. In 1982 Bertram replaced the original Nautilex cockpit sole with a fiberglass deck (a major improvement), and a teak interior became standard. A little wet at times, the 38 III is otherwise known as a capable sea boat. Nearly all were diesel powered. Cat 300-hp diesels (19–20 knots cruise) were popular as were the Cat 355-hp and Cummins 380-hp VT903 engines, both of which cruise around 23 knots. Production ceased in 1987 with the introduction of the Bertram 37. A total of 331 Bertram 38 IIIs were built making her one of the best-selling 38-foot sportfishing boats ever. ❏

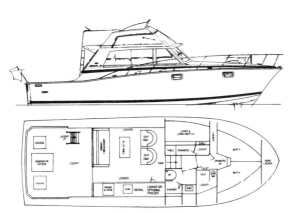

See Page 259 for Pricing Information

BERTRAM 38 SPECIAL

SPECIFICATIONS

Length	38'5"	Fuel	395 gals.
Beam	13'3"	Cockpit	97 sq. ft.
Draft	4'2"	Hull Type	Deep-V
Weight	27,000#	Deadrise Aft	17°
Clearance	9'11"	Designer	Bertram
Water	100 gals.	Production	1986–87

The Bertram 38 Special is a high-quality, fast-action sportfisherman with a huge fishing cockpit for serious tournament-level pursuits. Her hull is the same as that used in the 38 III Convertible but with balsa coring placed in the hullsides forward of the engine bulkhead. The design philosophy behind the 38 Special was to give the bluewater angler a pure, no-nonsense fishing machine with good performance and plenty of range. Although the interior is limited in size, the rounded bulkheads and radiused corners make the most of the available space. Visibility from the raised helm position is very good. A small hatch provides routine access to the engines, and the entire bridgedeck sole is removable for major work. Caterpillar 375-hp diesels were standard (23 knots cruise/27 knots wide open). GM 6V71TAs rated at 435-hp were optional and increased the cruising speed to about 25 knots and the top speed to 30 knots. A popular boat in resale markets, the Bertram 38 Special enjoyed limited market success due to her high cost and production ended after just two years. ❏

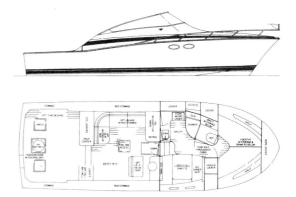

See Page 259 for Pricing Information

BERTRAM 42 CONVERTIBLE

SPECIFICATIONS

Length	42'6"	Fuel	488 gals.
Beam	14'10"	Cockpit	108 sq. ft.
Draft	4'0"	Hull Type	Deep-V
Weight	39,400#	Deadrise Aft	17°
Clearance	14'11"	Designer	Bertram
Water	150 gals.	Production	1976–87

One of Bertram's most successful boats, the 42 Convertible needs no introduction to anglers on either coast. A total of 329 of these boats were built, and her exceptional seakeeping abilities, superb fishability, long range, and top-quality construction have earned for the Bertram 42 a reputation as a classic design. Heavily built on a deep-V hull, numerous updates were made during her long production run. In 1981, the twin sliding salon doors were replaced with a single door, and the flybridge helm position was moved from portside to the centerline. In 1982, a teak interior replaced the earlier woodgrain mica decor (a welcome improvement). In another major upgrade, the original vinyl cockpit sole was replaced with fiberglass in 1982. In 1983, a queen bed became standard in the master stateroom. A restyled flybridge in 1986 added much to her profile, and an oak interior became standard in 1987. Cummins 420-hp diesels (popular through 1979) and 435-hp GM 6V92TAs (1980–84 models) cruise around 23–24 knots, and the more recent 475-hp 6V92TAs cruise at 25+ knots. ❏

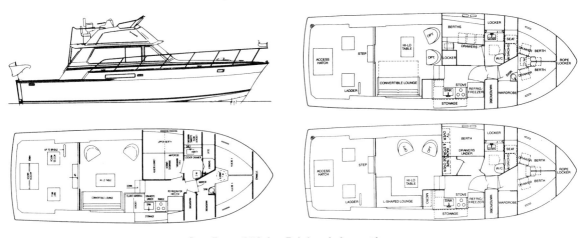

See Page 259 for Pricing Information

BERTRAM 43 CONVERTIBLE

SPECIFICATIONS

Length	43'4"	Fuel	546 gals.
Beam	14'11"	Cockpit	120 sq. ft.
Draft	4'4"	Hull Type	Deep-V
Weight	41,890#	Deadrise Aft	17°
Clearance	13'5"	Designer	Bertram
Water	160 gals.	Production	1988–Current

A popular boat since her introduction in 1988, the Bertram 43 Convertible is highly regarded among experienced, tournament-level anglers for her rugged construction, rakish appearance and superb open-water performance. She's built on a deep-V hull with cored hullsides, a well-flared bow and a solid fiberglass bottom. Her interior (several layouts have been offered over the years) is luxuriously appointed and finished with light oak or—since 1993—maple woodwork. Further updates in 1993 included a new U-shaped galley-up floorplan (that lasted one year) and direct cockpit access to the engine room. The current two-stateroom, mid-galley layout was introduced in 1994 with a dinette option in place of the second stateroom. Further improvements for '94 include moving the genset from under the cockpit sole to the engine room and restyled cabin windows. Additional features include side-dumping exhausts, wide sidedecks, a roomy engine room with good outboard access, molded tackle centers and a transom door. Twin 535-hp 6V92 Detroit diesels will cruise the Bertram 43 around 24–25 knots with a top speed of 28+ knots. In 1995, 655-hp MANs became available (27 knots cruise/30+ top). ❏

Original Galley-Up, Two-Stateroom Layout

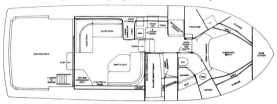

Original Galley-Down, Two-Stateroom Layout

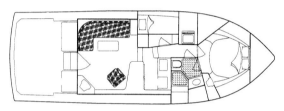

Standard Two-Stateroom, Mid-Galley Floorplan (Current)

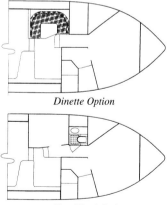

Dinette Option

Two-Head Option

See Page 260 for Pricing Information

37

BERTRAM 43 MOPPIE

Photo by Forrest Johnson

SPECIFICATIONS

Length	43'4"	Cockpit	106 sq. ft.
Beam	15'0"	Clearance	9'1"
Draft	4'8"	Hull Type	Deep-V
Weight	38,290#	Deadrise Aft	17°
Fuel	546 gals.	Designer	Bertram
Water	160 gals.	Production	1995–Current

Production express fishermen over forty feet have become popular in recent years and the new Bertram 43 Moppie is tough competition. This is certainly one of the best-looking boats Bertram has ever built. Like all Bertrams, she's heavily constructed on a rugged deep-V hull. Two different deck layouts are available: the cruising version has a radar arch and wraparound seating in the cockpit, and the sportfishing version has a completely unobstructed cockpit with a transom fish box, direct cockpit access to the engine room, rod storage, and a transom door and gate. Below decks, the Moppie's maplewood interior is arranged with a huge galley (with excellent storage), berths for four adults, and a spacious head with separate stall shower. Additional features include a molded bow pulpit, a double-wide helm seat with lounge seating opposite, and wide sidedecks. A good sea-boat, the 43 Moppie will cruise at a fast 27 knots with standard 550-hp 6V92 diesels and reach 30+ knots top. First available in 1996, the new 625-hp DDEC 6V92s will cruise at an honest 28 knots with a full tower and load.

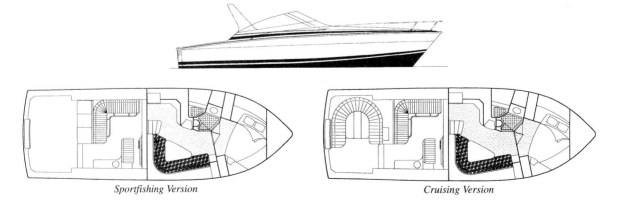

Sportfishing Version *Cruising Version*

See Page 260 for Pricing Information

BERTRAM 46 CONVERTIBLE (EARLY)

SPECIFICATIONS

Length	46'6"	Fuel	620/720 gals.
Beam	16'0"	Cockpit	117/130 sq. ft.
Draft	4'6"	Hull Type	Deep-V
Weight	44,900#	Deadrise Aft	19°
Clearance	15'6"	Designer	Bertram
Water	230/246 gals.	Production	1971–87

The Bertram 46 Convertible was for many years the standard by which other production sportfishing boats her size were measured. Her popularity has much to do with the precise handling and impressive seakeeping characteristics of the 46's deep-V hull design. Originally a two-stateroom boat with the galley down, a three-stateroom model (the 46 II) was available during 1983–85. Significant design changes include a single sliding salon door (replacing double doors) in 1981, a fiberglass cockpit sole (replacing the Nautilex liner) and a new teak interior in 1982, and a standard transom door in 1985. The 46 III model (1986–87) features an updated layout with oak woodwork and a centerline queen forward. Prior to 1981, the most popular engines were the 435-hp 8V71TIs, which will cruise around 20 knots and reach 23 knots top. In 1981, the 570-hp 8V92TIs became available (around 24 knots cruise), and the 600-hp versions (1985–87) added another knot of speed. Note that the fuel capacity was increased to 720 gallons in 1983. ❏

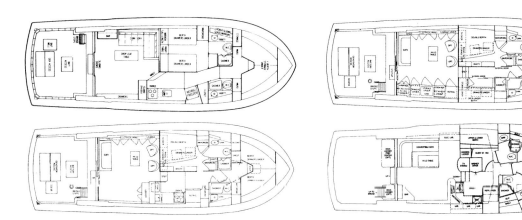

See Page 260 for Pricing Information

BERTRAM 46 CONVERTIBLE

SPECIFICATIONS

Length	46'3"	Cockpit	120 sq. ft.
Beam	15'1"	Clearance	13'5"
Draft	4'10"	Hull Type	Deep-V
Weight	46,100#	Deadrise Aft	17.5°
Fuel	800 gals.	Designer	Bertram
Water	175 gals.	Production	1995–Current

Few production boats attained the classic status enjoyed by the original Bertram 46 Convertible, a legendary tournament machine with superb all-weather handling characteristics. The new 46 is a completely redesigned boat with a greatly improved profile to go with her upgraded interior and faster cruising speeds. Her deep-V hull—basically a stretched version of the Bertram 43 hull—is very dry and a lot more more stable at trolling speeds than the original 46 thanks to the widened chine flats. Note the long fore-deck; the house sits well aft giving the boat a very rakish appearance. The standard two-stateroom floorplan is arranged with the mid-level galley two steps down from the salon level. The owner's stateroom is amidships (where it should be), and both heads are fitted with stall showers. The salon, with its raised dinette forward and maple woodwork, presents an altogether appealing and upscale decor. On the downside, the engine room (with cockpit access) is on the small side. A good performer, standard 8V92 diesels will cruise the Bertram 46 at a fast 27–28 knots (about 31 knots top). ❏

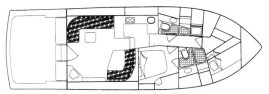

Standard Two-Stateroom Floorplan

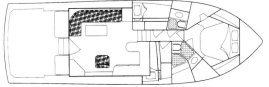

Optional Three-Stateroom Floorplan

See page 260 for pricing information

Don't Just Fish for the Day,
Fish For The Future.

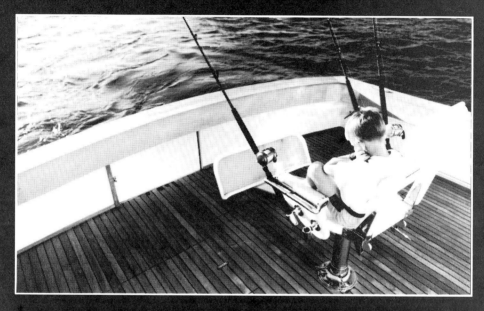

JOIN THE FOUNDATION.

Billfish are being withdrawn from our oceans faster than they can multiply. Commercial longlines and gillnets pose the greatest threat to these noble pelagics, the ultimate symbols of marine wildlife. For that reason, The Billfish Foundation has spent the last nine years investing member dollars in studying the biology and behavior of the world's billfish species. Now, TBF is the world's leading billfish conservation advocate, delivering the hard scientific facts necessary to rebuild the oceans' billfish populations.

Join The Foundation and participate in an organization that is securing the future of billfish. Your membership dollars will support such programs as the Youth Education Program, Tag & Release Program and No Marlin on the Menu. *To learn more about how you can make a difference, please call today.*

The Billfish Foundation · 2419 E. Commercial Blvd., Suite 303 · Ft. Lauderdale, FL 33308
(305) 938-0150 · FAX (305) 938-5311 · TOLL FREE 1-800-438-8247

BERTRAM 46 MOPPIE

SPECIFICATIONS

Length	46'0"	Fuel	650 gals.
Beam	14'11"	Cockpit	106 sq. ft.
Draft	4'8"	Hull Type	Deep-V
Weight	42,000#	Deadrise Aft	17°
Clearance	9'1"	Designer	Dave Napier
Water	135 gals.	Production	1993–Current

Introduced in 1993, the Bertram 46 Moppie is built on a stretched 43 Convertible hull with cored hullsides, a wide beam, and a fairly steep 17° of transom deadrise. This is one of the bigger express cruisers to be found and she's designed to meet the needs of fishermen and upscale sportcruisers alike. Offered with a choice of two floorplans, the single-stateroom layout (with two heads—very unusual) is aimed at the sportfish market while the two-stateroom layout is more suited for cruising activities. Either way, there's seating on the bridgedeck for a small crowd, and the sportfish version includes molded tackle centers in the cockpit. Until 1995, the Moppie had reversed engines with V-drive-like shaft couplers. The current engines, however, are straight inboards. Also in 1995, the genset was moved from under the cockpit into the more protected environment of the engine room. A good-running boat and a comfortable ride in a chop, a pair of 735-hp 8V-92s will cruise the Bertram 46 Moppie at a fast 28–29 knots and reach top speeds in the neighborhood of 32 knots. ❑

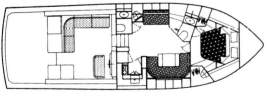

Standard Stateroom w/Sport Option (1993–94)

Double Stateroom Cruising Layout (1993–94)

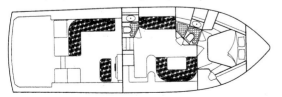

Standard Stateroom w/Sport Option (1995)

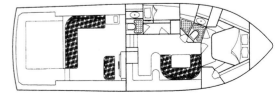

Double Stateroom Cruising Layout (1995)

See Page 260 for Pricing Information

BERTRAM 50 CONVERTIBLE

SPECIFICATIONS

Length	50'0"	Fuel	1,046 gals.
Beam	16'0"	Cockpit	108 sq. ft.
Draft	5'0"	Hull Type	Deep-V
Weight	56,531#	Deadrise Aft	17°
Clearance	15'9"	Designer	Bertram
Water	175 gals.	Production	1987–Current

A beautifully styled boat with a truly aggressive profile, the Bertram 50 Convertible is considered by many to represent the state of the art in production sportfishermen of her size. She's been a popular boat from the beginning and resale values are extremely strong in all markets. Built on a deep-V hull with cored hullsides and a relatively wide beam, her seakeeping qualities are excellent. Initially offered in a three-stateroom layout with the galley up, a spacious two-stateroom galley-down interior with an enormous salon became available in 1988. She received a complete update in 1994 including two new layouts and a fresh deckhouse profile with new windows and stripes. A transom door and tackle center are standard in the cockpit, and a wraparound helm console (also updated for '94) eliminates the need for an overhead electronics box. A good performer, 735-hp 8V92 diesels will cruise at 24 knots (27 knots top) with a range of over 400 miles. Twin 820-hp MAN diesels, introduced in 1989, provide cruising speeds of 26–27 knots (31 knots top) and, beginning in 1994, optional 900-hp 12V71s will cruise at a fast 29 knots. ❏

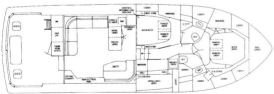

Original Galley-Up, Three-Stateroom Layout

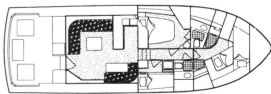

Current Galley-Up, Three-Stateroom Layout

Galley-Down, Two-Stateroom Layout

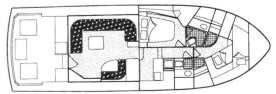

Current Galley-Down, Two-Stateroom Layout

See Page 260 for Pricing Information

BERTRAM 54 CONVERTIBLE

1981–93

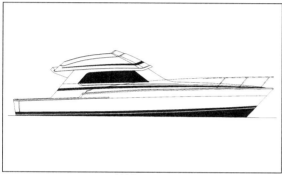

1995–Current

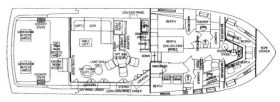

1981–83

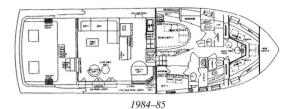

1984–85

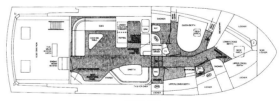

1987–89

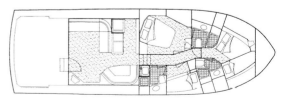

1990–93

1995–Current

SPECIFICATIONS

Length	54'0"	Fuel	1,200/1,450 gals.
Beam	16'11"	Cockpit	144 sq. ft.
Draft	5'2"	Hull Type	Deep-V
Weight	65,000#	Deadrise Aft	17°
Clearance	16'8"	Production	1981–93
Water	250 gals.		1995–Current

A proven tournament winner and sportfishing superstar, the Bertram 54 is built on a rugged deep-v hull with cored hull sides and plenty of beam. With her near perfect blend of design, engineering and construction, she delivers superb rough-water performance. Several three-stateroom/three-head interiors have been offered over the years. The generators were relocated from under the cockpit sole to the engine room in 1984. The front deckhouse windshield was eliminated in 1986, and updates for 1987 included a restyled flybridge, increased fuel capacity, and a light oak interior. The 54 was totally revised and reintroduced in 1995. She now features Bertram's latest and more rakish profile and an innovative new layout with a cutdown galley (with custom refrigeration), beautiful maple woodwork, and a stall shower in each head. The engine room was also completely re-engenered and much improved. The 800-hp 12V71 Detroits (optional 1981-84) cruise the Bertram 54 at 24-25 knots (29 knots top). The 900-hp 12V71s (1985-86) cruise at a fast 26 knots, and the 1,080-hp 12V92s (1987-93) cruise at an honest 29 knots and reach 33 knots wide open. First available in 1995, 1,250-hp Cats will *cruise* at 33 knots! ❑

See Page 260 for Pricing Information

BERTRAM 58 CONVERTIBLE

SPECIFICATIONS

Length	58'3"	Fuel, Std.	1,300 gals.
Beam	17'11"	Fuel, Opt.	2,020 gals.
Draft	5'6"	Cockpit	168 sq. ft.
Weight	90,000#	Hull Type	Modified-V
Clearance	19'5"	Deadrise Aft	15°
Water	300 gals.	Production	1977–83

The Bertram brochures hardly overstated the matter when they referred to the 58 Convertible as a "hugely elegant machine." Huge indeed—only the Hatteras 60 Convertible exceeded her in size among production sportfishing yachts of her era. The 58 Convertible's hull is solid fiberglass with a full keel below and just 15° of deadrise aft (the least amount of "V" in any Bertram hull). Notably, the decks and superstructure were built of aluminum. Among her many attributes is a ride that many consider to be the best in this size range. Designed for serious tournament level competition and comfortable offshore cruising, the Bertram 58's massive cockpit dimensions will accommodate two full-size fighting chairs. Her luxurious three-stateroom/three-head teak interior features a huge salon with extravagant entertaining potential. The flybridge is arranged with two helm stations—one well forward and one aft to view the cockpit action. At 90,000 lbs., the Bertram 58 Convertible is no lightweight, but her performance with 675-hp 12V71 diesels is a respectable 18 knots at cruise and around 21 knots top. ❑

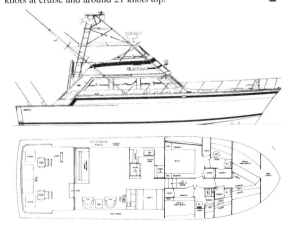

See Page 260 for Pricing Information

BERTRAM 60 CONVERTIBLE

SPECIFICATIONS

Length	60'0"	Fuel	1,630 gals.
Beam	16'11"	Cockpit	144 sq. ft.
Draft	5'4"	Hull Type	Deep-V
Weight	85,000#	Deadrise Aft	17°
Clearance	16'8"	Designer	D. Napier
Water	250 gals.	Production	1990–Current

A very popular model with well-heeled tournament anglers (over 20 have been built to date), the Bertram 60 projects the classic styling and aggressive good looks common to all modern Bertram designs. (Note that she's built on a stretched and re-worked version of the existing Bertram 54 hull—one of the best all-weather hulls in the business.) Construction and engineering are state-of-the-art inside and out. The original galley-up, three-stateroom floorplan is similar to that found in the Bertram 54 with the extra length used to enlarge the salon. A stall shower in the starboard guest head was added, and the entire layout is finished with maple paneling since 1993. A new four-stateroom layout became available in 1994. The cockpit comes complete with an oversized transom door, molded tackle center, and direct engine room access. The flybridge helm console is simply a work of art. Twin 1,400-hp 16V92 diesels will cruise the Bertram 60 at an honest 31 knots and reach 34–35 knots wide open. Cat 3412 diesels (1,250-hp) available since 1995 will cruise at a more efficient 28–29 knots. ❑

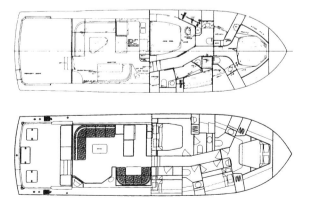

See Page 260 for Pricing Information

SPECIFICATIONS

Length	72'6"	Fuel	2,570 gals.
Beam	18'5"	Cockpit	193 sq. ft.
Draft	6'9"	Hull Type	Deep-V
Weight	120,000#	Deadrise Aft	17°
Clearance	19'10"	Designer	Bertram
Water	300 gals.	Production	1990–94

SPECIFICATIONS

Length	29'0"	Fuel	225 gals.
Beam	10'3"	Cockpit	65 sq. ft.
Draft	2'6"	Hull Type	Modified-V
Weight	8,100#	Deadrise Aft	NA
Clearance	NA	Designer	P. Patterson
Water	30 gals.	Production	1989–93

Designed to be one of the fastest yachts of her kind in the world, the Bertram 72 makes extensive use of balsa coring throughout the hull, including the bottom—a first for any Bertram yacht. The all-new hull is a deep-V design with 17° of deadrise and a sweeping sheer stepped just forward of the cockpit. The interior can be customized to an owner's specifications, however the three-stateroom, three-head layout with the galley up should prove to be popular among sportfishermen. (Note the full-width master stateroom below the galley.) The bridge is enclosed and air conditioned, and a second outside helm overlooks the massive cockpit. A convenient day head is provided on a small deck abaft the salon bulkhead. Additional features include a huge walk-in engine room, a sea chest to eliminate thru-hulls, trolling valves, and an optional bow thruster. The first hulls were fitted with 1,960-hp MTUs, although 1,440-hp 16V92s are standard. Speeds with the MTUs are reportedly 30 knots at cruise and 34 knots wide open. ❏

Bimini Marine acquired molds to the Topaz 29 SF in 1989 following that company's demise and reintroduced her the same year as the Bimini 29. Hull construction is solid fiberglass, and the layout of the Bimini is basically the same as the earlier Topaz model. A large hatch on the bridgedeck provides access to the engines, and visibility from the helm is excellent. The lower level of the cockpit is large enough for a mounted chair, and a large in-deck fish box and below-deck storage area keep the cockpit free of clutter. Inside, there are berths for three in the cabin along with a compact galley and a roomy stand-up head with shower. Most were sold with the optional factory tower. Several gas and diesel engines were offered in the Bimini 29 over the years. The popular 200-hp Volvo diesels will cruise at a fast 26–27 knots with a top speed of around 30 knots. Note that a Bimini 29 Sport model with an enlarged bridgedeck and smaller cabin was also available. ❏

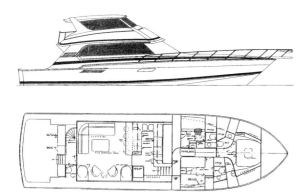

See Page 260 for Pricing Information

See Page 260 for Pricing Information

BLACK WATCH 30 SPORTFISHERMAN

SPECIFICATIONS

Length ....30'1"	Fuel ....240 gals.
Beam ....10'11"	Cockpit ....120 sq. ft.
Draft ....2'10"	Hull Type.................Deep-V
Weight ....9,000#	Deadrise Aft ....18°
Clearance ....7'0"	Designer ....Hunt Assoc.
Water ....50 gals.	Production 1986–Current

Introduced in 1986, the Black Watch 30 was well-received among serious anglers for her extraordinary handling abilities, handsome profile, and high-tech construction. Her balsa-cored deep-V hull is capable of slugging it out in some pretty mean seas and, with nearly 11 feet of beam, she's a stable platform at trolling speeds. The layout is dedicated to serious fishing activities, of course, and her large unobstructed cockpit is set low to the water. A transom door is offset to starboard, and a pair of fish boxes are built into the cockpit sole. Engine boxes make access to the engines easy, and the entire cockpit liner is removable for major service work. Inside, the cabin accommodations are fairly basic with berths for four (the backrests of the convertible dinette forward swing up to create single berths), an enclosed head with shower, and a small galley area. Headroom is adequate throughout. A good performer, 454-cid gas engines will cruise around 25 knots (34 knots top), and the 300-hp Cummins (or Cat) diesels will cruise economically at a fast 28–29 knots and reach 33 knots wide open.. ❏

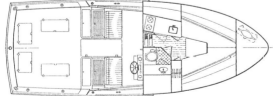

See Page 260 for Pricing Information

BLACK WATCH 30 FLYBRIDGE

SPECIFICATIONS

Length ....30'1"	Fuel ....270 gals.
Beam ....10'11"	Cockpit ....80 sq. ft.
Draft ....3'0"	Hull Type.................Deep-V
Weight ....12,000#	Deadrise Aft ....18°
Clearance ....9'6"	Designer ....Hunt Assoc.
Water ....40 gals.	Production 1989–Current

Serious anglers, whose lust for a high-performance sportfisherman often conflicts with the family's demand for a comfortable interior, will quickly appreciate the Black Watch 30 Flybridge. A little top-heavy in appearance (thanks to an oversize flybridge) but an otherwise rugged-looking boat, she's built on the same balsa-cored deep-V hull as the Sportfisherman model. The interior is surprisingly roomy for a 30-footer and features V-berths forward, a convertible dinette, compact galley, and an enclosed head. The headroom is very good, and the teak trim, quality fabrics, and teak and holly cabin sole add an upscale feel to the interior. Outside, a big fish box runs athwartships across the after part of the cockpit, and clever roll-back engine boxes provide excellent access to the engines. Standard 454-cid gas engines will cruise the Black Watch 30 Flybridge around 24–25 knots (about 33 knots top), and optional 300-hp Cummins diesels provide outstanding performance and economy at a hard 28-knot cruise. Top speed with these engines is about 32–33 knots. ❏

See Page 261 for Pricing Information

BLACK WATCH 36 FLYBRIDGE

SPECIFICATIONS

Length ....36'2"
Beam.............................11'4"
Draft ....2'7"
Weight ....13,900#
Clearance ....11'0"
Cockpit ....150 sq. ft.

Water ....60 gals.
Fuel ....300 gals.
Hull Type.................Deep-V
Deadrise Aft ....18°
Designer ....Hunt Assoc.
Production 1991–Current

Built on a semi-custom basis, the Black Watch 36 is a light-weight, high-tech flybridge fisherman with top-quality construction and superb offshore performance. Her hull—a relatively narrow deep-V—is fully balsa-cored, vacuum-bagged, and reinforced on the bottom with Kevlar. Aside from her graceful appearance and meticulous detailing, perhaps the most striking feature of the Black Watch 36 is her oversized fishing cockpit. Indeed, it's so big that the cabin layout is necessarily compact compared with other boats her size. With V-bunks, galley, dinette, and head, the Black Watch 36 provides accommodations for four with good headroom, overhead rod storage, and a stylish teak-and-holly sole. Note the absence of a stall shower in the head. The motors are easily accessed via engine boxes in the cockpit, and the bridge is arranged with a wraparound helm console, Panish controls, and guest seating forward. A economical boat with optional 291-hp Cummins diesels, she'll cruise at 24 knots (18–20 gph) and reach a top speed of 27–28 knots.

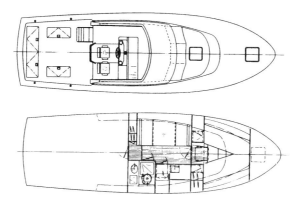

See Page 261 for Pricing Information

49

38' COMBI

WHY BE OPEN TO COMPROMISE?

You may not realize that nearly every open fisherman on the market is lighter than a flybridge or convertible. And for most boats, lighter weight means a less stable ride. Not so with the Blackfin line of open fishermen.

Our combis feature the acclaimed Blackfin high-density hull. With a beamy, deep "V" design, each model's hull is the heaviest in its size class. This means you get the most comfortable, smooth-riding fishing boat in the world plus the conveniences of a spacious open fisherman.

Contact your local Blackfin dealer today and test drive one of our remarkable combis from 29' to 38'. But do it today. Or you might be compromising something else tomorrow.

NEW   29' COMBI

31' COMBI

33' COMBI

Overbuilt By Any Standard Except The Sea's.

BLACKFIN YACHT CORPORATION, P.O. BOX 22982, FT. LAUDERDALE, FL 33335 • PHONE (305) 525-6314 • FAX (305) 523-7728

BLACKFIN 29 COMBI

SPECIFICATIONS

Length	29'4"	Water	30 gals.
Beam	10'6"	Fuel	250 gals.
Draft	2'5"	Cockpit	62 sq. ft.
Weight, Gas	10,025#	Hull Type	Deep-V
Weight, Dsl	12,120#	Deadrise Aft	22°
Clearance	7'5"	Production	1983–Current

A tournament-level offshore fisherman in spite of her small size, the Blackfin 29 Combi is built on a solid fiberglass deep-V hull with moderate beam and plenty of flare at the bow. Her relatively wide beam and low center of gravity make her a surprisingly stable trolling platform in spite of her deep-V hull. Below, the small cabin features a convertible dinette forward, together with a mini-galley and a stand-up head with shower. The cockpit can handle a small chair and engine boxes provide good access to the motors. A popular boat, she was updated in 1995 with an all-new deck mold with softer lines, a stylish curved windshield, an integral bow pulpit and a new helm console. Additional features include transom-mounted outboard rudders, cockpit washdowns, and an in-deck fish box. Standard 320-hp gas engines will cruise the 29 Combi at 24 knots, and optional 230-hp Volvo diesels will cruise at 26 knots. Those with Cummins (or Cat) 300-hp diesels will cruise at 28–29 knots. An outboard version (with brackets and a roomier cockpit) will deliver a top speed of 40+ knots with a pair of Yahama 225-hp motors. ❑

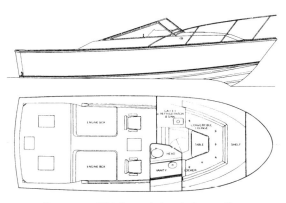

See page 261 for pricing information

BLACKFIN 29 FLYBRIDGE SF

SPECIFICATIONS

Length	29'4"	Water	50 gals.
Beam	10'6"	Fuel	250 gals.
Draft	2'6"	Cockpit	56 sq. ft.
Weight, Gas	11,109#	Hull Type	Deep-V
Weight, Dsl	13,604#	Deadrise Aft	22°
Clearance	9'4"	Production	1986–Current

The Blackfin 29 Flybridge is a great-looking small convertible and one of the few under-30-foot boats of her type capable of running with the heavy hitters in offshore conditions. She shares the same rugged deep-V hull as the 29 Combi with generous flare at the bow and unique outboard-mounted rudders. The Blackfin 29 is a superb fishing boat with a clean, unobstructed cockpit and an easy-to-reach flybridge with seating for five. The fact that she has a stylish and comfortable interior with 6'6" headroom only adds to her appeal. Finished with white mica countertops and cabinetry and trimmed in teak, the upscale accommodations allow her to serve as an occasional weekend cruiser. Raised engine boxes forward of the cockpit provide excellent access to the motors and double as bait-watching seats. Updates in 1995 include an integral bow pulpit and a new flybridge console. Twin 320-hp Crusaders will cruise the Blackfin 29 around 20 knots and reach a top speed of about 30 knots. Optional 230-hp Volvos will cruise at 24 knots (about 28 top), and those with 300-hp Cats cruise at 26 knots and reach 30 knots wide

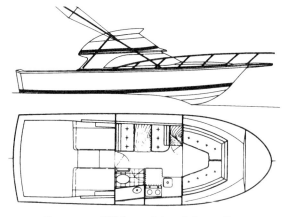

See page 261 for pricing information

BLACKFIN 31 COMBI

SPECIFICATIONS

Length	30'8"	Water	70 gals.
Beam	11'10"	Fuel	300 gals.
Draft	2'11"	Cockpit	75 sq. ft.
Weight, Gas	13,300#	Hull Type	Deep-V
Weight, Dsl	15,500#	Deadrise Aft	21°
Clearance	7'3"	Production	1993–Current

If the Blackfin 31 Combi has a different look than previous Combi models, it's because she's a remake of the earlier North Coast 31 (1988–90), a highly regarded deep-V fisherman from Massachusetts. In developing the 31 Combi, Blackfin engineers replaced the original strictly-fishing North Coast floorplan with a new dinette layout which is more open and suitable for family cruising. Lounge seating has also been added opposite the helm. The result is a proven offshore fisherman with civilized (almost upscale) cruising accommodations—a rarity in a serious fishboat. The original floorplan is a holdover from the original North Coast. An all-new floorplan for 1995 has a larger head compartment, a portside dinette, and a dinette/V-berth forward. Additional features of the 31 Combi include unusually wide sidedecks, hydraulically operated engine room hatches (from three hatches to one in 1995), a redesigned helm console, cockpit storage boxes and a transom door. An excellent sea boat with a notably sharp entry, standard 300-hp Cat diesels will cruise at 25–26 knots and reach a top speed of about

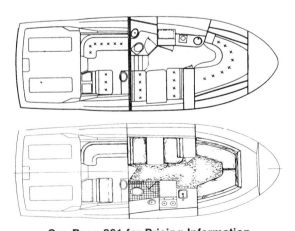

See Page 261 for Pricing Information

BLACKFIN 32 SPORTFISHERMAN

SPECIFICATIONS

Length	31'9"	Fuel	304 gals.
Beam	11'11"	Cockpit	71 sq. ft.
Draft, Dsl.	2'8"	Hull Type	Deep-V
Weight	17,800#	Deadrise Aft	21°
Clearance	NA	Designer	C. Jannace
Water	60 gals.	Production	1980–91

With her low and purposely aggressive profile, the Blackfin 32 SF has the unmistakable look of a serious bluewater tournament machine. Like all Blackfins, she was built on a solid fiberglass deep-V hull, and her wide beam adds stability not always found in deep-V boats this size. Not surprisingly, the good looks of the Blackfin 32 are backed up by solid construction, good open-water performance, and strong resale values. The cabin is attractively finished with off-white mica laminates trimmed in teak and offers comfortable—if basic—overnight accommodations for four. There's room in the cockpit for a full-size tuna chair. The raised (and dangerously heavy) engine boxes provide cockpit seating as well as good access to the motors. Standard 454-cid gas engines will cruise the Blackfin 32 around 18 knots and reach 27 knots top. Several diesel engine options were offered over the years. The popular 300-hp Cats will cruise about 23–24 knots, and the 375-hp versions cruise at 29 knots and reach around 33 knots wide open. ❏

See Page 261 for Pricing Information

BLACKFIN 32 COMBI

SPECIFICATIONS

Length	31'9"	Fuel	304 gals.
Beam	11'11"	Cockpit	80 sq. ft.
Draft	2'8"	Hull Type	Deep-V
Weight, Gas	15,081#	Deadrise Aft	21°
Weight, Dsl.	17,788#	Designer	C. Jannace
Water	50 gals.	Production	1988–92

The Blackfin marketing people once dubbed the 32 Combi the "944 Turbo of sportfishing boats"—a fair description for what many anglers regard as one of the premium day boats in the market. She was built using the already proven deep-V hull of the Blackfin 32 Sportfisherman with plenty of flare at the bow and a sharp 21° of transom deadrise. Like other Combi models, the 32 is a beamy, low-profile day boat that almost begs for a tower. Blackfins aren't inexpensive, and they're clearly aimed at the upscale end of the market. While the 32 Combi is designed for fishing, her accommodations below are surprisingly plush. Indeed, with berths for four inside and lounge seating opposite the helm on the bridgedeck, she can easily double as a weekend cruiser. A transom door was standard, and the cockpit can easily handle a full-size chair. Standard 454-cid Crusader gas engines will cruise the 32 Combi at 24 knots (31+ top), and the optional 300-hp Cat 3116 diesels will cruise economically at around 26 knots and reach 29–30 knots wide open. ❏

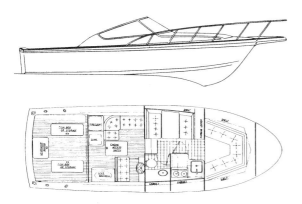

See Page 261 for Pricing Information

BLACKFIN 33 SPORTFISHERMAN

SPECIFICATIONS

Length	32'6"	Fuel	225 gals.
Beam	9'9"	Cockpit	NA
Draft	2'8"	Hull Type	Deep-V
Weight	10,470#	Deadrise Aft	24°
Clearance	10'8"	Designer	John Bird
Water	30 gals.	Production	1978–84

When Blackfin acquired the assets of Cary Marine back in the 1970s, included in the package was this 32'6" hull originally designed as an offshore racer. Long and slender with a drooped nose and low freeboard, Blackfin engineers took this hull, modified it for a sportfishing application, and introduced her in 1978 as the Blackfin 32 (later changed to 33) Sportfisherman. At the time, one writer referred to her as the Rolls Royce of open fishing boats. Serious anglers were impressed with the fishability of the Blackfin 33's large and unobstructed cockpit, and she soon became recognized as a rugged, hard-core sportfishing boat. She also has a reputation for truly awesome performance in nasty seas. Definitely a no-frills ride, the cuddy cabin consists only of two 7-foot berths and a marine toilet. Used Blackfin 33s are found today with a wide range of power, including outboards. The standard 454-cid gas engines cruise at a fast 26–27 knots and run at 36+ wide open. The optional 210-hp Cat diesels will cruise at 21–22 knots and reach 26 knots top. ❏

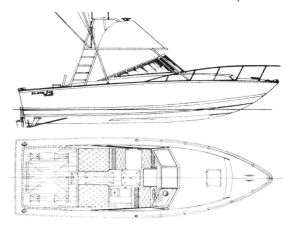

See Page 262 for Pricing Information

BLACKFIN 33 FLYBRIDGE

SPECIFICATIONS

Length	32'11"	Fuel	340 gals.
Beam	12'0"	Cockpit	75 sq. ft.
Draft	2'11"	Hull Type	Deep-V
Weight	20,169#	Deadrise Aft	22°
Clearance	10'0"	Designer	Blackfin
Water	80 gals.	Production	1990–Current

Replacing the classic Blackfin 32 in 1990, the 33 Flybridge is a better-handling boat in just about every respect. Blackfin does not use coring in their hulls, so there's nothing high-tech here in the way of construction. Indeed, the 33 is a straightforward deep-V design with a relatively wide beam. There are berths for four belowdecks along with a compact galley, dinette, and a head with a separate stall shower—a pleasant surprise. In 1993, a floorplan option has the dinette forward and an L-lounge in the cabin. The flybridge is large for a 33-footer with bench seating forward of the helm and a large console for flush-mounting electronics. Anyone who ever fished a 32 will appreciate the 33's enlarged cockpit and standard transom door. Engine boxes are retained in the new 33, and access to the motors is excellent. Standard 454-cid gas engines will cruise around 24 knots. Optional 320-hp or 375-hp Cats cruise at a fast 25 and 28 knots, respectively, and reach 30+ wide open. ❏

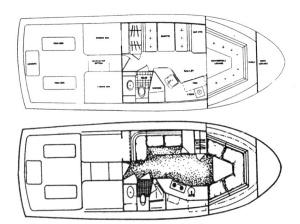

See Page 262 for Pricing Information

BLACKFIN 33 COMBI

SPECIFICATIONS

Length	32'11"	Water	80 gals.
Beam	12'0"	Fuel	340 gals.
Draft	2'11"	Cockpit	75 sq. ft.
Weight, Gas	16,428#	Hull Type	Deep-V
Weight, Dsl.	19,132#	Deadrise Aft	22°
Clearance	8'6"	Production	1994–Current

A good-looking boat with an upscale price tag to go with her strictly business appearance, the 33 Combi is about as good as it gets in a mid-size express fisherman. Like all Blackfins, she's built on a solid fiberglass deep-V hull (borrowed from the 33 FB) with considerably more transom deadrise than other production boats. Her profile is low, the beam is wide, and the ride is superb. Inside, the lush well-appointed interior will come as a surprise to those expecting the plain-Jane cabin accommodations common to most thoroughbred fishing machines. Indeed, the light ash woodwork, off-white cabinetry, Avonite countertops and halogen lighting present a warm and completely inviting appearance. The Combi's bi-level cockpit is ideally arranged with lounge seating opposite the helm and a big fishing platform aft. The helm and companion seats can be raised hydraulically for access to the engines, and the side decks are notably wide and well-secured. The finish work is excellent. Optional 425-hp Cats will cruise at a fast 28 knots and reach 33 knots wide open. ❏

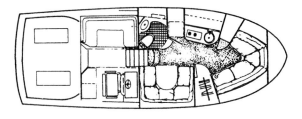

See Page 262 for Pricing Information

BLACKFIN 38 COMBI

SPECIFICATIONS

Length	38'3"	Fuel	514 gals.
Beam	14'5"	Cockpit	122 sq. ft.
Draft	3'9"	Hull Type	Deep-V
Weight	34,170#	Deadrise Aft	18°
Clearance	9'6"	Designer	C. Jannace
Water	135 gals.	Production	1989–Current

The 38 Combi is a hard-core express fisherman with the rugged good looks and built-in fishability one expects of a Blackfin product. She's actually a stretched version of the earlier Blackfin 36 Combi (1987–88) the difference being the larger cockpit of the 38 model. The Combi makes a great first impression on those who enjoy the open helm and bi-level cockpit layout of an express-type fishing boat. There's a full 120 sq. ft. of fishing platform on the lower level and L-shaped passenger seating opposite the helm on the raised deck. While the 38 may have less living space below than other day boats her size, the cabin nonetheless manages to include the necessities. First offered with a queen berth forward, a dinette floorplan with V-berths became standard in 1991, and in 1993 an optional layout with a U-shaped dinette became available. Optional 485-hp 6-71s will cruise at 27 knots (30 top) and 550-hp 6V92s cruise around 29–30 knots and reach 33 knots wide open. ❏

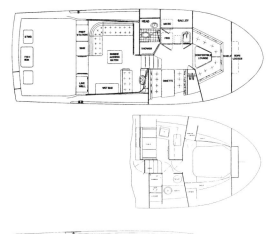

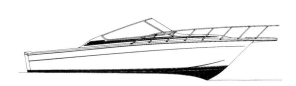

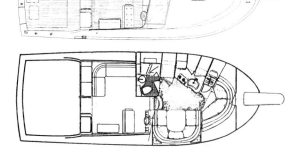

See Page 262 for Pricing Information

55

BLACKFIN 38 CONVERTIBLE

SPECIFICATIONS

Length	38'3"	Fuel	514 gals.
Beam	14'5"	Cockpit	122 sq. ft.
Draft	4'0"	Hull Type	Deep-V
Weight	35,970#	Deadrise Aft	18°
Clearance	13'0"	Designer	C. Jannace
Water	135 gals.	Production	1989–Current

The 38 Convertible pictured above is actually a stretched version of the earlier Blackfin 36 Convertible (1987–88), a heavy deep-V fisherman with a solid fiberglass hull and an attractive low-profile appearance. A better sea boat than the 36, the extra length went into the cockpit dimensions—a big improvement. A sportfisherman at heart, her upscale cabin accommodations allow the 38 to easily double as a weekend cruiser. The original two-stateroom, galley-up layout was replaced in 1990 with a new mid-level galley floorplan offering a choice of either a dinette or second stateroom. Where the early interiors were finished with teak, recent models use light oak woodwork. A good performer, twin 425-hp Cats will cruise the Blackfin 38 Convertible around 23 knots and reach 26 knots top. The 485-hp 6-71 diesels will deliver a cruising speed of about 28 knots and 31+ knots at full throttle, and the 550-hp 6V92s will produce an honest 28-knot cruise and a top speed of around 31–32 knots. ❏

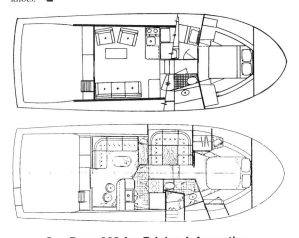

See Page 262 for Pricing Information

SPECIFICATIONS

Length	31'9"	Fuel	313 gals.
Beam	11'10"	Cockpit	74 sq. ft.
Draft	2'8"	Hull Type	Deep-V
Weight	12,500#	Deadrise Aft	20°
Clearance	7'6"	Designer	Whaler
Water	40 gals.	Production	1988–92

SPECIFICATIONS

Length w/Pulpit	30'8"	Water	40 gals.
Hull Length	28'8"	Clearance	5'0"
Beam	11'3"	Hull Type	Modified-V
Draft	2'4"	Deadrise Aft	15°
Weight	9,000#	Designer	Walter Schultz
Fuel	220 gals.	Production	1988–Current

The fact that you can't sink the Boston Whaler 31 will appeal to safety-conscious anglers who can afford to own this well-built inboard sportfisherman. Constructed on a rugged deep-V hull, a layer of urethane foam bonds the inner liner to the outer hull acting as a stiffener and providing enough flotation to keep the 31 afloat even when fully swamped! This is a proven offshore design with good trolling stability and better-than-average performance in rough water. Introduced in 1988, she was redesigned in 1991 with a new deckhouse profile, relocated engines, and fresh interior and cockpit layouts. (The private stateroom in early models was a rarity in a fishing boat this size.) The revised bi-level cockpit features an in-deck fish box, bait-prep center, lockable rod storage, and a fold-down jumpseat. The hinged bridgedeck tilts up for excellent engine access. Most early 31s were powered with 250-hp Cummins diesels (23 knots cruise/27 top). Later models with 300-hp Cummins cruise at 25 knots and deliver around 29 knots top. ❏

The Brendan 28 is a limited-production express sportfisherman with conservative lines and a practical fish-or-cruise layout. She's built on a fully cored deep-V hull with moderate beam and a shallow keel—an easy-riding design with good offshore handling characteristics. The interior of the Brendan is arranged with V-berths, a removable dinette table, convertible settee, a small galley and an enclosed head with shower. A well-crafted boat, the detailing and quality components found in the Brendan 28 are impressive. With over 100 sq. ft. of space, the cockpit is able to handle the installation of a fighting chair with no problem. Additional features include a transom door, two in-deck fish boxes, fairly wide sidedecks, a molded bow pulpit and plenty of storage. A pair of sliding deck covers behind the helm and companion seats provide excellent access to the motors. Standard 270-hp gas inboards will cruise the Brendan 28 at 20 knots and reach a top speed in the neighborhood of 29–30 knots. A limited-production boat, 22 hulls have been completed since 1988. ❏

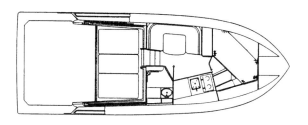

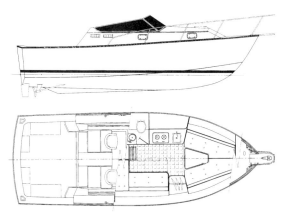

See Page 262 for Pricing Information

See Page 262 for Pricing Information

Cabo 35 Express

"...the best production inboard 35-foot fishing boat the world has to offer."

Dean Travis Clarke **Sportfishing magazine**

"You'll find everything aboard the Cabo that you'd ever expect to find in the cockpit of a top flight 50-foot sportfishing convertible..." **Dean Clarke**

boat you can love

Dean Travis Clarke has seen and run a lot of sportfishing boats. As executive editor of *Sport Fishing* magazine, Dean has evaluated the performance, handling and fishability of nearly the entire gamut of sportfishing boats on the market today. In Dean's words, "There are plenty of great boats to like out there, but when you start talking love, over the period of a lifetime there are very few...those who've spent their lives on boats will fall for this boat just as sure as ebb follows flood."

It's perfect for light tackle

Pam Basco is an internationally known angler who has captured seven world records on light tackle and was named by the IGFA as one of the outstanding anglers of the year in 1993. When searching for the ideal boat to try for a new world record for blue marlin on 8# test, Pam selected the Cabo 35. In her words, "The boat does great. We raised an awful lot of fish in two days, including 2 striped marlin, 11 blues and one sail. And the way it maneuvers and backs down, it's perfect for light tackle."

A war chest of fishing features

"You'll find everything aboard the Cabo that you'd ever expect to find in the cockpit of a top flight 50-foot sportfishing convertible: Bait prep station, bait freezer, live well, tackle storage center and rod storage for 19 rods are all standard fare. When you go aboard the Cabo, lift one of the big lids to a fishbox in the cockpit, then do something you know you shouldn't--let it fall shut. The hatches fit into their gasketed and drained lips so well that rather than slamming shut, the lid quietly goes 'boomph'."

Superior construction

"No boat, no matter how beautiful, is worth the effort if it isn't durable. Only the finest ingredients go into a Cabo: Vinylester resin for greater osmotic blistering protection, biaxial nonwoven fiberglass roving and balsa core from the waterline up offer strength with light weight in the hull, while the bottom is solid fiberglass. All hidden areas, like bilges and inside cabinets, are ground and then gelcoated for a smooth, flawless finish. Put your face right against the hull of a Cabo: Look for indentations, bumps and finish flaws. You won't find any."

Engine access without equal

"Touch a button at the threshold to the helm deck and the entire deck rises on electrically activated hydraulic rams, revealing the impressive power center--impressive mainly for its organization. Every single hose, wire, pipe and fitting in the engine room is run and labeled individually. All functions are segregated with the plumbing on one side, everything electrical on the other side..."

The best the world has to offer

"At the moment, Cabo arguably provides the best production inboard 35-foot fishing boat the world has to offer." Dean is not alone in his assessment of the Cabo 35. Other experts in the industry and professional anglers agree that the Cabo may be the finest 35-foot sportfishing boat ever.

To receive unedited full color reprints of test reports run by the experts at *Boating, Saltwater Sportsman, Sportfishing, Marlin* and *Powerboat Reports*, call, write or FAX:

CABO™ Sportfishers
by Cat Harbor Boats, Inc.
9780 Rancho Road
Adelanto CA. 92301
Fax. (619) 246-8970
Phone 800 647-8236

CAT® Diesel Power

CABO 31 EXPRESS

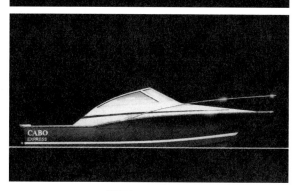

SPECIFICATIONS

Length w/Pulpit ....33'2"	Water ....80 gals.
Hull Length ....31'0"	Clearance ....NA
Beam..............................12'5"	Hull Type.................Deep-V
Draft ....3'2"	Deadrise Aft.................18.5°
Weight ....19,500#	Headroom......................6'6"
Fuel ....320 gals.	Production 1995–Current

Introduced in mid 1995, the new Cabo 31 Express is a premium offshore fisherman with tremendous eye appeal to go with her superb performance. She's built on an easy-riding deep-V hull with a wide beam, a sharp entry, and balsa coring in the hullsides. While the Cabo is obviously designed for serious anglers, the upscale cabin accommodations are surprisingly spacious for a boat of this type with berths for four adults, a complete galley area, decent storage, and an enclosed, stand-up head and shower. The interior is finished with varnished teak woodwork, and headroom is more than adequate throughout. Outside, the entire helm deck can be raised hydraulically for access to the motors. An L-shaped settee is opposite the helm, and the windshield has a center vent. Cockpit features include a bait prep center, transom fishbox, rod storage, fresh and salt water washdowns, and a transom door with gate. Among several engine options (gas engines are standard), twin 300-hp Cats will cruise the Cabo 31 Express at 26 knots and reach a top speed of about 30 knots. Note the generous 320-gallon fuel capacity. ❏

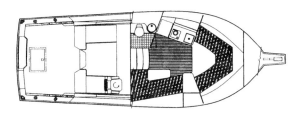

See Page 262 for Pricing Information

CABO 35 FLYBRIDGE SF

SPECIFICATIONS

Length w/Pulpit ....37'6"	Water ....100 gals.
Hull Length ....34'6"	Fuel ....400 gals.
Beam..............................13'0"	Cockpit ....80 sq. ft.
Draft ....2'6"	Hull Type.................Deep-V
Weight ....21,000#	Deadrise Aft................17.5°
Clearance ....11'3"	Production 1992–Current

A good-looking boat with a low-slung appearance and a huge cockpit, the Cabo 35 is a rugged West Coast design with a lot of built-in quality and sex appeal. She's built on a deep-V hull with a relatively wide beam and cored hullsides. Her low profile is the result of placing the motors in cockpit engine boxes, thus allowing the salon sole to be set low in the hull. Considering her oversized cockpit, the Cabo's interior is surprisingly spacious. The galley-up layout includes an 8-foot settee with hidden rod storage in the salon and an island berth in the stateroom, while the galley-down floorplan has a stall shower in the head. (There's a large storage area beneath the salon sole.) Additional features include two in-deck fish boxes, transom door and gate, good cabin headroom, single-lever helm controls, and wide side decks with sturdy rails. A popular boat since the day she hit the market (over 60 have been sold to date), optional 375-hp Cats will cruise the Cabo 35 at 27 knots and reach around 32 knots top. Note the generous 420-gallon fuel capacity. ❏

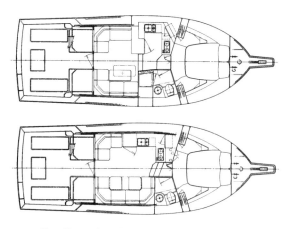

See Page 262 for Pricing Information

CABO 35 EXPRESS SF

SPECIFICATIONS

Length w/Pulpit ....37'6"	Water ....188 gals.
Hull Length ....34'6"	Fuel ....400 gals.
Beam.............................13'0"	Cockpit ....80 sq. ft.
Draft ....2'6"	Hull Type................Deep-V
Weight ....18,000#	Deadrise Aft.................17.5°
Clearance ....11'3"	Production 1993–Current

Using the hull of the Cabo 35 Flybridge model, the Cabo 35 Express is a rugged express fisherman with the kind of family-style interior accommodations that most dedicated fishboats lack. She's constructed on a deep-V hull with a relatively wide beam and Airex-cored hullsides. The Cabo's floorplan is arranged with a full-size double berth forward along with a roomy galley and dinette. Throughout, the Corian countertops, teak joinerwork, and upscale appliances combine to present an attractive and extremely well-crafted interior decor. Outside, the cockpit is big for a 35-footer and comes standard with a bait prep center, transom door, two in-deck storage boxes, cockpit coaming, and washdowns. An L-shaped settee is opposite the helm, and the entire bridgedeck lifts hydraulically for excellent access to the motors. A good performer with plenty of eye appeal (as well as an upscale price), optional 422-hp Cats will cruise at 29 knots and reach around 33 knots top. A good-selling boat, over 50 have been built to date. ❏

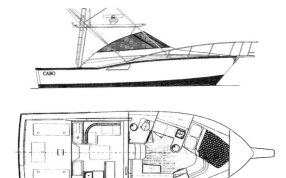

See Page 262 for Pricing Information

CALIFORNIAN 35 CONVERTIBLE

SPECIFICATIONS

Length ....34'11"	Fuel ....300 gals.
Beam..............................12'4"	Cockpit............................NA
Draft ....3'2"	Hull Type..........Modified-V
Weight ....18,000#	Deadrise Aft....................15°
Clearance ....10'8"	Designer.............J. Marshall
Water ....75 gals.	Production 1985–87

A stylish and good-looking boat, the 35 Convertible was introduced during the time of Wellcraft's ownership of Californian Yachts. A sporty profile and a unique window treatment give the 35 a distinctive look and make her an easy boat to spot in a crowd. She was built on the same hull used for the Californian 35 Motor Yacht—a conservative modified-V design with moderate beam and a short skeg below. Equally at home as a family cruiser or weekend fisherman, the interior of the Californian 35 is quite spacious and the grain-matched teak cabinetry is impressive. Berths for four are provided, and a stall shower is fitted in the head. The relatively small cockpit can support some light-tackle fishing, although a step along the cabin bulkhead prevents the installation of a tackle center. Molded cockpit steps lead to wide side decks making foredeck access easy and secure. Gas engines were standard, but 210-hp Cat diesels proved a popular option. At a 17-knot cruising speed, the Cats burn just 15 gph—better than 1 mpg. ❏

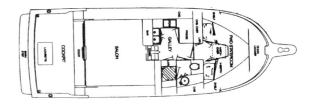

See Page 262 for Pricing Information

CALIFORNIAN 38 CONVERTIBLE

SPECIFICATIONS

Length	37'8"	Fuel	400 gals.
Beam	13'3"	Cockpit	NA
Draft	3'6"	Hull Type	Modified-V
Weight	25,000#	Deadrise Aft	15°
Clearance	14'6"	Designer	J. Marshall
Water	100 gals.	Production	1984–87

The Californian 38 Convertible is a modern and good-looking family cruiser with attractive styling and above-average finish work. (Interestingly, a lot of bow flare was used to create what appears to be a broad, trawler-style foredeck.) She's built of solid fiberglass on a low-deadrise hull with moderate beam and a shallow skeg below. Like all Californian models, the side decks of the 38 Convertible are notably wide with molded steps in the cockpit for easy access. The standard two-stateroom interior is arranged with an in-line galley to port opposite a built-in settee. Both staterooms are fitted with double berths, and there's a stall shower in the head. The woodwork is very good. Outside, the cockpit is large enough for the occasional fishing venture, however there are no in-deck storage bins, and the step along the salon bulkhead prevents the installation of a molded tackle center. Twin 210-hp Caterpillar diesels will cruise around 15 knots (18–19 knots top), and the larger 300-hp Cats will cruise at 21 knots and deliver 25 top. ❏

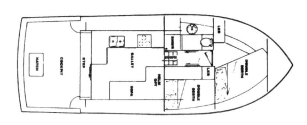

See Page 262 for Pricing Information

CALIFORNIAN 42 CONVERTIBLE

SPECIFICATIONS

Length	42'5"	Fuel	400/550 gals.
Beam	15'2"	Cockpit	NA
Draft	4'4"	Hull Type	Modified-V
Weight	38,000#	Deadrise Aft	15°
Clearance	13'4"	Designer	J. Marshall
Water	190 gals.	Production	1986–89

At 38,000 lbs., the Californian 42 Convertible is a relatively heavy boat for her size. She's built on a solid fiberglass hull with a shallow keel and moderate transom deadrise—the same hull used in the production of the Californian 42 Motor Yacht. A comfortable boat inside, her two-stateroom interior is finished with teak paneling and woodwork (pre-1988 models have a walnut interior) and features a tapered double berth in the master stateroom and stacked single berths in the guest cabin. An earlier two-stateroom layout had the galley at mid-level and a second head with a stall shower. Topside, the 42's tournament-style flybridge has the helm aft and bench seating forward. Note the cockpit engine room access door—an unusual feature in a boat under fifty feet. Caterpillar 375-hp diesels deliver a cruising speed of 20 knots, and the 485-hp 6-71s will cruise the 42 Convertible at 23 knots with a top speed of 26. The fuel capacity was increased in the 1989 models to 550 gallons. ❏

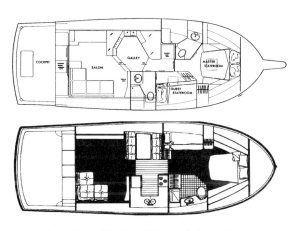

See Page 262 for Pricing Information

CALIFORNIAN 48 CONVERTIBLE

SPECIFICATIONS

Length	48'5"	Fuel	760 gals.
Beam	15'2"	Cockpit	NA
Draft	4'8"	Hull Type	Modified-V
Weight	40,000#	Deadrise Aft	NA
Clearance	14'1"	Designer	B. Collier
Water	210 gals.	Production	1986–89

Built on the standard hull used for the entire Californian line in the late 80s, the 48 was the largest convertible model the company ever built. The contemporary styling is accented by a glassed-over deckhouse windshield. Her attractive three-stateroom interior is visually impressive and finished throughout with well-crafted teak paneling (walnut in pre-1988 models). The salon dimensions are on the narrow side due to the wide side decks and relatively narrow beam of the 48's hull. Unlike a lot of other floorplans in convertibles this size, the Californian 48 has the master stateroom located amidships rather than forward in the bow—certainly a more comfortable place to sleep underway. Standard features included separate stall showers in both heads, a molded pulpit, transom door, and tackle center in the cockpit. Among several engine options, 550-hp 6V92s will cruise at 21 knots with a top speed of around 24 knots. The 650-hp 8V92s improve those speeds to 24 knots cruise and 27 knots top. Never a big seller, the 48 Convertible was withdrawn from production in 1989. ❏

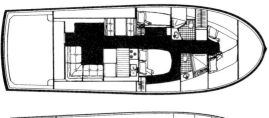

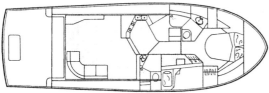

See Page 262 for Pricing Information

CAROLINA CLASSIC 28

SPECIFICATIONS

Length	28'5"	Water	55 gals.
Beam	10'6"	Clearance	NA
Draft	2'6"	Hull Type	Deep-V
Weight	13,000#	Deadrise Aft	24°
Cockpit	NA	Designer	Mac Privott
Fuel	290 gals.	Production	1994–Current

The Carolina Classic 28 is a sturdy, strictly-business offshore fisherman with clean lines and a seriously deep-V hull. Construction is solid fiberglass, and her 10-foot, 6-inch beam is wide for a 28-footer, resulting in a very roomy cockpit. In spite of the fact that she's a dedicated fishboat, the 28 has a surprisingly complete cabin below with a big V-berth, stand-up head with shower, a compact galley, air-conditioning, and teak-framed cabinetry. The engines, located near the center of the boat beneath the elevated bridgedeck, are accessed via a large deck hatch that raises hydraulically. The cockpit has plenty of room for a mounted chair and includes a pair of in-deck fish boxes, rod holders, a transom live well, tackle center with sink, and fresh- and saltwater washdowns. Additional features include side-dumping exhausts, wide side decks, and a well-arranged helm with room for flush-mounted electronics. Note that the Carolina Classic 28 is available with straight inboards or jackshafted I/O. A good open-water performer, standard 300-hp gas inboards will cruise at a fast 25–26 knots (about 38 knots top). ❏

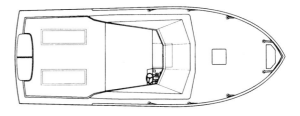

See Page 262 for Pricing Information

CHASE 38 SPORTFISHERMAN

SPECIFICATIONS

Length	38'0"	Fuel	500 gals.
Beam	13'9"	Cockpit	108 sq. ft.
Draft	4'9"	Hull Type	Deep V
Weight	28,000#	Deadrise Aft	18°
Clearance	NA	Designer	Hunt & Assoc.
Water	130 gals.	Production	1988–92

A distinctive boat, the Chase 38 is an upscale express fisherman with a very unusual layout. She was built in Costa Rica on a fully cored deep-V hull, and at 28,000 lbs., the Chase is no lightweight. Stepping below from the elevated bridgedeck, one is immediately confronted with an abundance of varnished teak woodwork and brass accessories more common to a sailboat than a serious sportfishing boat. (Too much teak in the eyes of a lot of anglers who'd rather invest in more practical fishing features.) The interior isn't notably spacious but includes a stall shower in the head and an island berth forward. Topsides, the huge bridgedeck features wraparound seating for a crowd—a superb entertaining platform several steps above the cockpit with a walk-thru to the foredeck. Access to the large engine room is from the cockpit. Cat diesels were standard, and GM 6-71s and 6V92s were optional. Cat 375-hp diesels will cruise a loaded Chase 38 around 23 knots, while the larger 550-hp 6V92s will cruise about 28 knots. ❑

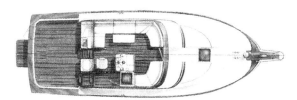

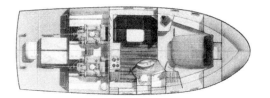

See Page 263 for Pricing Information

CHEOY LEE 48 SPORT YACHT

SPECIFICATIONS

Length	48'0"	Water	200 gals.
Length WL	43'0"	Fuel	1,000 gals.
Beam	15'0"	Cockpit	140 sq. ft.
Draft	4'0"	Hull Type	Modified-V
Weight	37,000#	Designer	Tom Fexas
Clearance	16'6"	Production	1980–1986

The 48 Sport Yacht was the first modern sportfishing boat ever offered by the Cheoy Lee yard. She's built on a lightweight fully cored hull with a relatively flat bottom and moderate beam. Big and dramatic with a flat black mask running around the deckhouse and a rakish flybridge, her long foredeck gives the 48 Sport Yacht a dramatic appearance. Conceived as a competent sportfisherman with elegant interior comforts, the European decor (painted walls) found in early models was quickly replaced with a more traditional teak interior. The original two-stateroom floorplan of the 48 Sport Yacht had the galley aft in the salon, and a unique curved corridor leads from the salon to the master stateroom. A three-stateroom layout with the galley forward in the salon (not shown) was also available. The cockpit, with a full 140 sq. ft. of space, is huge, but the raised deck along the salon bulkhead restricts the installation of a full-size tackle center. A good performer with 8V92 diesels, the Cheoy Lee 48 Sport Yacht will cruise around 27 knots and reach a top speed of 30+ knots. ❑

See Page 263 for Pricing Information

CHEOY LEE 50 SPORT YACHT

SPECIFICATIONS

Length	50'8"	Fuel	1,000 gals.
Beam	16'1"	Cockpit	115 sq. ft.
Draft	3'2"	Hull Type	Modified-V
Weight	36,000#	Deadrise Aft	NA
Clearance	14'0"	Designer	Tom Fexas
Water	200 gals.	Production	1987–Current

Introduced in 1987 as a replacement for the 48 Sport Yacht, the Cheoy Lee 50 features greater beam, a third stateroom, and more conservative styling than her predecessor. Airex coring is used extensively in the construction of the hull, deck, and superstructure, resulting in a strong lightweight fisherman with a very good turn of speed. At only 36,000 lbs.—very light indeed—the 50 Sport Yacht has the displacement of a much smaller boat. Her three-stateroom floorplan is efficiently arranged with the U-shaped galley forward and separated from the salon by a serving counter. A walkaround double berth is fitted in the master stateroom, and both heads are equipped with separate stall showers. Outside, the side decks are wide, and the uncluttered cockpit is designed for serious fishing activities. The tournament-style flybridge is large for a 50-foot convertible and features a built-in table and seating for eight. With standard 720-hp 8V92 diesels, the Cheoy Lee 50 Sport Yacht cruises at 25–26 knots and reaches a top speed of around 28 knots. ❏

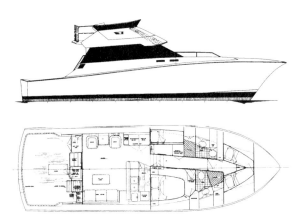

See Page 263 for Pricing Information

CHEOY LEE 58 SPORT YACHT

SPECIFICATIONS

Length	58'5"	Fuel	1,000 gals.
Beam	17'10"	Cockpit	138 sq. ft.
Draft	4'3"	Hull Type	Modified-V
Weight	58,500#	Deadrise Aft	NA
Clearance	15'10"	Designer	Tom Fexas
Water	150 gals.	Production	1986–93

Distinctively styled and featuring a unique underwater profile, the Cheoy Lee 58 Sport Yacht is certainly one of the more dramatic boats to be found among the ranks of big offshore production sportfishermen. This yacht is meant to go fast—construction is high-tech with lightweight Airex and Divinycell coring and unidirectional laminates throughout. The wide-open cockpit includes direct engine room access, molded tackle centers, flush fish boxes and built-in storage. The flybridge is huge with the helm console set well aft and circular guest seating forward. Inside, the innovative salon of the Cheoy Lee 58 is arranged with two facing sectional sofas forward and the dinette and galley aft—a practical arrangement that eliminates a good deal of traffic through the boat. There are three staterooms on the lower level, two with walkaround double berths. The interior is completely paneled and finished with varnished teak or ash woodwork. A fast boat with standard 870-hp 12V71 diesels, the 58 Sport Yacht will cruise fully loaded at 28 knots and reach a top speed of 30–31 knots. ❏

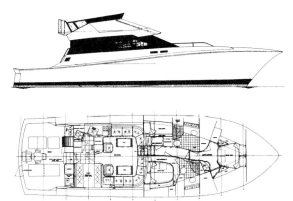

See Page 263 for Pricing Information

CHEOY LEE 66 SPORT YACHT

SPECIFICATIONS

Length	66'0"	Fuel	1,670 gals.
Beam	19'0"	Cockpit	176 sq. ft.
Draft	4'6"	Hull Type	Modified-V
Weight	65,000#	Deadrise Aft	NA
Clearance	19'10"	Designer	Tom Fexas
Water	370 gals.	Production	1984–1987

The Cheoy Lee 66 Sport Yacht is more than a little different from most other production yachts of her size. Dramatic in appearance, her high-tech construction and extensive coring materials have resulted in a lightweight hull with excellent performance. The Sport Yacht's unusual four-stateroom floorplan includes full crew quarters forward and features an opulent master stateroom beneath the salon—an arrangement made possible by placing the motors well aft in the hull (and increasing the shaft angles to the max). That the salon isn't especially roomy is due primarily to the very wide side decks. Outside, an observation deck overlooks the cockpit, giving the boat a distinct "yachtfish" profile. Additional features include cockpit access to the (small) engine room, foredeck lounge, and a full teak interior. The cockpit can easily handle a full-size chair, and a tackle center and cockpit controls were standard. A good performer with standard 870-hp 12V71 Detroit diesels, the Cheoy Lee 66 Sport Yacht will cruise at 20–21 knots and reach a top speed of 24 knots. ❏

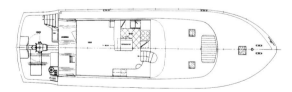

See Page 263 for Pricing Information

CHEOY LEE 70 SPORTFISHERMAN

SPECIFICATIONS

Length	70'10"	Clearance	18'9"
Beam	20'9"	Cockpit	NA
Draft	5'4"	Hull Type	Modified-V
Weight	89,000#	Deadrise Aft	14°
Fuel	2,200#	Designer	Tom Fexas
Water	400 gals.	Production	1992–Current

Few would argue that Tom Fexas designs aren't distinctive in the extreme. Indeed, the Cheoy Lee 70 is styled unlike any other production or custom sportfisherman in the world. Built on a "double-V" bottom (super-wide chine flats extending out from a deeper V on the centerline) and fully cored from the keel up, the ride is said to be very soft in a variety of sea consitions. Inside, the four-stateroom layout is plush in the extreme. The raised galley forward in the salon allows room for a huge master stateroom below, and each guest stateroom has its own private head. With more than a twenty feet of beam, it's hardly a surprise to note that the accommodations rival those of a good-sized motor yacht. The cockpit is fitted with in-deck fish boxes, a livewell, and direct access to the engine room. Topside, the enclosed bridge is very spacious and offers big-boat *skylounge* amenities including a settee and wet bar. Standard 1,000-hp Cat 3412 diesels will deliver a cruising speed of 21 knots and a top speed of about 25 knots. ❏

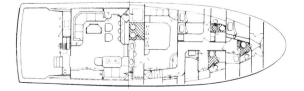

See Page 263 for Pricing Information

CHRIS CRAFT 30 TOURNAMENT SF

SPECIFICATIONS

Length	30'2"	Fuel	184 gals.
Beam	11'11"	Cockpit	120 sq. ft.
Draft	2'6"	Hull Type	Deep-V
Weight	13,500#	Deadrise Aft	21°
Clearance	11'8"	Designer	Hunt Assoc.
Water	45 gals.	Production	1975–77

Sporting a handsome profile and a notably wide beam, the Chris 30 Tournament Fisherman has the distinction of being the only Chris Craft ever built on a deep-V, Hunt-designed offshore hull. With a steep 21° of deadrise at the transom and six lifting strakes, this boat is clearly built to run in rough weather. Hull construction is solid fiberglass, and the engines rest on inverted aluminum mounts—a very heavy-duty installation. Inside, the wide beam provides for a roomy cabin with berths for four and a stand-up head. A privacy curtain separates the V-berths from the salon, and the woodwork throughout is teak. Hinged engine boxes are forward in the cockpit, and, with a full 120 sq. ft. of space, the cockpit is exceptionally large and easily fished. The flybridge is big, and the backrest on the aft bench seat folds down so the helmsman can get a view of the cockpit. Twin 250-hp gas engines will cruise the Chris 30 Tournament SF at 18 knots and reach a top speed of 25–26 knots. ❏

See Page 263 for Pricing Information

CHRIS CRAFT 315 SPORT SEDAN

SPECIFICATIONS

Length	30'10"	Fuel	250 gals.
Beam	11'10"	Cockpit	NA
Draft	2'4"	Hull Type	Modified-V
Weight	11,400#	Deadrise Aft	5°
Clearance	9'6"	Designer	Chris Craft
Water	40 gals.	Production	1983–90

The 315 Sport Sedan is a handsome flybridge fisherman with a big cockpit and basic cabin accommodations. She was built on the same flat-bottom hull used to build the 310 Catalina. To say that she's a hard ride in a chop is charitable; she'll knock your fillings out in a headsea. Her interior is rather cheery for a sportfishing boat with berths for four persons and room to store most of the things that cruising families will need for a few days away from home. Note that in 1988 Chris Craft designers replaced the engine boxes and flush cockpit sole with a raised bridgedeck arrangement—a definite improvement. The floorplan was redesigned at the same time by moving the head aft. Standard features included teak covering boards in the cockpit, a spacious flybridge with bench seating in front of the helm console and wide side decks for secure foredeck access. With the optional 330-hp gas engines, the 315 Sport Sedan will cruise around 22–23 knots and reach a top speed of 30+. ❏

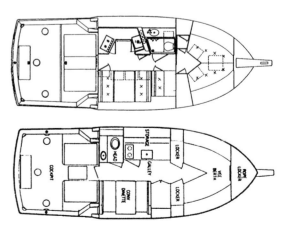

See Page 263 for Pricing Information

CHRIS CRAFT 360 SPORT SEDAN

1973–84

1985–86

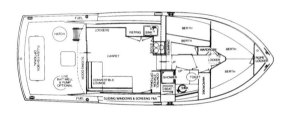

SPECIFICATIONS

Length	36'0"	Fuel	300/400 gals.
Beam	13'0"	Cockpit	NA
Draft	3'2"	Hull Type	Modified-V
Weight	22,600#	Deadrise Aft	NA
Clearance	11'11"	Designer	Chris Craft
Water	75/100 gals.	Production	1973–86

A long-time favorite with fishermen and family cruisers alike, the Chris 360 Sport Sedan enjoyed an unusually long production run (for a Chris Craft), and they remain reasonably popular today on the used markets. Introduced in 1973 as the 36 Tournament SF (she became the 360 Commander in 1981), she had a practical two-stateroom, galley-up interior until 1984 when a single-stateroom floorplan with a dinette became standard. Construction is solid fiberglass, and her low-deadrise hull generates good lift but produces a stiff ride in a chop. The profile of the original 36 (pictured above, top) remained the same until 1985 when the deckhouse and flybridge were dramatically restyled. An increase in fuel capacity (to 400 gallons) in 1983 improved the range considerably. Standard 454-cid gas engines will cruise at about 18 knots with a top speed of 27–28 knots. Among numerous diesel options, the 300-hp Cat (or 320-hp Cummins) diesels bring the cruising speed up to approximately 23 knots and the top speed to 26–27 knots. ❑

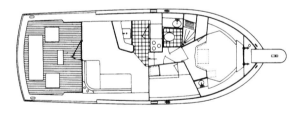

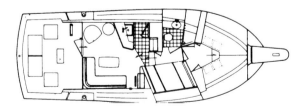

See Page 263 for Pricing Information

382 (1985)

392 (1986–90)

SPECIFICATIONS

Length	38'0"	Water	100 gals.
Length WL	33'0"	Fuel	350 gals.
Beam	13'11"	Cockpit	92 sq. ft.
Draft	3'9"	Hull Type	Modified-V
Weight	28,000#	Designer	Uniflite
Clearance	12'0"	Production	1985–90

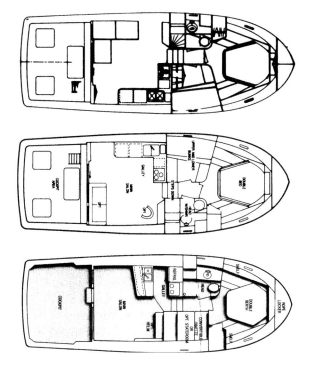

The Chris 392 Commander Sport Sedan is actually the old Uniflite 38 Convertible dressed up in a modern package. Chris Craft first marketed this boat in 1985 as the 382 Commander Sport Sedan—basically the late Uniflite 38 with a new name. The following year (1986) Chris Craft redesigned the deckhouse and flybridge resulting in a much-improved profile. Several two-stateroom floorplans were offered during her production run, and in 1990 (the final year) a single-stateroom floorplan with a mid-level galley and oak paneling became standard. While the Chris 392 is light-years ahead of the old Uniflite in appearance and decor, the well-known seakeeping properties of the original hull have been retained. The cockpit is large enough for a fighting chair, side decks are wide, and the bridge is arranged with bench seating forward of the helm. Standard 454-cid gas engines will cruise at 17–18 knots and reach 27 knots at full throttle. Optional 375-hp Cats will cruise at 24 knots and turn a top speed of 28 knots. ❏

See Page 263 for Pricing Information

CHRIS CRAFT 422 SPORT SEDAN

1974–84

1985–90

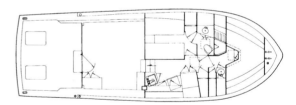

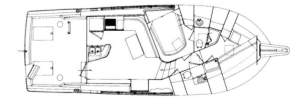

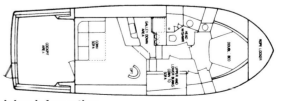

SPECIFICATIONS

Length	42'4"	Fuel	400/525 gals.
Beam	14'0"	Cockpit	110 sq. ft.
Draft	3'11"	Hull Type	Modified-V
Weight	33,000#	Deadrise Aft	8°
Clearance	13'7"	Designer	Chris Craft
Water	125 gals.	Production	1974–90

The Chris 422 Commander enjoyed the longest production run of any modern Chris Craft model. She was introduced as the 42 Tournament Fisherman in 1974, and critics were impressed with her comfortably dry ride and 24-knot cruising speed with then-new 8V71TIs. She was built on a shallow deadrise hull with a wide beam and a big fishing cockpit to go with her roomy two-stateroom interior. The 421 models (1983–84) are remembered for their gaudy hull graphics and cheap interiors. Chris Craft engineers thoroughly redesigned the boat in 1985 (new house, enlarged flybridge, glassed-over windshield, teak interior, etc.) with the introduction of the final 422 model. Throughout all the model changes the basic two-stateroom layout has been retained in one fashion or another. Retained too were the excellent seakeeping qualities that made her such a good performer. With either the original 8V71s or the later 485-hp 6-71s, the Chris 42 is a reasonably fast boat for her size with a cruising speed of 24 knots and a top speed of 27 knots. ❑

See Page 263 for Pricing Information

CHRIS CRAFT 45 COMMANDER SF

CHRIS CRAFT 482 CONVERTIBLE

SPECIFICATIONS

Length	45'6"	Fuel	600 gals.
Beam	16'0"	Cockpit	NA
Draft	3'11"	Hull Type	Modified-V
Weight	38,700#	Deadrise Aft	NA
Clearance	13'7"	Designer	Chris Craft
Water	150 gals.	Production	1972–81

SPECIFICATIONS

Length	48'10"	Fuel	780 gals.
Beam	15'9"	Cockpit	133 sq. ft.
Draft	4'9"	Hull Type	Modified-V
Weight	48,000#	Deadrise Aft	14°
Clearance	13'9"	Designer	A. Nordtvedt
Water	200 gals.	Production	1985–1988

Although the Chris 45 Commander Sportfisherman was in production for nearly a decade, she never achieved the widespread popularity among hard-core anglers of the Hatteras 45 and 46 convertibles or the Bertram 46. The 45 Commander went into production in 1972 on a heavy, broad-beamed hull with a sharp entry and a nearly flat bottom at the transom. A conventional two-stateroom, galley-down interior was standard and a three-stateroom layout was also available (one of the first three-stateroom arrangements ever offered in a production boat of this size). Notable features include overhead rod storage in the salon, a big tournament-style flybridge, and good storage throughout. The large and well-organized cockpit includes two fish boxes, a livewell on the centerline, and a wide transom door. After playing around with the idea of gas turbines in early production models, a variety of optional diesel engines were offered over the years. Among them, the popular 425-hp GM 8V71s will cruise the Chris 45 Commander SF at a respectable 20 knots and reach 23 knots wide open. ❑

Originally introduced in 1980 as the Uniflite 48 Convertible, the Chris 482 Commander was built on a rugged modified-V hull with moderate transom deadrise and balsa coring in the hullsides. Her long foredeck and huge cockpit mark her as a tournament-style fisherman although the luxurious interior of the 48 Commander is certainly one of her more desirable features. Various floorplans were offered when she was built by Uniflite, but Chris Craft settled on the popular three-stateroom arrangement with a queen berth in the starboard master stateroom. Rich teak paneling and a modern decor highlight the spacious salon. Chris Craft offered an optional glassed-in front windshield in later models in keeping with current design trends. With good offshore performance and 780 gallons of fuel, the Chris Craft 482 is a heavyweight tournament contender. With standard 8V92 diesels (600-hp), she can cruise at a steady 25 knots and reach a top speed of about 28 knots. Note that the Chris Craft 502 Convertible (1989 only) was built on a stretched 482 hull. ❑

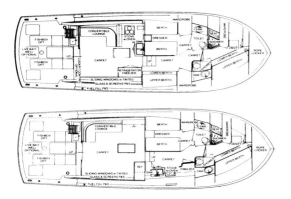

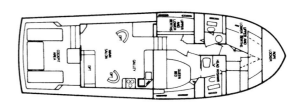

See Page 263 for Pricing Information

See Page 263 for Pricing Information

CONTENDER 35

SPECIFICATIONS

Length ....35'0'	Fuel ....250 gals.
Beam...............................10'0"	Cockpit.............................NA
Draft ....2'0"	Hull Type.................Deep-V
Hull Weight ....5,200#	Deadrise Aft ....24°
Clearance ....NA	Designer ....J. Nebber
Water ....45 gals.	Production 1989–Current

The Contender 35 is a high-performance, tournament-class fishing boat designed for serious offshore anglers. She's built on a narrow deep-V hull with balsa coring from the waterline up and a unique integral swim platform extension. A good-looking boat, the Contender is available with three separate cockpit configurations, however the aft-console/L-shaped settee layout (pictured above) is said to be the most popular. (Twin helm consoles can also be fitted aft, or the helm can be aft and midships.) Inside fold-up bunks provide berths for four with a stand-up head, high-low table and small galley. Notable features include good access to the engines on inboard models (the whole center section of the deck raises hydraulically), a well-arranged helm console with tilt wheel, livewell, removable fish boxes, and rod storage below. Available with inboard or outboard power (most late models have had the outboards), twin 250-hp Yamahas will deliver a top speed of 42+ knots while the 250-hp Cummins inboard diesels will cruise at a fast 32 knots (about 36 knots top). ❏

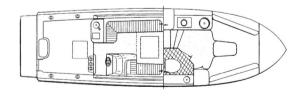

See Page 264 for Pricing Information

CRUISERS 3210 SEA DEVIL

SPECIFICATIONS

Length ....30'10"	Water ....45 gals.
Beam...........................10'10"	Fuel ....250 gals.
Draft ....2'10"	Hull Type.........Modified-V
Weight ....9,500#	Deadrise Aft....................18°
Clearance ....7'0"	Designer ....Jim Wynne
Cockpit.............................NA	Production 1988–90

The 3210 Sea Devil isn't noted for her long production run; she was dropped from the line after just three years. Construction was solid fiberglass, and she was built on the same 31-foot hull used in the production of the 3260 Esprit— a deep-V with moderate beam and prop pockets at the transom. The Sea Devil is a stylish design for anglers who like their boats with a little sex appeal. The cockpit is fitted with rod holders, built-in livewells, and a big fish box, and the transom door and integral swim platform are big pluses. Visibility from the raised helm console is excellent, and the instrument panel is very well arranged. The interior layout is nearly identical to that in the 3260 Esprit—very upscale and ideal for family cruising with berths for four. A good-running boat with standard 260-hp gas engines, she'll cruise easily at 19–20 knots and reach a top speed of about 30 knots. While it's fair to say that the Sea Devil is no tournament monster, she certainly is easy on the eye. ❏

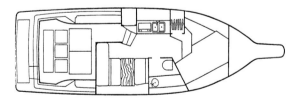

See Page 264 for Pricing Information

DAVIS 44 SPORTFISHERMAN

SPECIFICATIONS

Length ....44'5"	Fuel ....650 gals.
Beam..............................15'3"	Cockpit ....100 sq. ft.
Draft ....4'0"	Hull Type..........Modified-V
Weight ....35,000#	Deadrise Aft ....NA
Clearance ....NA	Designer......................Davis
Water ....135 gals.	Production 1991–93

Designed as an affordable alternative to the Davis 47, the 44 Sportfisherman displays the same incredibly well-proportioned profile of larger Davis models along with the smooth ride and proven offshore performance expected in a design from this highly regarded North Carolina builder. Her modified-V hull is constructed on a solid fiberglass bottom with cored hullsides, a fine entry, and greatly flared bow sections—the so-called "Carolina Flare." Several floorplans were offered, and each of the four 44s delivered had at least a few custom interior features. Not surprisingly, the cockpit is set up for tournament-level fishing activities, with plenty of workspace, direct engine room access, a huge in-deck fish box, and modular tackle centers. Note the extended flybridge overhang in the cockpit. Topside, the varnished teak helm console features Panish controls and a pop-up instrument pod. Standard engines in the Davis 44 SF were 485-hp 6-71s which cruise at 23 knots and reach 26–27 knots wide open. Optional 550-hp 6V92s cruise at 26 knots and deliver 30 knots wide open. ❏

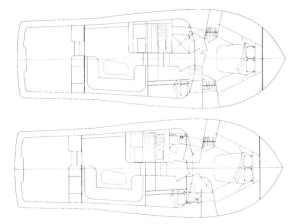

See Page 264 for Pricing Information

DAVIS 44 EXPRESS SF

SPECIFICATIONS

Length ....44'5"	Fuel ....500 gals.
Beam..............................15'3"	Cockpit ....100 sq. ft.
Draft ....4'0"	Hull Type..........Modified-V
Weight ....35,000#	Deadrise Aft ....NA
Clearance ....NA	Designer......................Davis
Water ....135 gals.	Production 1992–Current

An extremely good-looking boat with terrific lines, the Davis 44 Express is an upscale offshore fisherman with the look and feel of a custom-made boat. Like all Davis models, she's built on an easy-riding modified-V hull with a greatly flared bow, a wide beam, and moderate deadrise at the transom. The spacious cockpit (three steps below the bridgedeck level) is designed with low-freeboard gunwales and features a complete set of molded tackle centers, livewell, in-deck fish boxes, an offset transom door, and direct access to the large engine room. The helm is located on the centerline, and the varnished teak console and single-lever controls are impressive. There are several interior floorplans available, and each includes private stateroom forward, a small galley, and a separate stall shower in the head. Not surprisingly, handling characteristics are excellent, and the flared bow results in a dry ride. Twin 550-hp 6V92 diesels will cruise the 44 Express at 27 knots (about 30 knots top), and the 675-hp MANs will cruise at 29 knots and reach 33+ wide open. ❏

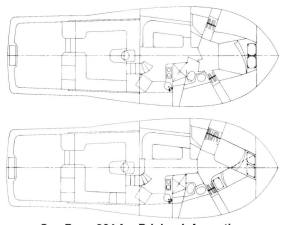

See Page 264 for Pricing Information

DAVIS 47 FLYBRIDGE SF

SPECIFICATIONS

Length	47'0"	Fuel	750/840 gals.
Beam	16'0"	Cockpit	NA
Draft	4'0"	Hull Type	Modified-V
Weight	45,000#	Deadrise Aft	NA
Clearance	12'10"	Designer	Davis
Water	150 gals.	Production	1986–93

While she has the distinctive appearance of a custom design, the Davis 47 was a full production boat and remains one of the more popular sportfishing boats of her size in the market. She's built on a modified-V hull with Divinycell coring in the hullsides from the waterline up. (The first six hulls were fully cored.) After experimenting with several floorplans, Davis in 1990 introduced two layouts (see below) that remained standard until she went out of production in 1993. The popular galley-down, two-stateroom version features a huge salon, and the galley-up floorplan has three staterooms—rare on a 47-footer. Access to the engine room is through a door in the cockpit. A teak console with single-lever controls dominates the flybridge. The cockpit features a molded tackle center, teak covering boards, transom door, and two in-deck storage boxes. Standard 735-hp 8V92s will cruise around 24 knots (29 knots top), and optional 820-hp MANs cruise around 28 knots (33 top). Fuel was increased for 1990. A total of 88 Davis 47s were built. ❏

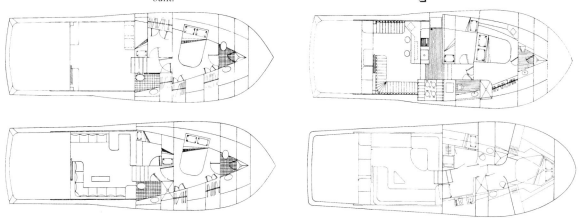

See Page 264 for Pricing Information

73

DAVIS 61 FLYBRIDGE SF

SPECIFICATIONS

Length ....61'0"	Fuel ....1,550 gals.
Beam.............................17'6"	Cockpit ....185 sq. ft.
Draft ....5'8"	Hull Type..........Modified-V
Weight ....80,000#	Deadrise Aft ....NA
Clearance ....18'0"	Designer ....G. Van Tassel
Water ....250 gals.	Production 1987–93

Behind the classic profile and aggressive styling of the Davis 61 lurks the heart of a proven big-game tournament-winner with truly outstanding performance capabilities. Indeed, it's been said many times that her ability to run into a head sea is better than any other boat in her class. In the Davis 61, a buyer can get the look and feel of an expensive custom boat for the price of a good quality production model. The result is an opulent and completely upscale sportfisherman with an elegant teak interior, four staterooms (two with double berths), and a huge fishing cockpit with a teak sole and teak covering boards. Other features include direct cockpit access to the engine room, a custom teak helm console on the flybridge with Panish controls and pop-up electronics display, and the availability of huge 1,400-hp 16V92s for an honest 30-knot cruising speed. Standard 1,040-hp 12V92s cruise at 26 knots (with a tower and full fuel) and reach a top speed of 31 knots. A popular boat, a total of 35 were built before production ended in 1993. ❑

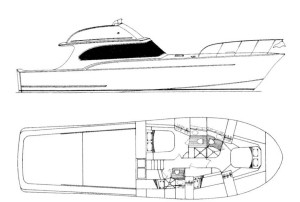

See Page 264 for Pricing Information

DAWSON 33 EXPRESS

SPECIFICATIONS

Length w/Pulpit ....35'10"	Water ....70 gals.
Hull Length ....33'0"	Clearance ....7'0"
Beam ....11'6"	Hull Type.................Deep-V
Draft ....2'6"	Deadrise Aft ....17°
Weight ....19,500#	Designer ....Dawson
Fuel ....300 gals.	Production 1995–Current

The Dawson 33 is a one of the better-looking express fisherman we've seen, and it's fair to say that her beauty is more than skin deep. She's built at a small yard in New Jersey on a beamy deep-V hull with a solid fiberglass bottom and cored hullsides. Like a lot of serious fishing boats, the Dawson is built close to the water, and she has a decidedly strictly-business appearance about her. The cockpit is large enough for a mounted chair and comes with a recirculating live well, bait rigging and tackle stations, saltwater washdown, padded coamings, and plenty of rod storage. A big U-shaped lounge with a removable table is opposite the helm. Inside, the Dawson's accommodations are limited (most of her length is devoted to cockpit and bridgedeck space) but efficiently arranged with V-berths, a small galley, dry storage, and an enclosed head. A good-running boat, twin Cummins 300-hp diesels will deliver a fast 26-knot cruising speed (burning *less* than 1 gpm—very impressive) with a top speed of around 31 knots. ❑

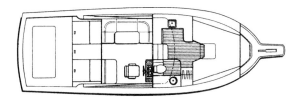

See Page 264 for Pricing Information

DAWSON 38 CONVERTIBLE SF

SPECIFICATIONS

Length ....38'0"	Fuel ....400 gals.
Beam..............................13'8"	Cockpit ....100 sq. ft.
Draft ....3'6"	Hull Type.................Deep-V
Weight ....28,000#	Deadrise Aft ....24°
Clearance ....NA	Designer ....T. Dawson
Water ....90 gals.	Production 1987–94

The Dawson 38 is a limited production fisherman designed to appeal to the tournament-level angler. The hull is not a new design; it was first developed back in 1975 in Pensacola and has since been used for commercial and charter service. The hulls were purchased and shipped to New Jersey where the 38s were finished out at the old Pacemaker yard. With a steep 24° of deadrise aft, the Dawson has more "V" than just about any other boat of her type on the market. An attractive design, her styling is on the conservative side, and most will view the Dawson as a strictly business sport-fisherman in spite of her comfortable interior. The two-stateroom, galley-up floorplan includes a centerline double bed forward, a separate stall shower, and bunk berths in the guest cabin. Standard 375-hp Cats will cruise the Dawson 38 around 25 knots (30 knots top) and optional 485-hp 6-71s cruise at a fast 30 knots (33–34 knots) wide open). A total of 26 Dawson 38 Convertibles were built during her production run. Note that an express model became available in 1991. ❏

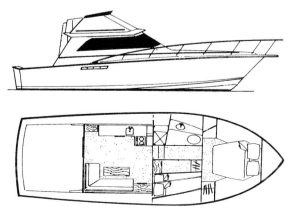

See Page 264 for Pricing Information

DELTA 36 SFX

SPECIFICATIONS

Length ....36'3"	Fuel ....400 gals.
Beam..............................12'2"	Cockpit ....98 sq. ft.
Draft ....3'0"	Hull Type................Deep-V
Weight ....17,200#	Deadrise Aft....................23°
Clearance ....NA	Designer.......................Delta
Water ....50 gals.	Production 1987–Current

Delta boats are well known in the charter boat trade for their no-nonsense approach to the basics. The hulls are generally Coast Guard certified, and the construction is rugged with the emphasis on reliability. In the Delta 36 SFX, however, there's more than just a tough deep-V hull and a big fishing cockpit. This is truly an innovative and practical boat with an outright aggressive appearance. What sets her apart from most other sportfishers in the mid-range market is her unique raised command bridge—a spacious platform that splits the difference between a true flybridge and the raised bridgedeck used in open express boats. Positioned about three feet above the cockpit level, this sensible concept provides a stand-up engine room (virtually unheard of in a small fisherman), with direct cockpit access and extraordinary headroom below. Inside, the layout is modern and very attractive with a circular pit-style dinette, linear galley, and double berth forward. A good sea boat, she'll cruise around 24–26 knots with 435-hp Cat (or 400-hp Cummins) diesels with a top speed of close to 30 knots. ❏

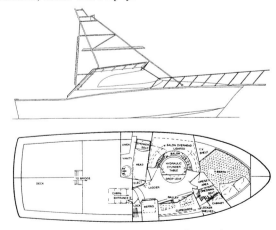

See Page 264 for Pricing Information

DELTA 38 SPORTFISHERMAN

SPECIFICATIONS

Length ....38'0"	Fuel ....300 gals.
Beam..............................12'5"	Cockpit ....120 sq. ft.
Draft ....3'0"	Hull Type.........Modified-V
Weight ....19,500#	Deadrise Aft....................13°
Clearance ....NA	Designer.......................Delta
Water ....50 gals.	Production 1984–Current

The first Delta 38s were commercial dive and charter boats, where they earned a reputation for dependability and offshore stability. A semi-custom model, about 70 have been built (most to USCG specifications), and, while the majority are used commercially, there are many that are privately owned as well. Her modified-V hull is narrow with moderate deadrise aft and a spray rail forward—a no-nonsense fishing platform with solid fiberglass construction and proven offshore performance. The cockpit in this boat is huge with low freeboard and plenty of space for tackle centers and a full-size chair. The interior dimensions are limited due to the oversize cockpit and the unique 4-foot collision bulkhead forward (a watertight compartment required by the CG in certified boats). A lower helm is standard, and V-berths are below, along with a galley and small head. The Delta 38 has been offered with a wide variety of power options including single or twin GM, Cat, Volvo, and Cummins diesels to 425-hp. A good-running boat, she'll appeal to anglers seeking simplicity and durability. ❏

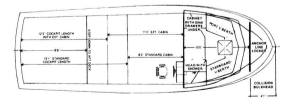

See Page 264 for Pricing Information

Why should you consider shopping through a member of the
FLORIDA YACHT BROKERS ASSOCIATION?

Each member has agreed to uphold a Code of Ethics to treat YOU, the customer, fairly and honestly.
These are people who know their business…people you can count on.

2 Hulls
Adventure Yacht Sales, Inc.
Alexander Yachts
Alexander Yachts, Inc.
Allied Marine Group
Altech Yachts Inc.
American Show Boats, Ltd., Inc.
Ameriship Corp.
Aqua Marine International, Inc.
Ardell Yacht & Ship Brokers
Atlantic Pacific Sailing Yachts
Atlantic Yacht & Ship
Aventura Yacht Charters & Sales
Bain Yacht Sales, Inc.
Bartram & Brakenhoff, Inc.
Bob Anslow Yacht Sales
Boger & Associates
Bollman Yachts
Boston Yacht Sales, Inc.
Bradford International
Burger Yacht Sales
Camper & Nicholson
Capt. Jack's Yacht Brokerage, Inc.
Card Sound Yachts, Inc.
Caretaker Yacht Sales
Carson Yacht Brokerage, Inc.
Castlemain ,Inc.
Castonguay Associates
Catamaran Sales, Inc.
Charles Morgan Associates
Charles P. Irwin Yacht Brokerage
Cliff Argue Yacht & Aircraft Sales
Coastal Marina Development, Inc.
Coconut Grove Yacht Sales
Colonial Yacht Brokerage, Inc.
Corporate Yacht Brokerage, Inc.
Cozy Cove Marina, Inc.
Dave D'Onofrio Yacht Sales, Inc.
David Lowe's Boatyard, Inc.
Daytona Marina and Boat Works
DYB Charters Inc. & Yacht Sales
East West Yachts, Inc.
First Coast Yacht Sales, Inc.
Florida Yacht Charters & Sales, Inc.
Florida Yacht Connection
Fraser Yacht Sales
Fredericks/Power & Sail

GDB Yachts
Gilman Yacht Sales, Inc.
Gulf Air Boats, Inc.
H & H Yacht Sales, Inc.
Hal Jones & Company
Helms, Kelly, MacMahon Int'l Yachting
Herb Phillips Yacht Sales, Inc.
Hidden Harbor Marine
High-Tech Yacht & Ship, Inc.
HMY Yacht Sales, Inc.
Hoffmann Yacht Sales,Inc.
Homestead Boat & Yacht Sales
Int'l Yachting Services of Naples, Inc.
Interyacht, Inc.
Jackson Marine Sales, Inc.
Jacksonville Beach Yacht Sales
John G. Alden of Boston, Inc.
Jordan Yacht & Ship Co.
J. Woods Marine Group
Luke Brown & Associates
Luxury Yacht Corp.
Mares
Marine Group, Inc.
Marine Unlimited
Melvin B. Gaines Yacht Brokerage, Inc.
Merle Wood & Associates, Inc.
Merrill-Stevens Yacht Sales
Merritt Boat & Engine Works
Mitchell's Yacht Brokerage
Monterey Marine Yacht Sales
Naples Yacht Brokerage
Nautor's Swan
Nautor's Swan Southeast
NI'O Yacht Group
Northrop & Johnson, Inc.
Northside Marine Sales, Inc.
Odyssey III Ltd.
Offer & Associates
Offshore Yacht Brokers
Ortega Yacht Sales
Oviatt Marine, Inc.
O'Brien Yacht Sales, Inc.
Palm Beach Yacht Brokerage, Inc.
Parrot & Herst Yacht & Ship Sales
Parrot, Elfenbein & O'Brien
Perdue Dean Co., Inc.
Peter Kehoe & Associates

Pilot Yacht Sales
Pilot Yachts
Regatta Pointe Yacht Sales, Inc.
Rhodes Yacht Brokers, Inc.
Richard Bertram, Inc.
Riverbend Marina
Robert Dean & Associates Yacht Brokerage
Roger Hansen Yacht Sales
Royce Yacht & Ship Brokers, Inc.
R.J.W. Moran Yacht & Ship, Inc.
Safe Harbour Marina
Sandy Hatton Yacht Sales, Inc.
Sarasota Yacht & Ship Services
Sea Lake Yacht Sales
Sea Ray Port Jacksonville
Seafarer Brokerage, Inc.
South Florida Boat Mart, Inc.
South Florida Marine Liquidators
Starboard Yacht Brokerage, Inc.
Starboard Yacht Sales & Service, Inc.
Stuart Cay Marina
St. Augustine Yacht Center, Inc.
St. Petersburg Yacht Charters & Sales, Inc.
Summerfield Yacht Sales, Inc.
Sustendal & Co.
The Moorings Yacht Brokerage
The Shaw's Yacht Brokerage & Marine Supply, Inc.
The William F. Nelson Co.
The Yacht Broker Marine Group
United /Derecktor Gunnell Yachts
Walsh Yachts, Inc.
Waterline Yacht Brokerage
Webster Associates
West Florida Yachts, Inc.
Whitney's Sailcenter, Inc.
Woods & Oviatt, Inc.
Yacht Perfection, Inc.
Yacht Search, Inc.
Yachtco International
Yacht-Eng Yacht Sales & Brokerage

Just look for the logo

FLORIDA YACHT BROKERS ASSOCIATION
P.O. Box 6524, Station 9 • Fort Lauderdale, FL 33316 • 305-522-9270 • Fax 305-764-0697

DONZI F-33

SPECIFICATIONS

Length	33'1"	Clearance	5'6"
Beam	9'0"	Hull Type	Deep-V
Draft	1'6"	Deadrise Aft	24°
Weight	5,300#	Max HP	600
Fuel	295 gals.	Designer	D. Riley
Water	20 gals.	Production	1987–92

Based on the hull of Donzi's Z-33 go-fast boat, the F-33 (the F stands for fishing) is a sporty center console with a well-established reputation for superior offshore performance and a great ride. She's built on a fully cored deep-V hull with a narrow beam and a steep 24° of transom deadrise. While the Donzi's cockpit dimensions are small compared to most 33-foot sportfisherman, there's still plenty of room for a couple of anglers to work without feeling cramped for deck space. At the helm, the wide console has space for mounting electronics, and there's a bench seat forward with storage under. Fishing features include an in-deck livewell, leaning post/rocket launcher, a flip-up cutting board at the transom, raw water washdown, and recessed storage compartments. Forward, the small cuddy provides basic overnight accommodations for three with V-berths and a quarter berth, a manual toilet and a mini-galley. Four full-size rod racks are mounted on the cabin wall. Twin 225-hp outboards will cruise the Donzi F-33 at 25 knots with a top speed of around 40 knots. ❏

See Page 264 for Pricing Information

DONZI 65 SPORTFISHERMAN

SPECIFICATIONS

Length	65'0"	Fuel	2,000 gals.
Beam	18'8"	Cockpit	NA
Draft	5'2"	Hull Type	Modified-V
Weight	72,000#	Deadrise Aft	12°
Clearance	14'4"	Designer	J. Garland
Water	350 gals.	Production	1987–Current

Built since 1988 by Roscioli International (when they purchased the molds from Donzi), the Donzi 65 is a magnificent display of big-time sportfishing elegance. The beauty is more than skin deep: construction of the Donzi 65 is state-of-the-art with Divinycell hull coring and a long list of exotic materials used to create a strong and relatively lightweight structure. The hull is a modified-V design with a sharp entry forward and 12° of transom deadrise. The Donzi's cockpit is huge, and the full-width flybridge above can accommodate a dozen people. Several three- and four-stateroom layouts have been offered over the years, and all feature a wide-open salon with the galley forward. The interior woodwork (teak, oak, or pecan) and decor appointments are opulent in the extreme. The stand-up engine room runs about a third of the boat's *length* and is accessed from the cockpit or through a door next to the crew quarters. A superb sea boat, twin 1,440-hp 16V92 DDEC diesels will cruise the Donzi 65 at 26 knots and deliver 30 knots of speed wide open. ❏

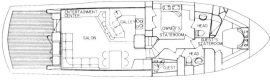

Four-Stateroom, Owner to Port

Four-Stateroom, Owner Forward

See Page 264 for Pricing Information

SPECIFICATIONS

Length	30'0"	Fuel	90 gals.
Beam	8'8"	Cockpit	40 sq. ft.
Draft	1'6"	Hull Type	Modified-V
Weight	4,900#	Deadrise Aft	8°
Clearance	NA	Designer	C. Werebach
Water	25 gals.	Production	1988–Current

The Dorado 30 is a semi-custom center console fisherman with a relatively narrow flat-bottom hull and a unique jackshaft drive system. Weighing in at less than 5,000 lbs., the Dorado is light for her size (and extremely fuel efficient) thanks to her Divinycell-cored hull construction and single engine power. The hull was first designed back in the 1950s for tarpon fishing and has been built of fiberglass since 1988. Although the transom deadrise is marginal, the ability to adjust the outdrive to sea conditions provides a dryer and softer ride than might otherwise be expected. The uncluttered cockpit is arranged with an in-deck livewell and fish box on each side of the boat and bench seating forward of the console. Storage is excellent (superior, actually), and V-berths and dry storage are provided in the cuddy cabin. Among several engine options, a single 230-hp Volvo diesel will cruise at 26 knots cruise and reach a top speed of around 32 knots. The range (at an easy 20-knot cruise) with this engine approaches 300 miles—very impressive indeed. ❏

(Floorplan Unavailable)

See Page 264 for Pricing Information

DUFFY 35 SPORT CRUISER

SPECIFICATIONS

Length	35'1"	Fuel, Std.	100 gals.
Length WL	33'4"	Fuel, Opt.	200 gals.
Beam	11'11"	Cockpit	NA
Draft	3'3"	Hull Type	Modified-V
Weight	12,000#	Designer	S. Lincoln
Water	50 gals.	Production	1983–Current

Designed with a greater emphasis on speed than most other Downeast-style boats of her type, the Duffy 35 is a well-built, semi-custom cruiser with distinctive lines and tremendous eye appeal. She's constructed on a solid fiberglass, modified-V hull with a fine entry, hard chines aft, and a full-length keel which provides protection for the underwater gear. Like most of the true Downeast designs, a fully equipped Duffy 35 is priced at the higher end of the market for boats in her size range. Aside from good looks and traditional charm, her great attraction is a superb blend of New England craftsmanship and lasting value. The Duffy is a versatile boat with a cockpit large enough for serious fishing and an efficient interior layout well-suited for extended cruising. Features include a deckhouse galley, complete lower helm station, a large stall shower, and excellent access to the engine. A seaworthy and economical boat, a single Cat 375-hp diesel will produce a surprisingly fast cruising speed of 24 knots and a top speed of around 28 knots. ❏

See Page 264 for Pricing Information

DUFFY 42 SPORT CRUISER

SPECIFICATIONS

Length	42'0"	Fuel	500 gals.
Beam	14'6"	Cockpit	NA
Draft	4'6"	Hull Type	Semi-Disp.
Weight	24,000#	Designer	S. Lincoln
Water	100 gals.	Production	1985–Current

A classic lobster boat profile and a high level of craftsmanship have made the Duffy 42 one of the more popular Downeast cruisers currently on the market. These are rugged semi-custom boats with cored hulls and a full length keel below—seaworthy designs with beautiful sheers, protected running gear, and generous cockpits. There are several versions of the Duffy 42, and each can be built to a buyer's specifications. The two-stateroom, galley-up floorplan of the FB Cruiser (pictured above) features an island berth forward and bunk berths in the guest cabin. A lower helm is standard, and the conservative interior decor is functional and well-finished. Engine room access is very good, and a transom door and swim platform are standard. Most of the Duffy 42s built for private use (many are used commercially) have been powered with a single 375-hp Cat which delivers a 14-15-knot cruising speed and around 18 knots wide open. Cruising range is an impressive 500+ miles. A class act, used Duffy 42s are considered premium boats on the used markets. ❏

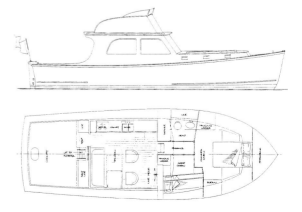

See Page 265 for Pricing Information

DYER 29

Trunk Cabin

Bass Boat

SPECIFICATIONS

Length	28'6"	Water	24 gals.
Beam	9'5"	Fuel	110 gals.
Draft	2'6"	Hull Type	Semi-Disp.
Weight	6,700#	Designer	Nick Potter
Clearance	6'0"	Production	1955–Current

Designed for cruising, fishing, or as a general utility boat, the durable Dyer 29 is a industry classic. Indeed, there are those who think she's one of the most alluring small boats ever designed. Production began over 35 years ago making her the longest-running fiberglass model in the business. Each of the over 300 sold has been customized to some extent, and no two are exactly alike. At only 6,700 lbs., the Dyer would be considered a light boat were it not for her narrow beam. She's built on a soft-chined hull with a fine entry, protected prop, and an uncommonly graceful sheer. The ability of the hull to tackle heavy sea conditions is legendary. Those who own Dyers tolerate her tight cabin quarters and inconvenient engine box and delight in the fingertip control and positive response of this easily driven hull. Among numerous engine options, a single 200-hp Volvo diesel will cruise the Dyer 29 efficiently at 16 knots (7 gph) and reach a top speed of 20–21 knots. In addition to the popular Trunk Cabin and Bass Boat models (pictured above), the 29 is available in hardtop and express versions. ❏

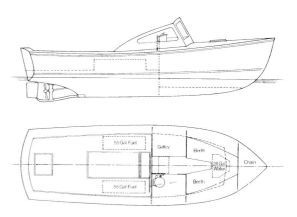

See Page 265 for Pricing Information

EGG HARBOR 33 SEDAN

1971–77

1978–81

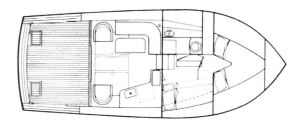

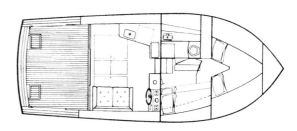

SPECIFICATIONS

Length	33'0"	Fuel	216 gals.
Beam	13'2"	Cockpit	NA
Draft	2'9"	Hull Type	Modified-V
Weight	13,000#	Deadrise Aft	8°
Clearance	NA	Designer	Egg Harbor
Water	50 gals.	Production	1971–81

The 33 Sedan was the first fiberglass hull ever built by the Egg Harbor Yacht Company. Designed primarily as a family cruiser, she was constructed with a mahogany deck and superstructure until 1978 when the switch was made to all-fiberglass construction. The standard floorplan arrangement has a two-stateroom layout with the galley in the salon. A galley-down version was offered in later models, and the head was also redesigned to accommodate a separate stall shower. Although the cockpit is small, and the range is limited, the great appeal of the Egg Harbor 33 Sedan lies in her graceful profile, rich mahogany interior, and the extensive use of exterior teak including teak covering boards and a solid teak cockpit sole. Her appearance improved dramatically when the fiberglass deck and house were introduced, and she remained in production until replaced in 1982 with the all-new Egg Harbor 33 Convertible. Twin 270-hp Crusader engines will cruise the Egg 33 at a modest 15–16 knots, and she'll reach a top speed of about 23 knots. ❏

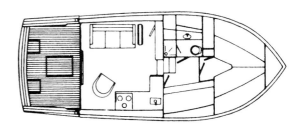

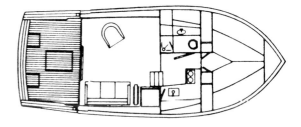

See Page 265 for Pricing Information

EGG HARBOR 33 CONVERTIBLE

SPECIFICATIONS

Length	33'0"	Fuel	320 gals.
Beam	13'2"	Cockpit	70 sq. ft.
Draft	2'5"	Hull Type	Modified-V
Weight	17,000#	Deadrise Aft	8°
Clearance	NA	Designer	W. Nickerson
Water	50 gals.	Production	1982–89

The 33 Convertible was the first of the new-style Egg Harbor designs when she came out in 1982. She evolved from the Pacemaker 33 SF, a good-looking flybridge sedan that went into production in 1979 and ended when Pacemaker closed down the following year. Egg Harbor picked up the tooling, revised the interior layout and reintroduced her as a replacement for the original 33 Sedan. In addition to the Convertible model, Egg Harbor also offered the 33 in an express fisherman version with no flybridge. Significantly, the fuel capacity of the newer Egg 33 is 320 gallons— a big improvement in range from the original 33 Sedan—and a teak interior replaced the original 33 Sedan's mahogany woodwork. From 1987 to 1989, a stretched version, the Egg Harbor 35 SF, was built with a larger cockpit and 400 gallons of fuel. Upgrades on both eliminated the front windshield in later models. Standard 350-hp gas engines cruise the Egg Harbor 33 around 19 knots with a top speed of 28–29 knots. ❏

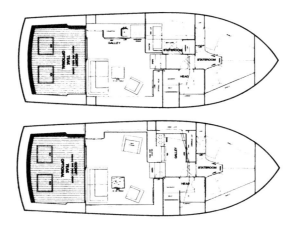

See Page 265 for Pricing Information

1990–94

1994–Current

SPECIFICATIONS

Length w/Pulpit..........37'8"	Cockpit...................85 sq. ft.
Hull Length ....34'6"	Water ....75 gals.
Beam...............................13'2"	Fuel ....406 gals.
Draft ....3'2"	Hull Type ....Modified-V
Weight ....20,925#	Deadrise Aft......................8°
Clearance ....12'3"	Prod........1990; 1993–Current

Renamed the Golden Egg 35 for 1996, the 34/35 Golden Egg is one of only a few production flybridge convertibles available in the under-35' range. She's built on the same rugged hull used in the production of the earlier 33 Convertible (1982–89)—a good all-around modified-V design with moderate beam, a flared bow and solid fiberglass construction. The black wraparound mask was dropped in mid-1994 when Egg Harbor designers softened the deckhouse windows, restyled the flybridge and eliminated the exterior teak trim. Two interior floorplans are offered: a two-stateroom layout with the galley up, and a single-stateroom, galley-down arrangement with a larger salon. Both floorplans have a stall shower in the head, and both have the traditional Egg Harbor full teak interior. The cockpit is roomy for a 34-footer although the flybridge is on the small side. Fishing features include a molded tackle center with sink and icebox, transom door, recessed storage lockers and inwale coaming. Standard 310-hp/454-cid gas engines will cruise at 19 knots and reach about 28 knots wide open. ❏

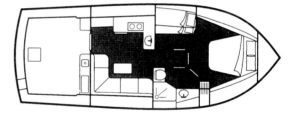

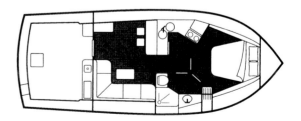

See Page 265 for Pricing Information

EGG HARBOR 36 SEDAN

SPECIFICATIONS

Length	36'0"	Clearance	NA
Beam	13'3"	Cockpit	NA
Draft	2'9"	Hull Type	Modified-V
Weight	17,000#	Deadrise Aft	6°
Water	75 gals.	Designer	Egg Harbor
Fuel	260/320 gals.	Production	1976–1985

A good many cruisers find the 34–36-foot size range to be ideal in a family boat. The cockpit is usually large enough for fishing, and a good design will retain the maneuverability of a much smaller hull. Such a boat is the Egg Harbor 36 Sedan. She's built on a modified-V hull designed by Egg Harbor with a deep forefoot and flat aftersections for quick planing. Early models were built with a glassed-over mahogany deckhouse, but in 1978 construction became all-fiberglass. The Egg 36 has the teak cockpit sole and covering boards that many owners find appealing in spite of the maintenance. The interior can accommodate up to six depending on the floorplan (there were a total of four). A Tournament Fisherman model in 1978 featured an improved bridge layout with bench seating forward of the helm. The standard 350-hp gas engines will cruise at about 19 knots and reach 28 knots top. Note that the Taiwan-built Pace 36 SF (1988–92) used the old Egg Harbor 36 Sedan molds. ❏

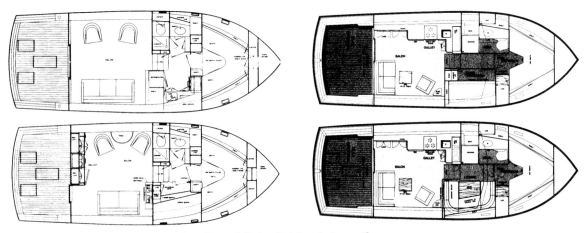

See Page 265 for Pricing Information

EGG HARBOR 37 CONVERTIBLE

SPECIFICATIONS

Length	37'5"	Fuel	340/400 gals.
Beam	14'5"	Cockpit	NA
Draft	3'0"	Hull Type	Modified-V
Weight	24,000#	Deadrise Aft	9°
Clearance	NA	Designer	W. Nickerson
Water	80 gals.	Production	1985–89

A scaled-down version of the Egg Harbor 41 SF, the 37 Convertible is a competent family cruiser with a smallish cockpit and a rather unattractive profile. She's built on a modified-V hull with balsa coring in the hullsides and a relatively flat bottom for lift and quick acceleration. Inside, the interior is every bit as impressive (and exactly the same size) as her bigger sister. The salon is clearly the centerpiece of the boat—a completely stylish and comfortable living area offered in a choice of two layouts. The 37's wide beam provides an interior volume seldom found on boats of her size, and the quality teak woodwork is typical of all Egg Harbor models. Outside, the sidedecks are wide enough to get forward, and the average-size bridge is arranged with guest seating forward of the helm. Twin 350-hp gas engines were standard in the Egg 37 for a cruising speed of 19 knots and a top speed of around 28 knots. The fuel was increased to 400 gallons in 1986 models. ❑

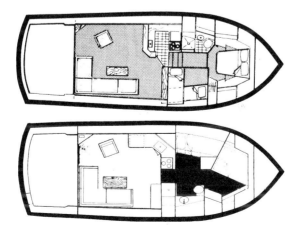

See Page 265 for Pricing Information

87

EGG HARBOR 38 GOLDEN EGG

1990–94

1995–Current

SPECIFICATIONS

Length w/Pulpit..........41'8"	Fuel, Gas ....400 gals.
Hull Length ....38'6"	Fuel, Dsl. ....500 gals.
Beam...............................15'0"	Cockpit....................90 sq. ft.
Draft ....3'10"	Hull Type ....Modified-V
Weight ....22,500#	Deadrise Aft ....8°
Water ....120 gals.	Prod. 1990; 1993–Current

Replacing the not-so-popular 37 Convertible, the Egg Harbor 38 is one of the biggest 38-footers around thanks to her super-wide 15-foot beam. When she was introduced in 1990, Egg Harbor designers gave her a distinctive wraparound "black mask' deck-house profile that many in the industry found quite attractive. Times change, however, and in 1994 the mask was dropped altogether, and the windows and flybridge were restyled to give the boat a softer, more traditional appearance. Built on a solid fiberglass hull with cored hullsides, the 38 Golden Egg is available with two floor-plans: a two-stateroom layout or a single-stateroom arrangement with a dinette in place of the second cabin. The full-teak interior is well crafted, and the quality hardware, fabrics and workmanship are impressive. The cockpit comes standard with a molded tackle center, livewell, transom door, and fish box. While gas engines have always been available, serious anglers have favored the 375-hp Caterpillar or 400-hp 6V53 Detroit diesels, either of which will cruise at 22–23 knots (about 25 knots top). The now-standard 430-hp Volvo diesels are a knot or two faster. ❏

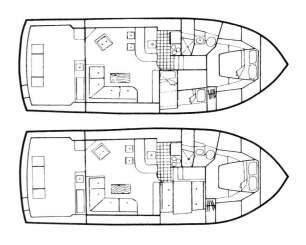

See Page 265 for Pricing Information

EGG HARBOR 40 SEDAN

SPECIFICATIONS

Length	40'0"	Fuel	338 gals.
Beam	14'0"	Cockpit	95 sq. ft.
Draft	2'9"	Hull Type	Modified-V
Weight	28,000#	Deadrise Aft	6°
Clearance	NA	Designer	D. Martin
Water	100 gals.	Production	1975–86

Introduced as a replacement for the Egg Harbor 38 Sedan in 1975, the principal difference between the Egg Harbor 40 Sedan and her predecessor is the 40's larger cockpit dimensions—something the Egg Harbor 38 sorely lacked. The original 38-foot hull was stretched, and the additional length adds much to her graceful profile. Her appearance was considerably enhanced when a new fiberglass deckhouse and flybridge replaced the wooden superstructure in 1978. Several interior floorplans were offered over the years with most of the recent models being two-stateroom layouts with a mid-level galley to port. In a significant production change, the original mahogany interiors were changed to teak in 1982. A large and unobstructed cockpit made the Egg Harbor 40 Sedan a popular and competent sportfisherman, and the teak sole and covering boards were standard. A Tournament Fisherman version introduced in 1978 moved the helm aft for better cockpit visibility. Optional 450-hp GM 6-71 diesels will cruise the Egg Harbor 40 Sedan around 24 knots and reach 27 knots wide open. ❑

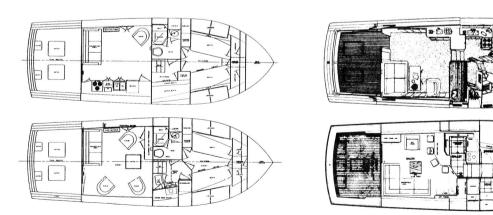

See Page 265 for Pricing Information

89

SPECIFICATIONS

Length	40'10"	Fuel	500 gals.
Beam	14'5"	Cockpit	NA
Draft	3'0"	Hull Type	Modified-V
Weight	28,000#	Deadrise Aft	8°
Clearance	13'0"	Designer	W. Nickerson
Water	80 gals.	Production	1984–89

The Egg Harbor 41 SF stands out among most mid-sized convertible models because of her huge cockpit and elegant interior accommodations. She's designed around a reworked Pacemaker 38 hull acquired by Egg Harbor when Pacemaker went out of business in 1980. A good-running boat with quick acceleration, the hull is a modified-V affair with a flat 8° of transom deadrise and balsa coring in the hullsides. She was introduced in 1984 in both a Sportfisherman and a Convertible Sedan version, the difference being the larger salon and smaller cockpit of the Convertible. The upscale interiors of both boats are lush with furniture-quality teak cabinetry and paneling throughout. Outside, the exterior styling of the Egg Harbor 41 is very graceful, and, when fitted with a full tower, she has a decidedly serious appearance. Gas engines were standard, but optional GM and Caterpillar diesels were the engines of choice for most. A pair of 375-hp Cats will cruise about 22 knots, and the 6-71TIs cruise in the 26+ range. ❑

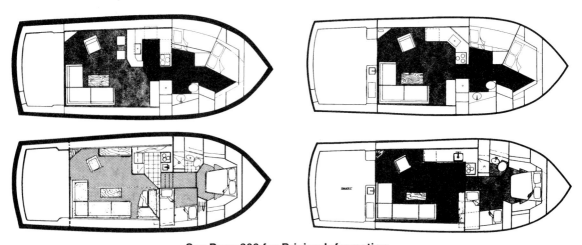

See Page 266 for Pricing Information

1990–94

1995–Current

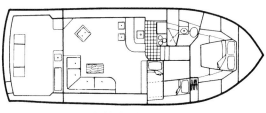

1990–94 Floorplans

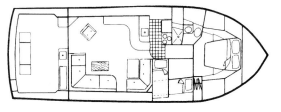

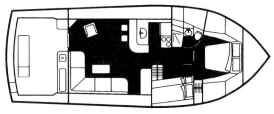

1995 – Current

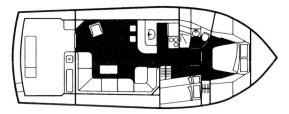

SPECIFICATIONS

Length w/Pulpit..........45'4"	Cockpit..................100 sq. ft.
Hull Length ....42'2"	Water ....120 gals.
Beam............................15'0"	Fue ....600 gals.
Draft ....3'10"	Hull Type ....Modified-V
Weight ....36,300#	Deadrise Aft ....8°
Clearance ....13'0"	Prod. 1990; 1993–Current

Introduced in 1990 to replace the Egg 41 and 43 Convertibles, the Egg Harbor 42 was restyled in 1994 with a fresh window treatment and an all-new flybridge profile. She's built on the same modified-V hull used for the 38 Golden Egg with cored hullsides, a well-flared bow and a relatively flat 8° of transom deadrise. The two-stateroom, mid-galley floorplans offered in the Egg 42 have all featured an abundance of varnished teak woodwork, quality appliances and plush decorator fabrics. Indeed, the upscale furnishings create on of the nicer interiors to be found in a 42-foot convertible. With 100 sq. ft. of space, the cockpit can easily handle a fighting chair and includes a tackle center, in-deck fish box, livewell and transom door. The teak trim and covering boards were eliminated in 1995. Topside, the tournament flybridge is arranged with the helm well aft for a good view of the cockpit. Among several engine options, early models with 375-hp Cats will cruise at 23–24 knots (about 27 top). The current 485-hp 6-71 Detroits cruise at 26 knots (29 knots top), and optional 535-hp 6V-92s run about a knot or two faster.   ❑

See Page 266 for Pricing Information

SPECIFICATIONS

Length	43'0"	Fuel	600 gals.
Beam	14'5"	Cockpit	NA
Draft	3'0"	Hull Type	Modified-V
Weight	32,000#	Deadrise Aft	8°
Clearance	NA	Designer	W. Nickerson
Water	80 gals.	Production	1986–89

The Egg Harbor 43 Sportfisherman is easily one of the better-looking boats in her size class. She's built on a stretched version of the Egg 41 SF hull—a relatively flat-bottom affair with moderate beam and cored hullsides—and she carries an extra 100 gallons of fuel for increased range. (The extra two feet of length has been used to enlarge the salon dimensions. Indeed, the 43's interior appears to be that of a much larger boat.) Several two-stateroom floorplans were offered, and all feature a single head and mid-level galley. The teak cabinetry and paneling used throughout is impressive and very well crafted. Taken together, the upscale decor and luxurious accommodations make the Egg Harbor 43 a comfortable boat for family cruising. Like many modern sportfishermen the front windshield area is glassed-over and painted to create a distinctive wraparound black "mask" surrounding the deckhouse. A pair of 375-hp Cats will cruise the 43 SF around 22 knots, and the larger 6-71TIs will cruise at 26 knots. ❑

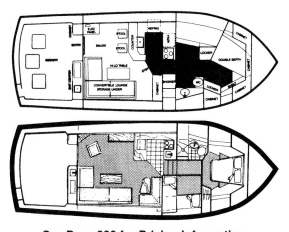

See Page 266 for Pricing Information

EGG HARBOR 46 SEDAN

1973–77

1978–83

SPECIFICATIONS

Length ....46'8"	Fuel ....500/628/788 gals.
Beam..............................15'0"	Cockpit............................NA
Draft ....3'8"	Hull Type ....Modified-V
Weight.....................38,000#	Deadrise Aft.....................2°
Clearance........................NA	Designer..............D. Martin
Water ....100 gals.	Production 1973–83

Considered a handsome boat in her day with good all-around accommodations, the 46 Sedan was a popular model for Egg Harbor during her decade-plus in production. Originally built with a fiberglass hull and mahogany deck and superstructure, Egg Harbor went to all-fiberglass construction in 1978, and the new tooling considerably improved her appearance. As a fisherman, she had the cockpit space and handling qualities then demanded by serious anglers. Several interior arrangements were available over the years including a three-stateroom version—a rarity in just a 46-foot boat. More popular, however, was the two-stateroom layout with the galley down and a more open salon. As the Egg 46 matured, she received the additional fuel capacity necessary for offshore work and a new teak interior in 1982 replaced the original mahogany woodwork used in the earlier models. GM 8V71TIs will cruise the Egg Harbor 46 Sedan around 20 knots and reach a top speed of 23. Note that this hull was stretched to create the Egg Harbor 48 in 1978. ❏

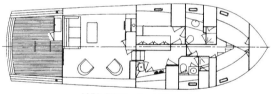

1973–77 Standard Floorplan

1978–83 Plan A

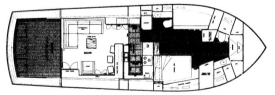

1978–83 Plan B

See Page 266 for Pricing Information

93

SPECIFICATIONS

Length	48'2"	Fuel	788 gals.
Beam	15'0"	Cockpit	NA
Draft	4'4"	Hull Type	Modified-V
Weight	44,000#	Deadrise Aft	2°
Clearance	13'1"	Designer	D. Martin
Water	110/210 gals.	Production	1978–86

Built on a stretched version of the flat-bottom hull first used for the Egg 46 Sedan, the Egg 48 SF represented the last of the classic old-style Egg Harbor convertible designs. Aimed at the luxury end of the sportfishing market, she was originally offered in either a two- or three-stateroom layout with a large portside master stateroom. The floorplans were revised in 1982 when the galley became a permanent part of the salon, and a new teak interior replaced the mahogany woodwork found in earlier models. Notably, the Egg Harbor 48 was one of the first production boats fitted out with the early 550-hp 8V92 diesels resulting in a fast 25-knot cruising speed. (Fast indeed for 1978, and very few other production boats her size could run with her.) Additional features include a very spacious engine room with flooring all around the motors, teak cockpit sole and covering boards, a spacious main salon with overhead grabrails, and large wraparound cabin windows. (Note that late model Egg 48s have a solid front windshield.) ❏

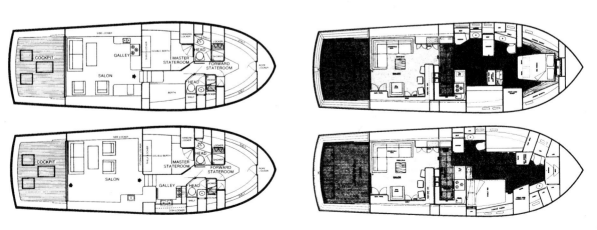

See Page 266 for Pricing Information

EGG HARBOR 54 GOLDEN EGG

1988–94

1995–Current

SPECIFICATIONS

Length w/Pulpit	57'8"	Water	220 gals.
Hull Length	54'6"	Fuel	1,000 gals.
Beam	17'6"	Hull Type	Modified-V
Draft	5'3"	Deadrise Aft	7°
Weight	72,600#	Production	1988–90
Clearance	15'10"		1995–Current

The 54 Golden Egg is a scaled-down version of the Egg Harbor 60 Convertible introduced back in 1986. She's a good-looking boat with her long foredeck and sensuous sheer and, after a few years out of production, Egg Harbor designers restyled the super-structure and flybridge and eliminated the exterior teak for her re-introduction in 1995. She's built on a beamy modified-V hull with cored hullsides, a well-flared bow and a relatively flat 7° of transom deadrise. Inside, the floorplan is arranged with the dinette and galley forward on the main deck and three staterooms on the lower level. The owner's stateroom is amidships in this layout (note the step-down dressing room under the salon floor) and includes a queen bed and a tub/shower in the head. With just over 100 sq. ft., the cockpit isn't large for a 54-footer (but certainly adaquate) and comes with a molded tackle center, in-deck fish box and transom door. The engine room is on the small side as well thanks to the extended lower-level accommodations. Standard 735-hp 8V92 Detroits cruise around 25 knots and deliver a top speed of 28 knots. ❏

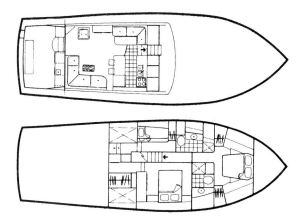

See Page 266 for Pricing Information

EGG HARBOR 58 GOLDEN EGG

1990–94

1995–Current

SPECIFICATIONS

Length w/Pulpit	62'8"	Water	220 gals.
Hull Length	58'6"	Fuel	1,200 gals.
Beam	17'6"	Hull Type	Modified-V
Draft	5'3"	Deadrise Aft	7°
Weight	82,000#	Production	1988–90
Clearance	20'10"		1995–Current

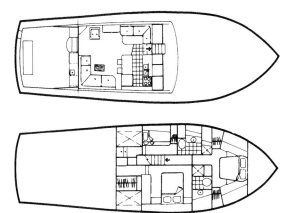

The 58 Golden Egg is a scaled-down version of the Egg Harbor 60 Convertible introduced back in 1986. She's a good-looking boat with her long foredeck and graceful sheer and, after a few years out of production, Egg Harbor designers restyled the superstructure and flybridge and eliminated the exterior teak for her re-introduction in 1995. She's built on a modified-V hull with cored hullsides, a well-flared bow and a relatively flat 7° of transom deadrise. Inside, the floorplan is arranged with the dinette and galley forward on the main deck and three staterooms on the lower level. The owner's stateroom is amidships in this layout (note the step-down dressing room under the salon floor) and includes a queen bed and a tub/shower in the head. Unlike her current 54-foot sistership, the cockpit of the 58 is huge with over 150 sq. ft. of deck space. A good performer, she'll cruise at a fast 27 knots with 1,100-hp 12V92 diesels and reach a top speed of around 30 knots. Optional 1,250-hp Cat 3412 diesels push those speeds up about two knots. ❑

See Page 266 for Pricing Information

EGG HARBOR 60 CONVERTIBLE

SPECIFICATIONS

Length	59'6"	Fuel	1,200/1,500 gals.
Beam	17'6"	Cockpit	111 sq. ft.
Draft	5'3"	Hull Type	Modified-V
Weight	72,000#	Deadrise Aft	8°
Clearance	18'5"	Designer	D. Martin
Water	300 gals.	Production	1986–89

Egg Harbor made a clean break with the past when they introduced the 60 Sportfisherman in 1986. Her high-tech construction (balsa-cored hullsides, triaxial/Kevlar composites, etc.) represented an engineering first for Egg Harbor. This luxury sportfisherman features an innovative floorplan on the lower level: by moving the engines aft and tightening up the engine room, Martin was able to fit a unique dressing area into the master stateroom and a separate utility room to port. The huge salon/galley layout is impressive in both size and decor. So too is the rest of the interior, including the expansive master stateroom with walkaround queen berth and a forward stateroom with yet another walkaround queen—accommodations on a scale more often found on motor yachts. Outside, the profile of the Egg Harbor 60 is classic Jersey-style sportfish with a graceful sheer and generously flared bow. On the downside, the engine room is small for a 60-footer. A good performer, 1,080-hp 12V92 diesels will cruise around 27 knots with a top speed of 30 knots. ❏

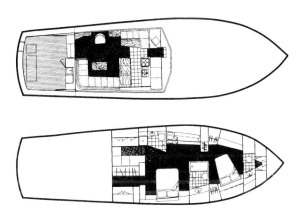

See Page 266 for Pricing Information

97

27 Center Console OB (1993)

29 Center Console OB (1994–Current)

SPECIFICATIONS

Length ....27'0"/29'0"	Clearance ....NA
Beam.................................8'4"	Water ....None
Hull Draft ....1'6"	Hull Type ....Deep-V
Weight w/motors.....4,900#	Deadrise Aft...................22°
Fuel ....207 gals.	Max HP 400
Cockpit............................NA	Production 1993–Current

Introduced in 1993 as a 27-footer (a redesigned transom the following year added 2 feet to the hull length), the Fountain 29 is a fast-action fishing machine for anglers who place a premium on performance. She's built on a very narrow, deep-V hull with a keel pad and a sharp 22° of transom deadrise. At only 4,900 lbs. the Fountain 29 is a light boat for her size, and a lot of high-tech construction techniques (including a fully cored hull) have gone into keeping the weight down. While there are many other 29-footers with larger cockpits, the deck layout of the Fountain is completely uncluttered and includes an in-deck fishbox, leaning post, an optional above-deck livewell, rod holders and a slightly raised casting platform forward. The console is well designed with a lockable electronics box and bench seating forward. This is a *very* fast boat with a reputation for capable handling in heavy sea conditions. Twin 200-hp outboards will cruise at 35 knots and reach a top speed of 50+ knots. Note that the props are very close together and handling in tight quarters requires skill. ❏

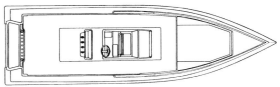

27 Center Console

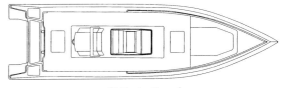

29 Center Console

See Page 266 for Pricing Information

Outboard

Stern Drive

SPECIFICATIONS

Length	27'0"/29'0"	Fuel	207 gals.
Beam	8'4"	Water	11 gals.
Hull Draft	1'6"	Cockpit	NA
Draft, I/O	2'4"	Hull Type	Deep-V
Weight with OBs	5,000#	Deadrise Aft	22°
Weight, I/O	5,800#	Production	1993–Current

The Fountain 29 SF Cruiser (she was introduced as a 27-footer in 1993, but a slightly redesigned transom the next year added 2 feet to her length) is a trailerable, downsized version of Fountain's popular 31 SF Cruiser. She's a lightweight, high-performance cuddy fisherman with fully-cored construction and an easy-riding deep-V hull. With only 8'4" of beam, she's a narrow boat and cockpit space is at a premium. Offered with stern drive or outboard power, the cabin of the I/O is smaller than the outboard version because the engine box requires that everything be moved forward at the expense of the cabin. Either way, the cockpit offers an unobstructed fishing platform with two fishboxes, flush rod holders, under-gunnel rod storage, washdown, and (on the outboard version) transom storage boxes. Inside, the cuddy has a V-berth with a dinette table filler, sink and icebox. A fast ride, the Fountain 29 will reach a top speed of over 50 knots with a pair of 200-hp outboards. The I/O version with a 350-hp Mercruiser will cruise at 30 knots and reach a top speed of 40+ knots. ❏

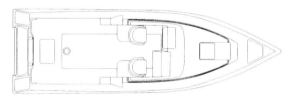

Outboard

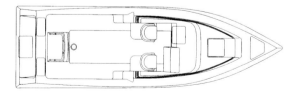

Stern Drive

See Page 266 for Pricing Information

FOUNTAIN 8.8 METER/31 SPORTFISH

8.8 Meter (1985–88)

Fountain 31 SF (1989–Current)

SPECIFICATIONS

Length ....29'/31'	Clearance ....7'8"
Beam................................8'4"	Hull Type ....Deep-V
Hull Draft ....1'6"	Deadrise Aft.................22.5°
Hull Weight...............4,300#	Max HP 600
Fuel ....207 gals.	Designer ....Fountain
Water ....None	Production 1985–Current

Today's high-performance Fountain 31 Sportfish evolved from the 8.8 Meter (29') Center Console Fountain introduced back in 1985. (She grew into the current 31-footer in 1989 when a molded engine step was added at the transom.) The deep-V hull is fully cored with Divinycell and, at just 4,300 lbs., the Fountain 31 is certainly one of the lightest (and strongest) boats in her class. The cockpit—where space is at a premium thanks to the very narrow beam—is free of obstructions, and there are molded steps at the forward corners to facilitate access to the elevated foredeck platform. Fishing features include a huge above-deck livewell at the transom, a wide foredeck walkaround, built-in tackle boxes and undergunnel rod storage. Two can sleep in the cuddy cabin where there's a manuel toilet, dry storage and overhead rod holders. A fast boat with the ability to run in some rough seas, the Fountain 31 Sportfish will attain a top speed of around 50 knots with a pair of 200-hp outboards. Note that the props are quite close together and close-in handling requires a skillful hand. ❏

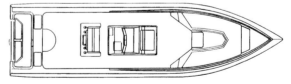

31 SF Layout

See Page 266 for Pricing Information

FOUNTAIN 31 & 32 SF CRUISERS

31 SF Cruiser (Outboard)

32 SF Cruiser (I/O)

SPECIFICATIONS

Length ....31'/32'	Fuel, 32 207
Beam................................8'4"	Hull Type ....Deep-V
Hull Draft ....1'8"	Deadrise Aft.................22.5°
Hull Weight, 31 ....4,800#	Max HP 600
Hull Weight, 32 ....7,650#	Designer ....R. Fountain
Fuel, 31 ....236 gals.	Production 1992–Current

The Fountain 31 and 32 SF Cruisers (the 31 is an outboard and the 32 is an I/O) are a pair of good-looking cuddy fishermen for anglers who place a premium on high speed and all-weather performance. The hull is a fully cored deep-V with a narrow beam and Fountain's unique notch-transom and pad keel bottom design—a hull designed specifically for high-speed operation in rough waters. The layout is simple and very workable, and four anglers can fish without being crowded. (Note that the cockpit in the I/O version is much smaller than in the outboard-powered 31.) The 31 has an above-deck livewell at the transom, and both boats have molded steps to the wide sidedecks. Below, the cabin includes a removable dinette table, V-berths, mini-galley, and an enclosed head and shower. Twin 200-hp outboards will cruise the Fountain 31 around 30 knots (45 knots top), while a pair of 385-hp 7.4-litre stern drives will cruise the Fountain 32 at 34 35 knots with a top speed in the mid-50s. Because of the narrow hull, the engines in both boats are quite close together requiring more skill for tight-quarters handling. ❏

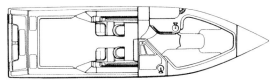

31 SF Cruiser (Outboard) Layout

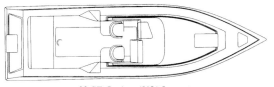

32 SF Cruiser (I/O) Layout

See Page 267 for Pricing Information

GAMEFISHERMAN 34

SPECIFICATIONS

Length ....34'0"	Headroom.......................6'3"
Beam..............................11'2"	Cockpit............................NA
Draft ....2'2"	Hull Type ....Modified-V
Weight ....14,500#	Deadrise Aft...................7.5°
Fuel ....270 gals.	Designer..........................NA
Water ....30 gals.	Production 1992–Current

A great-looking dayboat, the Gamefisherman 34 is a limited production sportfisherman with a graceful, unbroken sheer and a classic custom-boat profile. While most are built with fiberglass hulls, the Gamefisherman is also available with cold-molded construction for anglers who enjoy the feel of a wood boat. A strictly-business fishing machine, most of her length is dedicated to a large, uncluttered cockpit and a huge bridgedeck. Note that the helm console—with its solid mahogany fascia, Rybovich wheel, and custom single-lever controls—is located on the centerline, well aft on the bridgedeck with fore-and-aft settees on either side. This configuration provides the helmsman with quick access to the cockpit and lots of seating out of the sun. Additional features include an in-deck fish box, transom live well, and plenty of storage. The small cabin has an enclosed head and mini-galley along with upper/lower berths to starboard. Housed in a spacious engine room, twin 300-hp Cat 3116s will cruise the Gamefisherman at a fast 27-28 knots with a top speed of 30+ knots. ❏

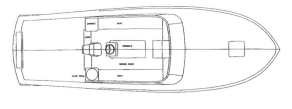

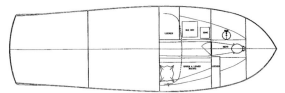

See Page 267 for Pricing Information

GAMEFISHERMAN 40

SPECIFICATIONS

Length ....40'0"	Fuel ....400 gals.
Beam..............................13'0"	Cockpit.................120 sq. ft.
Draft ....3'1"	Hull Type ....Modified-V
Weight ....22,000#	Deadrise Aft ....10°
Clearance ....13'4"	Designer ....B. Jackman
Water ....50 gals.	Production 1986–Current

Seemingly a modern version of the Merritt 37 or 43, the Gamefisher 40 is a better sea boat with superior rough-water capabilities. She's an open bulkhead design with a flush-deck layout from the transom to the forward cabin door. Hull construction is cold-molded mahogany planking with an epoxy glass outer covering. The flybridge and foredeck are laminated and epoxied, and the cockpit sole is teak. This hull is so well-balanced that trim tabs are not required (and not installed). The long narrow cockpit is excellent for all types of fishing and offers an in-deck livewell and fish box as well as a complete tackle center. The open deckhouse dinette and settee are slightly raised on engine boxes, and there are two big single berths below along with an enclosed head forward—the ideal day boat layout. Engine access is good, and there's space for a generator in the engine room. Volvo 380-hp diesels will cruise a tower-equipped Gamefisherman 40 at an economical 23 knots and reach a top speed of 27–28 knots. ❏

See Page 267 for Pricing Information

GARLINGTON 44

SPECIFICATIONS

Length ....44'6"	Fuel ....350–500 gals.
Beam.............................13'9"	Cockpit..................100 sq. ft.
Draft ....3'2"	Hull Type ....Modified-V
Weight ....22,000#	Deadrise Aft ....16°
Clearance ....NA	Designer ....D. McCarthy
Water ....75 gals.	Production 1990–Current

When custom boat builder Richard Garlington sat down to design a boat for himself, the Garlington 44 was the result, a good-looking express fisherman with classic South Florida custom styling. Rapidly growing in popularity (about ten have been built to date), the 44's state-of-the-art construction includes composite cores of Kevlar, carbon fiber, Airex foam and fiberglass. The hull is Awlgripped at the factory, and the sweeping sheer and flared bow make the Garlington 44 one of the most beautiful production fishermen available (and certainly one of the more expensive). The elegant teak interior includes a full dinette and galley along with a separate stall shower in the head. Outside, an L-shaped settee is opposite the helm on the raised bridgedeck, and there's over 100 sq. ft. of fishing space on the lower level. The engine room is tight. A superior sea boat with a great ride and incredible sex appeal (and resale), twin 460-hp Lugger diesels will cruise the Garlington 44 at 30 knots (at about 1 mpg!) and reach 34 knots top.   ❏

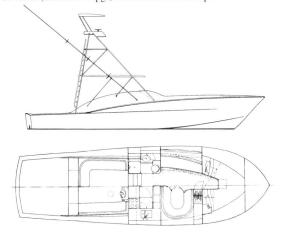

See Page 267 for Pricing Information

GRADY-WHITE MARLIN 280/300

SPECIFICATIONS

Length w/Pulpit ....32'7"	Water.......................35 gals.
Hull Length................28'0"	Fuel.......................306 gals.
Beam ....10'7"	Hull Type ....Deep-V
Hull Draft.....................1'7"	Deadrise Aft...................20°
Weight.......................7,000#	Designer.....Hunt & Assoc.
Cockpit ....60 sq. ft.	Production...1989–Current

The largest model in the Grady-White fleet, the Marlin 300 (called the Marlin 280 until 1995) is a popular walkaround cuddy design with a surprisingly generous cabin to go with her strictly fishing cockpit layout. Hull construction is solid glass, and the Marlin's deep-V hull was specifically designed by Hunt & Associates for outboard V-6 power—not V-8s. (Note that below-deck cavities are filled with polyurethane flotation, which makes the Marlin unsinkable—an uncommon feature in a boat this size.) With her walkaround deck layout and big cockpit, the interior dimensions are necessarily limited but hardly confining. Indeed, there are comfortable berths for four (including a big quarter berth that extends below the bridgedeck), plus a stand-up head compartment with shower, excellent headroom, and a compact galley. Standard features include an integral engine bracket platform with transom door and swim ladder, fish box, 30-gallon livewell, and tackle center. A good-running boat, twin 225 Yamaha O/Bs will cruise the Grady-White 280/300 at an easy 24 knots and deliver a top speed of 35–36 knots.   ❏

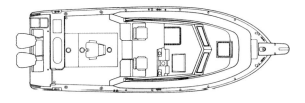

See Page 267 for Pricing Information

103

BEFORE BUYING YOUR NEW BOAT, MAKE SURE IT'S EQUIPPED WITH THIS ESSENTIAL PART.

Hatteras

This is the only way you can be sure your next boat is as good as a Hatteras. For more information, contact Hatteras Yachts, 2100 Kivett Drive, P.O. Box 2690, High Point, NC 27261. Or call (910) 889-6621.

HATTERAS 32 FLYBRIDGE & EXPRESS SF

Flybridge SF

Sport Fisherman

SPECIFICATIONS

Length	32'8"	Fuel	265 gals.
Beam	12'0"	Cockpit	95 sq. ft.
Draft	3'0"	Hull Type	Modified-V
Weight	18,000#	Deadrise Aft	18°
Clearance	10'6"	Designer	Jim Wynne
Water	50 gals.	Production	1982–86

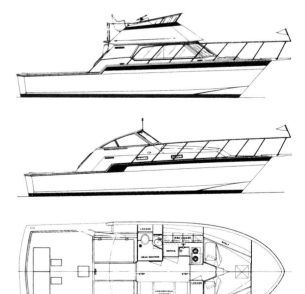

The Hatteras 32 Flybridge SF was built with the modern good looks and quality touches one expects in a Hatteras product. The hull is a Jim Wynne design with recessed propeller pockets and 18° of transom deadrise. The hullsides are balsa-cored from the waterline up, and considerable flare is used at the bow. Compared to other boats in her class, the Hatteras 32 is no lightweight. Inside, the cabin is arranged with a small galley, a roomy head compartment, and overnight berths for four. This is one of the more finely crafted and stylish interiors one is likely to find in a 32-foot fishing boat. The decor is bright and airy with only a modest amount of teak trim. Although not designed with any serious cruising in mind, the Hatteras 32 can provide comfortable accommodations for an extended weekend. Twin 300-hp Caterpillar diesels will cruise at 21–22 knots with a top speed of around 26 knots. Note that the Hatteras 32 Sport Fisherman (with no flybridge) has the same interior layout but smaller cabin windows. ❏

See Page 267 for Pricing Information

HATTERAS 36 CONV. (EARLY)

SPECIFICATIONS

Length ....36'1"	Fuel ....240/300 gals.
Beam ....12'9"	Cockpit ....NA
Draft ....3'0"	Hull Type ....Modified-V
Weight ....19,000#	Deadrise Aft ....NA
Clearance ....12'11"	Designer ....J. Hargrave
Water ....70 gals.	Production 1969–77

The original Hatteras 36 Convertible is still a popular boat on the used market in spite of her obviously dated profile and overbuilt hull construction. Equally adept as an offshore fishing boat or comfortable family cruiser, the Hatteras 36 features an all-teak interior with the galley and stateroom three steps down from the salon. A two-stateroom floorplan with deckhouse galley was made available in 1975. While the accommodations are not considered spacious by today's standards, the mahogany woodwork and quality hardware, fixtures, and systems installed aboard the Hatteras 36 make renovations practical and reasonably cost-effective. The cockpit is large enough for a mounted chair and tackle center, but the flybridge and (especially) the engine room are both small. Never known for her blinding speed, standard 330-hp gas engines will cruise the Hatteras 36 Convertible at 18 knots (26–27 top), while the optional Caterpillar 3160 diesels cruise around 15 knots with a top speed of 18 knots. Significantly, the fuel capacity was increased in 1971 to 300 gallons. ❏

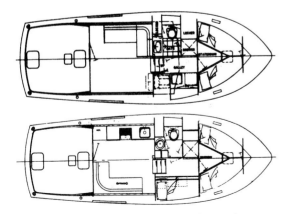

See Page 267 for Pricing Information

HATTERAS 36 CONVERTIBLE

SPECIFICATIONS

Length ....36'6"	Fuel ....355 gals.
Beam ....13'7"	Cockpit ....NA
Draft ....3'9"	Hull Type ......Mod. Deep-V
Weight ....26,500#	Deadrise Aft ....18°
Clearance ....12'6"	Designer ....Jim Wynne
Water ....115 gals.	Production 1983–1987

The most recent Hatteras 36 Convertible (the original 36 Convertible ran from 1969–77) was introduced in 1983. Designed as a replacement for the aging Hatteras 37, she's heavily built on a Jim Wynne-designed hull with a shallow keel and prop pockets. This is the same hull used in the Hatteras 36 Express—a capable offshore design but nowhere near the top of her class in performance. Well-engineered and impressively finished, the Hatteras 36 makes an excellent family cruiser with her deluxe interior accommodations and stylish decor. Buyers can chose between a single-stateroom floorplan with an open salon and the galley down or a two-stateroom layout with the galley up. A relatively small cockpit and moderate performance have made the 36 convertible more popular with cruisers and weekend fisherman than the hardcore tournament crowd. Standard 454-cid gas engines cruise at just 15 knots, and the optional 390-hp 6-71 diesels cruise around 22 knots (26 knots wide open). Note that the Hatteras 36 Sedan Cruiser (1986–87) is the same boat with an enlarged interior and an even smaller cockpit. ❏

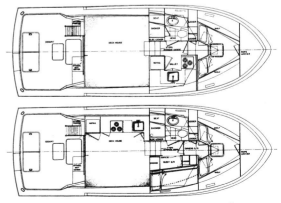

See Page 267 for Pricing Information

106

HATTERAS 36 SEDAN CRUISER

SPECIFICATIONS

Length	36'6"	Fuel	355 gals.
Beam	13'7"	Cockpit	NA
Draft	3'9"	Hull Type	Modified-V
Weight	25,500#	Deadrise Aft	18°
Clearance	12'6"	Designer	Jim Wynne
Water	115 gals.	Production	1986–87

Not remembered as a particularly successful model (production lasted only two years), the Hatteras 36 Sedan is basically the same boat as the Hatteras 36 Convertible (1983–87) with a larger interior and smaller cockpit dimensions. Hull construction is solid fiberglass, and the hull is designed with moderate beam, a shallow keel, and prop pockets. Two mid-galley interior layouts were available in the 36 Sedan: a dinette floorplan with a single stateroom and a two-stateroom arrangement without the dinette. Either way, the head compartment is very large and includes a separate stall shower. The interior is finished with traditional teak woodwork throughout, and it's notable that a lower helm option was never offered. While the salon is quite roomy for a 36-footer, the cockpit is too small for any serious fishing activities. Additional features include a big flybridge, good engine access, and fairly wide sidedecks. An unexciting performer with standard 350-hp Crusader gas engines, the Hatteras 36 Sedan will cruise at 15 knots and reach a top speed in the neighborhood of 24 knots. Diesels were optional and faster. ❏

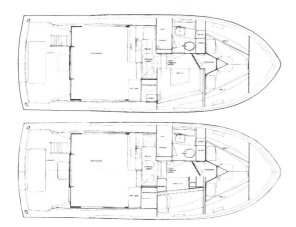

See Page 267 for Pricing Information

HATTERAS 36 SPORT FISHERMAN

SPECIFICATIONS

Length	36'6"	Fuel	355 gals.
Beam	13'7"	Cockpit	110 sq. ft.
Draft	3'9"	Hull Type	Deep-V
Weight	25,000#	Deadrise Aft	18°
Clearance	9'3"	Designer	Jim Wynne
Water	115 gals.	Production	1983–86

The Hatteras 36 Sport Fisherman is a heavy boat for her size, a fact that doubtless accounts for much of her somewhat sedate performance. Hull construction is solid fiberglass with balsa coring applied in the deck and superstructure. The 36 SF runs on a Jim Wynne-designed hull with recessed propeller pockets below for reduced shaft angles—the same hull used in the production of the Hatteras 36 Convertible (1983–87). Her open bi-level cockpit layout is well suited for serious deep-water fishing and comes standard with a transom door and a built-in fish box. Other features include wide walkaround sidedecks, an elevated helm position, a wraparound windshield, and easy cockpit access to the engines. Three steps down into the cabin reveals a practical layout with stylish fabrics, attractive high-pressure plastic laminates, and teak trim. Not only is this interior completely modern and appealing, it's easy to clean as well. The optional 390-hp GM 6-71s will cruise the Hatteras 36 Sport Fisherman around 24 knots and reach a top speed of 27–28 knots. ❏

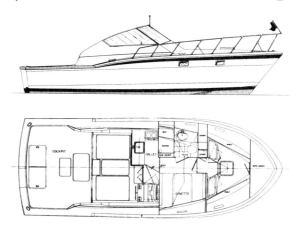

See Page 267 for Pricing Information

107

HATTERAS 37 CONVERTIBLE

SPECIFICATIONS

Length	37'0"	Fuel	330 gals.
Beam	14'0"	Cockpit	NA
Draft	3'3"	Hull Type	Modified-V
Weight	29,000#	Deadrise Aft	NA
Clearance	13'5"	Designer	J. Hargrave
Water	135 gals.	Production	1977–83

Introduced as a replacement for the very popular Hatteras 36 (1969–77), the 37 Convertible never achieved the widespread popularity of her predecessor among anglers in spite of her improved profile and roomier accommodations. She's built on a solid fiberglass hull with twin chines, a long keel, and moderate deadrise at the transom. With only 330 gallons of fuel, she's not a long-range boat. The interior is paneled in teak, and an offset double berth was offered in the forward stateroom beginning with the 1982 models. A stall shower is located in the double-entry head compartment. Large wraparound cabin windows give the salon a surprisingly spacious feeling for a 37-foot boat, and her tournament-style flybridge has seating for five. At 29,000 lbs., the Hatteras 37 Convertible is no lightweight. Those powered with the GM 6-71N diesels will cruise 18–19 knots with a top speed of about 21 knots. The optional 390-hp 6-71TIs will cruise the 37 Convertible around 21 knots and reach 23–24 knots wide open. ❏

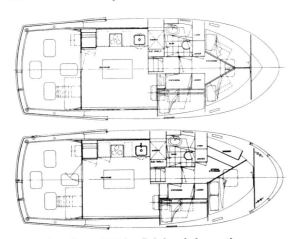

See Page 267 for Pricing Information

HATTERAS 38 CONVERTIBLE

SPECIFICATIONS

Length	38'10"	Fuel	490 gals.
Beam	13'5"	Cockpit	103 sq. ft.
Draft	4'8"	Hull Type	Modified-V
Weight	28,800#	Deadrise Aft	NA
Clearance	12'6"	Designer	Hatteras
Water	117 gals.	Production	1988–93

The 38 Convertible is one of a growing number of recent Hatteras models not designed by Jack Hargrave. A handsome boat with an aggressive profile, she's constructed on a modified-V hull with balsa coring in the hullsides and moderate transom deadrise. Aside from her stylish lines, the Hatteras 38 features a glassed-in front windshield and a luxurious two-stateroom teak interior layout with the galley in the salon. A centerline double berth is located in the master stateroom, and over/under single bunks are fitted in the guest cabin. While the cockpit dimensions are not notably deep, her beam is carried well aft providing ample space for the installation of a full-size fighting chair. A molded tackle center and a transom door were standard, and the engine room air intakes are located under the coaming. The aft-raking flybridge windshield is particularly stylish. An average performer, standard 485-hp Detroit 6-71 diesels will cruise the Hatteras 38 Convertible at a steady 23–24 knots and reach a top speed of around 27 knots. ❏

See Page 267 for Pricing Information

HATTERAS 39 CONVERTIBLE

SPECIFICATIONS

Length	38'10"	Fuel	490 gals.
Beam	13'5"	Cockpit	103 sq. ft.
Draft	4'8"	Hull Type	Modified-V
Weight	32,000#	Deadrise Aft	9°
Clearance	12'6"	Designer	Hatteras
Water	117 gals.	Production	1994–Current

Smallest boat in the current Hatteras fleet, the 39 Convertible is basically an updated version of the earlier Hatteras 38 Convertible with a restyled deckhouse and flybridge and a revised interior. She's built on a modified-V hull with cored hullsides, a solid fiberglass bottom, and a deep 4'8" keel. While the interior dimensions of the Hatteras 39 are about average for a boat this size, the mid-level galley configuration opens up the salon considerably (the 38 had a more confining galley-up layout). Outside, the cockpit comes with a transom door and gate, molded tackle center, and in-deck storage box. Additional features include light oak interior woodwork, a well-arranged helm console, side exhausts and expensive 5-bladed props. The real news about the Hatteras 39, however, is her low base price with standard 314-hp 4-71 diesels—a marketing choice that reduces cost at the expense of performance: 19 knots cruise/about 22–23 knots top. Optional (and much more practical) 465-hp 6-71s will cruise the Hatteras 39 at a respectable 25 knots and reach a top speed of around 28 knots. ❏

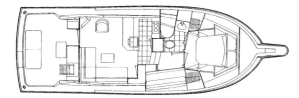

See Page 267 for Pricing Information

109

HATTERAS 39 SPORT EXPRESS

SPECIFICATIONS

Length	39'0"	Clearance	NA
Beam	13'5"	Cockpit	103 sq. ft.
Draft	4'8"	Hull Type	Modified-V
Weight	29,500#	Deadrise Aft	9°
Fuel	458 gals.	Designer	Hatteras
Water	117 gals.	Production	1995–Current

Tiara started the trend toward big, dual-purpose (fish or cruise) express boats with the introduction in 1991 of their 4300 Open. Viking and Bertram have since come out with 43-footers, and Hatteras introduced the 39 Sport Express in 1995. She is unquestionably a beautiful boat — perhaps the best in her class when it comes to styling. (The cruising version, with curved bridgedeck seating and a sport arch, is pictured above.) She's built on the same deep-draft hull used for the Hatteras 39 Convertible with moderate beam, a flared bow and cored hullsides. The Sport Express is a big boat on the outside with a party-size bridgedeck and a cockpit large enough to handle a full-size chair. (Note that the standard version has L-shaped settees on the bridgedeck—rather than the circular lounge—and no arch.) Cockpit features include an in-deck fishbox, molded tackle center, transom door and direct access to the engine room. Inside, the single-stateroom floorplan will sleep six and comes complete with a stall shower in the head. Optional 465-hp 6-71s provide a respectable 24 knots at cruise and 28–29 knots wide open. ❏

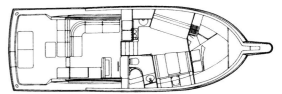

Curved Bridge Seating with Aft-Facing Cockpit Lounge

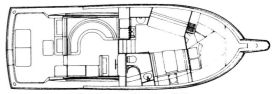

Offset Forward Berth and Dinette

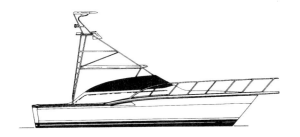

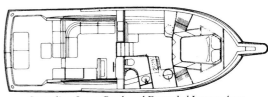

Centerline Queen Berth and Expanded Lounge Area

See Page 267 for Pricing Information

SPECIFICATIONS

Length	41'9"	Fuel	400/500 gals.
Beam	14'3"	Cockpit	120 sq. ft.
Draft	4'4"	Hull Type	Modified-V
Weight	35,400#	Deadrise Aft	NA
Clearance	13'9"	Designer	J. Hargrave
Water	150 gals.	Production	1986–91

SPECIFICATIONS

Length	42'8"	Fuel	400 gals.
Beam	13'10"	Cockpit	110 sq. ft.
Draft	3'5"	Hull Type	Modified-V
Weight	31,000#	Deadrise Aft	NA
Clearance	13'3"	Designer	J. Hargrave
Water	150 gals.	Production	1971–78

When the Hatteras 41 Convertible was introduced in 1986, she was widely hailed as the beginning of a new series of modern Hatteras designs. She was the first to have a fully cored hull (discontinued early in the production run), and vacuum-bagging was used extensively in the construction process. The "new look" window treatment, solid front windshield, stepped sheer, and rakish flybridge were the forerunners of today's Hatteras convertible styling. In the original two-stateroom layout, the in-line galley consumes a lot of the salon's living space. (A single-stateroom, galley-down floorplan was also offered.) In 1989, a revised two-stateroom floorplan greatly improved the original layout by moving the galley to starboard. A light ash interior became available in 1987. The transom door and tackle center were standard, and the engine air intakes are located under the gunwales. Fuel tankage was increased to 500 gallons in 1987. A good-running boat, standard 465-hp 6-71s diesels cruise at 23–24 knots, and the optional 535-hp 6V92s cruise at 26 knots with 29 knots top. ❏

The long-awaited replacement boat for the aging 41 Convertible, the Hatteras 42 Convertible represented a big step forward in convertible design in 1971 with her full-width flybridge (the first in any Hatteras model) and her bold, more aggressive exterior profile. Construction was on the heavy side, and considerable flare was added at the bow. Her large 110 sq. ft. cockpit easily accommodates a mounted chair and complete tackle center. The Hatteras 42 was offered with only one floorplan: a two-stateroom arrangement with the galley down to starboard. A stall shower is fitted in the double-entry head, and teak paneling and cabinetry are used throughout. The engine room is tight, but routine access is satisfactory. In 1977, the flybridge was restyled, and the galley was rearranged with the refrigerator moved forward (thus opening the galley up to the salon)—big improvements when compared against the earlier models. A comfortable offshore boat, the 42 Convertible will cruise around 19–20 knots with either the GM 6-71TIs or the Cummins VT-903 diesels. Top speed is 22–23 knots. ❏

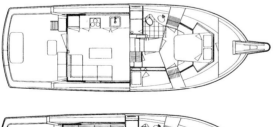

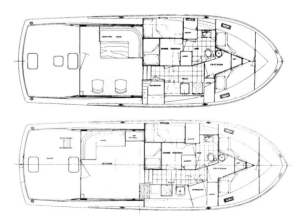

See Page 267 for Pricing Information

See Page 267 for Pricing Information

HATTERAS 43 CONVERTIBLE (EARLY)

SPECIFICATIONS

Length	43'8"	Fuel	470 gals.
Beam	14'6"	Cockpit	110 sq. ft.
Draft	4'2"	Hull Type	Modified-V
Weight	41,000#	Deadrise Aft	11°
Clearance	14'3"	Designer	J. Hargrave
Water	165 gals.	Production	1979–84

The Hatteras 43 Convertible was the replacement boat for the earlier Hatteras 42 Convertible. A good-looking boat, her new double-chined hull resulted in an enlarged engine room capable of handling the (then) recently introduced GM 6V92 diesels. In addition, her extra beam allowed for the installation of side-by-side berths in the master stateroom. (A double berth became available in 1982.) Other notable features of the Hatteras 43 include a spacious teak-paneled salon, an oversize flybridge with seating for eight, undercoaming air intakes in the cockpit, and a transom door with gate. The cockpit, while adequate for serious fishing activities, seems nonetheless small in an otherwise spacious boat. Note that a short-lived European arrangement (crew quarters forward with foredeck access) was offered in 1981–82 models. Never considered a particularly fast boat for her size, the early models with 450-hp 6V92s cruise around 20 knots. In 1981, the high-performance 6V92s (500-hp) were offered for a cruising speed of 22–23 knots and 26 knots at full throttle. ❏

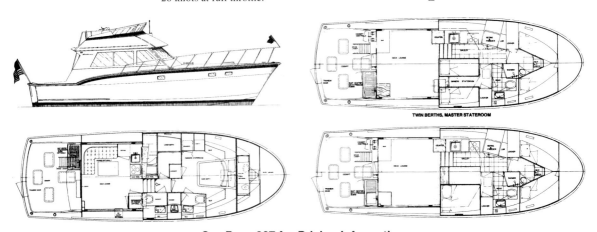

TWIN BERTHS, MASTER STATEROOM

See Page 267 for Pricing Information

HATTERAS 43 CONVERTIBLE

SPECIFICATIONS

Length ....43'2"	Fuel ....500 gals.
Beam..............................14'3"	Cockpit.................120 sq. ft.
Draft ....4'8"	Hull Type ....Modified-V
Weight ....40,000#	Deadrise Aft ....10°
Clearance ....12'4"	Designer ....Hatteras
Water ....154 gals.	Production 1991–Current

Sharing the same rakish profile and step-down sheer of her larger sisterships, the Hatteras 43 Convertible is a good-looking sportfisherman with the solid construction and improved performance typical of most recent Hatteras designs. She's built on a conventional modified-V hull with balsa coring in the hullsides, moderate beam, and a shallow keel below. A galley-down, two-stateroom layout is standard, and the optional single-stateroom floorplan trades out the guest cabin for a large U-shaped dinette. While the salon dimensions in both layouts are somewhat compact for a 43-footer, the light ash woodwork opens up the interior significantly. A washer/dryer is located in the companionway, and there's a stylish curved shower door in the head. Outside, the 43's large cockpit is tournament-grade all the way and includes direct access to the engine room—a feature seldom found in sportfisherman under 50 feet. A good running boat, standard 535-hp 6V92s will cruise the Hatteras 43 at 25 knots with a top speed of about 28 knots.   ❏

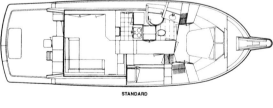

STANDARD

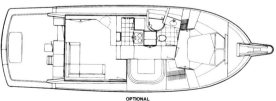

OPTIONAL

See Page 268 for Pricing Information

HATTERAS 45 CONVERTIBLE (EARLY)

SPECIFICATIONS

Length ....45'2"	Fuel ....650 gals.
Beam..............................14'7"	Cockpit...........................NA
Draft ....3'6"	Hull Type ....Modified-V
Weight ....37,000#	Deadrise Aft ....NA
Clearance ....13'10"	Designer ....J. Hargrave
Water ....180 gals.	Production 1968–74

There always seems to be a market for the old Hatteras 45 Convertible. Her profile is that of a classic sportfisherman with a high foredeck and sweeping sheerline ending with a low-freeboard cockpit. Solid hull construction and good seakeeping qualities have made the 45 Convertible a favorite among tournament-minded anglers. Her conventional two-stateroom, galley-down interior includes a spacious main salon with a complete lower helm station and built-in lounge seating to port. A less popular galley-up model was also available with an open day berth replacing the galley in the companionway. A versatile boat, the spacious cockpit in the Hatteras 45 gets high marks for good all-around fishability. The old-style flybridge, however, is small. (Note that the original centerline pedestal bridge layout was revised in 1970 to a more versatile tournament-style design.) The popular engine choices were 8V71Ns (15–16 knots cruise) and 8V71TIs (around 20 knots at cruise and 23 knots at full throttle). A wet ride in a chop, the resale values of early Hatteras 45 Convertibles are surprisingly good.   ❏

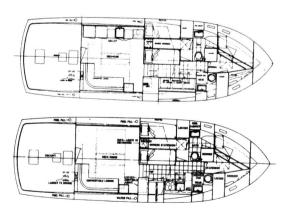

See Page 268 for Pricing Information

113

HATTERAS 45 CONVERTIBLE

1984–88

1989–91

SPECIFICATIONS

Length.........................45'8"	Fuel........................590 gals.
Beam ....14'6"	Cockpit................135 sq. ft.
Draft..............................4'6"	Hull Type........Modified-V
Weight....................45,000#	Deadrise Aft..................NA
Clearance....................14'3"	Designer ....J. Hargrave
Water....................165 gals.	Production.............1984–91

The Hatteras 45 Convertible began life in 1984 as simply an enlarged version of the previous Hatteras 43 Convertible (1979–84). The 45 kept the popular two-stateroom floorplan of the 43 intact (with its midships master stateroom and spacious salon) and used the additional hull length to create a bigger and much-improved fishing cockpit—something the 43 sorely lacked. A durable and popular boat, Hatteras dramatically updated her appearance in 1989 with a new deckhouse profile featuring the new-age Hatteras window treatment and a restyled flybridge. Note that a short-lived "Palm Beach" version of the 45 Convertible (1987 only) featured an optional two-stateroom, two-head layout with a glassed-in front windshield. In 1986 a contemporary light ash interior became available, and in 1988 the interior layout was revised to include an S-shaped forward companionway, a larger master stateroom, and two heads. Never known as a particularly fast boat, standard 535-hp 6V92s will cruise the Hatteras 45 Convertible at 23–24 knots and reach 27 knots wide open. ❑

See Page 268 for Pricing Information

HATTERAS 46 CONVERTIBLE (EARLY)

SPECIFICATIONS

Length ....46'2"	Fuel................650/710 gals.
Beam..............................14'9"	Cockpit..................125 sq. ft.
Draft ....4'2"	Hull Type ....Modified-V
Weight ....41,000#	Deadrise Aft ....NA
Clearance ....13'8"	Designer............J. Hargrave
Water ....180 gals.	Production 1974–85

One of the most popular big-boat convertibles ever produced, the Hatteras 46 was heavily built on the original single-chine Hatteras 45 hull with a deep, full-length keel and moderate transom deadrise. Aside from being an excellent fisherman with good handling characteristics, her spacious cabin accommodations and upscale teak interior have made her a popular boat with cruisers. Revised two- and three-stateroom floorplans were introduced in 1982 (each with two heads), and a new sliding door replaced the original hinged salon door in the same year. The original 46 Convertibles was powered with 8V71TIs and will cruise at 20 knots and deliver a top speed of 23–24 knots. In 1982, a high-performance version of the Hatteras 46 (with 650-hp 8V92TIs) featured a beefed-up hull with balsa coring in the hullsides and extra transverse frames in the bottom. (The keel was also shortened to improve handling and reduce wetted surface.) Speeds with the high-performance 8V92s are around 26 knots cruise and 29 knots top—not bad for any Hatteras of her era. ❏

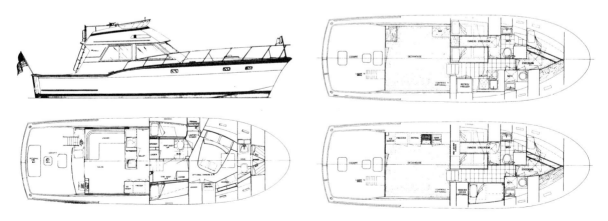

See Page 268 for Pricing Information

115

HATTERAS 46 CONVERTIBLE

SPECIFICATIONS

Length	46'10"	Fuel	775 gals.
Beam	15'7"	Cockpit	121 sq. ft.
Draft	4'11"	Hull Type	Modified-V
Weight	52,000#	Deadrise Aft	7°
Clearance	13'9"	Designer	Hatteras
Water	188 gals.	Production	1992–Current

Sharing the rakish profile and step-down sheer of all modern Hatteras sportfishermen, the 46 Convertible replaced the long-running 45 Convertible in the Hatteras fleet in 1992. She's heavily built on a beamy, low-deadrise hull with cored hullsides and a shallow keel—an in-house design with terrific lines and a lot of sex appeal. Inside, the two-stateroom ash interior is arranged with a mid-level dinette opposite the galley and a single head compartment. An alternate floorplan moves the dinette up into the salon and adds a second head with a stall shower. The cockpit—among the largest of any boat this size—comes with molded-in bait and tackle centers, an in-deck fish box, transom door, and direct access to a very well-engineered engine room with (wow!) standing headroom. (Note that the exhausts are underwater.) A good-running boat, a pair of 735-hp 8V-92s will cruise the Hatteras 46 at a steady 25 knots and reach 28–29 knots wide open. Hatteras also offers 780-hp MANs for the 46 Convertible. ❑

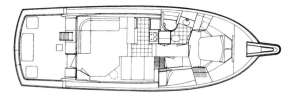

See Page 268 for Pricing Information

HATTERAS 48 CONVERTIBLE

SPECIFICATIONS

Length	48'8"	Fuel	812 gals.
Beam	16'0"	Cockpit	135 sq. ft.
Draft	5'5"	Hull Type	Modified-V
Weight	51,500#	Deadrise Aft	8°
Clearance	14'0"	Designer	J. Hargrave
Water	184 gals.	Production	1987–91

Modern construction, contemporary styling and good seakeeping characteristics personify the Hatteras 48 Convertible—a striking design aimed at the upscale end of the sportfish market. Somehow, her weight wasn't kept down very much in spite of the Divinycell coring used in the hullsides and bulkheads. Her big tournament-size cockpit came with a wide transom door and molded tackle center along with an engine room access door and under-coaming air intakes. Below, the spacious salon is laid out with a complete entertainment center, stylish fabrics, and teak paneling and cabinetry (light ash woodwork was also available) but with no dinette. Both staterooms have roomy head compartments with stall showers, and a convenient raised serving counter divides the salon from the mid-level galley area. Additional features include a solid front windshield, side exhausts, wide sidedecks, and a huge flybridge with plenty of guest seating. Standard 720-hp 8V92 diesels will cruise the Hatteras 48 at 24–25 knots and turn a top speed of 28 knots. (Note that the current Hatteras 50 Convertible rides on the 48's stretched hull.) ❑

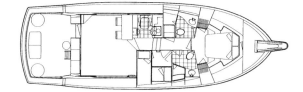

See Page 268 for Pricing Information

HATTERAS 50 CONV. (1980–83)

SPECIFICATIONS

Length	50'0"	Fuel	1,065 gals.
Beam	16'4"	Cockpit	NA
Draft	4'6"	Hull Type	Modified-V
Weight	56,500#	Deadrise Aft	NA
Clearance	15'10"	Designer	J. Hargrave
Fresh Water	185 gals.	Production	1980–83

Introduced in 1980, this second Hatteras 50 Convertible was designed to handle the then-new GM 8V92 diesels. Constructed on a beamy modified-V hull with balsa coring from the waterline up and a long keel, the Hatteras 50 is still regarded as a good-looking convertible. Her wide beam provides interior accommodations that are generous for a boat this size (especially considering the extra-wide sidedecks). Two floorplans were offered: a two-stateroom version with the galley down and a huge salon, and a more popular three-stateroom layout with a deckhouse galley. The cockpit (decidedly small for a 50-footer) came with a transom door, undercoaming air intakes, and direct engine room access. The flybridge is huge with bench seating for seven. The original 550-hp 8V92 diesels will cruise at 20 knots (22–23 top), while the high-performance 650-hp versions (introduced in 1982) cruise at 22 knots with a top speed of 25 knots. Note that the more recent Hatteras 52 Convertible (1984–91) is the same boat with a bigger cockpit. ❑

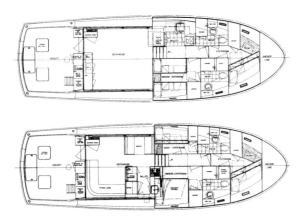

See Page 268 for Pricing Information

HATTERAS 50 CONV. (CURRENT)

SPECIFICATIONS

Length	50'10"	Fuel	890 gals.
Beam	16'1"	Cockpit	135 sq. ft.
Draft	5'9"	Hull Type	Modified-V
Weight	60,000#	Deadrise Aft	8°
Clearance	13'8"	Designer	J. Hargrave
Water	184 gals.	Production	1991–Current

The newest Hatteras 50—third in the company's history—replaced the popular 52 Convertible in the Hatteras lineup in 1991. The hull is a stretched version of the earlier 48 Convertible with a wide beam and modest transom deadrise. A handsome boat with her long foredeck, stepped sheer, and rakish flybridge, the Hatteras 50's standard three-stateroom, galley-up floorplan is arranged with the master stateroom amidships where the ride is most comfortable. By employing lighter woods and a cut-down galley, the salon has a surprisingly wide-open feeling. (A galley-down, two-stateroom floorplan is optional.) Additional features include cockpit access to the engine room (with near-standing headroom), a huge flybridge, underwater exhausts, and five-bladed props. A heavy boat for her size, performance is good but at a price. To achieve a competitive 26-knot cruising speed, the Hatteras 50 Convertible requires the optional 780-hp MANs or the 870-hp Detroit 12V71s. The standard 720-hp 8V92 diesels provide a modest 23–24 knots at cruise and 26 knots wide open. ❑

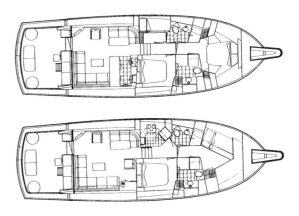

See Page 268 for Pricing Information

118

FREE Gift *for* Fishermen

When you join the International Game Fish Association

With your $25 membership in the International Game Fish Association you will receive the gift of your choice FREE!

Choice of:

- Guy Harvey's fine art Blue Marlin poster
- IGFA Loran book — includes 1,200 loran numbers
- IGFA crest pocket tee shirt
- IGFA sturdy fishing hat

In addition, you'll get as part of your membership:

- World Record Game Fishes book — 352 pages
- International Angler newsletter
- IGFA embroidered patch & membership decals
- Discounts on charters, fishing lodges, hotels, etc.
- Annual fishing contest
- World Record updates
- Tournament calendar
- Much, much more!

YOUR CHOICE

To Join, Complete Form Below and Mail TODAY!

Yes, I'll take your membership offer

Count me in! I want to join IGFA and support its many worldwide programs to benefit recreational fishermen. I understand my IGFA membership will start immediately upon receipt of this application and continue for 12 months.

FREE GIFT — your choice (please circle one)   1. Blue Marlin poster   2. IGFA Loran Book
3. IGFA crest pocket tee shirt (indicate size _____) 4. IGFA fishing hat.

IGFA membership starts at $25 ($30 foreign). Enclosed is my check for $_____ for _____ years membership. Or, please charge to my:

[ ] VISA   [ ] MASTERCARD   [ ] AMERICAN EXPRESS

Account No. _____Expiration Date_____

Signature_____

Name_____

Street Address_____

City/State_____Zip_____Country_____

Current IGFA members are eligible for free offer when extending membership for 1 or more years. An additional gift will be given for each extra year of membership requested. *Offer ends December 31.*
Make checks payable to: International Game Fish Association.
Mail to: IGFA, 1301 E. Atlantic Blvd., Pompano Beach, FL 33060
Fax (305) 941-5868 Phone (305) 941-3474

A copy of the Official Registration and financial information may be obtained from the Division of Consumer Services by calling 1-800-435-7352 within the state of Florida. Registration does not imply endorsement, approval or recommendation by the State of Florida.

MEMBERSHIP BEGINS AT $25 PER YEAR

Please check the category for which you are applying

[ ] $25 Regular Member (U.S.A.)
[ ] $30 Regular Member (Foreign)
[ ] $35 Contributing Member (U.S.A.)
[ ] $40 Contributing Member (Foreign)
[ ] $50 Fellow

1984–87

1987–91

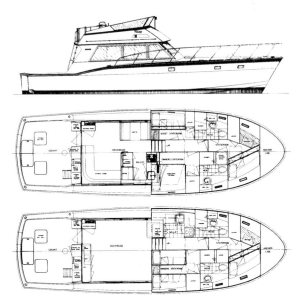

Original 52 Conv. (1984–87)

SPECIFICATIONS

Length	52'0"	Fuel	1,068 gals.
Beam	16'4"	Cockpit	153 sq. ft.
Draft	5'0"	Hull Type	Modified-V
Weight	55,400#	Deadrise Aft	NA
Clearance	15'10"	Designer	J. Hargrave
Water	188 gals.	Production	1984–91

The Hatteras 52 Convertible is virtually identical to the earlier Hatteras 50 Convertible with the extra length going into a larger cockpit—a big improvement. A popular design (just over 200 were built), she's constructed on a modified-V bottom with a long keel below and balsa coring in the hullsides. In mid-1987, the Hatteras 52 was dramatically restyled on the outside with a fresh deckhouse window treatment, solid front windshield, and a redesigned flybridge. Two floorplans were available—a galley-down layout with two staterooms, and a more popular deckhouse galley arrangement with three staterooms. Both floorplans include two heads with stall showers. A teak interior was standard, and light ash woodwork became optional in 1987. The large cockpit features a molded-in tackle center, transom door with gate, and an access door to the spacious engine room. A good sea boat, the Hatteras 52 will cruise around 23 knots with 720-hp 8V92s and reach a top speed of 26 knots. Notably, this was the first Hatteras convertible to use side-dumping exhausts. ❏

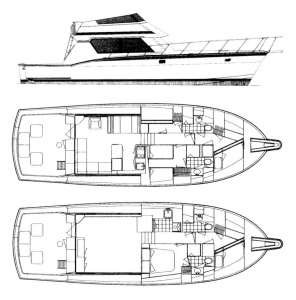

Hatteras 52 Conv. (1988–91)

See Page 268 for Pricing Information

HATTERAS 53 CONVERTIBLE

SPECIFICATIONS

Length ....53'7"	Fuel..............950/1,100 gals.
Beam.............................16'0"	Cockpit..................147 sq. ft.
Draft ....4'0"	Hull Type ....Modified-V
Weight.....................61,000#	Deadrise Aft...................NA
Clearance.....................15'2"	Designer...........J. Hargrave
Water ....250 gals.	Production 1969–80

Until she was retired from the fleet in 1980, the Hatteras 53 Convertible was the industry standard for over-50-foot sport-fishing yachts. Her long foredeck and sweeping sheer combine to present the aggressive appearance of a thoroughbred sportfisherman, and her low-freeboard fishing cockpit has never been surpassed for sheer fishability. Indeed, this boat is so well proportioned that she must be seen up close to fully appreciate her size. There have been several three-stateroom, galley-up layouts used in the 53 including a popular U-shaped galley to port with separate under-counter refrigeration. An alternate two-stateroom floorplan has the galley located forward of the dinette in the companionway. Significant updates include increased fuel and prop pockets in 1976 and a restyled flybridge in 1977. A comfortable boat offshore (but a wet ride in a chop), GM 12V71Ns (525-hp) will cruise the Hatteras 53 efficiently at 17 knots with a top speed of about 20 knots. The 8V92TIs (550-hp) will cruise around 19 knots and 12V71TIs (650-hp) cruise at 20 knots. Resale values are still very strong. ❏

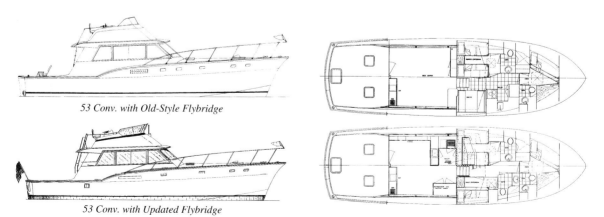

53 Conv. with Old-Style Flybridge

53 Conv. with Updated Flybridge

See Page 268 for Pricing Information

HATTERAS 54 CONVERTIBLE

SPECIFICATIONS

Length	54'11"	Fuel	1,320 gals.
Beam	17'4"	Cockpit	157 sq. ft.
Draft	5'10"	Hull Type	Modified-V
Weight	70,000#	Deadrise Aft	9°
Clearance	14'8"	Designer	Hatteras
Water	200 gals.	Production	1991–Current

The Hatteras 54—the replacement for the popular Hatteras 55 Convertible—is a completely impressive sportfisherman with the upscale interior accommodations of a fair-size motor yacht. A handsome boat with the aggressive profile and the rakish sheer found in all of the newer Hatteras convertibles, she's built on a new in-house hull design with a wide beam, shallow deadrise aft, and a *very* deep keel. Perhaps the most impressive feature of the Hatteras 54 is her innovative three-stateroom interior with its incredibly wide-open deckhouse and the largest master stateroom seen in a convertible this size. The diagonal galley configuration really opens up the salon and adds considerable living and entertaining space. Additional features include an immense flybridge, a helm console designed to flush-mount all necessary electronics, and a spacious walk-in engine room with near-standing headroom. No racehorse, standard 870-hp 12V71s cruise the Hatteras 54 at 22 knots with a top speed of about 24–25 knots. Optional 1,040-hp 12V92s (or 1,020-hp 12-cylinder MANs) will cruise around 25 knots with a top speed of 28–29 knots. ❏

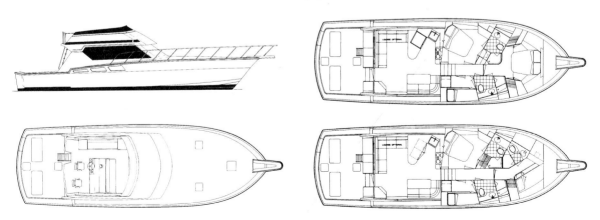

See Page 268 for Pricing Information

HATTERAS 55 CONVERTIBLE

1980–86

1987–89

SPECIFICATIONS

Length	55'8"	Fuel	1,285 gals.
Beam	17'6"	Cockpit	158 sq. ft.
Draft	4'10"	Hull Type	Modified-V
Weight	70,000#	Deadrise Aft	NA
Clearance	16'8"	Designer	J. Hargrave
Water	380 gals.	Production	1980–89

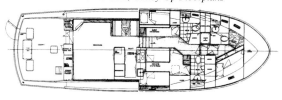

Three-Stateroom, Galley-Up Floorplans

Introduced in 1980 as the replacement for the Hatteras 53 Convertible, the 55 Convertible enjoyed a long and very successful production run. Her appearance was updated in 1987 when the front windshield was glassed over, and the cabin windows and flybridge were restyled in keeping with the current new look of the Hatteras convertibles. Two accommodation plans were offered with the three-stateroom, galley/dinette-up layout being the more popular. The huge cockpit came equipped with a molded tackle center, transom door, and direct access to the 55's spacious stand-up engine room. (Note that the air intakes for the engine room are located under the cockpit coaming.) The flybridge is huge with a superb helm layout and plenty of guest seating. No lightweight in spite of her cored hullsides, the Hatteras 55 is recognized as a stable fishing platform and a popular boat with anglers. Standard 650-hp 12V71TIs cruise at 19–20 knots (23 knots top), and 870-hp high-performance versions (available from 1982) cruise at 23+ knots (about 26 knots top). ❏

Two-Stateroom, Galley-Down Floorplans

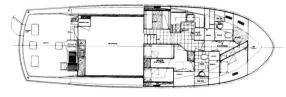

See Page 268 for Pricing Information

HATTERAS 58 CONVERTIBLE

SPECIFICATIONS

Length	58'10"	Fuel	1,660 gals.
Beam	17'9"	Cockpit	175 sq. ft.
Draft	5'11"	Hull Type	Modified-V
Weight	92,000#	Deadrise Aft	10°
Clearance	22'4"	Designer	Hatteras
Water	250 gals.	Production	1990–94

The Hatteras 58 Convertible is an in-house design built on a heavy modified-V hull with cored hullsides and a deep six-foot-deep keel. A good-looking boat, her three-stateroom, galley-up floorplan is arranged with the VIP guest suite equal in size and amenities to the master stateroom. The extravagant, high-style salon of the Hatteras 58 is impressive—closer to what one expects in a much bigger boat. Outside, the immense cockpit is set up for tournament-level fishing and includes an oversize transom door, live baitwell, molded tackle centers, engine room access, and a waist-level fish box built into the transom. The two-station flybridge can be fully enclosed and features a centerline helm. The Hatteras 58 is a heavy boat, and the added drag of her deep keel results in disappointing performance: standard 1,040-hp 12V92s cruise at just 22 knots (26 knots top). More popular (also costlier, heavier, and thirstier) 1,350-hp 16V-92s will cruise at 28–29 knots (140 gph!) with a top speed of 32 knots. ❑

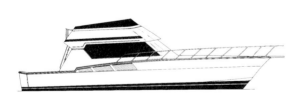

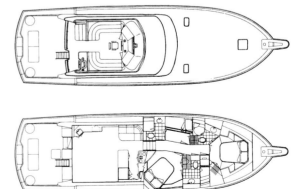

See Page 268 for Pricing Information

124

HATTERAS 60 CONVERTIBLE

SPECIFICATIONS

Length	60'11"	Fuel	1,555 gals.
Beam	18'0"	Cockpit	175 sq. ft.
Draft	4'11"	Hull Type	Modified-V
Weight	82,000#	Deadrise Aft	NA
Clearance	17'1"	Designer	J. Hargrave
Water	490 gals.	Production	1977–86

The 60 Convertible was a successful boat for Hatteras, and over 125 were built before she was replaced with the 65 Convertible in 1987. Offered with a fully enclosed and air conditioned flybridge, her three-stateroom, three-head floorplan is arranged with the galley and dinette on the deckhouse level and a midships master stateroom. A separate utility room forward of the engine compartment houses the air conditioning compressors, washer/dryer, etc., with room to spare. Additional features include a deep keel for prop protection, fore and aft flybridge helm stations, and a queen berth in the master stateroom. Her massive cockpit (175 sq. ft.) provides direct access to the well-arranged stand-up engine room. In 1968, the High-Performance model became available with more powerful motors, balsa coring in the hullsides, and beefed-up internal strengthening. A decent performer for her era, the standard 650-hp 12V71s will cruise the Hatteras 60 Convertible at 17–18 knots (about 20 knots top), and the high-performance 825-hp 12V71s cruise around 20 knots (23 knots top). ❏

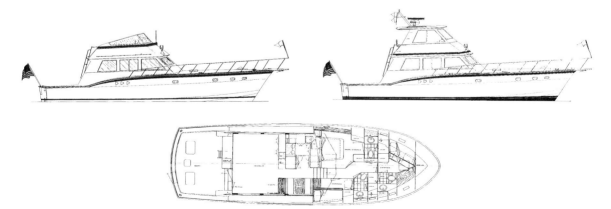

See Page 268 for Pricing Information

HATTERAS 65 CONVERTIBLE

SPECIFICATIONS

Length ....65'5"	Fuel ....1,674 gals.
Beam...........................18'0"	Cockpit.................183 sq. ft.
Draft ....5'11"	Hull Type ....Modified-V
Weight ....102,000#	Deadrise Aft ....NA
Clearance ....16'4"	Designer...........J. Hargrave
Water ....460 gals.	Production 1987–Current

A great-selling boat (over 100 have been sold to date), the Hatteras 65 Convertible is the most popular 60-foot-plus sportfisherman ever built. She's a step up from the earlier Hatteras 60 Convertible—not only are her lines more aggressive, but the performance is improved as well. The 65's hull is derived from an extension of the mold used in the production of the Hatteras 60 with a finer entry and the addition of lightweight Baltec coring in the hullsides. Her spacious three-stateroom layout is highlighted by an extravagant salon that many consider to be the ultimate in a production sportfisherman. The 183-sq. ft. cockpit is the largest found in a production boat this size. Topside, a second helm station is aft of the bridge enclosure for cockpit visibility. Standard 1,035-hp Detroit 12V92s will cruise the Hatteras 65 Convertible around 23 knots. Optional 1,235-hp MTUs (or 1,350-hp 16V92s) will cruise at 26–28 knots and reach a top speed of 30+ knots. Note the distinctive engine room air intakes on the hullsides. ❏

HATTERAS 82 CONVERTIBLE

SPECIFICATIONS

Length ....82'8"	Water ....840 gals.
Beam...........................21'5"	Fuel ....4,075 gals.
Draft ....6'6"	Hull Type ....Modified-V
Weight ....196,000#	Deadrise Aft ....NA
Clearance ....26'0"	Designer ....Hatteras
Cockpit...........................NA	Production 1992–Current

To begin with, the Hatteras 82 is the largest production convertible available. A production fiberglass sportfisherman over eighty feet was just a dream a few years ago, and Hatteras is finding that there's a market for such a boat with some very well-heeled sport fishermen. Designed as a crewed yacht (with crew quarters beneath the afterdeck, not forward), her extravagant triple-deck profile includes a two-station enclosed bridge, four staterooms with full heads, a vast salon/deckhouse galley living and entertainment area, and a huge tournament-style cockpit. Notable features of the Hatteras 82 include a circular stairwell in the salon for access to the bridge, a full-beam master suite with his-and-her heads, a utility/work room, a large observation deck overlooking the cockpit, and a convenient day head on the deckhouse level. The motors are almost lost in the huge stand-up engine room with its cockpit access. Powerful 16-cylinder Deutz diesels (2,540-hp each) are available in the Hatteras 82 Convertible as well as smaller 16V92s and 16V149s. ❏

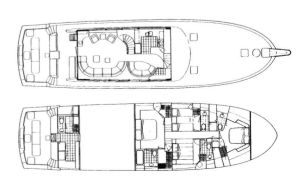

See Page 268 for Pricing Information

See Page 269 for Pricing Information

SPECIFICATIONS

Length	28'3"	Clearance	NA
Beam	10'2"	Cockpit	70 sq. ft.
Draft	2'6"	Hull Type	Modified-V
Weight	11,500#	Deadrise Aft	14°
Fuel	200 gals.	Designer	J. Henriques
Water	36 gals.	Production	1994–Current

The Henriques 28 is an inexpensive express fisherman with conservative styling and a no-nonsense layout. She's heavily built on a solid fiberglass hull with moderate beam and a relatively flat sheer. The cockpit—big for a 28-footer—has a fishbox/livewell built into the transom, transom door, and cockpit steps at the corners. A fishbox and a bait-rigging staion are located forward along with tackle lockers and a salt-water washdown. Twin bench seats with stowage under flank the bridgedeck, and the sole lifts up to provide good access the the motors. The belowdecks accommodations are basic but comfortable for two anglers with a V-berth/dinette forward, small galley area and a stand-up head with shower. Standard features include a welded aluminum tower hardtop and controls, Panish helm controls and recessed trim tabs. Note that the exhausts are channeled out through the trim tabs to reduce diesel fumes in the cockpit. Twin Volvo 200-hp diesels (or 170-hp Yanmars) provide a cruising speed of 23–24 knots and a top speed of about 28 knots. The standard 150-hp Volvos run about 4 knots slower. ❑

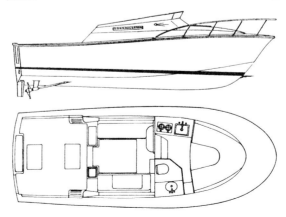

See Page 269 for Pricing Information

Sportfisherman

Open Fisherman

Workboat

SPECIFICATIONS

Length ....35'4"	Fuel ....320 gals.
Beam..............................12'0"	Cockpit, SF/Open ..120 sq. ft.
Draft, SF & Open ....3'1"	Cockpit, Workboat .165 sq. ft.
Draft, Workboat.............3'9"	Hull Type ....Modified-V
Weight, SF................22,000#	Production:
Weight, Open ....14,000#	SF................1977–Current
Weight, Workboat ..18,000#	Open SF...............1985–87
Water ....60 gals.	Workboat 1993–Current

The Maine Coaster 35s have been around in one form or another since Henriques first started building boats back in 1977. First came the Sportfisherman, a conservative all-fiberglass flybridge sedan with a deckhouse galley, lower helm and V-berths forward. With a full 120 sq. ft. of cockpit, a good-running hull (although her flat aftersections makes her difficult to handle in a following sea) and an attractive price, she became a popular boat over the years along the East Coast. The Open Fisherman came along in 1985, and her primary appeal was a simple layout (including a nice interior for a dayboat), easy engine access and of course that *huge* cockpit. The 35 Workboat is the most recent entry in the Maine Coaster series. She's basically a single-screw pilothouse design with an enlarged keel and integral skeg for prop protection. The helm is fully enclosed, and there are bunk berths forward along with a head and small galley. The SF, with 250-hp Cummins diesels, will cruise at about 20 knots, and the Open Fisherman will cruise at about the same speed with a pair of 240-hp Perkins diesels. ❏

See Page 269 for Pricing Information

HENRIQUES 38 SPORTFISHERMAN

SPECIFICATIONS

Length ....38'0"	Fuel ....415 gals.
Beam............................13'10"	Cockpit..................140 sq. ft.
Draft ....3'10"	Hull Type ....Modified-V
Weight ....28,000#	Deadrise Aft ....14°
Clearance ....21'0"	Designer ....J. Henriques
Water ....75 gals.	Production 1988–Current

The Henriques 38 SF is a sturdy East Coast sportfisherman with a no-nonsense profile to go with her practical layout. She's built on a conventional modified-V hull with moderate beam, a flared bow, a gently curved sheer, and Divinycell-cored hullsides. The house, deck, and cockpit are constructed in a single mold (no leaks) and, with a full 140 sq. ft. of space, the cockpit is among the largest to be found in a boat this size. Nearly all Henriques 38s have been built with the dinette (single-stateroom) layout, although a second stateroom can be added in place of the dinette. The somewhat dark interior is tastefully finished with traditional teak cabinetry and woodwork throughout. Outside, cockpit controls, transom door, tackle center, rod storage, and two 70-gallon recessed fish boxes are standard. Note the side-facing bridge ladder. A good-running boat, the Henriques 38 will cruise at 24–25 knots with the 375-hp Cat diesels (or 380-hp Volvos) and reach a top speed of about 30 knots. ❏

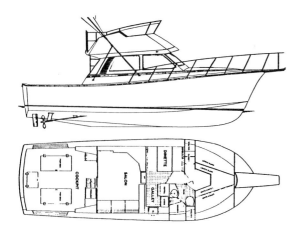

See Page 269 for Pricing Information

HENRIQUES 38 EL BRAVO

SPECIFICATIONS

Length ....38'0"	Fuel ....415 gals.
Beam............................13'10"	Cockpit..................130 sq. ft.
Draft ....3'4"	Hull Type ....Modified-V
Weight ....28,000#	Deadrise Aft ....14°
Clearance ....9'3"	Designer ....J. Henriques
Water ....60 gals.	Production 1991–Current

Based on the proven hull of the Henriques 38 Sportfisherman with moderate beam and cored hullsides, the 38 El Bravo is a good-looking express fisherman with an array of features that serious anglers will appreciate. Foremost among her attributes is an absolutely huge fishing cockpit—only the Blackfin 38 rivals the El Bravo in cockpit space for a boat this size. Not surprisingly, the El Bravo's single-stateroom interior is small for a 38-footer since so much of the hull's LOA has been given over to the cockpit. A wraparound helm console provides space for flush-mounting most electronics and a centerline hatch on the bridgedeck provides quick and easy access to the motors. Standard features include a tuna tower, generator, in-deck fish boxes, transom door, fresh- and salt-water washdowns, and lots of tackle and rod storage. Fully loaded with tower and gear, the 38 El Bravo will cruise economically at 25 knots with optional 435-hp Cats (375-hp Cats are standard) and reach a top speed of 29–30 knots. ❏

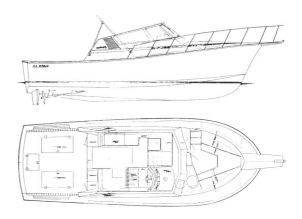

See Page 269 for Pricing Information

130

HENRIQUES 44 SPORTFISHERMAN

SPECIFICATIONS

Length ....44'0"	Fuel ....600 gals.
Beam.......................14'10"	Cockpit.................170 sq. ft.
Draft ....3'8"	Hull Type ....Modified-V
Weight ....37,000#	Deadrise Aft ....12°
Clearance ....NA	Designer ....J. Henriques
Water ....120 gals.	Production 1983–Current

The Henriques 44 SF is a dedicated Jersey-style sportfisherman with a conservative profile and the largest fishing cockpit in her class. She's built on a solid fiberglass hull with moderate beam, a shallow keel, and 12° of deadrise at the transom. While many convertible builders are quick to sacrifice cockpit space for a bigger interior, Henriques boats are well known in the trade for their big cockpits. In the case of the Henriques 44, that translates into a huge and completely uncluttered 12' x 14' cockpit—more than enough space to satisfy the requirements of the most demanding tournament activities. Insulated fish boxes, a transom door, tackle center, and teak covering boards are all standard. Several one- and two-stateroom floorplans have been offered over the years—the latest has an island berth in the forward stateroom—all fully paneled and finished with traditional teak woodwork. Most have been sold with the hard enclosure. Standard 550-hp 6V92s will cruise the Henriques 44 around 25 knots and reach 29 knots wide open. ❑

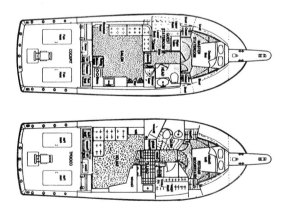

See Page 269 for Pricing Information

HYDRA-SPORTS 2800 SF

SPECIFICATIONS

Length w/Pulpit..........30'1"	Fuel ....300 gals.
Beam.............................10'7"	Cockpit.............................NA
Draft ....2'3"	Hull Type ....Deep-V
Hull Weight ....7,900#	Deadrise Aft ....19°
Clearance ....NA	Max HP 500
Water ....31 gals.	Production 1991–Current

A good-running boat with an integrated outboard bracket and efficient deck plan, the Hydra-Sports 2800 manages to combine all the necessary elements of a good offshore fishing boat. Hull construction is solid fiberglass, and the wide 10'7" beam makes for a stable fishing platform with plenty of elbow room for a couple of anglers. A bait-prep station and baitwell are built into the 2800's full-height transom, and a big lift-out fish box resides in the cockpit sole. Visibility from the raised bridgedeck is excellent, and a chart flat is built into the dash in front of the companion seat. Belowdecks is a well-arranged cabin with an enclosed head, a fully equipped galley, storage areas and plenty of headroom. The dinette converts into a double bed, and a small aft cabin is located below the bridgedeck. Additional features include trim tabs, a large transom door, tackle drawers, molded pulpit, and cockpit washdowns. Designed to handle up to 500 horsepower, twin 225-hp outboards will cruise the Hydra-Sports 2800 SF at an easy 25 knots and hit 40+ knots top. ❑

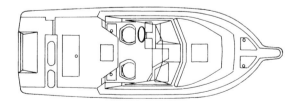

See Page 269 for Pricing Information

HYDRA-SPORTS 3300 SF

SPECIFICATIONS

Length	32'11"	Clearance	5'6"
Beam	9'6"	Hull Type	Deep-V
Hull Draft	1'6"	Deadrise Aft	24°
Hull Wgt. (approx.)	5,300#	Maximum HP	600
Water	40 gals.	Designer	D. Riley
Fuel	270 gals.	Production	1989–92

Based on the hull of the Donzi F-33, the Hydra-Sports 3300 is a high-performance offshore fisherman with a center console/cuddy deck plan and bracket-mounted engines aft. The 3300's deep-V hull is balsa-cored from the waterline up, and the narrow 9'6" beam allows her to be trailerable with a permit. A good-looking boat with an aggressive profile, the 3300 features a wide helm console with space for flush-mounting (and securing) the basic electronics. Cockpit seating is excellent: a bench seat behind the helm seat faces aft, and a full-width bench seat folds flush against the transom for more cockpit space. Inside the small cuddy, a V-berth will sleep two adults, and the compact galley has a stove and sink. Note that the 3300 was one of the earlier designs to feature a stand-up head compartment inside the console. A good heavy-weather performer (but a wet ride in a chop), twin 300-hp V8 outboards will cruise the Hydra-Sports 3300 at a fast 28 knots and reach a top speed of 40+ knots. ❏

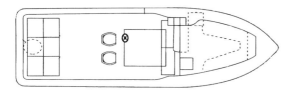

See Page 269 for Pricing Information

INNOVATOR 31

SPECIFICATIONS

Length	30'10"	Fuel	265 gals.
Length WL	NA	Cockpit	75 sq. ft.
Beam	10'4"	Hull Type	Modified-V
Weight	11,000#	Deadrise Aft	12°
Clearance	9'0"	Designer	Ed Monk, Jr.
Water	60 gals.	Production	1988–91

The Innovator 31 is a well-built West Coast design with a single-minded objective: catching fish. Introduced in 1988, she was updated in late 1991 and re-introduced as the Innovator 30 (see lower floorplan below). Only a few of the 30s were built, however, and of the two models the original 31 sold better (about 35 were built) and remains better-known today. The hull is solid glass, and the deadrise at the transom is a modest 12°. Inside, the cabin is arranged with berths for four along with a compact galley and a stand-up head with shower. The cockpit comes with two in-deck fish boxes along with washdowns and rod holders. Engine boxes provide excellent access to the motors, and molded cockpit steps at the cockpit corners lead to extra-wide sidedecks. Gas engines were standard, but most Innovators were delivered with one of several diesel options. Among them, Cummins 210-hp diesels will deliver an impressive cruising speed of 23–24 knots and a top speed of around 28 knots. ❏

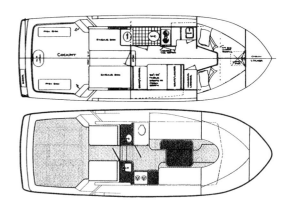

See Page 269 for Pricing Information

INTREPID 30 OPEN

SPECIFICATIONS

Length w/Bracket ....32'1"	Fuel ....170 gals.
Beam..............................8'6"	Cockpit............................NA
Draft ....2'0"	Hull Type ....Deep-V
Weight......................3,250#	Deadrise Aft ....22°
Clearance ....5'5"	Designer...............J. Wynne
Water ....None	Production 1991–Current

A popular boat, the Intrepid 30 is a high-performance center con-sole fisherman with the same lightweight, high-tech construc-tion common to all recent Intrepid products. Offered with or with-out a cuddy cabin, the 30 is among the lightest and most fuel-efficient boats in her class, and she has a reputation for superb offshore performance. This exilerating, high-performance person-ality comes at a price, however. Like all narrow deep-Vs, she's not the most stable fishing platform at trolling speeds, and the cockpit is much smaller than that of a conventional 30-foot fishing boat. Fishboxes and baitwells are found in the cockpit sole, and there's space at the helm for securing the electronics. The Open model has a casting platform, and the Cuddy has V-berths and rod storage below. The fully integrated bracket brings the motors close to the transom and reduces the possibility of a snagged line while working a rodtip around the engines. A fast ride, twin 250-hp Yamaha out-boards will cruise the Intrepid 30 at a brisk 33 knots and reach a top speed of 46+ knots. ❏

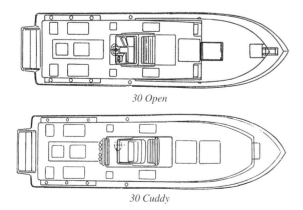

30 Open

30 Cuddy

See Page 269 for Pricing Information

INTREPID 31 WALKAROUND

SPECIFICATIONS

Length w/Bracket ....33'0"	Clearance ....5'0"
Beam............................10'0"	Hull Type ....Deep-V
Hull Draft ....2'0"	Deadrise Aft................20.5°
Hull Weight ....5,500#	Max HP 500
Fuel ....245 gals.	Designer.................Intrepid
Water ....22 gals.	Production 1995–Current

The Intrepid 31 is something different in a walkaround design. In addition to the center console and cuddy, the 31 has circular lounge seating forward of the helm—a civilized touch that family and guests will find most useful. While this pit-style entertainment area uses up some cockpit space, the extra seating turns the 31 into a fine family boat which is something few walkarounds can claim. She's well built on a deep-V hull with cored hullsides and a solid fiberglass bottom. The Intrepid 31 carries more beam than most high-performance fishermen, and the cockpit is roomier than you might expect in a boat of this type. Two 6-foot fishboxes and a big 35-gallon livewell are fitted beneath the sole, and a leaning post/rocket launcher, raw-water washdown and recessed rod storage are standard. The cabin comes with V-berths, an enclosed head compartment with toilet and shower, mini-galley and overhead rod storage. The full walkaround sidedecks complete the utility of this versatile design. With a pair of 225-hp outboards, the Intrepid 31 will cruise at 30 knots and reach 40+ knots wide open. ❏

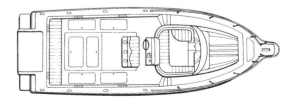

See Page 269 for Pricing Information

INTREPID 33 CUDDY

SPECIFICATIONS

Length	35'6"	Fuel	250 gals.
Beam	10'6"	Cockpit	NA
Draft	2'0"	Hull Type	Deep-V
Weight	5,500#	Deadrise Aft	22°
Clearance	8'0"	Designer	M. Peters
Water	40 gals.	Production	1993–Current

An incredibly lightweight boat for her size, the Intrepid 33 is a high-performance day fisherman with plenty of sex appeal to go with her practical layout. Her raceboat-style stepped hull is built on a solid fiberglass bottom with Divinycell coring in the hullsides, and multidirectional pre-impregnated fabrics are used along with vacuum-bagging in the high-tech construction process. The 33's center console deck plan will appeal to those seeking plenty of guest seating in addition to good overall fishability. The layout features a semi-circular settee forward of the helm and a wide-open cockpit with three in-deck storage boxes and a below-deck livewell. There's room in the console for flush-mounting electronics and convenient swim steps are outboard of the integral engine bracket. Belowdecks, the cabin will sleep three and comes with a small galley and a private head with shower. A good sea boat, the Intrepid 32 will cruise economically at a fast 33 knots and reach a top speed of around 42 knots with twin 275-hp outboards. ❏

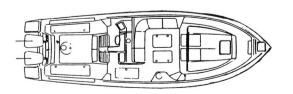

See Page 269 for Pricing Information

INTREPID 38 EVOLUTION

SPECIFICATIONS

Length	37'6"	Fuel	300 gals.
Beam	12'0"	Cockpit	108 sq. ft.
Draft	2'6"	Hull Type	Deep-V
Weight	14,000#	Deadrise Aft	NA
Clearance	NA	Designer	M. Peters
Water	52 gals.	Production	1991–93

With her high-tech materials and state-of-the-art construction, the Intrepid 38 is a very specialized boat with a price tag to match. She's built on a stepped deep-V hull similar to that used by racing boats. Her primary purpose is offshore fishing, and (to the best of our knowledge) she's the largest production inboard center console dayboat ever built. The walkaround deck layout will appeal to light-tackle and stand-up anglers. The cockpit will easily handle a full-size chair, and there are molded steps port and starboard. The helm is set well aft on the bridgedeck with seating forward—innovative but windy with no screen. The compact helm console provides space for flush mounting most electronics, and a hydraulically operated hatch provides excellent access to the motors below. Inside, the accommodations are basic with a small galley, king-size V-berths, a stand-up head, and a unique double berth below the helm. Twin 400-hp Merlin inboard diesels will cruise at 28–29 knots and reach 35 knots top, and 425-hp Cats are capable of 40 knots top. ❏

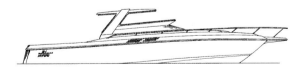

See Page 269 for Pricing Information

134

ISLAND GYPSY 32 FISHERMAN

SPECIFICATIONS

Length	32'1"	Water	120 gals.
Length WL	29'8"	Fuel	250 gals.
Beam	11'6"	Cockpit	110 sq. ft.
Draft	3'8"	Hull Type	Semi-Disp.
Weight	13,000#	Designer	H. Halvorsen
Clearance	NA	Production	1987–Current

A good-looking boat with a distinctive profile, the Island Gypsy 32 Fisherman uses the same two-piece semi-displacement hull mold used in the 32 Sedan model. Said to be based on a traditional Australian fishing boat design (yeah, sure), she's built at the Halvorsen yard in mainland China. This is a handsome little fisherman with a spacious cockpit and a straightforward, business-like appearance. The floorplan—basic but comfortable overnight accommodations for two—includes V-berths forward, an enclosed head with stand-up shower, compact galley and dinette. The lower helm (optional) is uniquely located just inside the cockpit door where forward and portside visibility are limited. The flybridge is rather small with passenger seating aft of the helm. Engine access is from inside the cabin as well as via a raised cockpit hatch, and the transom door and swim platform are standard. A single 275-hp Sabre diesel will cruise the Island Gypsy 32 Fisherman at an economical 15 knots (17–18 knots top), and optional twin 210-hp Cummin diesels will cruise at a brisk 20+ knots. ❏

See Page 269 for Pricing Information

135

JEFFERSON FS 35

SPECIFICATIONS

Length	35'0"	Fuel	240 gals.
Beam	9'2"	Water	31 gals.
Draft, Up	1'8"	Hull Type	Deep-V
Draft, Down	2'5"	Deadrise Aft	24°
Hull Weight	4,150#	Designer	David Shaw
Clearance	6'0"	Production	1994–Current

If the Jefferson FS 35 looks familiar, check out the Marlin 35. That's right, the Jefferson is an unabashed knock-off of the Marlin with the same sexy profile, efficient deck plan, and attractive price. She's built on a fully cored deep-V hull with a sharp entry and a narrow beam. A keel pad and stepped transom help get the hull on plane quickly. While the FS 35 dosen't have the cockpit space of wider center consoles her size, there's still enough room for a few anglers to work without feeling cramped. There are a pair of fishboxes in the deck and a livewell flanked by saltwater and freshwater sinks at the transom. The console is particularly well arranged with a large area for electronics, tackle drawers on both sides and a tilt wheel. There's a cooler/jump seat behind the leaning post and under-gunnel rod storage. The basic cabin has a V-berth and an MSD between the bunks. A light boat for her size, twin 200-hp Mercs will cruise the Jefferson at a fast 28–30 knots a reach and about 45 knots top. ❏

See Page 269 for Pricing Information

JERSEY 36 CONVERTIBLE SF

SPECIFICATIONS

LOA	39'4"	Fuel	365 gals.
Beam	13'4"	Cockpit	90 sq. ft.
Draft	2'6"	Hull Type	Modified-V
Weight	23,500#	Deadrise Aft	10°
Clearance	11'0"	Designer	F. McCarthy
Water	75 gals.	Production	1986–92

A handsome sportfisherman with flowing, almost custom lines, the Jersey 36 is built on a solid fiberglass hull with moderate beam, a sharp entry, and substantial flare at the bow. Her original single-stateroom interior is arranged with the galley down, a big head compartment with stall shower, and an offset double berth forward. A new floorplan introduced in 1991 offered a centerline double berth forward with the addition of a dinette (or second stateroom) at the expense of the stall shower and some engine room and salon space. The bridge layout was also rearranged in 1991 with the helm console now on the centerline rather than to starboard—a big improvement. The Jersey 36 came with a long list of standard equipment including a factory hardtop. Her large fishing cockpit features very low freeboard with plenty of room for tackle centers and a mounted chair. With standard 350-hp/454-cid gas engines, the Jersey 36 Convertible will cruise at 19–20 knots and reach 29 knots wide open. Optional 375-hp Cat diesels cruise efficiently at 24–25 knots and top out at around 28 knots. ❏

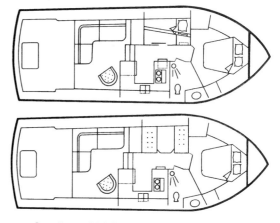

See Page 269 for Pricing Information

JERSEY 40 DAWN CONVERTIBLE

SPECIFICATIONS

Length ....40'0"	Fuel ....400 gals.
Beam.............................14'6"	Cockpit...........................NA
Draft ....3'5"	Hull Type ....Modified-V
Weight ....28,000#	Deadrise Aft ....10°
Clearance ....NA	Designer ....F. McCarthy
Water ....100 gals.	Production 1973–88

No longer in production, the 40 Dawn is a classic East Coast fisherman with a low-deadrise bottom, a sweeping sheerline, and a greatly flared bow. Her wide beam and relatively deep keel insure stable handling characteristics in most weather conditions, and a spacious cockpit provides plenty of room for tournament-level fishing activities. Two interior floorplans were offered with the single-stateroom dinette layout proving more popular than the two-stateroom, galley-up version. The interior—which is a little dark—is completely finished with teak woodwork and cabinetry. (Note that the switch from woodgrain mica to an all-teak interior was made in 1979.) Standard features include bow pulpit, air conditioning, generator, stereo, and color TV. Still popular with experienced fishermen, many of the Jersey 40s were powered with economical 235-hp Volvo diesels which cruise around 18 knots at only 18 gph, or 1 mpg—very efficient indeed. Later models with the optional 325-hp Cats are capable of cruising around 20 knots and reaching 23–24 knots wide open. ❏

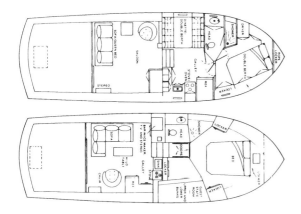

See Page 270 for Pricing Information

JERSEY DEVIL 44 SF

SPECIFICATIONS

Length ....44'0"	Fuel ....400 gals.
Beam.............................14'6"	Cockpit.................154 sq. ft.
Draft ....3'10"	Hull Type ....Modified-V
Weight ....34,800#	Deadrise Aft ....10°
Clearance ....14'2"	Designer ....F. McCarthy
Water ....100 gals.	Production 1980–85

When it comes down to cockpit size, the Jersey Devil 44 is simply in a class by herself. Eight of these durable canyon runners were built during a 6-year production run and several can be found today operating as charter boats along the East Coast. She was built using a stretched version of the Jersey 40 hull with a deep entry and a slightly rounded bottom. Transom deadrise is a modest 10°. The basic two-stateroom interior is arranged with the galley up on the salon level. (The front windshield panels are glassed over.) Early interiors were finished with simulated teak laminates, but Jersey went to an all-teak interior in 1979. A very useful feature is the huge storage bin below the galley sole—large enough for an inflatable and extra ground tackle. The cockpit has lockable rod racks under the gunwales and a tackle center to port. A good-running boat with a strictly-business appearance, all Jersey Devil 44s were powered with 450-hp GM 6-71 diesels. She'll cruise around 24–25 knots and reach a top speed in the neighborhood of 27 knots. ❏

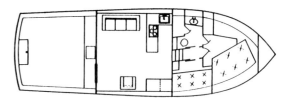

See Page 270 for Pricing Information

JERSEY 42/44 CONVERTIBLE SF

SPECIFICATIONS

LOA	45'6"	Fuel	400/476 gals.
Beam	15'8"	Cockpit	114 sq. ft.
Draft	3'6"	Hull Type	Modified-V
Weight	30,500#	Deadrise Aft	10°
Clearance	17'0"	Designer	F. McCarthy
Water	100 gals.	Production	1989–92

Introduced as the Jersey 42, the 44 Convertible retains the distinctive styling characteristics—the long foredeck, sweeping sheer, and graceful profile—common to all Jersey boats. (The see-thru front windshield is almost a rarity on big convertibles these days). Construction is solid fiberglass, and her relatively flat after sections make her a quick boat to accelerate out of the hole. Aside from building a tough hull, the more recent Jersey boats have very tastefully finished interiors. Several accommodation plans have been offered during her production years, and the popular dinette layout (two staterooms with the galley down to starboard) features upper/lower berths in the guest stateroom and a breakfast bar in the salon. Throughout, the interior is fully paneled with dark teak woodwork and cabinetry. The large fishing cockpit is free of obstructions, and a factory hardtop and flybridge enclosure were standard. Caterpillar 375-hp diesels will cruise the Jersey 42 around 22 knots with a top speed of 26. The optional 485-hp 6-71s cruise at a fast 27 knots and reach 30 knots wide open. ❏

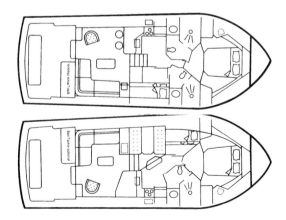

See Page 270 for Pricing Information

JERSEY 47 CONVERTIBLE

SPECIFICATIONS

Length	47'4"	Fuel	600 gals.
Beam	15'8"	Cockpit	124 sq. ft.
Draft	3'10"	Hull Type	Modified-V
Weight	36,000#	Deadrise Aft	10°
Clearance	17'0"	Designer	F. McCarthy
Water	150 gals.	Production	1987–92

Introduced in 1987, the 47 Convertible is the largest boat ever offered by this small New Jersey manufacturer. Notably, Jersey was one of the few builders that never abandoned single-skin fiberglass hull construction, thus avoiding the complexities (and the benefits) of cored hulls. The graceful profile of the Jersey 47 is quite distinctive, and her extra-long foredeck and cockpit bridge overhang make her an easy boat to recognize. Note the use of front windows—most modern sportfisherman have glassed-over windshields (although that option was available from the factory). Three interior plans were offered with the three-stateroom, galley-up layout being the most popular. Both guest staterooms are small, but the heads are very large and fitted with shower stalls. Traditional teak woodwork is used extensively throughout the interior. Outside, the uncluttered cockpit is arranged for serious fishing pursuits, and the flybridge is huge with seating for eight. Reliable 6-71 Detroit diesels (485-hp) were standard, and the Jersey 47 Convertible will cruise at a fast 26 knots with a top speed of 30 knots. ❏

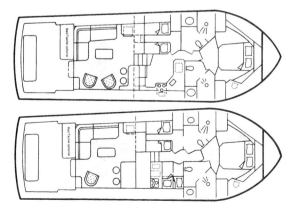

See Page 270 for Pricing Information

JUPITER 31 CENTER CONSOLE

SPECIFICATIONS

Length	30'8"	Hull Type	Deep-V
Beam	9'6"	Cockpit	NA
Hull Draft	1'9"	Clearance	6'8"
Hull Weight	4,500#	Deadrise Aft	24°
Fuel	250 gals.	Max HP	600
Water	40 gals.	Production	1989–Current

The Jupiter 31 is a big outboard center console with a growing following among hard-core anglers with an eye for quality. Available as an open fisherman or cuddy cabin, the Jupiter is built on a high-performance, super-deep-V hull with a fairly wide beam and cored hullsides. The bottom of the Jupiter 31 incorporates a flat lifting pad from the stern forward for quick and efficient planing. Available as an open-bow center console (pictured above) or as a center colsole cuddy, both models share many of the same features such as a bait-rigging station with sink, an 80-gallon livewell, storage space below the deck and a spacious enclosed head in the cosole with standing headroom. The open fisherman also has a second livewell forward along with additional dry storage. The cuddy cabin features a full inner liner with a dinette/V-berth and a compact galley along with molded steps from the cockpit for easy foredeck access. With twin 200-hp outboards, the Jupiter 31 will cruise at 30 knots and reach a top speed of 40+ knots. ❏

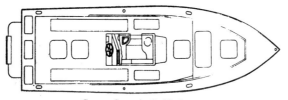

Center Console Cuddy Layout

See Page 270 for Pricing Information

LUHRS TOURNAMENT 290 (EARLY)

SPECIFICATIONS

Length	29'0"	Fuel	200/260 gals.
Beam	10'9"	Cockpit	60 sq. ft.
Draft	2'5"	Hull Type	Mod. Deep-V
Weight	9,000#	Deadrise Aft	17°
Clearance	14'6"	Designer	Mike Peters
Water	40 gals.	Production	1986–88

The first of three models to carry the same name, the Tournament 290 pictured above is notable for her ungainly and somewhat top-heavy bridgedeck profile. She's built on a modified-V hull with a double chine and a relatively steep 17° of deadrise at the transom. An out-and-out fishing boat, the Tournament 290 has a large bi-level cockpit with roughly 60 sq. ft. of fishing area on the lower level. All were delivered with a standard factory tower. Three lift-out fish boxes provide good access to the rudder posts and bilges, and a cockpit washdown and coaming padding were standard. The accommodations below are simple but nicely finished with oak paneling and a teak and holly sole. Cabin headroom is 6'2". The full-width of the cabin results in narrow sidedecks, and walking forward to the bow is difficult. Twin 270-hp Crusaders were standard with GM 6.2 diesels offered as an option. The 270s will cruise the Luhrs Tournament 290 around 24 knots with a top speed of 30+ knots. ❏

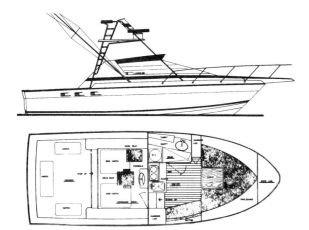

LUHRS TOURNAMENT 290

SPECIFICATIONS

Length	29'6"	Fuel	250 gals.
Beam	10'9"	Cockpit	NA
Draft	2'5"	Hull Type	Mod. Deep-V
Weight	7,480#	Deadrise Aft	17°
Clearance	NA	Designer	Mike Peters
Water	40 gals.	Production	1989–91

With her large cockpit and walkaround decks, the Luhrs Tournament 290 will appeal to the fisherman who requires basic cabin accommodations to go with a good day-boat layout. The second of three 290 express models from Luhrs, she was built on the same hull as the original Tournament 290 (1986–88) with steep deadrise at the transom and solid fiberglass construction. Dedicated anglers will appreciate the wide sidedecks and efficient cockpit. Fishing features include rod storage under the gunwales, a drop curtain to enclose the lower helm, standard bait center, a large livewell in the transom, and a standard factory tower with controls. Note the lack of a windshield at the helm. Below, the cabin is surprisingly spacious. The dinette converts to a double berth, and the galley and head are adequate for weekend service. The seat at the lower helm also folds out when two extra berths are required. A good-running boat with standard 350-cid gas engines, the Tournament 290 will cruise around 23 knots and reach 31–32 knots wide open. ❏

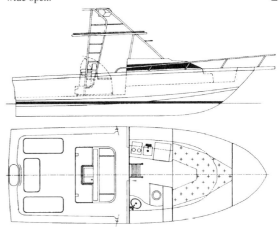

See Page 270 for Pricing Information

See Page 270 for Pricing Information

LUHRS TOURNAMENT 290 OPEN

LUHRS ALURA 30

SPECIFICATIONS

Length	29'10"	Fuel	300 gals.
Beam	11'6"	Cockpit	NA
Draft	2'9"	Hull Type	Deep-V
Weight	8,000#	Deadrise Aft	18°
Clearance	16'6"	Designer	Luhrs
Water	30 gals.	Production	1992–Current

The Tournament 290 Open is a scaled-down version of the Tournament 380 introduced in 1991. Luhrs is building some good-looking fishing boats these days, and the 290 Open will appeal to anglers seeking a capable offshore fishing platform at an affordable price. She's built on a lightweight deep-V hull with cored hullsides and a wide 11-foot, 6-inch beam. Her cockpit is large enough for a full-size chair and includes two in-deck fish boxes, a unique lift-out transom door, and a smaller fish box built into the transom. The helm is located on the centerline, and the bridgedeck sole lifts up for easy access to the step-down engine compartment. There are overnight accommodations for four in the small cabin which is arranged with the head in the forepeak. Notable features include a full tower with buggy top and controls, electronics box, entertainment center, bait-prep station, and side exhausts. Standard 350-cid gas engines will cruise at 16–17 knots and reach a top speed of about 27 knots. ❏

SPECIFICATIONS

Length	30'0"	Water	38 gals.
Length WL	28'0"	Fuel	196 gals.
Beam	10'3"	Cockpit	110 sq. ft.
Draft	2'11"	Hull Type	Semi-Disp.
Weight	7,800#	Designer	Luhrs
Clearance	NA	Production	1987–90

Featuring a distinctive Downeast profile, the Alura 30 is a versatile weekender with a large cockpit and comfortable cabin accommodations. She's built of solid fiberglass on a semi-displacement hull with a sweeping sheer and moderate beam. A long keel provides a measure of prop protection while ensuring good handling characteristics at low speeds. Although not considered a beamy boat, the cockpit is exceptionally large and includes built-in baitwells and fish boxes. Helm visibility is good, and the windshield can be opened for ventilation. The wide sidedecks are notable. Inside, the cabin layout is clean and simple, and the teak and holly sole is especially attractive. Two people can cruise aboard this boat for a few days without problem. A good all-purpose design, the Alura 30 will do well as a dive boat or as an inexpensive fisherman and weekend cruiser. Note that the keel was redesigned in 1988 to reduce vibration problems. Her single 270-hp gas engine provides an efficient cruising speed of 14–15 knots and a top speed of around 22 knots. ❏

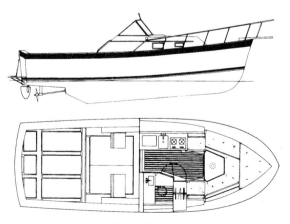

See Page 270 for Pricing Information

See Page 270 for Pricing Information

LUHRS TOURNAMENT 300

SPECIFICATIONS

LOA	34'6"	Water	40 gals.
Hull Length	31'6"	Fuel	250 gals.
Beam	10'9"	Hull Type	Deep-V
Draft	2'6"	Deadrise Aft	18°
Weight	12,000#	Designer	Luhrs
Clearance	11'6"	Production	1991–Current

The Tournament 300 SF is an updated version of the earlier Tournament 290 model with several improvements including a windshield and molded swim platform. A good-looking boat, she's built on a deep-V hull with average beam and cored hullsides. The cockpit is large enough to handle a fighting chair, and comes standard with an in-deck fish box, tackle drawers, bait-prep center, and two built-in seats with rod gimbals. The helm is set behind a center-vent windshield, and there's space in the console for flush-mounting electronics. A baitwell is located on the transom platform, and the full-length helm seat features a hydraulic lift mechanism for easy access to the (tight) engine compartment. Cabin accommodations include a dinette that converts to a double berth, a small galley, and a stand-up head with shower—a generous layout for a walkaround boat. Twin 350-cid gas engines are standard (21 knots cruise and 28 top), and 170-hp Yanmar diesels (21 knots at cruise and 24–25 knots wide open) are a popular option. ❏

See Page 270 for Pricing Information

LUHRS TOURNAMENT 320

SPECIFICATIONS

Length w/Pulpit	34'8"	Water	60 gals.
Hull Length	31'6"	Fuel	300 gals.
Beam	13'0"	Cockpit	NA
Draft	3'1"	Hull Type	Deep-V
Weight	15,000#	Deadrise Aft	18°
Clearance	NA	Production	1988–Current

The Luhrs Tournament 320 has the classic profile of a high-dollar custom fisherman. Indeed, her graceful lines are unusually attractive, and the affordable price of the Tournament 320 has already made her a popular boat in a short period of time. Note that she was built on a fully cored hull until 1991 when Luhrs went to a solid fiberglass bottom and cored hullsides. Inside, her surprisingly roomy cabin can accommodate six in reasonable comfort. An island berth is fitted in the stateroom and the salon—with facing settees—is open to the mid-level galley. The 320's uncluttered cockpit has enough room for a small mounted chair, and the flybridge is arranged with bench seating forward of the helm. Additional features include in-deck storage boxes, livewell, tackle center with controls, fresh and saltwater washdowns, and a transom door. A good-running boat, standard 310-hp/454-cid gas inboards will cruise the Luhrs Tournament 320 around 20 knots and reach a top speed of 29–30 knots. Note that the dinette was eliminated from the layout in 1992. ❏

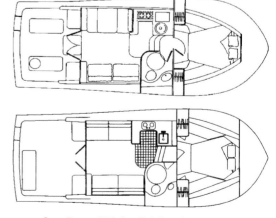

See Page 270 for Pricing Information

LUHRS TOURNAMENT 320 OPEN

SPECIFICATIONS

LOA	34'8"	Water	60 gals.
Hull Length	31'6"	Fuel	340 gals.
Beam	13'0"	Cockpit	60 sq. ft.
Draft	3'1"	Hull Type	Deep-V
Weight	15,000#	Deadrise Aft	18°
Clearance	15'9"	Production	1994–Current

The Tournament 320 Open is a good-looking express fisherman with a good deal of value built into her affordable base price. Designed as a smaller alternative to the popular 380 Open, the 320 is built on a deep-V hull with cored hullsides, a wide beam, and a considerable amount of flare at the bow. The deck plan is arranged with a walkaround center console and flanking bench seats on the bridgedeck level and a big fishing cockpit aft with a transom door, molded tackle center, and stand-up livewell. Inside, the 320 Open has berths for five with a V-berth/dinette forward and a convertible settee whose hinged backrest becomes a pilot berth at night. The teak woodwork, Corian countertops, and upscale fabrics make this an attractive and easily cleaned interior. The list of standard equipment is impressive: full tower with controls, hardtop with electronics box, enclosure panels, and cockpit washdowns. Standard 340-hp gas engines will cruise the Luhrs Tournament 320 Open around 21 knots and reach a top speed of 30–31 knots. Optional 3116 Cat diesels (291-hp) will cruise at a fast 28 knots (about 32 knots top). ❏

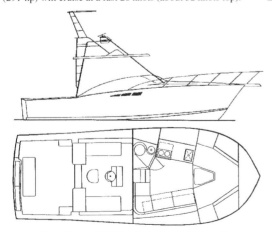

See Page 270 for Pricing Information

LUHRS 340 SPORTFISHERMAN

SPECIFICATIONS

Length	34'0"	Fuel	260 gals.
Beam	12'6"	Cockpit	67 sq. ft.
Draft	3'0"	Hull Type	Modified-V
Weight	12,300#	Deadrise Aft	15°
Clearance	11'5"	Designer	J. Fielding
Water	60 gals.	Production	1983–87

The Luhrs 340 Sportfisherman shares the same hull as the Silverton 34 Convertible—a proven and well-tested design with generous flare at the bow, plenty of beam, and moderate transom deadrise. She was marketed as an inexpensive and fully equipped fisherman with a marlin tower, fish boxes, salt- and freshwater washdown, side exhausts, and recessed rod storage in the cabin—all standard. The Luhrs 340 has a large bi-level cockpit (the bridgedeck is raised two feet from the cockpit sole) resulting in good helm visibility and adequate working space in the engine compartment. The helm console is positioned on the centerline with the companionway offset to starboard. Below, the 340's cabin is arranged in the normal fashion with a convertible dinette and V-berths forward. Teak-trimmed white mica cabinetry and a teak and holly sole highlight the interior. Standard 454-cid gas engines will cruise at 21 knots (about 30 top), and optional 210-hp GM 8.2 diesels will cruise around 23 knots and reach 25–26 knots wide open. ❏

See Page 270 for Pricing Information

144

LUHRS TOURNAMENT 342

SPECIFICATIONS

Length	34'0"	Fuel	300 gals.
Beam	12'6"	Cockpit	67 sq. ft.
Draft	3'2"	Hull Type	Modified-V
Weight	13,500#	Deadrise Aft	15°
Clearance	11'5"	Designer	J. Fielding
Water	60 gals.	Production	1986–89

The Luhrs Tournament 342 shares the same hull as the Luhrs 340 but with a different superstructure and a much larger interior. She was sold as a fairly complete package in keeping with the long-standing Luhrs practice of marketing a well-equipped boat at an affordable price. Her cockpit will handle a mounted chair and comes equipped with fresh- and saltwater washdowns, in-deck storage boxes, and padded coaming. The flybridge is particularly spacious with bench seating forward of the console. The original layout featured two staterooms, a deckhouse dinette, and oak woodwork. A much-revised layout was introduced in 1988 with only one stateroom, a more open salon/galley arrangement and an updated decor with an absence of any wood. The 342 also has a unique cabin ventilation system with hidden air intakes located beneath the forward bridge overhang. A good-running boat with brisk acceleration, the Luhrs Tournament 342 will cruise at 19–20 knots with standard 454-cid Crusaders gas engines and reach a top speed of 28 knots. ❑

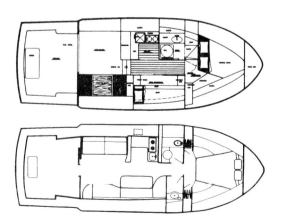

See Page 270 for Pricing Information

LUHRS ALURA 35

SPECIFICATIONS

Length	35'5"	Fuel	260 gals.
Beam	12'2"	Cockpit	NA
Draft	2'11"	Hull Type	Modified-V
Weight	12,800#	Deadrise Aft	NA
Clearance	NA	Designer	Luhrs
Water	55 gals.	Production	1988–89

The appealing Downeast character of the Alura 30 is missing from the more recent Alura 35. Here, the styling is more contemporary, and the accent is on the sportboat image. As such, the Alura 35 was designed to appeal to the price-conscious buyer. She's a straightforward express design without the curved windshield, radar arch, or the integral swim platform found in many of today's modern sportboats. What the Alura 35 does provide is a lot of boat for the money. If not plush, the mid-cabin interior accommodations are nonetheless roomy and very comfortable. The decor is light and airy, and the teak-and-holly cabin sole is especially attractive. Outside, the 35's large bi-level cockpit is well-suited to the demands of family cruisers as well as weekend anglers. A small tackle center is behind the helm seat; a swim platform was standard; and foredeck access is easy thanks to the wide sidedecks. Twin 270-hp Crusader gas engines will cruise the Alura 35 at around 17 knots with a top speed of 25–26 knots. ❑

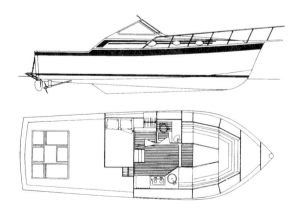

See Page 271 for Pricing Information

LUHRS TOURNAMENT 350

SPECIFICATIONS

L.O.A.	38'6"	Water	93 gals.
Hull Length	35'0"	Fuel	390 gals.
Beam	12'10"	Cockpit	94 sq. ft.
Draft	3'4"	Hull Type	Deep-V
Weight	19,000#	Deadrise Aft	17°
Clearance	16'0"	Production	1990–Current

Designed to fill the gap between the Tournament 320 and 380 models, the Luhrs 350 is built on modified deep-V hull design with balsa coring in the hullsides, a wide beam and a good deal of flare at the bow. Her aggressive profile and custom-style appearance are accented by darkly tinted wraparound windows and a rakish flybridge with its stylish cockpit overhang. The original single-stateroom floorplan is arranged with the mid-level galley open to the salon and an island berth in the stateroom. A new two-stateroom floorplan for 1995 has the galley in the salon and a smaller forward cabin. Either way, the interior of the 350 is large for a 35-footer and it's almost a surprise to note that the cockpit is still big enough for the installation of a fighting chair and a full tackle center. A transom door and in-deck storage boxes are standard. Twin 454-cid gas engines will cruise the Tournament 350 at an easy 17 knots with a top speed of around 25-26 knots. The optional Cat 350-hp (or Volvo 370-hp) diesels cruise around 24 knots and reach 28 knots top. ❏

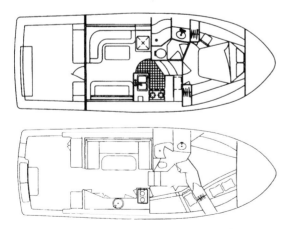

See Page 271 for Pricing Information

LUHRS TOURNAMENT 380

SPECIFICATIONS

Length w/Pulpit	40'10"	Water	100 gals.
Hull Length	37'9"	Fuel	450 gals.
Beam	14'11"	Cockpit	100 sq. ft.
Draft	3'7"	Hull Type	Deep-V
Weight	28,000#	Deadrise Aft	18°
Clearance	16'0"	Production	1989–Current

The Tournament 380 is a good-looking convertible with a classic sportfish profile and a surprisingly affordable price tag. She's built on a beamy deep-V hull designed with generous flare at the bow and balsa coring in the hullsides. The half-tower is standard, and her tournament-style flybridge and the large cockpit with molded tackle centers will satisfy the demands of most serious anglers. Inside, the original two-stateroom interior was arranged with the galley to port on the salon level. The floorplan was restyled in 1990 with an athwartships galley forward of the salon—an unusual but still-practical layout. Storage is excellent, and the head compartment is very large. Interestingly, the front windows are real and not fiberglassed-over, although the wraparound deckhouse mask does a good job of concealing them. A popular model with the lines of a custom boat, 310-hp/454-cid gas engines were standard (15 knots cruise/about 25 knots top) until 1991. Detroit 485-hp 6-71s (23 knots cruise/28 knots top) are now standard. ❏

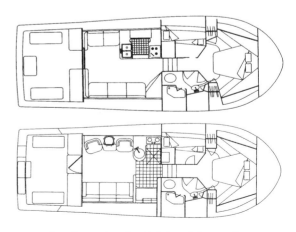

See Page 271 for Pricing Information

LUHRS TOURNAMENT 380 OPEN

LUHRS TOURNAMENT 400

SPECIFICATIONS

Length	37'10"	Fuel	600 gals.
Beam	14'11"	Cockpit	100 sq. ft.
Draft	3'7"	Hull Type	Deep-V
Weight	24,000#	Deadrise Aft	18°
Clearance	22'0"	Designer	Luhrs
Water	85 gals.	Production	1991–Current

SPECIFICATIONS

Length	40'0"	Fuel	400 gals.
Beam	14'0"	Cockpit	NA
Draft	3'2"	Hull Type	Modified-V
Weight	25,500#	Deadrise Aft	14°
Clearance	14'0"	Designer	Bob Rioux
Water	100 gals.	Production	1987–90

Luhrs has come up with a real beauty in the Tournament 380 Open, a versatile and feature-packed fishing machine with a very inviting price tag. Open sportfishermen have been growing in length and popularity in recent years, and this is becoming a very competitive market. Built on a wide, low-profile hull with cored hullsides, the 380 Open is a roomy and capable offshore boat. Her large bi-level cockpit layout includes a unique centerline helm console, flanking full-length lounge seating with rod storage under, molded transom fish box, and P&S molded tackle centers which double as bait-watching seats. Below, the interior is notable for its spacious layout and stylish decor—impressive indeed for a serious fishboat. Additional features include a standard tuna tower, hydraulic bridgedeck lift mechanism for superb engine room access, pop-up electronics display at the helm, and side exhausts. A good-running boat with excellent range, standard 485-hp 6-71 diesels will cruise the Tournament 380 Open around 26 knots and deliver 29–30 knots wide open. ❏

Built on the same hull as the Silverton 40 Convertible, the Luhrs Tournament 400 was a moderately priced convertible sportfisherman with aggressive lines and comfortable accommodations. With her rakish flybridge and black wraparound deckhouse mask, the Luhrs 400 has a very distinctive profile. Her two-stateroom interior is arranged with the galley down and an L-shaped dinette in the salon. The forward stateroom has an offset double berth, and over/under bunks are fitted in the guest cabin. The 400's interior originally featured oak paneling but was revised in 1988 with updated fabrics and off-white mica surfaces trimmed in teak. Fishing accessories in the cockpit include fresh- and salt-water washdowns, an in-deck fish box, rocket launchers, and flush rod holders. The half tower was standard, and the flybridge is notably large compared to other convertibles her size. The cruising speed with 454-cid gas engines is a sluggish 15–16 knots (around 25 knots top). Optional 375-hp Cats will cruise the Tournament 400 around 22 knots and reach 26 wide open. ❏

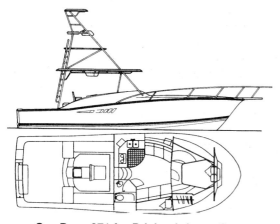

See Page 271 for Pricing Information

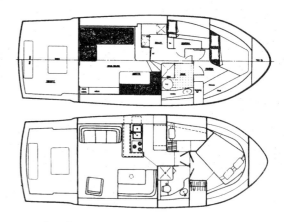

See Page 271 for Pricing Information

MAKO 282 CENTER CONSOLE

SPECIFICATIONS

Length	28'1"	Water	None
Beam	8'6"	Transom Height	25"
Hull Draft	1'4"	Hull Type	Deep-V
Hull Weight	4,100#	Deadrise Aft	23°
Fuel, Std.	185 gals.	Max HP	450
Fuel, Optional	50 gals.	Production	1995–Current

Among Mako's newest models is the 282 bracket model center console, a particularly good-looking fisherman with an integrated outboard mount and a dive platform with ladder. This is the largest trailerable Mako model and she's loaded with practical and well-thought-out fishing features. Her uncluttered cockpit is huge with enough space for four anglers to work all day without feeling confined or cramped. The wide helm console has room for most necessary electronics and, unlike other consoles, you access the interior (with its toilet, batteries, and storage bins) from the front rather than the side. A choice of two seating options is offered: twin pedestal chairs, or a leaning post with rocket launchers. Standard fishing amenities include an above-deck 42-gallon livewell and sink in the transom, two in-deck fish boxes, a center casting platform storage box, flush-mounted rod holders and two recessed rod lockers. There's also lockable forepeak storage. A good-running boat, twin 225-hp outboards will cruise the Mako 282 at a fast 30 knots (about 45 knots top). ❑

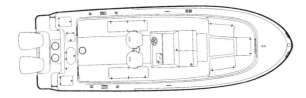

See Page 271 for Pricing Information

MAKO 286 INBOARD

SPECIFICATIONS

Length	28'5"	Water	30 gals.
Beam	9'10"	Fuel	213/230 gals.
Draft	2'6"	Hull Type	Modified-V
Weight	8,000#	Deadrise Aft	13°
Clearance	6'6"	Designer	Mako
Cockpit	NA	Production	1985–Current

A popular boat for Mako (and the largest boat in the fleet for several years), the 286 Inboard is a dual console fisherman with a practical deck layout and good overall performance. She's built on a rugged deep-V hull with a relatively wide beam and positive foam floatation. Like all of the larger Makos, the 286 performs well in rough weather and tracks nicely in a chop. The single-level cockpit is large enough to handle a full-size fighting chair, and there's a large fish box built into the cockpit sole near the transom. The portside console includes a sink with storage below, and there's built-in bench seating forward of the helm. Belowdecks, the lockable cuddy cabin contains adult-size V-berths, storage lockers, and a plumbed marine head. Additional features include teak covering boards, under-gunwale rod storage, companion seat, and very sturdy bow rails. An easy-riding boat with standard 350-cid gas inboards, the Mako 286 will cruise at 23 knots and reach a top speed of 30–31 knots. ❑

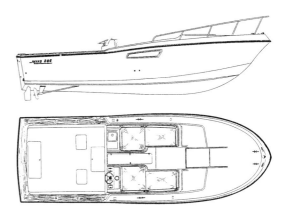

See Page 271 for Pricing Information

SPECIFICATIONS

Length w/Pulpit	30'10"	Water	25 gals.
Hull Length	28'7"	Fuel	240 gals.
Beam	9'6"	Hull Type	Deep-V
Draft	1'7"	Deadrise Aft	23°
Weight	5,000#	Max HP	550
Clearance	8'0"	Production	1993–Current

Beginning life in 1993 as the Mako 263, the 293 Walkaround is an extremely stylish walkaround cuddy with just about every feature an angler could ask for on a boat this size. She's built on a deep-V hull with a solid fiberglass bottom and cored hullsides, and there's enough foam packed into the hull to provide positive floatation. The deck layout boasts a full-height transom with a built-in livewell, shower, and two storage bins. There are two big fish boxes in the cockpit sole, and tackle drawers are located behind the helm and companion seats. Rod storage is under the gunwales. The sidedecks are wide, deep and well-secured, and bench seating is built into the forward part of the house. Inside, the mid-cabin floorplan sleeps four and includes a galley and an enclosed head with shower. A good performer, the Mako 293 will cruise efficiently at 29 knots with a pair of 275-hp outboards and reach about 40 knots wide open. ❏

SPECIFICATIONS

Length w/Bracket	31'9"	Water	39 gals.
Hull Length	28'3"	Fuel	300 gals.
Beam	10'0"	Hull Type	Deep-V
Hull Draft	1'11"	Deadrise Aft	19°
Hull Weight	6,800#	Max HP	400
Clearance	6'0"	Production	1993–Current

The largest Mako ever, the 295 is a long-range dayboat with a wide-open deck plan and a low-profile appearance. She's built on a deep-V hull with a full-length inner liner, cored hullsides, and a relatively wide beam. The cockpit is large enough for a mounted chair and features two 6-foot fish boxes in the sole, an in-deck 165-qt. livewell, bait-prep station, and transom door. (A storage bin built into the full-height transom can also be plumbed as a livewell.) While the cabin is small, it can still sleep four in a pullman-type V-berth. There's also a private head with a sink. The sidedecks leading around the cuddy are narrow, and the low bow rails don't add much in the way of foredeck access. Notably, the outboards are mounted on 32" centers (rather than the 28" centers seen in most outboards this size), and low-speed handling is impressive. A heavy boat, twin 250-hp Yamahas will cruise efficiently at 26 knots (about 1 gpm) and reach 37–38 knots top. ❏

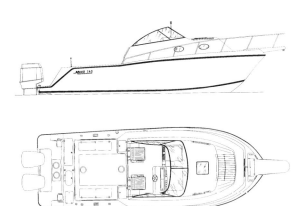

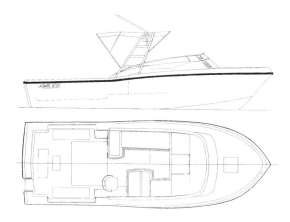

See Page 271 for Pricing Information

See Page 271 for Pricing Information

MARLIN 350 SPORTFISHERMAN

Center Console Cuddy

Open Bow

SPECIFICATIONS

Length	35'6"	Fuel	230 gals.
Beam	9'4"	Cockpit	NA
Draft	1'6"	Hull Type	Deep-V
Weight	4,500#	Deadrise Aft	24°
Clearance	8'0"	Max. HP	600
Water	40 gals.	Production	1991–Current

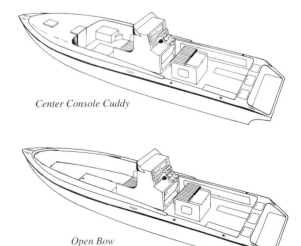

Center Console Cuddy

Open Bow

The Marlin 35 is a solid offshore fisherman with excellent speed and stability and a notably affordable price. Built in Ft. Lauderdale and sold factory-direct, the Marlin is unique in its construction technique. A quarter-inch layer of foam core (made of pre-expanded polyester resin) is sprayed between layers of mat and woven roving. The hull, deck and liner are then glassed—not bolted—together. The result is a rigid, lightweight and stable hull capable of handling some rough seas. The fishing appointments include a bait-prep station and two sinks built in along the transom, two big in-deck fish boxes, and a 50-gallon recirculating livewell. The helm console has space for flush-mounting the necessary electronics, and the console itself lifts to reveal a large storage area below. A marine toilet and two berths comprise the small cuddy cabin which is probably best used for dry storage. A very fuel-efficient boat, the Marlin's top speed is better than 40 knots with twin 200-hp O/Bs and well over 45 knots with twin 225-hp engines. ❏

See Page 271 for Pricing Information

350 FORWARD CUDDY

A high performance, semi-custom boat designed by bluewater fishermen, manufactured with top quality materials, using the latest technology in modern boat building. It's built for the purist who demands and appreciates reliability, performance, strength, craftsmanship, and ease of maintenance. Trips of up to 100 miles or more offshore in four to six foot seas and returning the same day are routine, safe and extremely comfortable.

350 OPEN BOW

IMPRESSIONS

The Marlin 350 is an excellent, mid-speed offshore boat with unusually good stability. Although it looks for all the world like a high-speedracer, Marlin hasn't made the common mistake of sacrificing weight (and attendant smoothness of ride) for pure speed. All thing considered, this boat offers an awful lot for the money. *"Sportfishing"*

FACTORY DIRECT

MEDITERRANEAN 38 CONVERTIBLE

SPECIFICATIONS

LOA w/Pulpit	42'10"	Water	100 gals.
Hull Length	38'4"	Fuel	300/450 gals.
Beam	12'6"	Cockpit	NA
Draft	3'2"	Hull Type	Deep-V
Weight	25,000#	Deadrise Aft	18°
Clearance	11'6"	Production	1985–Current

The Mediterranean 38 is a sturdy-looking flybridge sedan with a good deal of value packed into her low factory-direct price. She's built on a balsa-cored deep-V hull, and the construction involves some 65 individual molds resulting in a finished, gelcoated surface everywhere you look. Two interior layouts are offered with the single-stateroom floorplan being more popular. An overhead compartment in the salon can store six rods and reels. The interior is comprised of laminated teak cabinets and decorator fabrics. Outside, the sidedecks are very wide, and a cockpit tackle center, transom door, and fish box are standard. The step in the sheer was eliminated in 1987, and in 1988 the cockpit was rearranged and the fuel increased to 450 gallons. The flybridge can be ordered with the helm console forward or aft: either way, the bridge dimensions are comparatively moderate. Cummins 300-hp diesels will cruise at an economical 22 knots (27 knots top), and the larger 388-hp Cummins will cruise at 24–25 knots and reach 30 knots wide open. ❏

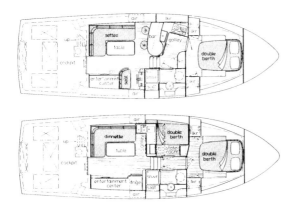

See Page 271 for Pricing Information

MEDITERRANEAN 54 CONVERTIBLE

SPECIFICATIONS

Length	53'7"	Clearance	NA
Beam	16'6"	Cockpit	180 sq. ft.
Draft	4'6"	Hull Type	Modified-V
Weight	55,000#	Deadrise Aft	15°
Fuel	1,400 gals.	Designer	S. Turner
Water	365 gals.	Production	1994–Current

Built in California and sold factory-direct, the Mediterranean 54 is a well-styled convertible with serious sportfishing potential and a very competitive price. She's constructed on a solid fiberglass modified-V hull and, at 55,000 lbs, she's a relatively light boat for her size (the Hatteras 54 and Viking 53 convertibles both weigh in at about 70,000 lbs). Several floorplans are available, and the factory promotes its ability to custom-design the interior to an owner's requirements. (Two versions of the standard galley-up, three-stateroom layout are pictured below.) Outside, the huge cockpit is arranged with molded steps at the corners, an engine room access door, two in-deck fish boxes and a bait well in the transom. The helm is aft on the oversize flybridge with lounge seating and a wet bar forward. Like most West Coast designs, the Mediterranean 54's sidedecks are very wide, and she carries a hulluva lot of fuel. Note that a Pilothouse (enclosed bridge) version is also available. Standard 550-hp Detroit 6V92s (small engines for a 54-footer) will cruise at 20 knots and reach 24 knots top. ❏

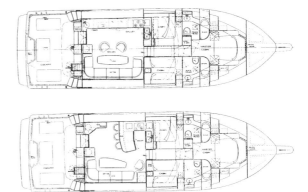

See Page 271 for Pricing Information

48 Sedan

50 Sport Fisherman

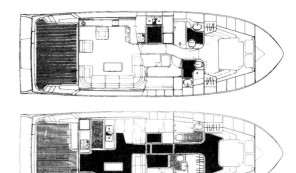

48 Sedan

SPECIFICATIONS

Length, 48 Sedan ....48'6"	Fuel ....1,000 gals.
Length, 50 SF...............50'6"	Cockpit...................90 sq. ft.
Beam.............................16'8"	Hull Type ....Modified-V
Draft ....3'10"	Deadrise Aft ....12°
Weight ....45,000#	Designer ....Tom Fexas
Water ....300 gals.	Production 1990–Current

The Mikelson 48 Sedan and 50 SF are a pair of innovative designs from the drawing board of Tom Fexas. (The difference between the two is in the cockpit where the 48 Sedan has an intergral swim platform compared to the built-in bait tanks found on the 50 SF.) Built in Taiwan on a fully cored hull with rounded bilges and a wide beam, the 48 and 50 are notably light boats for their size — a feature that results in some surprising performance figures with relatively small engines. A choice of two- or three-stateroom interiors have been available in both models. All of the interiors are finished out with an abundance of teak woodwork, and the large cabin windows make for a wide-open and very spacious salon. The cockpit gets small when a full set of tackle centers is added. Perhaps the most interesting feature of the Mikelson 48/50 is the huge flybridge with its circular dinette and fore and aft helm consoles. Twin 425-hp V-drive Cat diesels will cruise at 23 knots and reach a top speed of around 26 knots. A good-selling model with excellent range, the Mikelson 48/50 is primarily a West Coast boat. ❏

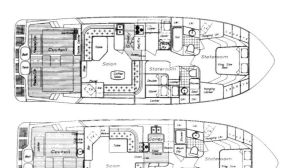

50 Sport Fisherman

See Page 271 for Pricing Information

MIKELSON 60 SPORTFISHER

SPECIFICATIONS

Length	59'1"	Fuel	1,000 gals.
Beam	17'2"	Cockpit	NA
Draft	4'4"	Hull Type	Modified-V
Weight	55,000#	Deadrise Aft	14.5°
Clearance	NA	Designer	Tom Fexas
Water	300 gals.	Production	1992–Current

Designed by Tom Fexas and built in Taiwan, the Mikelson 60 is an innovative West Coast sedan fisherman with a dramatic profile and plenty of built-in sex appeal. She's built on a lightweight, fully cored hull with a wide beam, prop pockets, and moderate transom deadrise—a notably efficient hull requiring relatively small engines for her size. Two floorplans are available: the standard galley-down layout has three staterooms, and the alternate arrangement calls for two staterooms with an enlarged galley. Either way, the wide-open salon comes with built-in settees and plenty of teak cabinetry and woodwork. Stepping outside, an unusual aft deck platform overlooks the cockpit. The flybridge is huge with a wraparound helm console and seating for a crowd. The engines are located under the aft deck where they're accessed via hydraulically operated hatches in the sole. The Mikelson 60 also has a rather unique underwater exhaust system with a transom bypass for quiet operation. A good performer with 735-hp 8V92s, she'll cruise at 23 knots and reach 26–27 knots wide open. Note that the Mikelson 56 is the same boat with a smaller cockpit. ❏

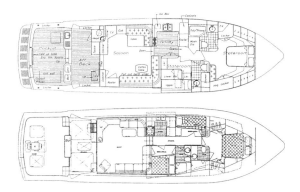

MIKELSON 72 SPORTFISHER

SPECIFICATIONS

Length	72'6"	Clearance	NA
Beam	20'6"	Cockpit	NA
Draft	5'6"	Hull Type	Modified-V
Weight	95,000#	Deadrise Aft	12°
Fuel	3,200#	Designer	Tom Fexas
Water	420 gals.	Production	1994–Current

Built by Knight & Carver in San Diego, the Mikelson 72 is a long-range sportfisher with a rakish profile and motor yacht-style accommodations. She's built on a fully cored hull with a very wide beam, and her sleek appearance makes her a clear standout among today's crop of mostly conservative production 65-foot-plus sportfishermen. While Mikelson promotes its ability to custom-design each 72 to an owner's requirements, the standard floorplan has the galley forward and *elevated* from the salon. This allows for the placement of an absolutely huge master stateroom beneath the galley floor. Note that each of the other three staterooms has a double bed and that all four heads have stall showers. An observation deck (with the engine room below) overlooks the spacious cockpit, and the flybridge (which may be enclosed) is the largest of any boat in her class and can even be ordered with a day head. Twin 1,000-hp 12-cylinder MTUs will cruise at 22 knots and deliver a top speed of 26–27 knots. With a 3,000-gallon fuel capacity and an easily-driven hull, the Mikelson 72 SF has excellent economy and range. ❏

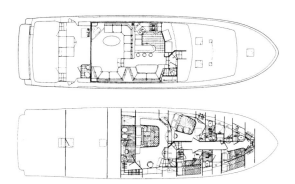

See Page 271 for Pricing Information

See Page 271 for Pricing Information

NAUSET 35 SPORT CRUISER

SPECIFICATIONS

Length	35'0"	Water	40 gals.
Beam	12'0"	Fuel	150 gals.
Draft	3'0"	Hull Type	Semi-Disp.
Weight	17,000#	Designer	R. Lowell
Clearance	NA	Production	1984–94

Nauset Marine is a well-known New England builder of commercial workboats and custom cruisers, and among their more notable products is the 35 Sport Cruiser, a boat the company produced for more than a decade. She's constructed on the old Bruno-Stillman 35 hull—an extremely popular design used in the production of some 350 boats from 1973 until 1984 when the company closed down. Nauset bought the molds and have since built about forty 35 Sport Cruisers for private use. Construction is solid fiberglass with a single-piece inner liner and a deep, prop-protecting keel. The interior has changed little from the original Bruno-Stillman layout, although the deckhouse profile is completely new. Features include a standard lower helm, wide sidedecks (well-protected with raised bulwarks and high railings), a prominent bowsprit, and a large cockpit with room for a mounted chair. Among several single- and twin-engine options, a single 375-hp Cat (17–18 knots cruise/24 top) has proven most popular. With her classic profile and seakindly hull, the Nauset 35 is a very appealing design. ❏

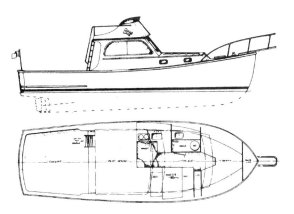

See Page 271 for Pricing Information

NORTH COAST 31 SPORTFISHERMAN

SPECIFICATIONS

Length	30'8"	Fuel, Std.	275 gals.
Beam	12'0"	Fuel, Opt.	410 gals.
Draft	3'2"	Cockpit	77 sq. ft.
Weight	11,300#	Hull Type	Deep-V
Clearance	8'0"	Deadrise Aft	23°
Water	50 gals.	Production	1988–90

Several builders inaccurately apply the "Deep-V" label to their hulls in an attempt to curry favor with offshore fishermen convinced of the superiority of a deep-V design. In the case of the North Coast 31 the claim is more than just advertising hype—the transom deadrise is a steep 23°. In a field crowded with small inboard sportfisherman, the North Coast 31 has several features that anglers will admire. The helm visibility is particularly good, and the unique console provides space for flush-mounting most electronics. The cockpit has molded steps for easy access to the recessed sidedecks, and there are two removable fish boxes in the sole. Below, the well-finished cabin has a teak-and-holly sole, attractive light ash trim work, and a head with stall shower. A good-running boat, twin 250-hp Cummins diesels will cruise the North Coast 31 at an economical 25 knots with a top speed of about 29 knots. Note that Blackfin recently acquired the molds to this model, and she's now marketed as the Blackfin 31 Combi. ❏

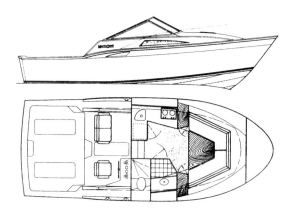

See Page 271 for Pricing Information

OCEAN 29 SUPER SPORT

SPECIFICATIONS

Length	29'0"	Fuel	215 gals.
Beam	11'6"	Cockpit	68 sq. ft.
Draft	2'5"	Hull Type	Modified-V
Weight	13,500#	Deadrise Aft	14°
Clearance	10'6"	Designer	D. Martin
Water	35 gals.	Production	1990–92

The Ocean 29 SS is one of the smallest flybridge boats ever offered by a major builder. Even with her wide beam and relatively heavy displacement, however, she's a small boat, and the addition of a flybridge results in a little more weight up high than is desirable. Like the earlier 32 and 35 SS models, the 29 SS carries more transom deadrise than most previous Ocean hulls. Inside, the floorplan includes a small salon/dinette level with a step-down galley to starboard and an offset double berth in the stateroom. The interior is attractively furnished with varnished teak woodwork, wall-to-wall carpeting, mini-blinds, and decorator fabrics. The good-size cockpit is fitted out with an in-deck storage box, tackle centers, and rod lockers. Standard 350-cid gas engines deliver a cruising speed of around 22 knots and a top speed of 30 knots. Larger 454-cid gas engines will cruise around 25 knots (34 knots top). Optional 250-hp Cummins diesels deliver 26 knots at cruise (at only 16 gph) and 30 knots wide open. ❏

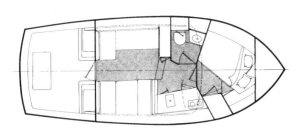

See Page 271 for Pricing Information

OCEAN 32 SUPER SPORT

SPECIFICATIONS

Length	32'0"	Fuel	280 gals.
Beam	12'4"	Cockpit	NA
Draft	2'6"	Hull Type	Modified-V
Weight	17,043#	Deadrise Aft	13°
Clearance	11'1"	Designer	D. Martin
Water	60 gals.	Production	1989–92

The Ocean 32 Super Sport has the classic raked-back cabin profile and aggressive performance found in all of the larger Ocean models. Indeed, she's a good-looking boat with a roomy cockpit and a surprisingly open interior layout. The fact that she has a real salon—and a stylish one at that—is notable in a 32-footer, and the walkaround island berth in the stateroom is a comfort seldom found in a boat this size. There's plenty of room in the cockpit for a mounted chair, and the flybridge will seat six. Competitively priced, standard features included a central vacuum system, bimini with enclosure panels, and distinctive teak covering boards in the cockpit. Twin 320-hp Crusader gas engines will cruise the Ocean 32 at about 23 knots cruise (30 knots top). Optional 250-hp Cummins diesels will cruise economically at 22 knots (at 1 mpg) and reach 25–26 knots wide open. The larger 300-hp Cummins will cruise at a fast 25 knots (about 29 knots top). The engine compartment is a seriously tight fit. ❏

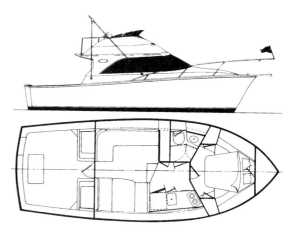

See Page 271 for Pricing Information

156

OCEAN 35 SUPER SPORT

SPECIFICATIONS

Length	35'0"	Fuel	320 gals.
Beam	13'0"	Cockpit	NA
Draft	2'5"	Hull Type	Modified-V
Weight	19,800#	Deadrise Aft	13°
Clearance	11'9"	Designer	D. Martin
Water	70 gals.	Production	1988–94

The Ocean 35 SS is a fast convertible sportfisherman with the sleek Jersey-style profile of the larger Ocean yachts. She's built on a modified-V hull with considerable beam forward, Divinycell-cored hullsides, and more transom deadrise than earlier Ocean hulls. The interior is roomy for a 35-footer with the salon completely open to the galley and dinette. The list of standard equipment includes a generator, air conditioning, and central vacuum system. The use of interior teak woodwork is notably scaled-back in the 35 SS compared to other Ocean models. Outside, the cockpit is fitted with a standard transom door, molded-in tackle center, side lockers, and teak covering boards. The Ocean 35 does not have the teak cockpit sole or toe rail found in previous Ocean yachts. Standard 320-hp Crusaders will cruise at 21 knots and reach 30 knots wide open. The optional 300-hp Cummins diesels will cruise the Ocean 35 SS around 25 knots (at an economical 23 gph) and reach 30 knots top. The engine room is a tight fit. ❏

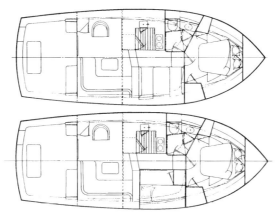

See Page 272 for Pricing Information

OCEAN 35 SPORT FISH & SPORT CRUISER

Sport Fish

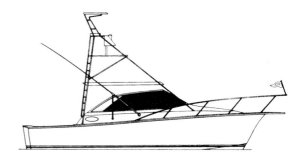

Sport Cruiser

SPECIFICATIONS

Length	35'0"	Fuel	280 gals.
Beam	13'0"	Cockpit	74 sq. ft.
Draft	2'11"	Hull Type	Modified-V
Weight	18,000#	Deadrise Aft	13°
Clearance	8'9"	Designer	D. Martin
Water	55 gals.	Production	1990–92

In general, express-style designs from manufacturers of sportfishing boats tend to be at the high end of the price spectrum. The Ocean 35 Sport Cruiser is unusual in that respect—she's an affordable and competent express cruiser equally at home as a family cruiser or weekend fisherman. Available in a Sportfish version as well as the Sport Cruiser model pictured above, the difference between the two is the extra cockpit seating and radar arch found in the Sport Cruiser and the teak covering boards, tackle lockers, and hinged transom gate of the Sportfish. The interiors are identical in both boats with a centerline double berth in the forward stateroom, a nifty mid-cabin fitted beneath the bridgedeck, a head with shower stall, and a portside galley with dinette opposite. Standard equipment includes air conditioning, generator, washdowns, rod storage, and a bimini with enclosure. Twin 320-hp gas engines will cruise at 22–23 knots and exceed 30 knots wide open. The optional 300-hp Cummins diesels cruise around 26 knots with a top speed of 29–30 knots. ❏

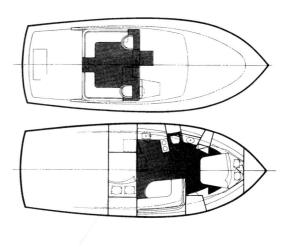

See Page 272 for Pricing Information

OCEAN 38 SUPER SPORT (EARLY)

SPECIFICATIONS

Length	38'4"	Fuel	354 gals.
Beam	13'8"	Cockpit	NA
Draft	3'2"	Hull Type	Modified-V
Weight	23,000#	Deadrise Aft	NA
Clearance	13'1"	Designer	D. Martin
Water	80 gals.	Production	1984–91

The 38 Super Sport was one of Ocean's best-selling models with 158 built during her long production run. She's a big boat for her length with the speed and performance of a sportfisherman and the upscale interior of a family cruiser. Indeed, the 38 SS has the aggressive good looks that many other convertibles her size can only admire. Note the glassed-over deckhouse windshield panels and wraparound black mask. Most 38s were delivered with the two-stateroom layout (the alternate single-stateroom floorplan has a more open salon), and the varnished teak woodwork is impressive. One of the more appealing aspects of the Ocean 38 is her serviceable engine room. The cockpit is set up for serious fishing and includes a tackle center, freezer, teak sole, and teak covering boards. A sistership—the Ocean 38 Super Sportfisherman (1984–87)—was also available with a larger cockpit and no fixed salon bulkhead. A stiff ride in a chop, 375-hp Caterpillar diesels will cruise at a fast 26–27 knots and reach 30+ knots top. ❏

OCEAN 38 SUPER SPORT

SPECIFICATIONS

Length	38'9"	Fuel	400 gals.
Beam	14'2"	Cockpit	85 sq. ft.
Draft	3'8"	Hull Type	Modified-V
Weight	27,000#	Deadrise Aft	NA
Clearance	15'6"	Designer	D. Martin
Water	80 gals.	Production	1992–Current

The new Ocean 38 SS looks a lot like the original 38 SS on the outside, but she's an entirely different boat below. Built on a slightly wider (and heavier) hull with a sharper entry and cored hull-sides, the new 38 has a smaller cockpit than her predecessor but a much larger interior. Indeed, the two-stateroom floorplan is innovative and completely unique for a boat of this size. Stepping into the salon, one is confronted with a surprisingly spacious and efficient layout with the dinette positioned forward (beneath the windshield panels) and an open galley to starboard. The companionway is all the way to port (there's a 7-foot rod locker in the outside wall) and leads down to a midships master stateroom of truly remarkable proportions. The engine room, however, is a tight fit. Note that the hardtop is standard. The Ocean 38 SS comes standard with a choice of 425-hp Cats (22–23 knots cruise/28 knots top) or the new 430-hp Volvo diesels (26 knots cruise/31 top). ❏

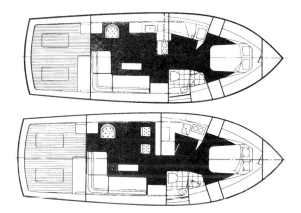

See Page 272 for Pricing Information

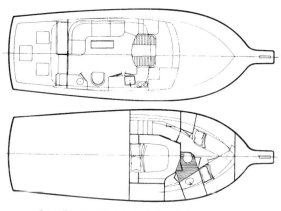

See Page 272 for Pricing Information

OCEAN 40 SUPER SPORT

SPECIFICATIONS

Length	40'2"	Fuel	450 gals.
Beam	14'4"	Cockpit	80 sq. ft.
Draft	3'0"	Hull Type	Modified-V
Weight	30,000#	Deadrise Aft	NA
Clearance	12'0"	Designer	D. Martin
Water	100 gals.	Production	1977–80

The Ocean 40 Super Sport was the first production design built by Ocean Yachts. Introduced to enthusiastic reviews in 1977, the 40 SS was a breakthrough boat capable of reaching a top speed of 30 knots—unheard-of performance back then in a production boat this size. The cockpit is adequate for serious fishing activities and came with a teak sole and teak covering boards. Delivered with a long list of standard equipment (generator, air conditioning, cockpit freezer, etc.), the Ocean 40 was available with a two-stateroom, galley-down floorplan or a two-stateroom, galley-up layout with a day berth in the companionway. The interior is a blend of varnished teak woodwork and vinyl wall coverings, and large cabin windows in the salon allow for plenty of natural lighting. A good-running boat, with the standard 410-hp 6-71 diesels, she'll cruise around 25 knots and reach a top speed of 28–29 knots. Stretched to 42 feet in 1980, the Ocean 40 SS marked the beginning of a long series of Ocean sportfishing designs. ❏

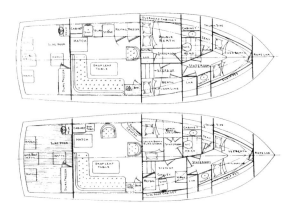

See Page 272 for Pricing Information

OCEAN 42 SUPER SPORT (EARLY)

SPECIFICATIONS

Length	42'0"	Fuel	480 gals.
Beam	14'4"	Cockpit	100 sq. ft.
Draft	3'4"	Hull Type	Modified-V
Weight	30,000#	Deadrise Aft	1.5°
Clearance	12'0"	Designer	D. Martin
Water	100 gals.	Production	1980–83

One of the best-selling Oceans ever, the 42 Super Sport is a stretched (and much-improved) version of the earlier 40 Super Sport with the additional length used to create a full 100-sq. ft. fishing cockpit. A good-looking boat with a clean-cut profile and excellent performance, her nearly flat bottom (just 1.5° of transom deadrise) provides a nice turn of speed with relatively small engines but makes for a hard ride in a chop. Oceans are noted for their attractive teak interiors, and the 42 is no exception. The standard two-stateroom layout is well arranged and suited to the needs of anglers and family cruisers alike. Additional features included a cockpit control station, tackle center, freezer, transom door, teak cockpit sole, central vacuum system, and a generator. On the downside, the engine room is a tight fit, and there's plenty of exterior teak trim to maintain. A good-running boat, the 42 SS will cruise at a fast 26 knots and reach a top speed of about 30 knots with standard 6-71 diesels. ❏

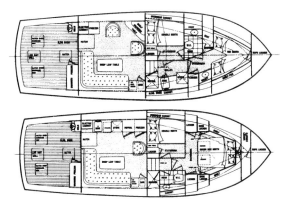

See Page 272 for Pricing Information

OCEAN 42 SUPER SPORT

SPECIFICATIONS

Length	42'0"	Fuel	466 gals.
Beam	15'0"	Cockpit	100 sq. ft.
Draft	3'7"	Hull Type	Modified-V
Weight	35,466#	Deadrise Aft	NA
Clearance	12'0"	Designer	D. Martin
Water	100 gals.	Production	1991–Current

One of the so-called "new generation" of Super Sport models, the Ocean 42 (note that an earlier Ocean 42 SS model ran from 1980–83) has a more streamlined deckhouse than earlier Ocean models together with an all-new hull design with additional transom deadrise and a shallower, slightly longer keel. Notably, most of the outside teak trim is gone. But the real story is below, where the Ocean 42 lays claim to one of the more impressive galley-up salon layouts to be found in a boat this size. It's an overused refrain, but this is a spacious floorplan. The master stateroom is very roomy, and a unique midships guest stateroom extends beneath the salon sole and includes a double and single berth. Additional features include a stylish hardtop, separate pump room below the galley sole, a huge fish box in the cockpit, and good engine access. Cat 425-hp diesels are standard in the Ocean 42 (24 knots cruise/27 knots top), and 485-hp 6-71s (26 knots cruise/30 top) are optional. ❏

OCEAN 44 SUPER SPORT

SPECIFICATIONS

Length	44'0"	Fuel	480 gals.
Beam	15'2"	Cockpit	130 sq. ft.
Draft	3'6"	Hull Type	Modified-V
Weight	36,000#	Deadrise Aft	1.5°
Clearance	13'3"	Designer	D. Martin
Water	100 gals.	Production	1985–91

The Ocean 44 Super Sport was built on a shortened 46 Super Sport hull with a restyled deck and superstructure. A popular boat (111 were built) with a particularly handsome profile, she was designed to replace the original 42 SS in 1985. With her flat bottom (1.5° transom deadrise) and narrow aftersections, the 44 is quick to accelerate but a hard ride in a chop. Below, the two-stateroom layout is arranged with the galley down from the salon. This is a notably wide-open and comfortable floorplan, and both heads have stall showers. Also notable is the more serviceable engine room in the Ocean 44—an improvement from that found in many earlier Ocean models. The large and unobstructed cockpit came standard with a tackle center, cockpit controls, washdown, a teak sole, and teak covering boards. Later models powered with the 485-hp versions of the GM 6-71s will cruise the Ocean 44 around 27 knots and reach 30+ knots top. Earlier 450-hp versions of the same engines are about a knot slower. ❏

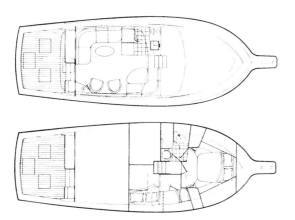

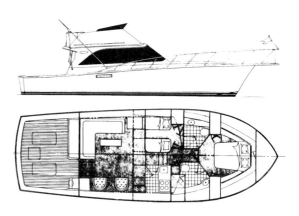

See Page 272 for Pricing Information   **See Page 272 for Pricing Information**

OCEAN 46 SUPER SPORT

SPECIFICATIONS

Length	46'0"	Fuel	580 gals.
Beam	15'2"	Cockpit	NA
Draft	3'6"	Hull Type	Modified-V
Weight	40,000#	Deadrise Aft	1.5°
Clearance	13'3"	Designer	D. Martin
Water	150 gals.	Production	1983–85

Introduced in 1983 as a bridge between the 42 and 50 Super Sport models, the Ocean 46 is a typical Jersey-style canyon runner with a relatively flat bottom and very quick performance. For a fishing boat, the interior was considered lush (by mid-'80s standards), and the attractive teak woodwork and cabinetry and high-style decors helped make this a very popular boat. While a conventional two-stateroom layout was available, the three-stateroom floorplan with mid-level galley is an unusual find in a 46-footer. The list of standard equipment was equally impressive—teak cockpit sole and covering boards, molded-in tackle center, freezer, vacuum system, etc. Most were sold with the optional factory hardtop. Access to the engines and generator is fair. A fast boat, the 46 SS will cruise at 25 knots and reach a top speed of 29–30 knots with standard 450-hp 6-71s. Optional 475-hp 6V92s cruise at 27 knots (about 30 top). With over 160 built, the 46 SS became one of Ocean's best-selling models.❏

OCEAN 48 SUPER SPORT (1986-90)

SPECIFICATIONS

Length	48'0"	Fuel	580 gals.
Beam	15'2"	Cockpit	152 sq. ft.
Draft	3'6"	Hull Type	Modified-V
Weight	40,000#	Deadrise Aft	2°
Clearance	13'3"	Designer	D. Martin
Water	150 gals.	Production	1986–90

A best-seller for Ocean, the 48 SS was built on a stretched 46 SS hull with all-new deck and superstructure styling. She's a good-looking boat with her stylish profile and aggressive appearance, but even more notable is the fact that she can turn an honest 30 knots with standard 485-hp 6-71 diesels. That spells economy: at a hard 27-knot cruising speed, she's burning only 44–46 gph. Built on a light-weight hull with a narrow beam and 2° of transom deadrise, she's quick to accelerate but a stiff ride in a chop thanks to her flat-bottom design. Ocean 48s were offered with a very popular three-stateroom, mid-galley interior (unusual in just a 48-footer) in addition to a conventional two-stateroom, galley-down floorplan. The interior cabinetry and woodwork are varnished teak, and the array of standard equipment included cockpit controls, tackle center with freezer, teak cockpit sole, and teak covering boards. A total of 167 Ocean 48 Super Sports were built during her 5-year production run. ❏

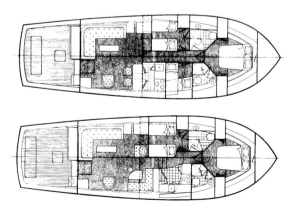

See Page 272 for Pricing Information

See Page 272 for Pricing Information

SPECIFICATIONS

Length	48'0"	Fuel	580 gals.
Beam	15'2"	Cockpit	NA
Draft	3'6"	Hull Type	Modified-V
Weight	40,000#	Deadrise Aft	2°
Clearance	13'3"	Designer	D. Martin
Water	150 gals.	Production	1991–94

The second Ocean 48 SS is basically a restyled version of the original 48 SS model (1986–90) with a more streamlined deck and superstructure, built-in hardtop with arch, less exterior teak, and a completely revised three-stateroom interior layout. The hull, tankage, power, and performance remain unchanged. The urethaned teak interior of the Ocean 48 is lush indeed and decorated with designer-style fabrics throughout. The galley is open to the salon in this floorplan, and the result is a very spacious and well-appointed living area with a built-in entertainment center and full dinette. The midships location of the master stateroom is ideal, although the deep overhead intrusion from the dinette above is discomforting. There's a double berth in the forward stateroom, and both heads are fitted with stall showers. Additional features include good engine room access and a revised cockpit layout. The 48 SS will cruise at 26–27 knots with 485-hp 6-71 diesels and reach a top speed of 30+ knots. She was replaced with an all-new 48 Convertible in 1995. ❑

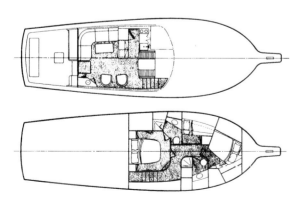

See Page 272 for Pricing Information

SPECIFICATIONS

Length	48'8"	Water	150 gals.
Beam	16'0"	Clearance	15'6"
Draft	4'2"	Hull Type	Modified-V
Weight	45,000#	Deadrise Aft	NA
Fuel, 6V92s	540 gals.	Designer	D. Martin
Fuel, 8V92s	685 gals.	Production	1995–Current

Latest in a series of 48-foot convertibles from Ocean Yachts, the new 48 Super Sport is built with a wider beam than her predecessor with a much more rakish profile (the house is carried way forward on the deck), greater bow flare, and a deeper forefoot for a softer ride in headseas. Like all Ocean yachts, the low deadrise, tapered hull shape is quick to plane and fast across the water. Inside, the plush decor of the newest 48 SS is very impressive and the spacious three-stateroom floorplan (two with walkaround queen beds) are comparable to those found in a bigger boat. The cockpit comes standard with a bait-prep station, freezer, engine controls, transom door, teak covering boards and an in-deck fishbox. Additional features include cockpit access to the engine room, modular interior construction, and a well-arranged helm console. Standard 535-hp Detroit 6V-92s will cruise at 24+ knots (28 knots top), and optional 735-hp 8V92s cruise at an honest 29–30 knots (about 33 knots top) making her one of the faster boats in her class. ❑

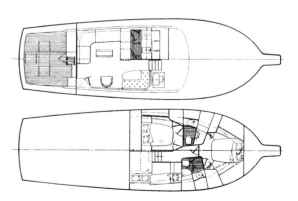

See Page 272 for Pricing Information

OCEAN 50 SUPER SPORT

SPECIFICATIONS

Length	50'0"	Fuel	750 gals.
Beam	16'0"	Cockpit	NA
Draft	4'2"	Hull Type	Modified-V
Weight	50,000#	Deadrise Aft	5°
Clearance	14'2"	Designer	D. Martin
Water	200 gals.	Production	1982–85

The Ocean 50 SS was built on a shortened 55 SS hull with balsa coring in the hullsides, a wide beam, and a flat 5° of deadrise at the transom. The result was a fast and easily powered yacht capable of a good turn of speed with standard 8V92 diesels. Unlike the earlier Ocean 55s with their see-thru front cabin windows, the windshield panels of the Ocean 50 are solid fiberglass. Below, two- and three-stateroom floorplans were offered with the two-stateroom version notable for its huge master stateroom dimensions. Both layouts feature an expansive salon with the galley down to starboard. The cockpit came standard with molded tackle centers, freezer, baitwell, transom door, and a teak sole. The engine room is entered directly from the cockpit, but access to the engines and generator is poor—a serious drawback. A hard-riding boat in a chop, the Ocean 50 SS will cruise at a brisk 25–26 knots with standard 675-hp 8V92 diesels and reach a top speed of about 29 knots. ❏

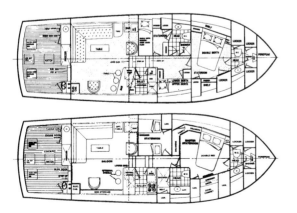

See Page 272 for Pricing Information

OCEAN 53 SUPER SPORT

SPECIFICATIONS

Length	53'0"	Fuel	860 gals.
Beam	16'4"	Cockpit	118 sq. ft.
Draft	4'4"	Hull Type	Modified-V
Weight	52,000#	Deadrise Aft	8°
Clearance	16'3"	Designer	D. Martin
Water	200 gals.	Production	1991–Current

Replacing the very popular 55 Super Sport, the 53 SS is built on an all-new Ocean hull design with a sharper entry and slightly increased transom deadrise. The hull changes make the Ocean 53 a generally better headsea boat than her predecessor with a notably dryer ride. The standard three-stateroom, galley-up layout is arranged with a midships master suite and another double berth forward. The alternate (and less popular) two-stateroom floorplan has the galley down and a dinette in the salon. While the salon dimensions are slightly smaller than the 55 SS, there's still room for a small crowd, and the upscale furnishings and teak woodwork create a very inviting atmosphere. A transom door is standard in the cockpit, and the fish box has been repositioned behind the chair for improved access to the rudder posts. Competitively priced, additional features include a factory hardtop, a well-arranged (but not overly spacious) engine room, and cockpit controls. Note the absence of exterior teak trim. A fast boat with standard 760-hp 8V92s (28 knots cruise/30 top), optional (and popular) 820-hp MANs are a couple of knots faster. ❏

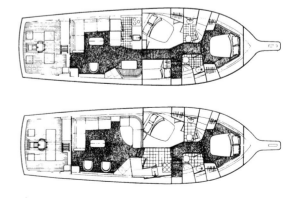

See Page 272 for Pricing Information

OCEAN 55 SUPER SPORT

OCEAN 58 SUPER SPORT

SPECIFICATIONS

Length	55'8"	Fuel	1,000 gals.
Beam	16'4"	Cockpit	130 sq. ft.
Draft	4'4"	Hull Type	Modified-V
Weight	58,000#	Deadrise Aft	4°
Clearance	14'6"	Designer	D. Martin
Water	200 gals.	Production	1981–90

The Ocean 55 Super Sport combines two essential elements of any modern tournament fisherman: speed and beauty. Her long foredeck, unbroken sheerline, and sleek cabin profile are pure Jersey-style sportfish. Inside—luxury on a grand scale. The three-stateroom layout with three heads and deckhouse galley proved more popular than the mid-level galley version with two heads and a huge salon. The 55 SS was restyled in 1986 with a new flybridge, a solid front windshield, and a black mask running around the deckhouse. The foredeck seat was also eliminated in 1986 for a more streamlined appearance. Whereas most big sportfishermen in this size range require the heavier 12-cylinder diesels to reach (or even approach) the magic 30-knot number, the Ocean 55 SS gets the job done with lighter, more efficient (and far less expensive) 8V92s. Top speed with the 735-hp versions of the 8V92s is 31 knots, and she'll cruise at a fast 27 knots. A total of 170 were built, making her the most popular big Ocean model ever. ❏

SPECIFICATIONS

Length	58'0"	Fuel	1,100 gals.
Beam	17'6"	Cockpit	131 sq. ft.
Draft	4'10"	Hull Type	Modified-V
Weight	72,215#	Deadrise Aft	NA
Clearance	14'11"	Designer	D. Martin
Water	250 gals.	Production	1990–Current

First of the so-called "new generation" Ocean yachts in 1990, the muscular 58 Super Sport is built on an efficient modified-V hull design with cored hullsides, modest deadrise at the transom, and a good deal of flare at the bow. Belowdecks, her innovative three-stateroom, three-head layout is arranged with the huge full-width master stateroom located *beneath* the raised salon sole—a giant departure from conventional convertible floorplans. Like all Ocean models, the 58 features a beautiful varnished teak interior with upscale furnishings and color-coordinated fabrics throughout. The tournament-sized cockpit features molded tackle centers, cockpit controls, teak covering boards, transom door, and direct engine room access. The flybridge is extremely large with three helm chairs and U-shaped lounge seating forward of the helm console. A factory option allows the flybridge to be fully enclosed and air conditioned. A good-running boat with plenty of eye appeal, standard 1,080-hp 12V-92 diesels (or 1,100-hp MANs) will cruise the fully loaded Ocean 58 Super Sport at a fast 29–30 knots. ❏

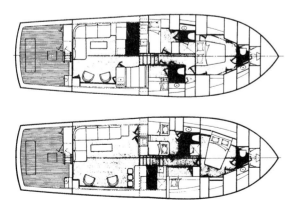

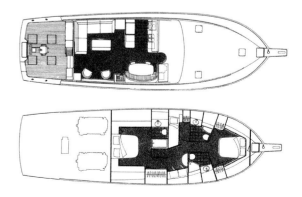

See Page 272 for Pricing Information

See Page 272 for Pricing Information

OCEAN 63 SUPER SPORT

SPECIFICATIONS

Length	63'0"	Fuel	1,200 gals.
Beam	17'8"	Cockpit	150 sq. ft.
Draft	4'8"	Hull Type	Modified-V
Weight	74,000#	Deadrise Aft	3°
Clearance	14'9"	Designer	D. Martin
Water	300 gals.	Production	1986–91

Once the largest boat in the Ocean fleet, the 63 SS was for a time one of the largest production sportfisherman built in the U.S. Constructed on a relatively lightweight flat-bottom hull with cored hullsides, the Ocean 63 is a classic Jersey-style tournament sportfisherman with an opulent interior to go with her stylish profile. Inside, the innovative floorplan is arranged with four staterooms—two extending beneath the salon sole and two others with a queen bed. An eye-catching glass-enclosed rod locker is recessed into the wall in the forward passageway. Outside, the massive flybridge and equally spacious cockpit are fitted with an impressive array of standard features. A good performer for her size, standard 900-hp 12V71s will cruise the Ocean 63 Super Sport at 25 knots (about 29 knots top). Optional 1,050-hp 12V92s will cruise around 27–28 knots with a top speed of 32 knots. During 1990–91 MAN 1,050-hp diesels were also available (28 knots cruise/32–33 knots top). A total of 32 Ocean 63s were built. ❏

OCEAN 66 SUPER SPORT

SPECIFICATIONS

Length	66'0"	Fuel	1,400 gals.
Beam	17'8"	Cockpit	135 sq. ft.
Draft	5'0"	Hull Type	Modified-V
Weight	80,000#	Deadrise Aft	3°
Clearance	18'9"	Designer	D. Martin
Water	300 gals.	Production	1993–Current

Sportfishing luxury on a grand scale describes the 66 Super Sport, the largest boat yet from Ocean Yachts. She's basically an improved (easier riding) version of the previous 63 Super Sport with a deeper forefoot, a reshaped transom, additional fuel, and a newly configured flybridge. She's built on a tapered modified-V hull with cored hullsides and a nearly flat 3° of transom deadrise. Inside, the lavish (and innovative) floorplan is arranged with the galley and dinette forward and a step up from the huge salon. There are four staterooms on the lower level with the full-beam master suite located beneath the galley. The cockpit comes with molded tackle centers, cockpit controls, in-deck fish box, and direct engine room access. Topside, the factory hardtop and built-in radar arch are standard, and the massive flybridge includes three pedestal seats, a wet bar, and lounge seating for a crowd. A good-running boat with plenty of eye appeal, standard 1,040-hp 12V-92s will cruise the Ocean 66 at 25 knots and deliver a top speed of 28–29 knots. ❏

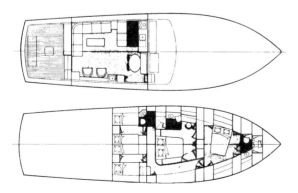

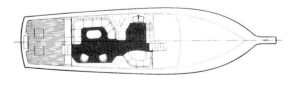

See Page 273 for Pricing Information

See Page 273 for Pricing Information

OCEAN MASTER 31 CENTER CONSOLE

SPECIFICATIONS

Length	30'7"	Fuel	300 gals.
Beam	10'3"	Cockpit	90 sq. ft.
Draft	1'4"	Hull Type	Modified-V
Hull Weight	5,140#	Deadrise Aft	16°
Clearance	NA	Designer	J. Hargrave
Water	None	Production	1975–Current

First of the big outboard-powered offshore day boats, the Ocean Master 31 is a classic center console fisherman with a production record (over 360 built) unmatched by the competition. These boats have a well-known reputation for being seriously overbuilt: the hull is laid up with 20 layers of solid fiberglass, and the inner liner is glassed directly to the stringers and hullsides. Designed for the serious angler, the deck layout boasts 90 sq. ft. of space aft of the console and 55 sq. ft. of elevated casting platform forward—enough room for four or five people to fish. Standard features include a 52-gallon livewell and an 850-gallon fish box, and an excellent non-skid cockpit surface. Note that the hard chines were reconfigured in 1993, softening amidships and running all the way to the transom for a dryer ride. In 1995 the deck was re-tooled, raising the sheer about 3" to form a deeped cockpit. Aside from the center console, a walk-around version with a small cuddy is also offered. Twin 225-hp outboards will cruise around 26 knots and reach about 40 knots top. ❑

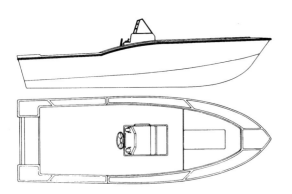

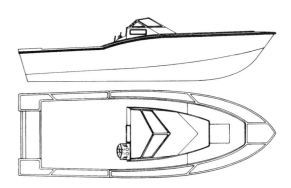

See Page 273 for Pricing Information

ORCA 36

SPECIFICATIONS

Length ....36'0"	Fuel ....500 gals.
Beam..............................13'0"	Cockpit.............................NA
Draft ....3'0"	Hull Type ....Deep-V
Weight ....15,000#	Deadrise Aft ....23°
Clearance ....17'3"	Designer.............C. Jannace
Water ....50 gals.	Production 1990–Current

The Orca 36 is a West Coast stand-up fisherman with an unconventional profile and plenty of space-age engineering. Her deep-V hull (23° deadrise aft) is fully cored with Airex, reinforced with Kevlar and carbon fiber, and vacuum bagged with vinylester resins. The unique, aerodynamically shaped marlin tower permits true 360° walkaround fishing access, and the hardtop is canted down 4° to match the boat's running angle for reduced windage. The Orca's bottom is also clean—no thru-hulls, just a sea chest in the engine room fed from the transom. There are two fish boxes in the cockpit sole, and the helm seat module rolls aft to expose the engine compartment. The interior is one of the more spacious found in a boat of this type with good headroom, an oversized head, and berths for four. A superb performer, 300-hp Cummins diesels deliver a top speed of 34 knots—hard to believe in a 36-foot boat. At a steady 25 knot cruise (16 gph) the Orca's range is around 700 miles! ❏

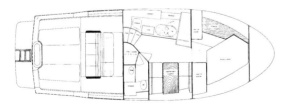

See Page 273 for Pricing Information

PACE 36 SPORTFISHERMAN

SPECIFICATIONS

Length ....36'0"	Fuel ....400 gals.
Beam..............................13'3"	Cockpit.............................NA
Draft ....2'9"	Hull Type ....Modified-V
Weight ....20,000#	Deadrise Aft ....NA
Clearance ....12'2"	Designer ....Egg Harbor
Water ....75 gals.	Production 1988–92

The classic Egg Harbor 36 Sedan (1976–85) was reborn for a time in the Pace 36 Sportfisherman. Built in Taiwan using the original molds, the relatively flat-bottom Egg Harbor hull was first used some years ago in the Pacemaker 36 (1973–80) and only later served as the platform for the Egg 36 Sedan. The Pace 36 is a good-looking boat with her traditional Jersey-style profile accented with a black wraparound deckhouse mask. Two floorplans were offered: a two-stateroom layout with the galley up, and a single-stateroom, galley-down arrangement with a much more open salon plus an island berth forward. The interior woodwork is teak, of course, and the Pace 36 uses plenty of teak trim outside as well, just like the original Egg Harbors. Crusader 454-cid gas engines were standard and will cruise the Pace 36 at 18 knots with 27 knots top. The optional 320-hp Cat diesels will cruise around 22 knots and turn 26 knots wide open. She's a good-handling boat overall but a hard ride in a chop. ❏

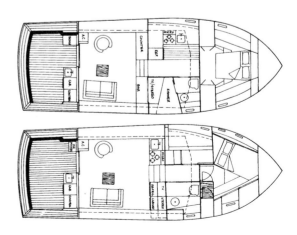

See Page 273 for Pricing Information

PACE 40 SPORTFISHERMAN

SPECIFICATIONS

Length ....40'0"	Fuel ....450 gals.
Beam.............................14'0"	Cockpit....................95 sq. ft.
Draft ....2'9"	Hull Type ....Modified-V
Weight ....28,000#	Deadrise Aft ....NA
Clearance ....NA	Designer...............D. Martin
Water ....100 gals.	Production 1988–92

The Pace 40 Sportfisherman is a re-creation of the earlier Egg Harbor 40 Sedan built from 1975 until early 1986. (The molds for five Egg Harbor designs were purchased and sent to Taiwan, where the Pace series was built by Nautique Yachts.) Aside from her solid front windshield and bold deckhouse mask, the Pace 40's styling remains very close to the original Egg Harbor 40 Sedan. The interior arrangement is also similar to that used in (later-model) Egg 40s with a mid-level galley, two staterooms below, and a single head compartment. The breakfast bar found in the original Egg 40 is eliminated in the Pace, thereby opening up the salon considerably. A generous amount of well-crafted teak cabinetry and paneling is applied throughout. The cockpit features a teak sole and covering boards, bait-prep center, and a transom door. Caterpillar 375-hp diesels will cruise around 22 knots, and the larger 485-hp 6-71s cruise about 25 knots. A handsome boat, the Pace 40 is a good reproduction of a classic Jersey-style sportfisherman. ❏

PACE 48 SPORTFISHERMAN

SPECIFICATIONS

Length ....48'2"	Fuel ....720 gals.
Beam.............................15'0"	Cockpit............................NA
Draft ....4'4"	Hull Type ....Modified-V
Weight ....40,000#	Deadrise Aft ....2°
Clearance ....NA	Designer...............D. Martin
Water ....200 gals.	Production 1987–92

Purists will recognize the familiar lines of the Pace 48 SF as those of the old Egg Harbor 48. Indeed, this is the same boat right down to the foredeck storage box and the teak cockpit, but with a new wraparound black mask and solid front windshield panels. Built in Taiwan, the original Egg Harbor molds were reworked for the new production run. Construction is identical to the earlier specifications with a solid fiberglass hull and balsa coring in the decks and superstructure. This is a narrow hull design with a fine entry and a nearly flat 2° of deadrise at the transom. Teak cabinetry is applied throughout the interior, and those who enjoy the ambience of a traditional interior will like the feel of the Pace 48's salon. The two-stateroom, two-head layout is very similar to the later-model Egg 48s. Power is 735-hp 8V92 diesels which fit nicely in the large engine room. A good-running boat, her cruising speed is an honest 26 knots, and the top speed is around 29 knots. ❏

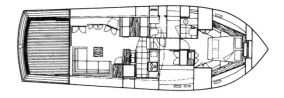

See Page 273 for Pricing Information

See Page 273 for Pricing Information

PACEMAKER 30 SPORTFISHERMAN

SPECIFICATIONS

Length	30'8"	Fuel	140 gals.
Beam	11'6"	Cockpit	80 sq. ft.
Draft	2'6"	Hull Type	Modified-V
Weight	10,000#	Deadrise Aft	NA
Clearance	9'11"	Designer	Pacemaker
Water	20 gals.	Production	1973–80

The Pacemaker 30 SF is a good-looking boat with a still-modern profile and comfortable accommodations below. She was offered with or without the lower helm station which came at the expense of one of the salon settees. Both floorplans have the galley and head aft in the salon where access from the cockpit is the most convenient. The Pacemaker 30 SF proved to be a popular design over the years due to her clean lines and affordable price. A competent sportfishing boat, her large cockpit should easily satisfy the requirements of most weekend anglers. In 1978, Pacemaker engineers combined the flybridge into the deck/cabin mold thus making the bridge an integral part of the superstructure. Standard 225-hp Chryslers cruise at 18–19 knots, and the top speed is around 27 knots. Note that the Pacemaker 31 Convertible (introduced by the new Pacemaker Yachts in 1988 and no relation to the old Pacemaker company) uses the same Pacemaker 30 tooling but includes several modern updates and design improvements. ❏

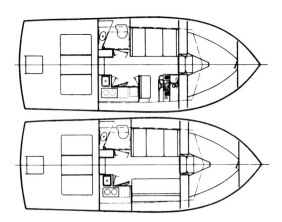

See Page 273 for Pricing Information

PACEMAKER 34 CONVERTIBLE

SPECIFICATIONS

Length	33'10"	Water	85 gals.
Beam	13'10"	Fuel	340 gals.
Draft	3'6"	Hull Type	Modified-V
Weight	15,000#	Deadrise Aft	8°
Clearance	12'0"	Designer	Pacemaker
Cockpit	75 sq. ft.	Production	1988–92

Built by the new Pacemaker company (the original firm went under in 1980), the Pacemaker 34 is built on a solid fiberglass low-deadrise hull with an exceptionally wide beam. Not surprisingly, the interior dimensions are spacious indeed, and the fact that she has a real salon is notable in just a 34-foot boat. There's also a separate dinette (not jammed into the salon) as well as a separate stall shower in the head compartment. Completely finished with teak cabinetry, doors, and woodwork, the full wraparound cabin windows provide plenty of outside natural lighting. The cockpit is too small for a fighting chair, although there's room for a couple of light-tackle anglers and their gear. Teak covering boards, washdowns, and a transom door are standard. Price-wise, the Pacemaker 34 was an inexpensive boat compared with other convertibles her size. Standard 454-cid gas engines cruise at 20–21 knots with a top speed of around 30 knots. Note that the Sportfish model is the same boat with a larger cockpit and reduced salon dimensions. ❏

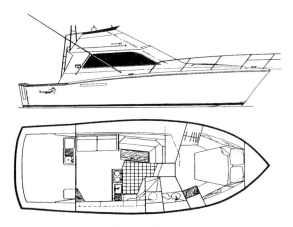

See Page 273 for Pricing Information

172

PACEMAKER 36 SPORTFISHERMAN

SPECIFICATIONS

Length	36'0"	Fuel	260 gals.
Beam	13'3"	Cockpit	80 sq. ft.
Draft	2'3"	Hull Type	Modified-V
Weight	17,100#	Deadrise Aft	NA
Clearance	12'2"	Designer	Pacemaker
Water	75 gals.	Production	1973–80

Introduced back in 1973 and enjoying a long and successful production run, the Pacemaker 36 SF has the traditional sportfish profile typical of many Jersey-style sportfishermen of the mid-1970s. Her large tournament flybridge and a roomy fishing cockpit made her a popular boat with a great many anglers over the years. Built on a low-deadrise, solid fiberglass hull with a wide beam, early models came with a standard two-stateroom floorplan with a salon galley and a stall shower in the head. A revised layout in 1976 moved the galley down and offered the option of replacing the guest stateroom with a dinette. This later floorplan results in a more open salon but eliminates the separate stall shower in the head. Either layout offers generally comfortable accommodations and adequate storage for brief trips. Several power options were offered. The standard 270-hp gas engines will run at 16–17 knots cruise and 25 knots top. Twin 350-hp Crusaders gas engines will cruise the Pacemaker 36 Sportfisherman around 17–18 knots and reach 26 knots wide open. ❏

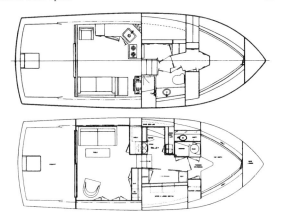

See Page 273 for Pricing Information

PACEMAKER 37 SPORTFISHERMAN

SPECIFICATIONS

Length	36'10"	Water	85 gals.
Beam	14'0"	Fuel	450 gals.
Draft	3'8"	Hull Type	Modified-V
Weight	22,000#	Deadrise Aft	8°
Clearance	16'6"	Designer	Pacemaker
Cockpit	110 sq. ft.	Production	1990–92

Introduced in 1988 by the new Pacemaker company (now deceased), the 37 SF is a classic Jersey-style sportfisherman with conservative lines and the traditional Pacemaker profile. She was available in two versions: the Sportfisherman (pictured above) came out in 1990 with a huge cockpit, optional front windshield, and standard hardtop; and the original Convertible model with a smaller cockpit, increased interior dimensions, and standard front cabin windshield. The oversize cockpit of the SF—one of the largest in her class—mandates a rather small interior for a boat of this size. Several floorplans were offered, and the factory was able to accommodate those seeking semi-custom layouts. The interior is finished out with teak woodwork and cabinetry, and there's a big fish box in the cockpit along with molded tackle centers and a transom door. Standard 454-cid gas engines will cruise the Pacemaker 37 SF around 19–20 knots and reach 29 knots top. Optional 450-hp Merlin diesels deliver a cruising speed of 25 knots and 29 knots wide open. ❏

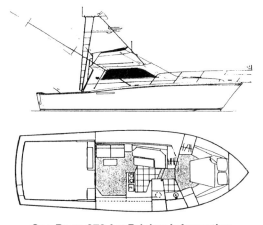

See Page 273 for Pricing Information

173

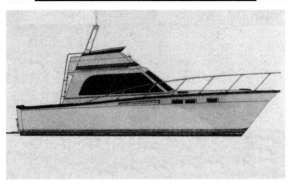

SPECIFICATIONS

LOA	41'11"	Cockpit	80 sq. ft.
Hull Length	38'5"	Water	150 gals.
Beam	14'5"	Fuel	512 gals.
Draft	3'6"	Hull Type	Modified-V
Weight	21,639#	Deadrise Aft	9°
Clearance	12'9"	Production	1979–80

A good-looking fisherman with a still-modern profile, the Pacemaker 38 was the last boat introduced by Pacemaker before the company went under in 1980. (Note that the molds were later used by Egg Harbor in the production of their 37 and 41 SF models.) Constructed on a solid fiberglass, low-deadrise hull with a comparitively wide beam, the 38 SF came with a standard two-stateroom floorplan with the galley and dinette up. This was a very open layout for a boat this size, and the large wraparound cabin windows provide excellent outside visibility. Teak woodwork is used throughout the interior, and the head compartment includes a stall shower. Outside, the cockpit features a teak sole and covering boards in addition to under-gunnel rod storage, a transom door, and room for a full-size fighting chair. The small flybridge has the controls well aft for an unobstructed view of the cockpit. Standard 350-hp gas engines will cruise the Pacemaker 38 SF at 18 knots and reach a top speed of about 28 knots. ❑

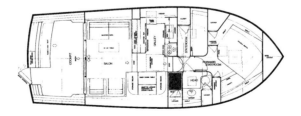

See Page 273 for Pricing Information

SPECIFICATIONS

Length	39'11"	Fuel, Std	260 gals.
Beam	13'10"	Fuel, Opt	330 gals.
Draft	2'8"	Cockpit	NA
Weight	20,098#	Hull Type	Modified-V
Clearance	12'3"	Deadrise Aft	8°
Water	69 gals.	Production	1973–79

With her classic sportfish styling and an aggressive profile, the Pacemaker 40 SF has the appearance of a much larger boat. She's built on a solid fiberglass hull with shallow deadrise aft and moderate beam—the same hull used for the Pacemaker 40 MY. Typical of most Jersey-style boats, the Pacemaker 40 has a flared bow and a notably attractive sheer. Two basic floorplans were offered: a two-stateroom layout (very popular), and a single-stateroom version with a dinette replacing the guest cabin. The galley is down in both arrangements, and the head has a shower stall. The engine room is small enough when equipped with the standard gas engines but becomes too small with diesels. Topside, the tournament-style flybridge offers an excellent view of the cockpit where a full-size fighting chair can easily be installed. Even with the optional 330-gallon fuel capacity, the cruising range is limited for a sportfisherman. GM 6-71s (325-hp) will cruise the Pacemaker 40 SF around 22 knots with a top speed of 24–25 knots. ❏

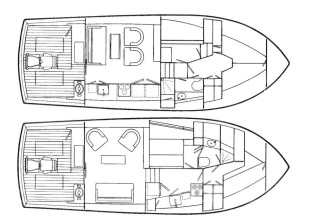

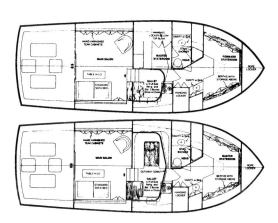

See Page 273 for Pricing Information

175

FISHING ADVENTURE IN EVERY ISSUE!

Join the thousands of other smart anglers who find new and better ways to help them catch and release salt water fish, every month in America's #1 sport fishing magazine!

Inside each jam-packed issue, you'll find accurate and up-to-date information on fishing trends, techniques and destinations, both local and international, written by our award-winning editorial staff of experienced fishermen. Each exciting issue reviews offshore and inshore fishing boats, high-tech marine electronics, innovative tackle, engines and other new products that today's sport fishermen demand. All this has made *Salt Water Sportsman* the **Fishing Authority for 56 Years**!

Subscribe to *Salt Water Sportsman* NOW and SAVE UP TO 53%! Mail this coupon or call toll-free: **1-800-238-4455**

SAVINGS CERTIFICATE

YES, I want to receive *Salt Water Sportsman* every month and save on every issue!
Check one:

☐ One year for $24.95
-Save 30%

☐ Two years for $38.95
-Save 45%

☐ Three years for $49.95
-Save 53%

☐ Payment enclosed   ☐ Bill me later

Name _____

Address _____

City _____ State _____ Zip _____

Outside U.S. add $10 postage. U.S. funds only.
Mail to: Salt Water Sportsman• P.O. Box 11357 Des Moines, IA 50347-1357

PACEMAKER 48 SPORTFISHERMAN

SPECIFICATIONS

Length	48'4"	Fuel	610/700/880 gals.
Beam	14'11"	Cockpit	105 sq. ft.
Draft	3'10"	Hull Type	Modified-V
Weight	40,000#	Deadrise Aft	NA
Clearance	NA	Designer	Pacemaker
Water	155 gals.	Production	1971–1980

The largest sportfishing model ever built by Pacemaker (and by far the best looking), the Pacemaker 48 SF was also one of the first boats to offer the new GM 8V92TI diesels as an option back in 1978. A pure tournament machine in all that the name implies, the 48 is a big boat designed for serious deepwater pursuits. Construction is solid fiberglass, and the long foredeck and sweeping sheer mark her as a classic East Coast fisherman. Two interior arrangements were available: a galley-down layout with two staterooms, or a galley-up version with three staterooms. Outside, the large and uncluttered fishing cockpit came with a teak sole and covering boards, a standard transom door, and molded tackle centers. The flybridge was restyled in 1976, and the fuel was increased to 880 gallons in 1978. Most Pacemaker 48s were powered with 425-hp 8V71s and cruise at 19–20 knots (23 top). Later models equipped with the 8V92TIs are capable of 24-knot cruising speeds and around 26–27 knots wide open. ❏

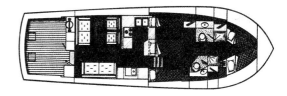

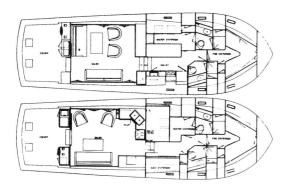

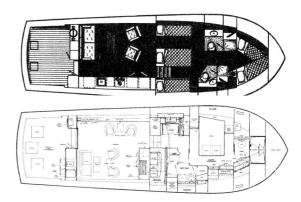

See Page 273 for Pricing Information

PACIFICA 36 SPORTFISHERMAN

SPECIFICATIONS

Length	36'0"	Fuel	300 gals.
Beam	13'0"	Cockpit	83 sq. ft.
Draft	3'4"	Hull Type	Modified-V
Weight	16,000#	Deadrise Aft	12°
Clearance	NA	Designer	John Norek
Water	90 gals.	Production	1974–92

A handsome boat with a distinctive profile, the Pacifica 36 is a limited-production sportfisherman designed for serious anglers. She's constructed on a modified-V hull form with a relatively deep keel for stability and generous flare at the bow. The Pacifica 36 is primarily aimed at the West Coast market and features wide sidedecks and a forward helm console on the flybridge (an East Coast, tournament-style flybridge was available). The cockpit—with just over 80 sq. ft. of usable space—isn't large compared to others in her class. Inside, the Pacifica 36 can sleep six with the salon dinette and settee converted. V-berths are located in the stateroom, and the split head features a huge shower to starboard. A lower helm was standard, and the interior is finished with laminate countertops and teak trim. At 16,000 pounds, the Pacifica 36 SF is a light boat, and her performance with 375-hp Cat diesels (26 knots cruise/30 knots top) is impressive. About 25 of these boats were built during her production run. ❑

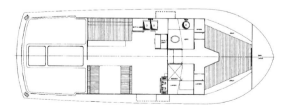

See Page 273 for Pricing Information

PACIFICA 44 SPORTFISHERMAN

SPECIFICATIONS

Length	44'0"	Fuel	650/750 gals.
Beam	15'0"	Cockpit	148 sq. ft.
Draft	4'2"	Hull Type	Modified-V
Weight	33,000#	Deadrise Aft	11°
Clearance	NA	Production	1970–92
Water	120 gals.		1995-Current

The Pacifica 44 SF has been in production for two decades without undergoing any significant design changes—a remarkable testament to her popularity among West Coast sportfishermen. She's never been a high-production model (about 65 have been sold), but the 44 remains Pacifica's most popular boat ever. Built on a modified-V hull with a wide beam and considerable flare at the bow, the 44 is notable for her huge fishing cockpit and rugged construction. Her interior consists of two staterooms (each with a double bed), two heads, and a handy midships lounge in the companionway that converts to over/under berths. Note that in 1995, a new Pacifica 44 was introduced with the same hull but an all-new superstructure and layout. As is the case with many West Coast sportfishermen, the wide sidedecks result in a salon of limited dimensions. A good performer, many were equipped with the 435-hp 8V71 diesels which cruise at 22–23 knots and reach 26 knots top. The larger 550-hp 6V92s will cruise around 26 knots and turn 30 wide open. ❑

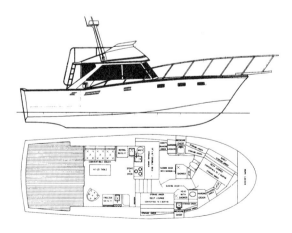

See Page 274 for Pricing Information

179

Why should you consider shopping through a member of the
FLORIDA YACHT BROKERS ASSOCIATION?

**Each member has agreed to uphold a Code of Ethics to treat YOU,
the customer, fairly and honestly.
These are people who know their business…people you can count on.**

2 Hulls
Adventure Yacht Sales, Inc.
Alexander Yachts
Alexander Yachts, Inc.
Allied Marine Group
Altech Yachts Inc.
American Show Boats, Ltd., Inc.
Ameriship Corp.
Aqua Marine International, Inc.
Ardell Yacht & Ship Brokers
Atlantic Pacific Sailing Yachts
Atlantic Yacht & Ship
Aventura Yacht Charters & Sales
Bain Yacht Sales, Inc.
Bartram & Brakenhoff, Inc.
Bob Anslow Yacht Sales
Boger & Associates
Bollman Yachts
Boston Yacht Sales, Inc.
Bradford International
Burger Yacht Sales
Camper & Nicholson
Capt. Jack's Yacht Brokerage, Inc.
Card Sound Yachts, Inc.
Caretaker Yacht Sales
Carson Yacht Brokerage, Inc.
Castlemain ,Inc.
Castonguay Associates
Catamaran Sales, Inc.
Charles Morgan Associates
Charles P. Irwin Yacht Brokerage
Cliff Argue Yacht & Aircraft Sales
Coastal Marina Development, Inc.
Coconut Grove Yacht Sales
Colonial Yacht Brokerage, Inc.
Corporate Yacht Brokerage, Inc.
Cozy Cove Marina, Inc.
Dave D'Onofrio Yacht Sales, Inc.
David Lowe's Boatyard, Inc.
Daytona Marina and Boat Works
DYB Charters Inc. & Yacht Sales
East West Yachts, Inc.
First Coast Yacht Sales, Inc.
Florida Yacht Charters & Sales, Inc.
Florida Yacht Connection
Fraser Yacht Sales
Fredericks/Power & Sail

GDB Yachts
Gilman Yacht Sales, Inc.
Gulf Air Boats, Inc.
H & H Yacht Sales, Inc.
Hal Jones & Company
Helms, Kelly, MacMahon Int'l Yachting
Herb Phillips Yacht Sales, Inc.
Hidden Harbor Marine
High-Tech Yacht & Ship, Inc.
HMY Yacht Sales, Inc.
Hoffmann Yacht Sales,Inc.
Homestead Boat & Yacht Sales
Int'l Yachting Services of Naples, Inc.
Interyacht, Inc.
Jackson Marine Sales, Inc.
Jacksonville Beach Yacht Sales
John G. Alden of Boston, Inc.
Jordan Yacht & Ship Co.
J. Woods Marine Group
Luke Brown & Associates
Luxury Yacht Corp.
Mares
Marine Group, Inc.
Marine Unlimited
Melvin B. Gaines Yacht Brokerage, Inc.
Merle Wood & Associates, Inc.
Merrill-Stevens Yacht Sales
Merritt Boat & Engine Works
Mitchell's Yacht Brokerage
Monterey Marine Yacht Sales
Naples Yacht Brokerage
Nautor's Swan
Nautor's Swan Southeast
NI'O Yacht Group
Northrop & Johnson, Inc.
Northside Marine Sales, Inc.
Odyssey III Ltd.
Offer & Associates
Offshore Yacht Brokers
Ortega Yacht Sales
Oviatt Marine, Inc.
O'Brien Yacht Sales, Inc.
Palm Beach Yacht Brokerage, Inc.
Parrot & Herst Yacht & Ship Sales
Parrot, Elfenbein & O'Brien
Perdue Dean Co., Inc.
Peter Kehoe & Associates

Pilot Yacht Sales
Pilot Yachts
Regatta Pointe Yacht Sales, Inc.
Rhodes Yacht Brokers, Inc.
Richard Bertram, Inc.
Riverbend Marina
Robert Dean & Associates Yacht Brokerage
Roger Hansen Yacht Sales
Royce Yacht & Ship Brokers, Inc.
R.J.W. Moran Yacht & Ship, Inc.
Safe Harbour Marina
Sandy Hatton Yacht Sales, Inc.
Sarasota Yacht & Ship Services
Sea Lake Yacht Sales
Sea Ray Port Jacksonville
Seafarer Brokerage, Inc.
South Florida Boat Mart, Inc.
South Florida Marine Liquidators
Starboard Yacht Brokerage, Inc.
Starboard Yacht Sales & Service, Inc.
Stuart Cay Marina
St. Augustine Yacht Center, Inc.
St. Petersburg Yacht Charters & Sales, Inc.
Summerfield Yacht Sales, Inc.
Sustendal & Co.
The Moorings Yacht Brokerage
The Shaw's Yacht Brokerage & Marine Supply, Inc.
The William F. Nelson Co.
The Yacht Broker Marine Group
United /Derecktor Gunnell Yachts
Walsh Yachts, Inc.
Waterline Yacht Brokerage
Webster Associates
West Florida Yachts, Inc.
Whitney's Sailcenter, Inc.
Woods & Oviatt, Inc.
Yacht Perfection, Inc.
Yacht Search, Inc.
Yachtco International
Yacht-Eng Yacht Sales & Brokerage

Just look for the logo

FLORIDA YACHT BROKERS ASSOCIATION
P.O. Box 6524, Station 9 • Fort Lauderdale, FL 33316 • 305-522-9270 • Fax 305-764-0697

PHOENIX 29 CONVERTIBLE

SPECIFICATIONS

Length	28'10"	Fuel	160/260 gals.
Beam	10'0"	Cockpit	75 sq. ft.
Draft	2'4"	Hull Type	Deep-V
Weight	8,500#	Deadrise Aft	21°
Clearance	9'6"	Designer	Jim Wynne
Water	50 gals.	Production	1977–87

The Phoenix 29 Convertible had a long and successful production run before being replaced with an all-new model in 1988. Over 750 were built, and during that time she earned the respect of many anglers and cruisers for her clean styling and durable construction. She has a surprisingly large interior for a boat of her size and type. There's plenty of elbow room throughout the cabin, and both the head and galley are conveniently located just inside the salon door. Berths are provided for four adults and two kids. Topside, a bench seat on the small flybridge will seat three. The cockpit is free of obstructions and well-designed for fishing. Because of her recessed prop pockets, shaft angles are significantly reduced allowing her to run in reasonably shallow waters. On the downside, some consider the Phoenix 29 to be a bit tender. Several engine choices were offered over the years. The popular 124-hp Volvo diesels will cruise efficiently at 18 knots and turn 22 knots top. Later models with the 165-hp Volvos cruise at 20–21 knots. ❑

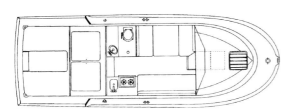

See Page 274 for Pricing Information

PHOENIX 29 SF CONVERTIBLE

SPECIFICATIONS

Length	31'11"	Fuel	180/300 gals.
Beam	10'0"	Cockpit	75 sq. ft.
Draft	2'4"	Hull Type	Deep-V
Weight	9,450#	Deadrise Aft	22°
Clearance	9'6"	Designer	Jim Wynne
Water	50 gals.	Production	1988–Current

The Phoenix 29 SF is an updated and restyled version of the original Phoenix 29 (1977–87). She replaces the straightforward and businesslike profile of her predecessor with the aggressive lines of the larger Phoenix 33 Convertible. Indeed, the oversized flybridge seems almost too large for a 29-footer. Phoenix has introduced a number of desirable features in this model including a transom door, molded pulpit, aluminum rails, and a revamped and updated interior layout with berths for six. Stoutly built, the all-new hull features a slightly wider beam at the waterline, a redesigned entry, and extra strakes for improved lift and stability. Like the 29 Convertible, the absence of a forward stateroom bulkhead results in a more open interior. Borrowing again from the 33 Convertible, a unique air duct system is used to rid the cockpit of exhaust fumes while underway. Standard 350-cid gas engines will cruise about 22 knots (30 knots top). Optional 200-hp Volvo diesels cruise about 25 knots (30 knots top), and the newer Volvo 225-hp diesels cruise at 27 knots (32 top). ❑

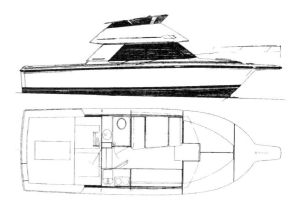

See Page 274 for Pricing Information

181

PHOENIX 33/34 CONVERTIBLE

SPECIFICATIONS

Length	33'9"	Fuel	300 gals.
Beam	13'0"	Cockpit	114 sq. ft.
Draft	2'9"	Hull Type	Deep-V
Weight, Dsl	23,600#	Deadrise Aft	17°
Clearance	10'9"	Designer	Jim Wynne
Water	70 gals.	Production	1987–Current

Well-built and realistically priced, the Phoenix 33 Convertible (note that she's been re-named the 34 Convertible for 1995) is loaded with the kind of features sure to please hard-core anglers and cruisers alike. She's a good-looking boat with a huge flybridge and a notably aggressive profile. Construction is solid fiberglass, and she rides on a beamy deep-V hull with prop pockets and a full-length inner liner. Underway, a unique vent ducting system directs fresh air into the cockpit to disperse fumes that might collect in that area. The stylish decor is impressive, with berths for six and several thoughtful design features. In 1991, Phoenix introduced the SFX model with a larger salon (but no stall shower), berths for four, and a revised helm console with additional room for flush-mounting electronics. Engine boxes make access to the motors easy, and the cockpit has a transom door, in-deck storage, and washdowns as standard. Standard 454-cid gas engines cruise the Phoenix 33/34 at 19 knots and reach a top speed of 30. The optional 435-hp Cats cruise around 26 knots. ❏

PHOENIX 33/34 TOURNAMENT

SPECIFICATIONS

Length	33'9"	Fuel, Std	300 gals.
Beam	13'0"	Fuel, Opt	400 gals.
Draft	2'9"	Cockpit	114 sq. ft.
Weight	20,520#	Hull Type	Deep-V
Clearance	8'4"	Deadrise Aft	17°
Water	70 gals.	Production	1990–Current

The Phoenix 33 Tournament (called the 34 Tournament beginning in 1995) is a good-looking express with a low profile and a large, unobstructed fishing cockpit. She's built on the same hull as the 33 Convertible—a rugged deep-V with a full inner liner and recessed prop pockets. The single-level cockpit of the 33/34 is arranged with a dinette/lounge opposite the helm, bait and tackle centers, and lockable rod storage. The engine boxes double as convenient bait-watching seats. Additional cockpit features include an in-deck fish box, seawater washdown, excellent non-skid, and a transom door with gate. (A reinforcing plate is provided in the cockpit sole for the installation of a mounted chair.) Below, the small (but very upscale) cabin can be fitted with an island berth or V-berths. While 454-cid gas engines are standard, most anglers will likely go for one of the several diesel options available. The popular 375-hp Cats cruise at 26–27 knots (30 knots top), and the newer 412-hp Cats will cruise at a fast 28 knots and reach 32 knots wide open. ❏

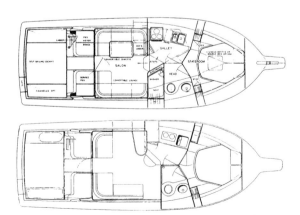

See Page 274 for Pricing Information

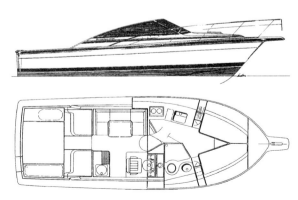

See Page 274 for Pricing Information

PHOENIX 37/38 CONVERTIBLE

SPECIFICATIONS

Length	37'10"	Fuel	440 gals.
Beam	14'0"	Cockpit	93 sq. ft.
Draft	3'7"	Hull Type	Modified-V
Weight	30,800#	Deadrise	18°
Clearance	12'7"	Designer	Jim Wynne
Water	110 gals.	Production	1989–Current

Bold styling and rugged construction characterize the 378 Convertible, currently the largest boat in the Phoenix fleet. (Note that she was called the Phoenix 37 until 1995.) She's built on basically the same hull as the earlier Phoenix 38 with a full inner liner, prop pockets, and a steep 18° of deadrise at the transom. New features include a molded pulpit, enlarged salon dimensions, a revised flybridge profile, and recessed trim tabs. Her two-stateroom, galley-up interior is arranged with an island berth forward and stacked single berths in the guest stateroom. Teak or white ash interior woodwork is offered, and a glassed-over deckhouse windshield is optional. With her large and uncluttered cockpit, the 37/38 is designed to meet the needs of serious fishermen. A transom door is standard along with a molded tackle center, livewell, rod storage, and two in-deck fish boxes. With the optional 375-hp Cat diesels, the Phoenix 37 will cruise at 22–23 knots and reach a top speed of 26 knots. The 485-hp 6-71s will cruise around 26–27 knots and turn 30 knots top. ❏

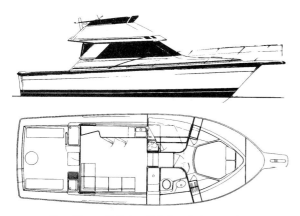

See Page 274 for Pricing Information

PHOENIX 38 CONVERTIBLE

SPECIFICATIONS

Length	38'0"	Fuel	400 gals.
Beam	14'0"	Cockpit	NA
Draft	3'7"	Hull Type	Deep-V
Weight	25,000#	Deadrise Aft	18°
Clearance	12'1"	Designer	Jim Wynne
Water	100 gals.	Production	1982–88

A good-looking fisherman with a huge cockpit to go with her aggressive profile, the Phoenix 38 is built on a solid fiberglass deep-V hull with a wide beam, a full-length inner liner, and prop pockets. Note that the salon's aft bulkhead is angled to improve the flow of fresh air in the cockpit while underway. Inside, one is immediately confronted with one of the smallest salons seen in a boat this size—a genuine drawback in an otherwise competent design. Her wide sidedecks, roomy cockpit, and excellent bridge layout make the Phoenix 38 a comfortable boat to fish. Engine room access is via a hatch in the cockpit—an innovative approach in a 38-foot boat, but the engine room is a tight fit. (Interestingly, this is the smallest production boat with a cockpit engine room door.) A solid front windshield became optional in 1988. The 375-hp Cats cruise at 20 knots and reach 24 at the top. The optional 450-hp 6-71s cruise the Phoenix 38 about 23 knots and reach 26 knots wide open. ❏

See Page 275 for Pricing Information

SOME NAMEPLATES COMMAND BIG BUCKS,

OTHERS COMMAND RESPECT.

38 Years of Uninterrupted Production
Says A Lot About A Company

...especially one in the boating business. Stable, reputable, well-managed and quality-minded are the traits most often attributed to Post Marine—the small New Jersey builder with the big reputation for quality.

Post has earned the trust and loyalty of a very select fraternity of seasoned skippers who recognize and appreciate those subtleties that often separate the truly fine yachts from the good ones. It is our owners who continue to perpetuate the Post reputation.

We now invite you to discover The Post Difference. We invite you to take the helm of a new Post *43, 46 or 50, and discover for yourself why Post remains one of the most revered nameplates in yachting today.

For further details,
and the name of your nearest dealer,
call Post Marine at 609-625-2434.

* Because of considerable refinements in both hull design and weight distribution, our '95 models feature the best performance and handling characteristics (in all conditions including following seas) of any previous model year. To arrange a sea trial, call Post Marine or your nearest dealer.

POST 42 SPORTFISHERMAN

SPECIFICATIONS

Length ....42'0"	Fuel.................460/500 gals.
Beam..............................15'9"	Cockpit..................115 sq. ft.
Draft ....3'0"	Hull Type ....Modified-V
Weight ....30,000#	Deadrise Aft ....2°
Clearance ....12'6"	Designer............Russel Post
Water ....120 gals.	Production 1975–83

With over 230 built, the 42 SF remains the best-selling Post ever. She was introduced in 1975 as a replacement for the all-wood Post 40, and she shares her predecessor's striking Jersey-style profile. As a fishing platform, most tournament veterans rank the Post 42 among the best of the mid-range sportfishermen. Her flat aftersections and flared bow produce a relatively dry boat with good lift and speed. The glassed-over deckhouse windshield seen in later models first became available in 1979. Inside, somewhat dated mahogany woodwork was standard (a teak interior became optional in 1979), and the salon appears larger than the dimensions suggest. Her two-stateroom layout has the master stateroom located amidships and stacked single berths in the forward stateroom. Always built on a solid fiberglass hull, the Post 42 was constructed with a glass-over-wood deck and superstructure until mid-1976. Nearly all were delivered with 310-hp 6-71N diesels (18–19 knots cruise/22 knots wide open) or 410-hp 6-71s (22–23 knots cruise/26 knots top). ❑

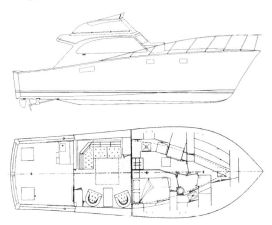

See Page 275 for Pricing Information

POST 43 SPORTFISHERMAN (EARLY)

SPECIFICATIONS

Length ....43'8"	Fuel.................500/550 gals.
Beam..............................15'9"	Cockpit..................125 sq. ft.
Draft ....3'6"	Hull Type ....Modified-V
Weight ....33,000#	Deadrise Aft...............2°/7°
Clearance ....13'7"	Designer.......W. Nickerson
Water ....120 gals.	Production 1984–89

The Post 43 is a revised and updated version of the classic Post 42 Sportfisherman. Introduced in 1984, the 43 underwent significant design changes for 1989 when she became the 43 II. Featuring a redesigned bottom with a deeper forefoot and increased transom deadrise (for a measurably improved ride), the Post 43 II also received a revised flybridge layout, more fuel, and a molded-in tackle center. The previously optional solid front windshield became standard, and a second sprayrail was added for improved lift and a dryer ride. Her two-stateroom interior is a blend of traditional teak woodwork and decorator fabrics. The cockpit is very large and includes a bait freezer, teak covering boards, a transom door, and two in-deck fish boxes. The bridge ladder is stepped on the tackle center and leads through a (small) opening in the flybridge overhang—a Post trademark. Twin 485-hp 6-71s will cruise the Post 43 around 25 knots with a top speed of 28 knots. The optional 550-hp 6V92s cruise at a fast 27 knots (31 knots wide open). ❑

See Page 275 for Pricing Information

185

POST 43 SPORTFISHERMAN

SPECIFICATIONS

Length	43'9"	Clearance	13'7"
Beam	15'9"	Cockpit	NA
Draft	3'6"	Hull Type	Modified-V
Weight	40,000#	Deadrise Aft	7°
Fuel	543 gals.	Designer	Post
Water	120 gals.	Production	1995–Current

The new Post 43 (an earlier version ran from 1984 to 1989) uses the same modified-V hull and superstructure as the Post 44, the boat she replaced in 1995, but with several notable improvements. Instead of two head compartments, the 43 has only a single large head, and the extra space allows the salon to be opened up to the point where a laundry center and deckhouse-level dinette have been added to the floorplan. The abundant teak joinerwork, quality appliances and upscale decor are impressive and typical of past Post interiors. There are improvements in the engine room as well. Traditionally, Post models built on this hull have had compact engine rooms, but by locating the fuel tanks aft (rather than between the engines) the headroom is significantly increased and serviceability enhanced. Additional features of the Post 43 include cockpit access to the engine room, a superb helm console, excellent storage and — in the cockpit — two in-deck fishboxes and a transom door. A fast ride with optional 535-hp 6V-92s, she'll cruise at 28 knots and reach a top speed of 31–32 knots. ❏

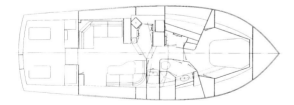

See Page 275 for Pricing Information

POST 44 SPORTFISHERMAN

SPECIFICATIONS

Length	43'9"	Fuel	570 gals.
Beam	15'9"	Cockpit	125 sq. ft.
Draft	3'6"	Hull Type	Modified-V
Weight	33,000#	Deadrise Aft	7°
Clearance	13'7"	Designer	W. Nickerson
Water	120 gals.	Production	1990–94

The profile of the Post 44 is virtually identical to that of the 43 II model, the boat she replaced in 1990. Indeed, both are built on the same hull, and the cockpit dimensions and bridge layout are identical. But where the Post 43 II has a two-stateroom, galley-down layout, the newer 44 has a two-stateroom, two-head floorplan with a smaller salon and a mid-level galley. While the actual salon dimensions of the Post 44 are about average, the meticulous woodwork and upscale decor are characteristic of Post's elegant teak interiors. Built for the serious angler, the cockpit has a molded tackle center, two in-deck fish boxes, transom door, and teak covering boards. The helm console and flybridge layout are state of the art. On the downside, the engine room is rather a tight fit and there isn't much headroom. (Note that cockpit engine room access was added beginning with the 1992 models.) A limited-production boat, only a few Post 44s were built every year, and most had the optional 550-hp 6V92s. She'll cruise at a fast 27–28 knots and deliver a top speed of 31 knots. ❏

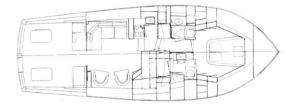

See Page 275 for Pricing Information

POST 46 SPORTFISHERMAN

SPECIFICATIONS

Length	46'9"	Fuel	635 gals.
Beam	15'9"	Cockpit	NA
Draft	3'6"	Hull Type	Modified-V
Weight	44,000#	Deadrise Aft	2°/7°
Clearance	13'7"	Designer	W. Nickerson
Water	120 gals.	Production	1978–Current

The Post 46 was introduced in 1978 as a stretched version of the popular Post 42. Hull construction is solid fiberglass, and her tapered form and low deadrise hull resulted in a boat that's quick to accelerate and fast over the water. Originally built with a galley-down floorplan with the master suite amidships, a new and more open mid-galley layout in 1985 moved the owner's stateroom forward and placed the dinette in the salon—a popular arrangement that lasted until 1995 when new floorplans became available. In 1988, the Post 46's hull was redesigned with slightly increased transom deadrise and a deeper forefoot for a better headsea and following sea performance. Cockpit access to the engine room became standard in 1992, and in 1995 a much-improved stand-up engine room resulted from moving the fuel tanks aft. A well-regarded boat with a strong East Coast following, used models are nearly always in demand. With the now-standard 535-hp 6V92s, she'll cruise around 27 knots (30 knots wide open). Earlier models with 450-hp 6-71s will cruise at 23 knots (about 27 knots top). ❏

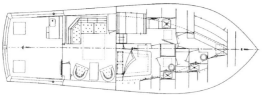

Galley & Dinette Down, Owner Amidships (1978–84)

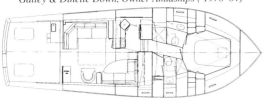

Mid-Galley, Owner Forward (1985–94)

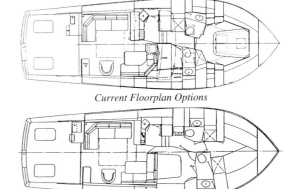

Current Floorplan Options

See Page 275 for Pricing Information

SPECIFICATIONS

Length ....50'7"	Fuel ....850 gals.
Beam............................16'11"	Cockpit.................147 sq. ft.
Draft ....4'0"	Hull Type ....Modified-V
Weight ....49,000#	Deadrise Aft ....8°
Clearance ....13'10"	Designer........W. Nickerson
Water ....240 gals.	Production 1989–Current

A great-looking boat with her long foredeck and sexy profile, the Post 50 combines the elegance of a yacht-style interior with the brute force of a well-bred offshore fishing machine. She's built on a low-deadrise modified-V hull with cored hullsides and a solid glass bottom. Note that unlike other Post designs, the hull is not tapered at the transom. The original three-stateroom, galley-down floorplan is unique in a convertible of this size (most three-stateroom 50' convertibles have the galley up), and a new mid-galley floorplan in 1995 moved the owner's stateroom aft. As usual, the interior woodwork and detailing are finished to high standards, and the stylish decor is very impressive. The huge cockpit comes with a full array of fishing gear including a molded tackle center, cockpit controls, transom door, and access to the engine room (where headroom was improved dramatically in 1995 when the fuel tanks were moved aft). Performance with standard 735-hp 8V92s is excellent—29 knots at cruise and 33 knots wide open. Optional 820-hp MANs boost the cruising speed to a *very* fast 32–33 knots (about 37 knots top). ❑

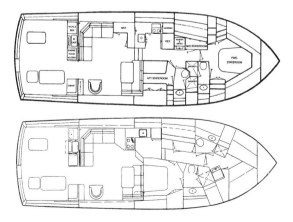

See Page 275 for Pricing Information

SPECIFICATIONS

Length w/Pulpit..........29'7"	Water ....22 gals.
Hull Length ....28'0"	Fuel ....204 gals.
Beam.............................10'0"	Waste ....25 gals.
Draft ....2'9"	Hull Type ....Modified-V
Weight ....7,900#	Deadrise Aft ....16°
Clearance ....8'3"	Production 1992–94

The Precision 2800 has that aggressive, low-slung profile that experienced anglers have come to associate with good fishing platforms. A light boat at just 7,900 pounds, her solid fiberglass hull is designed with a well-flared bow, shallow 6-foot keel, and a relatively steep 16° of deadrise at the transom. Note the absence of front windows in the house. The cabin sole is a step down from the cockpit level, and engine boxes flank the entryway. Inside, there are accommodations for four with V-berths forward and a convertible dinette opposite the galley. Outside, the roomy cockpit is arranged with two in-deck fish boxes along with padded coamings, washdowns, and a transom door. A helm and companion seat are fitted on the flybridge. Additional features include wide walkaround sidedecks with waist-high railings, a molded bow pulpit, and a stand-up head with shower. An efficient boat with 4-cylinder Yanmar 170-hp diesels, the Precision 2800 will cruise at 25 knots and reach a top speed of around 29–30 knots. Note that production of this boat lasted only a couple of years. ❑

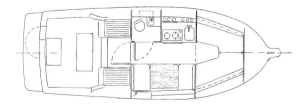

See Page 275 for Pricing Information

PRO-LINE 2950 MID-CABIN W/A

SPECIFICATIONS

Length	30'0"	Fuel	300 gals.
Beam	10'9"	Cockpit	80 sq. ft.
Hull Draft	1'10"	Hull Type	Deep-V
Hull Weight	7,500#	Deadrise Aft	19°
Clearance	6'0"	Designer	Pro-Line
Water	42 gals.	Production	1992–Current

A popular boat, the Pro-Line 2950 Mid-cabin Walkaround is one of the more affordable fishing boats in her size range. Construction is solid glass, and the wide-beam hull is packed with foam flotation. A distinguishing feature of the 2950 is her wide, deep walkaround sidedecks—the high freeboard provides unusual security, although it's a long reach over the gunwale to the water. Visibility from the raised bridgedeck is excellent, and the big 80-sq. ft. cockpit is fitted with a jump seat, in-deck fish box, rod storage, tackle drawers, and transom door. A bait-prep station is built into the transom complete with livewell and sink. Belowdecks, the cabin is arranged with V-berths, a compact galley, enclosed head and a mid-cabin berth aft. The headroom is excellent—about 6'4". Additional features include a stylish curved windshield, molded pulpit, a well-arranged helm console, and foredeck seating. A good-looking boat in spite of her no-frills construction, bracket-mounted 250-hp Yahamas will cruise the Pro-Line 2950 at an easy 28 knots and reach 40+ knots wide open. ❏

PURSUIT 2800 OPEN

SPECIFICATIONS

LOA w/Pulpit	30'4"	Water	22 gals.
Hull Length	28'2"	Fuel	290 gals.
Beam	10'0"	Cockpit	NA
Hull Draft	1'9"	Hull Type	Deep-V
Weight	5,500#	Deadrise Aft	20°
Clearance	6'9"	Production	1989–92

A stylish design with plenty of eye appeal, this outboard-powered day fisherman manages to combine excellent offshore performance with a practical cockpit layout and surprisingly spacious cabin accommodations. (While she's better known among anglers as the 2800 Open—her original name—she was also called the 2800 Express Fisherman during 1991–92.) Her deep-V hull is balsa-cored from the chines up, and the wide ten-foot beam results in a stable fishing platform easily able to handle a small tower. Her cockpit is arranged with a 5-foot in-deck fish box plus rod holders and storage under the cabin wings. An insulated cooler is built into the companion seat, and a tackle center is behind the helm seat. Note the attractive curved windshield and molded pulpit. Inside, the well-finished cabin includes berths for two in addition to a roomy galley and stand-up head compartment. The level of finish and detailing is excellent. Twin 225-hp outboards will cruise the Pursuit 2800 easily at 26 knots and deliver top speeds in the neighborhood of 38–39 knots. ❏

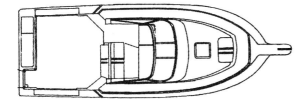

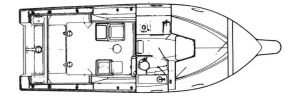

See Page 275 for Pricing Information

See Page 275 for Pricing Information

PURSUIT 2855 EXPRESS FISHERMAN

SPECIFICATIONS

Length w/Pulpit..........33'3"	Water ....30 gals.
Hull Length ....31'0"	Fuel ....300 gals.
Beam.............................10'3"	Cockpit....................57 sq. ft.
Hull Draft ....1'9"	Hull Type ....Deep-V
Weight ....6,500#	Deadrise Aft ....20°
Clearance ....8'6"	Production 1993–Current

The Pursuit 2855 Express Fisherman is a rugged offshore fisher-man whose well-designed helm and roomy cabin make her a pleasure to fish in all kinds of weather. She's a good-looking boat with her crisp styling and integrated outboard bracket, and the layout and detailing are well above average—a first-class boat from a top-quality builder. The cockpit is completely unobstructed and includes a transom door as well as a bait and tackle-rigging station in the transom bulkhead. A pair of molded fish boxes are located behind the companion seats, and the stylish helm console is wide enough for flush-mounting most necessary electronics. Belowdecks, the 2855 will sleep four (the dinette converts to a double berth, and the seat backs swing up to form pilot berths) and includes a compact galley area and a stand-up head with shower. Additional features include fairly wide sidedecks, a molded bow pulpit, balsa coring in the hull-sides and a windshield center vent. Twin 250-hp outboards will cruise the Pursuit 2855 Express at 25 knots and reach a top speed of around 38 knots. ❏

PURSUIT 3000 EXPRESS

SPECIFICATIONS

Length w/Pulpit..........31'2"	Water ....40 gals.
Hull Length ....29'1"	Cockpit 57
Beam.............................12'0"	Hull Type ....Deep-V
Draft ....2'9"	Deadrise Aft....................19°
Weight ....10,800#	Designer ....Pursuit
Fuel ....250 gals.	Production 1995–Current

A great-looking boat with a sexy, semi-custom profile, the Pursuit 3000 Express is loaded with a blend of practical fea-tures that place her among the best production designs ever built in this class. She's constructed on a solid fiberglass, deep-V hull with a relatively wide beam and a well-flared bow. The cockpit (about 60 sq. ft.) is completely unobstructed and comes with a transom door, a centerline bait station (with an above-deck live well), and a fish-box in the transom. Note that the helm is located on the centerline, and the entire bridgedeck can be hydraulically raised for engine access. There are berths for four below in the spacious cabin—two pilot berths to starboard and a double berth forward—as well as a roomy head, a backlit rod storage showcase, and a complete gal-ley. The stylish marlin tower includes a hardtop and bench seating. Standard 320-hp gas inboards will cruise at 22 knots (about 30 knots top), and optional 230-hp Volvo diesels will cruise efficiently at 26 knots (20 gph) and reach 30 knots wide open. ❏

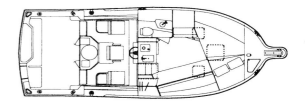

See Page 275 for Pricing Information

See Page 275 for Pricing Information

PURSUIT 3250 EXPRESS

SPECIFICATIONS

Length	33'0"	Fuel	305 gals.
Beam	12'6"	Cockpit	115 sq. ft.
Draft	2'8"	Hull Type	Modified-V
Weight	13,500#	Deadrise Aft	18°
Clearance	8'4"	Designer	L. Slikkers
Water	50 gals.	Production	1990–93

Largest of the Pursuit series of offshore fishermen, the 3250 (note that she was called the Pursuit 3300 Express in 1993) is an upscale canyon runner designed to appeal to well-heeled anglers with a taste for quality. She's built on a reworked version of the popular 3300 hull—a deep-V design with a wide beam and balsa coring in the hullsides. An inner liner is used to create a rugged one-piece hull of extraordinary strength. Below, the cabin layout is arranged with V-berths forward, a compact galley, dinette, and stand-up head. The 3250's bi-level fishing cockpit features an over-size transom door, an in-deck fish box, livewell, molded steps, and fresh- and salt-water washdowns. Push a button and hydraulic hatches rise to expose both engines. Gas engines were standard (just 15 knots cruise/24 top), but most 3250s were delivered with one of several diesel installations. The 300-hp Cummins, 296-hp Volvos, and 300-hp Cats will all cruise around 26-28 knots and deliver top speeds of 30+ knots. ❏

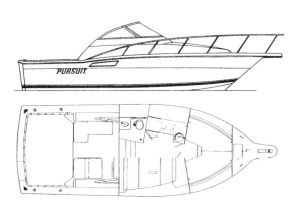

See Page 275 for Pricing Information

RADOVICH 34 SF

SPECIFICATIONS

Length	34'8"	Fuel, Std	360 gals.
Beam	13'0"	Fuel, Opt	500 gals.
Draft	2'8"	Hull Type	Modified-V
Weight	19,500#	Deadrise Aft	15°
Clearance	NA	Designer	V. Radovich
Water	100 gals.	Production	1987–94

The Radovich 34 is a conservative West Coast fisherman with a huge cockpit, basic interior accommodations, and a distinctive low-profile appearance similar to early Luhrs, Tollycraft and Silverton designs. She's heavily built on a solid fiberglass hull, and a 15-inch keel runs about two-thirds the length of the bottom. The Radovich is a beamy boat for her length, and that—together with her raised cockpit sole—allows the motors to be mounted further outboard for improved low-speed handling. An aluminum bait tank occupies the center of the cockpit, and extra-wide sidedecks make foredeck access easy. Topside, the bridge is arranged in typical West Coast fashion with the helm forward (although variations were available). Offered with or without a lower helm, the modest no-glitz interior of the Radovich includes a dinette, stand-up head, an efficient galley, good headroom and berths for four. Several engine options were offered over the years. Among them, twin 320-hp Cat diesels will cruise the Radovich 34 at 20 knots with a top speed of around 26 knots. ❏

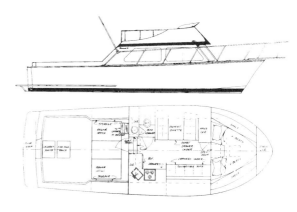

See Page 275 for Pricing Information

RAMPAGE 28 SPORTSMAN

SPECIFICATIONS

Length w/Pulpit..........29'6"	Fuel ....240 gals.
Hull Length ....28'0"	Cockpit...................80 sq. ft.
Beam.............................11'0"	Hull Type ....Modified-V
Draft ....2'6"	Deadrise Aft ....10°
Weight ....8,200#	Designer ....Dick Lema
Water ....25 gals.	Production 1986–Current

The Rampage 28 Sportsman is a good-looking day boat with a well-arranged cockpit and generous cabin accommodations. She's built on a fully cored hull with a sweeping sheer, modest transom deadrise, and a relatively sharp entry. Her relatively wide beam gives the 28 Sportsman the look and feel of a much bigger boat. About half of her length is given over to cockpit space, where there's plenty of room for a full-size fighting chair in addition to a standard livewell and transom door. Inside, the cabin is clean and attractive with enough teak woodwork and trim to keep things from looking too plain. There are berths for three (the portside backrest of the dinette/settee swings up to create the third berth), and an enclosed stand-up head compartment and compact galley complete the accommodations. Separate engine boxes below the helm and companion seats provide good access to the motors. A good performer, twin 350-cid gas inboards will cruise the Rampage 28 at a brisk 24 knots and deliver 33–34 knots top. ❑

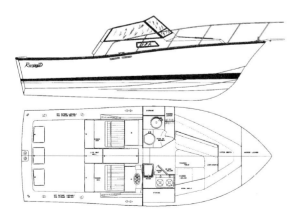

See Page 275 for Pricing Information

RAMPAGE 31 SPORTFISHERMAN

SPECIFICATIONS

Length w/Pulpit........31'10"	Fuel ....256 gals.
Hull Length ....30'10"	Cockpit.................114 sq. ft.
Beam...........................11'11"	Hull Type ....Modified-V
Draft ....2'9"	Deadrise Aft ....10°
Weight ....12,000#	Designer ....Dick Lema
Water ....50 gals.	Production 1986–Current

The Rampage 31 is a good example of how a modern express fisherman combines the stringent requirements of offshore fishing with the high-tech construction techniques rapidly taking hold throughout the industry. She rides on a fully cored hull with a flared bow and moderate deadrise at the transom. Below, the cabin is snug but adequate for the needs of weekend anglers. The dinette/settee converts into a V-berth, and the backrests fold up to become bunks—a total of four berths. The bi-level cockpit is particularly well-designed with an extra-wide transom door, lockable rod storage, and a huge in-deck 85-gallon circulating livewell. There's room in the console for electronics installation, and a unique system of sliding hatches make engine access about as painless as it gets. Note the wide sidedecks and sturdy rails. Standard 454-cid gas engines will cruise the Rampage 31 around 24 knots (33 top). The popular 300-hp GM 8.2 diesels will cruise at a fast 28 knots with a top speed of 31–33 knots. ❑

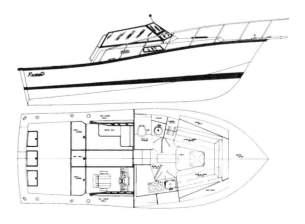

See Page 276 for Pricing Information

RAMPAGE 33 SPORTFISHERMAN

SPECIFICATIONS

Length w/Pulpit........34'10"	Water ....58 gals.
Hull Length ....32'4"	Fuel ....300 gals.
Beam..............................12'4"	Hull Type ....Deep-V
Draft ....2'7"	Deadrise Aft ....18°
Weight ....14,500#	Designer.............Dick Lema
Clearance ....11'2"	Production 1986–Current

The Rampage 33 is designed for experienced anglers who don't mind paying for the quality that goes into a stylish and well-built offshore day boat. She's built on a fully cored deep-V hull, and her wide beam and flared bow insure a dry and stable fishing platform in a variety of weather conditions. Belowdecks, the roomy cabin will sleep four and includes a stand-up head, a big U-shaped dinette, and a compact galley. The Rampage 33 is loaded with thoughtful features sure to appeal to hard-core fishermen—good engine access, an oversized transom door, big in-deck fish boxes, lockable rod storage space, a hinged helm console, underwater exhausts, windshield vents, and a completely removable aft cockpit sole. There's space in the console for most electronics, and the sidedecks are quite wide. Gas engines are standard, but most buyers will opt for diesel power. Optional Cummins 300-hp diesels will cruise economically at 24–25 knots and reach about 29 knots wide open. The bigger 320-hp Cats will run a knot faster. ❏

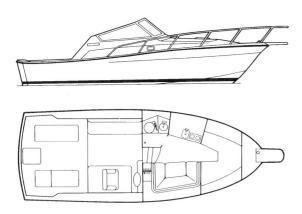

See Page 276 for Pricing Information

RAMPAGE 36 SPORTFISHERMAN

SPECIFICATIONS

Length w/Pulpit..........37'8"	Water ....70 gals.
Hull Length ....35'6"	Fuel ....435 gals.
Beam..............................13'9"	Hull Type ....Deep-V
Draft ....2'9"	Deadrise Aft ....17°
Weight ....19,000#	Designer.............Dick Lema
Clearance ....8'10"	Production 1986–Current

Built on a full-cored deep-V hull, the Rampage 36 is a beamy off-shore fisherman with the aggressive good looks and rugged construction common to all Rampage products. Chief among her attributes is a spacious bi-level fishing cockpit with insulated fish boxes, concealed rod storage, huge livewell, extra-large transom door, and molded tackle center. The helm position is elevated and features a lockable electronics panel and excellent visibility. A convenient settee is abaft the companion seat, and easy engine access is provided via a centerline hatch in the cockpit sole. Inside, the cabin layout is comfortable and well-arranged with a small galley, a full-sized convertible dinette, and an enclosed head with the toilet concealed in the shower stall. Additional features include side-dumping exhausts, chart table, and molded bow pulpit. Several diesel options have been offered. With 291-hp Cummins diesels, the Rampage 36 will cruise efficiently around 22 knots (25 knots top) and, with the big 435-hp Cats, will cruise at 25 knots and deliver 29–30 knots wide open. ❏

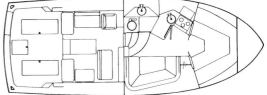

See Page 276 for Pricing Information

RAMPAGE 40 SPORTFISHERMAN

SPECIFICATIONS

Length	41'9"	Fuel	575 gals.
Beam	15'2"	Cockpit	102 sq. ft.
Draft	3'6"	Hull Type	Modified-V
Weight	25,000#	Deadrise Aft	NA
Clearance	13'3"	Designer	Rampage
Water	100 gals.	Production	1988–90

Not a notably popular boat, the styling of the Rampage 40 is unusual in that she features a rather unattractive trunk cabin foredeck rather than the conventional flush foredeck seen in most convertibles this size. Like all Rampage products, the 40 is constructed on a fully cored hull with a wide beam and moderate deadrise at the transom. A unique underwater exhaust system is located midships, just below the salon. The roomy two-stateroom interior is arranged with the galley aft in the salon (unusual in a fishing boat). A cavernous rod locker is built into the salon overhead, and the cherry woodwork is impressive. Topside, the wraparound helm console has two large electronics lockers properly angled for easy viewing. A transom door, circulating livewell, bait prep station, and two fish boxes were all standard. A well-built boat, 485-hp 6-71s will cruise the Rampage 40 around 23–24 knots. The bigger 550-hp 6V92 diesels will cruise at 27 knots and reach 30 knots top. Note that she was called the Rampage 42 Sportfisherman in 1990. ❏

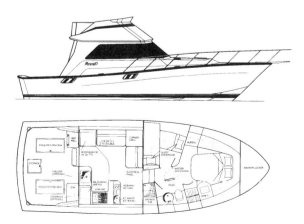

See Page 276 for Pricing Information

RIVIERA 33 CONVERTIBLE

SPECIFICATIONS

Length	33'0"	Clearance	NA
Beam	12'6"	Cockpit	NA
Draft	2'7"	Hull Type	Modified-V
Weight	20,500#	Deadrise Aft	16°
Fuel	300 gals.	Designer	Riviera
Water	100 gals.	Production	1992–Current

There are only a few production 33-foot convertibles being built these days, and the Riviera 33 from Australia certainly ranks among the better-looking of the lot. She's a well-proportioned boat with an aggressive, business-like profile remarkably similar to the old Bertram 33. Hull construction is solid fiberglass and, like all Riviera models, she has a collision bulkhead forward and two watertight bulkheads aft. Originally offered with two small staterooms (with the owner's cabin amidships), the current mid-galley layout has a single stateroom along with a separate stall shower in the head—a convenience seldom found in a boat this size. Note that current models have a glassed-over front windshield panel while earlier Riviera 33s have full wraparound cabin windows and a lower helm. The molded tackle center in the cockpit is actually an entryway to the engine room, a feature not found on *any* other production boat under 36 feet. The flybridge is very big. Among several engine options, twin 210-hp Cummins diesels will cruise the Riviera 33 at 22 knots and reach a top speed of about 27 knots. ❏

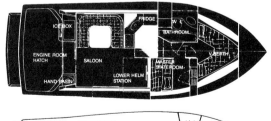

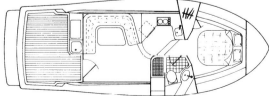

See Page 276 for Pricing Information

197

RIVIERA 36 CONVERTIBLE

SPECIFICATIONS

Length	36'0"	Clearance	NA
Beam	13'6"	Cockpit	NA
Draft	3'5"	Hull Type	Modified-V
Weight	22,800#	Deadrise Aft	16°
Fuel	350 gals.	Designer	Riviera
Water	100 gals.	Production	1993–Current

With her rakish flybridge and long foredeck, it's hard to believe that the Riviera 36 isn't a pure-bred American sportfisherman. This Australian import is definitely a looker—certainly one of the best-looking 36-footers around—and a favorable exchange rate makes her something of a bargain as well. Hull construction is solid fiberglass, and she's designed with a collision bulkhead forward as an extra margin of safety. A lot of anglers like the 35–36-foot size range since you can get a good-size cockpit as well as a two-stateroom interior without breaking the bank. The Riviera's mid-galley floorplan is unusual only in that it has a built-in dining area in the salon (rather than a sofa) along with a lower helm station that cold-weathers anglers will appreciate. A transom door and an engine room access hatch are standard in the cockpit, and the big tournament-style flybridge has bench seating forward of the rather plain-Jane helm console. The Riviera 36 has a cruising speed of 23 knots with a pair of 315-hp Cummins diesels and a top speed of around 26 knots. ❑

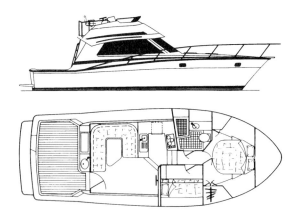

See Page 276 for Pricing Information

RIVIERA 39 CONVERTIBLE

SPECIFICATIONS

Length	39'4"	Clearance	NA
Beam	14'6"	Cockpit	NA
Draft	3'7"	Hull Type	Modified-V
Weight	28,400#	Deadrise Aft	15°
Fuel	400 gals.	Designer	Riviera
Water	100 gals.	Production	1993–Current

A stylish convertible with a rakish flybridge and sturdy profile, the Riviera 39 combines the requirements of a sportfisherman with the accommodation of a comfortable family cruiser. She's built in Australia on a solid fiberglass hull with a short keel and a collision bulkhead forward—a safety feature seldom seen in American boats. The mid-galley, two-stateroom floorplan of the Riviera 39 includes an island bed in the owner's stateroom, a unique double bed that converts to upper and lower berths in the guest stateroom, and a lower helm station in the salon. Like all Riviera convertibles, the salon comes with a built-in dinette (with a real teak table) which consumes a good deal of floor space. The full wraparound cabin windows, however, do much to open up the salon. The cockpit has room for a mounted chair and comes with a tackle center, transom door and direct access to the engine room—an excellent feature on any convertible. Among several engine options, a pair of 375-hp Cat diesels will cruise at 23 knots and reach a top speed of around 28 knots. ❑

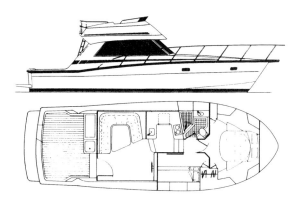

See Page 276 for Pricing Information

RIVIERA 42 CONVERTIBLE

SPECIFICATIONS

Length	43'4"	Clearance	NA
Beam	15'0"	Cockpit	80 sq. ft.
Draft	3'6"	Hull Type	Modified-V
Weight	35,000#	Deadrise Aft	17°
Fuel	425 gals.	Designer	Riviera
Water	130 gals.	Production	1992–95

The Riviera 42 Convertible is an Australian-built sportfisherman with an American-style profile, a somewhat unusual interior layout and—during her production years—a very affordable price tag. Like all Rivieras, the 42 is heavily built on a solid fiberglass, low-deadrise hull with a short keel and a collision bulkhead forward. Inside, the two-stateroom, single-head floorplan is arranged with a mid-level galley that extends well into the salon. Both staterooms have double berths, and there's a settee in the passageway that converts to over-and-under bunk berths. Because she comes standard with a lower helm, the front windows are not glassed over (as they are in most American boats) which adds to the impression of space in the salon. The cockpit is large enough for some serious fishing pursuits and includes a molded tackle center, walk-in access to the engine room, and steps at the corners leading to the wide sidedecks. Among several engine options, twin 375-hp Cat diesels will cruise efficiently at 21 knots and reach 26–27 knots wide open. ❑

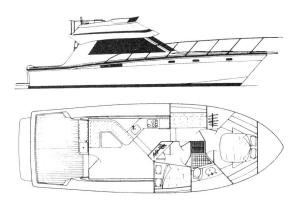

See Page 276 for Pricing Information

RIVIERA 48 CONVERTIBLE

SPECIFICATIONS

Length	48'0"	Clearance	16'6"
Beam	15'9"	Cockpit	NA
Draft	3'6"	Hull Type	Modified-V
Weight	45,000#	Deadrise Aft	12°
Fuel	650 gals.	Designer	Riviera
Water	210 gals.	Production	1993–Current

With her long foredeck, rakish flybridge and sweeping sheer, the Riviera 48 has the lean, business-like appearance of a hard-core sportfishing machine. She's heavily built on a solid fiberglass, modified-V hull with a short keel and a substantial 16° of transom deadrise. (For safety, there's a massive collision bulkhead forward and two watertight bulkheads in the engine room.) The tooling and gelcoat work is very good, and exterior maintanance has been kept to a minimum. The standard three-stateroom, mid-galley floorplan is arranged with the owner's stateroom forward and stall showers in boths heads. A built-in dining area dominates the salon and cold-weather anglers will like the lower helm and wraparound cabin windows. The cockpit is huge and so is the flybridge, but the helm console is a little old-fashioned. Additional features include a side-dumping exhaust system, transom door, molded tackle center, swim platform and direct cockpit access to the engine room. A good performer, twin 600-hp 8-cylinder MTUs will cruise the Riviera 48 Convertible at 26 knots and deliver a top speed of about 30 knots. ❑

See Page 276 for Pricing Information

RONIN 38 CONVERTIBLE

SPECIFICATIONS

Length	38'3"	Fuel	370 gals.
Beam	13'11"	Cockpit	108 sq. ft.
Draft	3'6"	Hull Type	Modified-V
Weight	26,000#	Deadrise Aft	15°
Clearance	12'8"	Designer	Unknown
Water	100 gals.	Production	1986–89

Built in Taiwan, the Ronin 38 is constructed on a conventional modified-V hull with a wide beam and balsa coring in the hullsides. Three separate molds were required—hull, superstructure, and flybridge—so there are no seams in the cockpit or screws on the bridge. A good-looking boat with a handsome profile, the Ronin 38 was available with a galley-down, single-stateroom layout or with the galley in the salon and two staterooms forward. The interior is finished in solid teak or light oak woodwork, and good craftsmanship is evident throughout. A hatch in the salon sole reveals a well-organized engine room with good access to motors and generator. Outside, the large cockpit is set up for serious fishing and includes a transom door and gate, livewell, freezer, and freshwater washdown. Standard Cat 375-hp diesels cruise the Ronin 38 at 22–23 knots and reach a top speed of 27. The optional 485-hp 6-71s provide a cruising speed of 25–26 knots and a top speed of about 29 knots. ❏

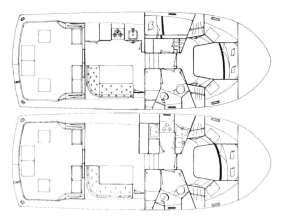

See Page 276 for Pricing Information

RONIN 48 CONVERTIBLE

SPECIFICATIONS

Length	48'8"	Fuel	850 gals.
Beam	15'10"	Cockpit	NA
Draft	4'0"	Hull Type	Modified-V
Weight	46,000#	Deadrise Aft	15°
Clearance	14'3"	Designer	Unknown
Water	200 gals.	Production	1987–89

To date, Ronin is one of the very few Taiwan sportfishermen to have at least cracked the long-standing resistance to Asian imports among hard-core anglers. Like the smaller Ronin 38, the 48 Convertible is built on a conventional modified-V hull with generous flare at the bow and 15° of deadrise at the transom. The hullsides are cored with balsa, and the boat is assembled with only three separate molds, which adds strength and rigidity while reducing seals and leaks. In appearance, the Ronin 48 Convertible has a strong resemblance to Brand H (as in Hatteras). The styling is contemporary and completely in line with popular sportfish trends. Inside, the 48 offered a choice of two or three staterooms with the galley up or down. The teak (or light oak) interior woodwork is very attractive, and the large engine room is arranged with good access to the motors. With optional 735-hp 8V92s, the Ronin 48 will cruise around 27 knots and reach 30+ knots wide open. Twin 840-hp MAN diesels were optional. ❏

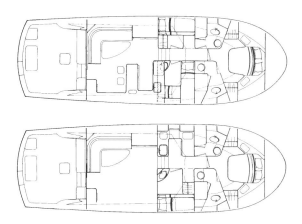

See Page 276 for Pricing Information

RYBO RUNNER 30 CENTER CONSOLE

SPECIFICATIONS

Length	30'0"	Fuel	200 gals.
Beam	10'8"	Hull Type	Deep-V
Draft	3'0"	Deadrise Aft	24°
Weight	6,500#	Designer	Rybovich
Clearance	NA	Production	1983–89
Water	None		1995–Current

The Rybo Runner is a high-speed fisherman from Rybovich with a unique double-step hull designed to reduce wetted area when planing by creating air pockets behind the steps. Hull construction is solid fiberglass, and a full-length inner liner adds a good deal of rigidity to the hull. The center console has space for flush-mounting some electronics, and there's room inside the console for a stand-up head and shower. Abaft the console, the leaning post is a molded fiberglass unit with rod holders, tackle storage, and an optional baitwell. In the cockpit sole are two long lift-out fish boxes, and there are four rod holders in the gunwales. The cockpit can easily accommodate a fighting chair. Rybo Runners were semi-custom boats, and most were equipped with an optional Rybovich tower and outriggers. Power options included twin outboards, 205-hp OMC SeaDrives, twin 270-hp gas inboards, or a single 8.2 diesel. The Sea Drives will cruise at 24 knots (42–43 knots top), and the gas inboards also cruise around 24 knots (31 top). Note that a new Rybo 30, with a fully cored hull, was re-introduced in 1995. ❑

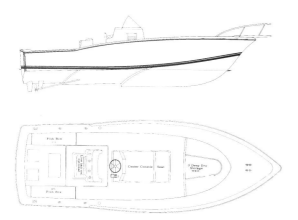

See Page 276 for Pricing Information

SEA RAY 310 AMBERJACK (LAGUNA 31)

SPECIFICATIONS

Length	31'2"	Water	40 gals.
Beam	11'5"	Fuel	296 gals.
Draft	3'1"	Hull Type	Deep-V
Weight	10,500#	Deadrise Aft	18°
Cockpit	57 sq. ft.	Designer	Sea Ray
Clearance	NA	Production	1991–Current

Sportboat enthusiasts will find much to like in the Sea Ray 310 Amberjack, a good-looking dayboat with the aggressive low-profile silhouette of a small Bertram or Blackfin. She's built on a deep-V hull with cored hullsides, a wide beam, prop pockets, and 18° of transom deadrise. The Amberjack's original design emphasis was in the large and well-organized cockpit. In 1994, Sea Ray engineers replaced the dinette opposite the helm with an elevated lounge area. The cockpit can be fitted with in-deck fish boxes, rod holders, and a transom livewell. While cabin space is at a premium, the 310 AJ manages to include overnight berths for two plus a stand-up head with shower, small galley, and convertible dinette. The side-decks are a foot wide, and the motors are accessed via engine boxes. A good performer with twin 454-cid MerCruiser gas engines, she'll cruise at an easy 24 knots and reach 31–32 knots top. Note that she was marketed as the Sea Ray 31 Laguna for the 1993 model year. ❑

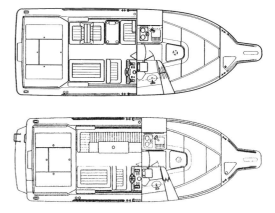

See Page 276 for Pricing Information

SEA RAY 310 SPORT BRIDGE

SEA RAY 390 SEDAN SF

SPECIFICATIONS

L.O.A.	33'8"	Cockpit	57 sq. ft.
Hull Length	31'2"	Water	40 gals.
Beam	11'5"	Fuel	296 gals.
Draft	3'1"	Hull Type	Deep-V
Weight	11,500#	Deadrise Aft	18°
Clearance	9'6"	Production	1992–93

A great-looking boat with aggressive styling and a low-profile appearance, the 310 Sport Bridge is basically a 310 Amberjack with a flybridge and semi-enclosed lower helm. She's built on an easy-riding deep-V hull with a wide beam, side-dumping exhausts and prop pockets. With no salon bulkhead, the lower helm is wide open to the huge cockpit, which consumes well over half of the boat's L.O.A. There's plenty of guest seating, including a sunpad and dinette, and the cockpit can be fitted with in-deck storage boxes, rod holders, and a transom livewell. While cabin space is at a premium, the 310 manages to include overnight berths for two plus a stand-up head with shower, small galley, and convertible dinette. The bridge is small, with seating for two. Hinged motor boxes provide good access to the engines, and the sidedecks are a foot wide. Twin 454-cid gas engines will cruise at 23 knots (30–31 knots top), and optional 291-hp Cummins diesels will cruise around 27 knots (31 knots top). ❏

SPECIFICATIONS

Length	39'0"	Fuel	400 gals.
Beam	13'11"	Cockpit	116 sq. ft.
Draft	2'5"	Hull Type	Deep-V
Weight	18,400#	Deadrise Aft	19°
Clearance	NA	Designer	Sea Ray
Water	100 gals.	Production	1983–86

The 390 Sedan SF is a stretched version of the popular Sea Ray 360 Sedan built from 1980 to 1983. The extra length went into the cockpit, which is easily the boat's most impressive feature. She was built on the same one-piece fiberglass hull as the 360 and 390 Express Cruisers—a deep-V design with a relatively wide beam, 19° of transom deadrise, and propeller pockets. The original floorplan was updated in 1985 to include a centerline queen berth in the forward stateroom and a more open salon area. Single berths are located in the guest cabin, and a serving counter separates the galley from the salon. The comfortable interior arrangements of the 390 Sedan make her an excellent all-purpose family cruiser, and, with plenty of fuel and a big cockpit, she's capable of fishing activities. Standard 350-hp gas engines will cruise around 17 knots and reach a top speed of 25 knots. Optional 320-hp Cat diesels cruise the 390 Sedan SF at an economical 21 knots and reach 24 knots top. ❏

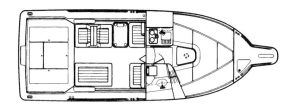

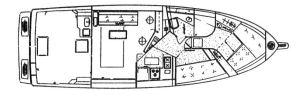

See Page 276 for Pricing Information

See Page 276 for Pricing Information

SEA RAY 440 CONVERTIBLE

SPECIFICATIONS

LOA	49'1"	Water	132 gals.
Hull Length	43'6"	Fuel	500 gals.
Beam	13'11"	Cockpit	NA
Draft	2'8"	Hull Type	Deep-V
Weight	23,000#	Deadrise Aft	17°
Clearance	10'9"	Production	1988–91

Aimed at the market for offshore fishermen, the 440 Convertible was styled after the larger Sea Ray 460 Convertible (1987–88) with a low foredeck, stepped sheer, and modern deckhouse profile. Introduced in 1988 as the 430 Convertible, the 440 designation came in 1989. Built on a rugged deep-V hull with plenty of beam, she's more family cruiser than fishing boat. Below, the high-style European interior theme of the 440 (no teak anywhere) was updated in 1990 with a modest amount of teak trim and compares well with many of today's contemporary family convertibles. The floorplan—with its mid-level galley and athwartships guest stateroom—is innovative and well-arranged. Also unusual (in a 43-foot boat) is the cockpit engine room access where a hatch opens into a somewhat tight engine compartment. Standard features include a transom door, removable fish box, salon and flybridge wet bars, cockpit shower, and a swim platform. With the optional 375-hp Cat diesels, the 440 Convertible will cruise around 21 knots and reach 25 knots wide open. ❏

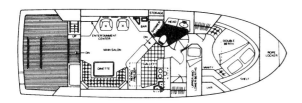

See Page 277 for Pricing Information

SHAMROCK 31 GRAND SLAM

SPECIFICATIONS

Length	31'0"	Fuel, Std.	290 gals.
Beam	11'4"	Fuel, Opt.	340 gals.
Draft	3'4"	Cockpit	142 sq. ft.
Weight	9,250#	Hull Type	Deep-V
Clearance	18'0"	Deadrise Aft	19°
Water	40 gals.	Production	1987–94

Shamrock Marine is a well-regarded South Florida builder of small fishing and utility boats featuring unique "keel drive" hull designs. Unlike the rest of the Shamrock series, however, the 31 Grand Slam is built on a conventional deep-V hull. At first glance, she appears to be a fairly standard open sportfisherman with attractive lines and a large fishing cockpit. A closer look reveals several interesting features. The helm seat, for example, can be converted into a leaning post. Engine access is good—a unique central service bay houses all the mechanical and electrical systems. The cockpit features modular tackle centers, rod holders, and storage bins. For accommodations, there are four single berths below (the dinette seatbacks convert to single bunks) and a stand-up head with shower. Standard gas engines have not proved popular with buyers. Early models with optional 250-hp Cummins diesels cruise at 28 knots (2 mpg!) and reach 33 wide open. Cummins 300-hp diesels (available since 1990) cruise at 31 knots and deliver 34–35 knots top. Over 160 were built. ❏

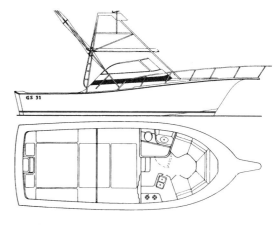

See Page 277 for Pricing Information

203

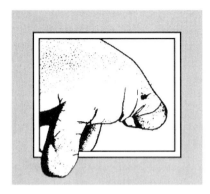

Get Your M.A. (Manatee Awareness) Degree In Recreational Watersports:

Tips To Protect Manatees

There are many things YOU can do to protect manatees from a watercraft collision or other human-related injuries:

❖ Wearing polarized sunglasses can help eliminate the glare of the sun and helps boaters to see below the water's surface.

❖ Stay in deep water channels when boating. Avoid boating over seagrass beds and shallow areas where manatees might be feeding (but be aware that manatees also use deep water channels when traveling).

❖ Look for a snout, back, tail, or flipper breaking the surface of the water, or a swirl or a flat spot on the water that is created by the motion of the manatee's paddle-shaped tail when it dives or swims.

❖ If you see a manatee when operating a powerboat, remain a safe distance away — 50 feet is suggested. If you want to observe the manatee, cut the motor, but do not drift over the animal.

❖ If you like to jet-ski, water-ski, or participate in high-speed water sports, choose areas that manatees do not, or cannot frequent, such as a land-locked lake.

❖ Obey posted speed zone signs and keep away from posted manatee sanctuaries.

❖ Keep your litter on board your vessel. Recycle it or throw it in a trash container when you get back on shore.

❖ Discard monofilament line or hooks properly. Discarding monofilament line into or onto the waters of the state of Florida is against the law.

❖ Look, but don't touch manatees. If manatees become accustomed to being around people, it can alter their behavior in the wild, perhaps causing them to lose their natural fear of boats and humans, and this may make them susceptible to harm. Passive observation is the best way to interact with manatees and all wildlife.

❖ Resist the urge to feed manatees or give them water. Remember, passive observation!

❖ When swimming or diving, the key words are _____ _____ (right! passive observation). You may not know it, but your presence might accidentally separate a mother manatee and calf or keep a manatee away from its warm water source — both of which are potentially life-threatening situations.

❖ Call the Manatee Hotline at 1-800-DIAL-FMP if you happen to spot an injured, dead, tagged, or orphaned manatee, or if you see a manatee that is being harassed.

Save the Manatee₍ₑ₎ Club
500 N. Maitland Avenue • Maitland, FL 32751

1 - 800 - 432 - JOIN

SILVERTON 37 CONVERTIBLE

SPECIFICATIONS

Length	37'4"	Fuel	375 gals.
Beam	13'11"	Cockpit	80 sq. ft.
Draft	3'9"	Hull Type	Modified-V
Weight	21,000#	Deadrise Aft	17°
Clearance	14'0"	Designer	M. Peters
Water	100 gals.	Production	1990–Current

With her good looks, a long list of standard equipment, and a budget-level price, the newest Silverton 37 (the original 37 Convertible ran from 1980 to 1989) is generally thought of as a lot of boat for the money. Her solid fiberglass modified-V hull is designed with a wide beam and a fairly steep 17° of deadrise at the transom. Belowdecks, the spacious single-stateroom interior is arranged with the galley and dinette down but still open to the salon. The light oak interior woodwork, white galley laminates, and wraparound cabin windows create a bright and pleasant interior. The cockpit is too small for a fighting chair, but coaming pads, an in-deck fish box, and a transom door and swim platform are standard. The flybridge seats six with bench seating forward of the helm, and the well-planned console has space for flush-mounting some electronics. No racehorse, the performance of the Silverton 37 with standard 454-cid gas engines is 15–16 knots at cruise, and the top speed is about 25 knots. ❏

SILVERTON 41 CONVERTIBLE

SPECIFICATIONS

Length	41'3"	Water	200 gals.
Beam	14'10"	Fuel	516 gals.
Draft	3'9"	Hull Type	Modified-V
Weight	27,000#	Deadrise Aft	NA
Clearance	15'5"	Designer	Silverton
Cockpit	98 sq. ft.	Production	1991–Current

The Silverton 41 Convertible is a moderately priced sedan cruiser with a clean-cut profile and a practical two-stateroom interior layout. With her long foredeck, step-down sheer, and raked bridge, the 41 has the look of a sportfisherman (although Silvertons have never been noted for building tournament-level boats). The cockpit is large enough for a fighting chair, and there's a good-size fish box below the sole. Inside, wraparound cabin windows provide excellent natural lighting. The light oak interior is arranged with the galley and (big) dinette down from the salon level, a double-entry head with a stall shower, over/under single berths in the guest cabin, and an island berth in the master stateroom. Additional features include a reasonably spacious flybridge with plenty of seating, side exhausts, transom door, and swim platform. Standard 502-cid gas engines will cruise the Silverton 41 Convertible at 19–20 knots (about 28 knots top), and the optional 425-hp Caterpillar diesels will cruise at 24–25 knots and reach 28 knots wide open. ❏

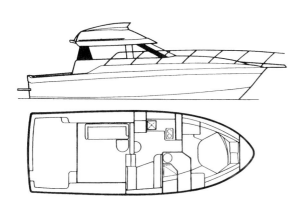

See Page 277 for Pricing Information

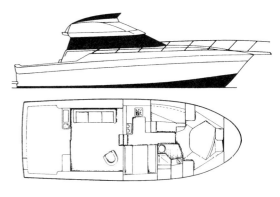

See Page 277 for Pricing Information

SOUTHERN CROSS 44 SF

SPECIFICATIONS

Length	44'2"	Fuel	550 gals.
Beam	14'6"	Cockpit	110 sq. ft.
Draft	3'0"	Hull Type	Modified-V
Weight	28,000#	Deadrise Aft	NA
Clearance	12'6"	Designer	Tom Fexas
Water	100 gals.	Production	1987–90

A great-looking design from Tom Fexas, the Southern Cross 44 is an Australian import with a number of innovative and practical design features. Beginning with a fully cored hull, her unique chamfered transom allows the 44 to back down hard with less tendency to flood the cockpit. The air intakes are hidden in the after edge of the house, and underwater exhausts run through the stringers. At 28,000 lbs., the Southern Cross 44 is a relatively light boat for her size, and those who have run her agree that her seakeeping characteristics are good. The cockpit is equipped with controls, a bait-prep station, transom door, and livewell. Access to the spacious engine room is provided via a cockpit door. Four steps up from the cockpit, the salon features silver ash woodwork and stylish fabrics to create an especially attractive interior. A good-running boat with a comfortable ride, twin 540-hp 6V92 diesels will cruise the Southern Cross 44 Convertible around 27 knots, and the top speed is 30 knots. ❑

SOUTHERN CROSS 52 SF

SPECIFICATIONS

Length	52'0"	Fuel	1,000 gals.
Beam	15'6"	Cockpit	144 sq. ft.
Draft	3'6"	Hull Type	Modified-V
Weight	38,000#	Deadrise Aft	NA
Clearance	NA	Designer	Tom Fexas
Water	150 gals.	Production	1986–1990

Southern Cross was the Australian builder who ran those full-page ads some years ago promising to blow Bertram and Hatteras out of the "bloody water." They were talking about the Southern Cross 52, a sleek Fexas design with plenty of high-tech construction and not a lot of weight. She never really caught on with serious anglers (her eagerly awaited introduction at the '85 Lauderdale boat show was a bust), and only seven were sold before Southern Cross closed down in 1991. In some ways, she was ahead of her time—lightweight, fully cored construction, and ash interiors have since become popular in the sportfishing community. Several floorplans were offered (early models had the galley aft in the salon) with the three-stateroom, galley-up layout preferred. Narrow in the beam and with a very low cockpit, the 52 SF never attained the promised 37-knot performance. Instead, she turned a still-fast 34 knots wide open with just 740-hp 8V92s (which isn't bad—a late model Hatteras 52 barely manages 27 knots top with the same motors). ❑

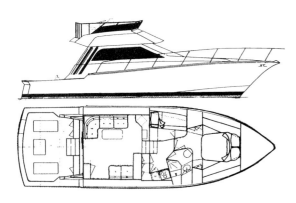

See Page 277 for Pricing Information

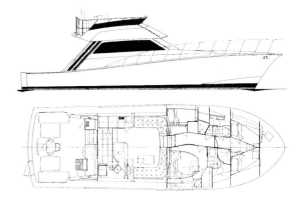

See Page 277 for Pricing Information

STAMAS 288 LIBERTY

SPECIFICATIONS

Length w/Pulpit..........30'2"	Water ....20 gals.
Hull Length ....28'4"	Fuel ....196 gals.
Beam.............................11'2"	Cockpit ....NA
Draft ....1'6"	Hull Type ....Modified-V
Weight ....9,500#	Deadrise Aft....................18°
Clearance ....7'6"	Production 1987–94

The 288 Liberty is an affordably priced express cruiser/family fisherman with conservative styling, an unusually large cockpit (for a 28-footer), and a straightforward and well-arranged interior with good accommodations. A popular model (she's was also called the Stamas 288 Family Fisherman), the hull is constructed of solid fiberglass with a wide beam and a gently flared bow. Key to the success of the boat is her practical deck plan and spacious mid-cabin interior layout. The single-level cockpit is arranged with two forward fish wells, two live baitwells, and an icebox. The helm is elevated, and a motor box occupies the aft end of the cockpit in the stern drive version. Inside, there are berths for four in the cabin with a stand-up head and a small galley—accommodations suitable for a small family. Additional features include wide sidedecks, a molded pulpit, and excellent storage. Those with 230-hp I/Os will cruise around 23 knots (36 knots top). Bracket-mounted 200-hp outboards will cruise around 21 knots and reach 30+ knots wide open. ❏

STAMAS 290 EXPRESS

SPECIFICATIONS

Length w/Pulpit..........31'7"	Clearance ....7'2"
Beam.............................10'4"	Water ....27 gals.
Draft, O/B ....1'7"	Fuel ....200 gals.
Draft, I/B ....2'4"	Hull Type ....Deep-V
Weight, O/B ....7,000#	Deadrise Aft....................18°
Weight, I/B................8,600#	Production 1992–Current

The 290 Express is a scaled-down version of the Stamas 310 Express with a similar profile and the exact same mid-cabin interior layout. A good-looking boat with a molded pulpit and a fully integrated bracket platform, the 290 Express is a versatile boat with the ability to serve as a competent offshore fisherman or capable family cruiser. The single-level cockpit is arranged with a transom baitwell, washdowns, and a starboard-side transom door. The helm seat is elevated (to make room for the mid-cabin below), and visibility is excellent. Belowdecks, the cabin has a V-berth/dinette forward, stand-up head with shower, compact galley, and an athwartships double berth in the small mid-cabin. The accommodations are basic but well finished and comfortable. Additional features include wide sidedecks, a stylish curved windshield, and four opening ports for ventilation. Available with inboard or outboard power, twin 200-hp Yamahas will cruise the 290 Express at a respectable 24 knots and reach just under 40 knots top. An optional 315-hp Yanmar diesel inboard will cruise at 21 knots (28–29 knots top) with a range of almost 450 miles. ❏

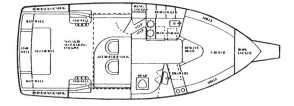

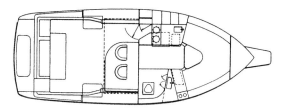

See Page 277 for Pricing Information

See Page 277 for Pricing Information

STAMAS 290 TARPON

SPECIFICATIONS

Length w/Pulpit	31'7"	Clearance	6'10"
Beam	10'4"	Water	20 gals.
Draft, O/B	1'7"	Fuel	302 gals.
Draft, I/B	2'4"	Hull Type	Deep-V
Weight, O/B	5,000#	Deadrise Aft	18°
Weight, I/B	6,000#	Production	1995–Current

The 290 Tarpon is a long-range center console designed to appeal to serious sportfisherman with an appreciation for the rugged durability long associated with the Stamas nameplate. Hull construction is solid fiberglass, and a sleek profile and full-height transom make her one of the best-looking rigs of her type on the market. A 302-gallon fuel capacity provides good range, even with the biggest outboards. (She's rated for 500-hp max.) The standard leaning post incorporates a rigging station with a freshwater sink and a large livewell. A second livewell is built into the walk-through transom and two lockable in-deck storage boxes flank the console. There's space at the helm for flush-mounting the necessary electronics, and a private head compartment is accessed from the front of the console. The deck is flush from the stern to the bow where a filler converts the U-shaped seating into a large casting platform. Available with a single inboard (gas or diesel) or twin outboards, a pair of 250-hp Yamahas will deliver top speed of 40+ knots and a cruising speed of around 26 knots. ❏

STAMAS 310 EXPRESS

SPECIFICATIONS

Length w/Pulpit	32'6"	Fuel	204 gals.
Beam	11'2"	Cockpit	106 sq. ft.
Draft	1'7"	Max HP	500
Weight, O/B	8,800#	Hull Type	Deep-V
Weight, I/B	10,500#	Deadrise Aft	18°
Water	40 gals.	Production	1993–Current

The Stamas 310 Express is an enlarged version of the smaller 290 Express with a similar profile and the same mid-cabin interior layout. She's well-built on a solid fiberglass hull with moderate beam and prop pockets to reduce the draft. While the 310 is likely to be viewed by many as a strictly-business fishing boat (thanks to the Stamas nameplate), the roomy mid-cabin accommodations are well suited to family cruising. There are berths for four with a convertible dinette/V-berth forward and a double berth in the mid cabin. Outside, the cockpit is big enough for three or four anglers, and the flush-deck layout results in an excellent fishing platform. A transom door is standard, and a deep fish box is built into the transom. Two hatches in the cockpit sole provide excellent access to the motors, and visibility from the elevated helm is outstanding. Available with inboard or outboard power, standard 250-hp MerCruiser inboards will cruise efficiently at 20 knots (about 20 gph) and reach 28–29 knots wide open. Optional 225-hp outboards will cruise the Stamas 310 at 25 knots with a top speed of 36–37 knots. ❏

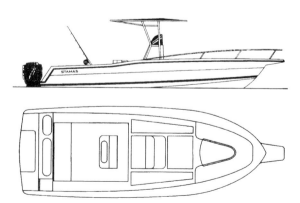

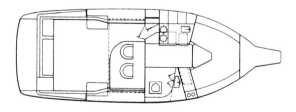

See Page 277 for Pricing Information

See Page 277 for Pricing Information

Sport Sedan

Sport Fisherman

SPECIFICATIONS

Length ....32'3"	Fuel, SF..................250 gals.
Beam............................12'0"	Cockpit....................70 sq. ft.
Draft: ....2'9"	Hull Type ....Modified-V
Weight ....12,800#	Designer...........Pete Stamas
Clearance ....11'6"	Production:
Water ....55 gals.	Sedan 1977–87
Fuel, Sedan ....200 gals.	SF.........................1978–87

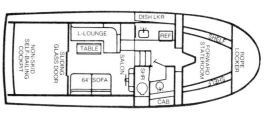

Sport Sedan Layouts

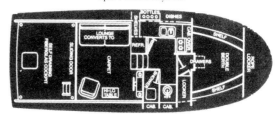

A popular boat during her long production run, the 32 Sport Sedan and Sport Fisherman each had long production runs for Stamas. They were built on an easy-riding solid fiberglass hull with a relatively wide beam, plenty of flare at the bow, and moderate deadrise at the transom. Aside from the Sport Sedan's deckhouse graphics, the two boats are much alike. The Sport Fisherman had a more flexible layout, however, and she was available with or without a salon bulkhead enclosure for anglers who wanted a more open cockpit configuration. Too, the SF had a dinette opposite the lower helm where the Sedan had a settee. Both had galley-down floorplans with V-berths forward, good storage and a roomy head with shower. Outside, the cockpit is large enough to handle a mounted chair, and there's seating for three on the flybridge. Note that the sidedecks on both boats are extremely wide and foredeck access is excellent. Several engine options were offered over the years. Among the most popular, a pair of 255-hp MerCruisers will cruise the Stamas 32s at 17 knots (about 20 gph) and reach 25–26 knots top. ❏

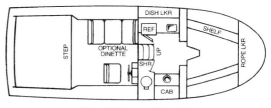

Sport Fisherman Floorplan

See Page 277 for Pricing Information

209

STAMAS 360 EXPRESS

SPECIFICATIONS

Length w/Pulpit	36'6"	Fuel	372 gals.
Beam	13'2"	Cockpit	155 sq. ft.
Draft	2'4"	Hull Type	Modified-V
Weight	16,975#	Deadrise Aft	18°
Clearance	8'3"	Designer	Jim Wynne
Water	90 gals.	Production	1992–Current

At first glance the Stamas 360 appears to be just another attractive mid-cabin family express with contemporary styling and a big cockpit. But Stamas has built their reputation on fishing boats, and the 360 Express is more than a good-looking express. Like the Tiara 36, she's designed to serve as a stable fishing platform as well as a comfortable cruiser. Hull construction is solid fiberglass with a wide beam, prop pockets, and a steep 18° of transom deadrise. Note that she has a long keel of sufficient depth to protect the running gear. In a departure from most of today's mid-cabin designs, the Stamas 360 has a single-level cockpit instead of a raised bridgedeck. Her mid-cabin accommodations are attractive and well-arranged, however the forward stateroom lacks a privacy door—a disappointing omission in a boat this size. Cockpit features include flush-mounted rod holders, an insulated fish box, baitwell, and transom storage. An competent performer with 454-cid gas engines, she'll cruise around 18–19 knots and reach 27 knots wide open. ❏

STRATOS 3300 CENTER CONSOLE

SPECIFICATIONS

Length	32'5"	Clearance	5'6"
Beam	9'0"	Hull Type	Deep-V
Hull Draft	1'6"	Deadrise Aft	23°
Hull Weight	5,800#	Max HP	600
Fuel	295 gals.	Designer	D. Riley
Water	27 gals.	Production	1992–Current

The Stratos 3300 is a big outboard-powered center console with a high-performance, deep-V hull and a raceboat profile. She's really a Donzi 33 in drag; OMC, who owned both companies at the time, decided to share the Donzi F33 molds with Stratos in order to give Stratos an entry into the high-performance center console market. (The same molds were also used to create the Hydra-Sports 3300.) The narrow, deep-V hull of the Stratos 3300 (which is cored) was designed for hard offshore running; her reputation for handling rough seas is well known. The cockpit has about 40 sq. ft. of fishing platform behind the console and includes a leaning post/rocket launcher, recessed rod storage, an in-deck baitwell and padded bolsters. A small fishbox is forward of the console along with port and starboard settees. The small cuddy cabin comes with V-berths, a manual head, a sink, and room for a stove. Like many narrow deep-Vs, the Stratos 3300 can be a wet ride in a chop. She'll cruise at 25 knots with a pair of 225-hp outboards with a top speed of around 36 knots. ❏

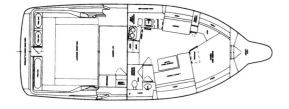

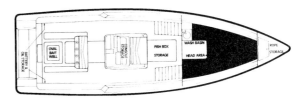

See Page 277 for Pricing Information

See Page 277 for Pricing Information

STRIKE 29 SPORTFISHERMAN

SPECIFICATIONS

Length w/Pulpit	31'7"	Water	20 gals.
Hull Length	29'0"	Fuel	225 gals.
Beam	10'11"	Hull Type	Deep-V
Draft	2'6"	Deadrise Aft	23°
Weight	7,500#	Production	1985–89
Clearance	7'6"		1995–Current

A serious offshore boat, the aggressive, low-profile appearance of the Strike 29 makes her an easy boat to pick out in a sea of look-alike designs. She's built on a solid fiberglass, deep-V hull with very low freeboard, a wide beam and propeller pockets for reduced shaft angles. The deck plan is ideal for fishermen who want the overnight capability of a small cuddy while still retaining the walk-around fish-fighting attributes of a center console. The cabin accommodations are basic—V-berths with a head under and rod storage. The cockpit is huge with plenty of room for a full-size chair. With the engines mounted close together, the extra-wide console house both and lifts up for easy access. The Strike 29 can easily handle the addition of a tower thanks to her wide beam and low center of gravity. A total of 35 were built through 1989. The boat was reintroduced in 1995 with a molded pulpit and an all-new inner liner. Early models with 240-hp Perkins diesels will cruise at 25 knots (29 knots top), and newer models with 250-hp Cummins diesels will cruise efficiently at 26 knots (about 30 knots top). ❏

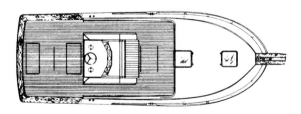

See Page 277 for Pricing Information

211

STRIKER 34 CANYON RUNNER

SPECIFICATIONS

Length	34'0"	Fuel	400 gals.
Beam	13'7"	Cockpit	100 sq. ft.
Draft	2'3"	Hull Type	Modified-V
Weight	16,500#	Construction	Aluminum
Clearance	NA	Designer	T. DeGroot
Water	100 gals.	Production	1973–75

The 34 Canyon Runner was introduced in 1973 as a scaled-down version of the popular Striker 44 SF. She was built of welded aluminum in Norway and utilized the same exclusive hull design of the bigger Strikers. With her serious profile and ship-like construction, the 34 set the tone for future models in the Canyon Runner series. She was specifically designed for the type of offshore running typical of the Jersey and Maryland coasts. Her wide beam provides a stable fishing platform, and she has the range to go long distances without refueling. Inside, the cabin is arranged to meet the basic overnight needs of a couple of anglers with V-berths, a convertible dinette area, and a small galley and head. The interior is trimmed with teak woodwork and Formica counters—not a particularly stylish decor, but maintenance is easy. A rugged little vessel still occasionally found on the used market, the Striker 34 Canyon Runner with the 240-hp V555M Cummins diesels will cruise at 15 knots and reach a top speed of 18–19 knots. ❏

See Page 278 for Pricing Information

STRIKER 37 CANYON RUNNER

SPECIFICATIONS

Length	37'4"	Fuel	750 gals.
Beam	14'7"	Cockpit	100 sq. ft.
Draft	2'8"	Hull Type	Modified-V
Weight	24,000#	Construction	Aluminum
Clearance	13'1"	Designer	T. DeGroot
Water	150 gals.	Production	1988–90

The 37 Canyon Runner is an enlarged version of the original 34 Canyon Runner. She started out as a 36-foot prototype in 1987 but was lengthened the following year to gain additional cockpit space. The 37 can be characterized as a serious gamefishing machine with battleship construction. Like all Strikers, the 37's hull and superstructure are heavy-gauge welded marine aluminum. The beam is unusually wide, and the deepest part of the keel provides protection for the props. (Notably, she's the only US-built Striker ever.) Inside, the compact layout has a single stateroom forward, a small head (without a shower stall), convertible dinette, and a very small galley. What appears to be a window in the aft bulkhead is actually a complete fold-up bait-prep center. A good-looking boat with a lean and mean appearance, standard 485-hp 6-71 diesels will cruise at 27–28 knots. Note the large 750-gallon fuel capacity. For the record, the Striker 37 Canyon Runner was at the top of the scale when it came to price. ❏

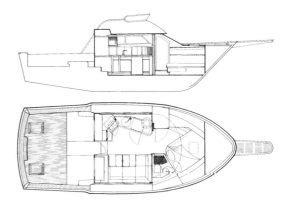

See Page 278 for Pricing Information

STRIKER 41 SPORTFISHERMAN

SPECIFICATIONS

Length	41'0"	Fuel, Std.	650 gals.
Draft	2'4"	Cockpit	NA
Beam	14'9"	Hull Type	Modified-V
Weight	16,250#	Deadrise Aft	NA
Clearance	13'6"	Construction	Aluminum
Water	100 gals.	Production	1981–83

A good-looking boat, the Striker 41 SF is a stable offshore fisherman built for serious tournament-level pursuits. She was constructed of aluminum on a wide-beam hull with a shallow draft, and at only 16,250 lbs. she's an incredibly light boat for her size. Her two-stateroom layout is very spacious and open (in spite of the dark teak woodwork) and includes two heads as well as a big galley on the lower level. Thanks to her wide beam, the generous interior accommodations of the Striker 41 don't intrude into the cockpit, where there's space for a complete set of tackle centers and a mounted chair. The flybridge is large for a 41-footer, and the sidedecks are very wide. Additional features include a teak cockpit sole and covering boards, foredeck seating, sturdy tubular deck rails, and a big engine room with good outboard service access. All six Striker 41s were fitted with 410-hp 6-71s which will cruise around 23 knots and reach a top speed of 26–27 knots. ❑

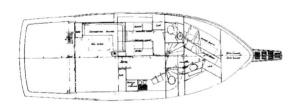

See Page 278 for Pricing Information

STRIKER 44 SPORTFISHERMAN

SPECIFICATIONS

Length	44'0"	Fuel, Opt.	705 gals.
Beam	15'9"	Cockpit	NA
Draft	2'9"	Hull Type	Modified-V
Weight	20,000#	Deadrise Aft	NA
Clearance	14'6"	Construction	Aluminum
Water	235 gals.	Designer	Tom DeGroot
Fuel, Std	470 gals.	Production	1968–75

The 44 Sportfisherman was the best-selling Striker ever. A total of 99 were built in Norway, and used models still seem to be in demand around serious sportfishing markets. Her popularity stems from the rugged welded aluminum construction and the massive brawn common to all Striker yachts. The 44 quickly gained a reputation as a capable offshore sportfisherman with a distinctive profile and superb offshore handling characteristics. As a fishing boat, she has very good range, a first-class working cockpit, and unusually wide and secure sidedecks with beefy deck hardware and rails. The more popular two-stateroom, galley-down layout is well suited to the needs of extended cruising. Among many notable features are a sea chest to eliminate unnecessary through-hull fittings, a serviceable engine room, an expansive flybridge, teak cockpit sole, and teak covering boards. Most Striker 44s were powered with 310-hp 6-71s and cruise at around 17 knots with a top speed of 20 knots. The 370-hp Cummins cruise at 20 knots and top out at 23. ❑

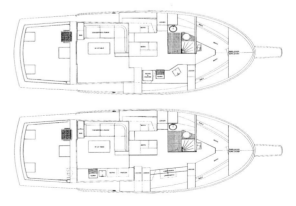

See Page 278 for Pricing Information

STRIKER 50 SPORTFISHERMAN

SPECIFICATIONS

Length ....49'11"	Cockpit..................100 sq. ft.
Beam..............................16'8"	Clearance ....12'6"
Draft ....3'9"	Hull Type ....Modified-V
Weight.....................41,000#	Designer ....T. DeGroot
Fuel ....1,100 gals.	Production 1979–82
Water ....250 gals.	1987–89

The first Striker 50s were built in Korea beginning in 1979. Five were constructed through 1982, and each was a semi-custom yacht built to suit the needs of her owner. Production was resumed in 1987 when a yard in Chile was selected to build the boats. These newer Striker 50s incorporated major design changes in the deck-house, cockpit, engine room, and flybridge. Her two-stateroom interior was available with the galley up or down, the difference being the size of the owner's stateroom and the salon arrangement. Featuring a luxurious decor (for her day), the spacious accommodations available in the Striker 50's living areas are impressive. Outside, the cockpit is set up for serious fishing with cockpit controls and a teak sole standard together with direct access to the roomy engine room. Additional features include wide sidedecks with sturdy rails, an upright rod locker in the cockpit, a huge flybridge, and an unusually long welded pulpit. A good-running boat, she'll cruise at a fast 25 knots and reach a top speed of 28 with 735-hp 8V92 diesels. ❏

STRIKER 54 SPORTFISHERMAN

SPECIFICATIONS

Length ....54'0"	Water ....350 gals.
Beam..............................17'0"	Clearance ....14'9"
Draft ....3'6"	Hull Type ....Modified-V
Weight.....................34,000#	Deadrise Aft ....NA
Fuel, Std. ....925 gals.	Designer ....T. DeGroot
Fuel, Opt. ....1,275 gals.	Production 1970–75

The Striker 54 evolved from the successful Striker 36 and 44 models, and all were designed for long-range, tournament-level events. A total of 18 were built in Norway. Her distinctive profile, welded aluminum construction, super-wide beam, and unique modified-V hull design set her apart from the competition. The first impression of a Striker 54 is of size—she's a big 54-footer. Inside, her three-stateroom interior is finished in solid teak and features an expansive 20-foot-long salon wide open to the galley. Each stateroom is fitted with twin berths, and each has a private head. Like all Strikers, the 54 features a sea chest to eliminate through-hull fittings, self-cooling integral fuel tanks, protection for the underwater running gear, very wide sidedecks, and massive aluminum rails for on-deck security. Still in demand as a used boat, she'll cruise at 17 knots and run 20 knots wide open with 12V71N diesels. With the larger 12V71TI versions she'll cruise at 21 knots and reach a top speed of 24 knots. Note that the published weight of 34,000 lbs. is *extremely* light for a boat this size and may well be inaccurate. ❏

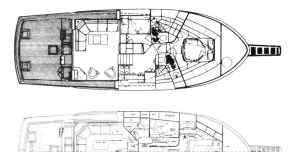

See Page 278 for Pricing Information

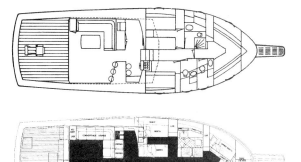

See Page 278 for Pricing Information

215

STRIKER 58/60 SPORTFISHERMEN

SPECIFICATIONS

Length	58'6"	Fuel	1,550 gals.
Beam	19'6"	Cockpit	149 sq. ft.
Draft	3'11"	Hull Type	Modified-V
Weight	51,480#	Construction	Aluminum
Clearance	15'6"	Production	1988–91
Water	315 gals.		1995–Current

Built in Chile, the Striker 58 SF (pictured above) is actually a revised and updated version of the earlier Striker 60 SF built in Korea from 1979–82. She has the same hull, but changes were made to the deckhouse, cockpit, engine room, and flybridge. Like all Striker yachts, she was constructed of welded aluminum on a wide-beamed hull with the shallow keel providing protection to the props and running gear. At heart, the Striker 58/60 is a world-class tournament fisherman with the strength and endurance to match any boat in the fleet. The spacious cockpit is set up for serious fishing and—as with the Striker 62 and 70 models—the 58 also has a unique on-deck day head. While all were delivered with semi-custom layouts, the interior of the 58 was redesigned early in her production run (see lower floorplan) and featured an all-new decor package. A good-running boat, 1,080-hp 12V92s will cruise the Striker 58/60 at 26 knots and reach a top speed of around 28 knots. Note that the Striker 58 is still available on a custom basis. ❏

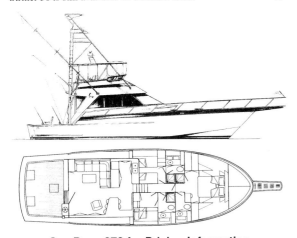

See Page 278 for Pricing Information

STRIKER 62 SPORTFISHERMAN

SPECIFICATIONS

Length	62'0"	Fuel	2,280 gals.
Beam	21'0"	Cockpit	146 sq. ft.
Draft	3'10"	Hull Type	Modified-V
Weight	68,000#	Construction	Aluminum
Clearance	NA	Production	1986–91
Water	315 gals.		1995–Current

Only a few production yachts received the media attention of the Striker 62 SF when she was introduced in 1986. Aside from the fact that she was at the time the largest all-aluminum sportfisherman ever built, what set her apart from earlier Strikers was her lush interior decor and incredible 21-foot beam. Built in Holland (a total of nine have been delivered), the Striker 62s were priced at the top of the chart compared to other yachts in this size range. The lavish three-stateroom accommodations must be seen to be appreciated—indeed, with a 21-foot beam, the floorplan dimensions are huge and the equal of many motor yachts. Among several innovative design features, the steps in the cockpit can be raised hydraulically for engine room access, and the electronics can be hidden within the flybridge helm console until needed. Standard 1,080-hp 12V92s cruise about 23 knots (at around 100 gph) and reach a top speed of 26–27 knots. Optional 1,300-hp 12-cylinder MTUs offer a 27-knot cruising speed and about 30 knots wide open. ❏

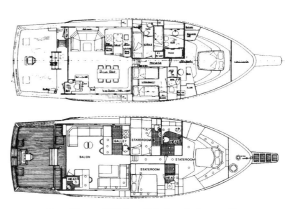

See Page 278 for Pricing Information

216

STRIKER 70 SPORTFISHERMAN

SPECIFICATIONS

Length	70'6"	Fuel	4,000 gals.
Beam	23'6"	Cockpit	221 sq. ft.
Draft	3'4"	Hull Type	Modified-V
Weight	75,000#	Deadrise Aft	NA
Clearance	17'4"	Production	1983–89
Water	450 gals.		1995–Current

The 70 Sportfisherman is the largest model ever built by Striker Yachts. A total of seven of these custom yachts have been constructed to date—two in Korea and five in Holland. With her welded aluminum construction, beefy systems, and enormous interiors, the Striker 70 is actually a small ship with the range to reach the most remote fishing grounds. The huge 221-sq. ft. cockpit is awesome in size and comes equipped with a vast array of features including the popular day head seen in some smaller Striker models. The salon steps lift up at the touch of a button to provide direct cockpit access to the engine room, and (like all Strikers) the gin pole serves as an air duct to ventilate the engine room. The interior layout and decor of the 70s were generally customized to meet the tastes of the owner. Those powered with the 1,300-hp MTUs will cruise at 17–18 knots. The 1,900-hp MTUs will cruise at 22 knots and reach a top speed of 25 knots. The 70 is one of several models currently offered by Striker Yachts on a custom basis. ❏

See Page 278 for Pricing Information

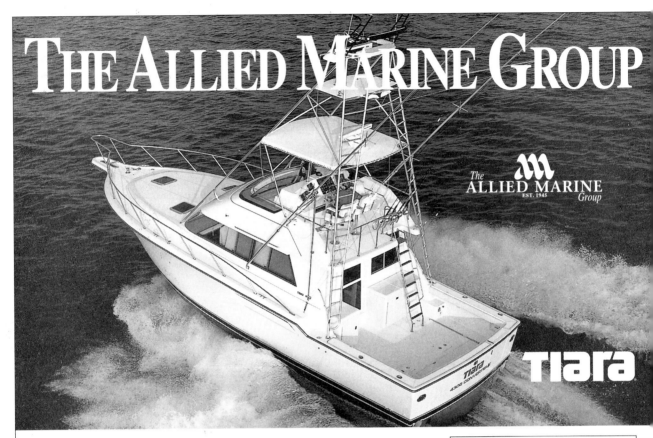

TIARA 2900 OPEN

SPECIFICATIONS

LOA w/Pulpit ....30'9"	Water ....30 gals.
Hull Length ....28'9"	Fuel ....200 gals.
Beam.............................11'4"	Cockpit....................60 sq. ft.
Hull Draft ....2'2"	Hull Type ....Deep-V
Weight ....10,000#	Deadrise Aft...................19°
Clearance ....7'8"	Production 1993–Current

With her conservative styling and quality construction, the Tiara 2900 Open will appeal to those looking for an upscale express cruiser with genuine offshore capabilities. She's built on a proven deep-V hull design with cored hullsides, a wide beam, and a relatively steep 19° of deadrise at the transom. Note the lack of an integrated swim platform—the 2900 retains a traditional full-height transom configuration with a bolt-on platform. Unlike most other contemporary family sportboats, the 2900 does not have a mid-cabin interior layout (but neither does she require the V-drives found in mid-cabin designs to deliver the power). The cabin appointments are lush indeed, and the level of finish is excellent. Additional features include hide-away bench seating at the transom, a hinged helm console, molded pulpit, and a transom door. The bridge deck can be raised hydraulically for engine access. Standard 260-hp gas inboards will cruise the 2900 Open at 18 knots (about 30 knots top), and optional 170-hp Yanmar diesels will cruise efficiently at 25 knots (29–30 top). ❏

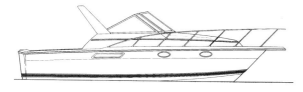

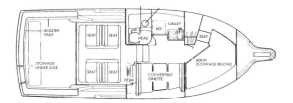

See Page 278 for Pricing Information

TIARA 3100 OPEN (EARLY)

SPECIFICATIONS

Length ....31'3"	Fuel, Std. ....196 gals.
Beam.............................12'0"	Cockpit.................144 sq. ft.
Draft ....2'9"	Hull Type ....Modified-V
Weight ....10,500#	Deadrise Aft....................16°
Clearance ....7'6"	Designer.............L. Slikkers
Water ....36 gals.	Production 1979–92

Originally called the 3100 Pursuit, the Tiara 3100 Open has long been a popular model with family cruisers and anglers alike. After more than a decade in production she remained basically unchanged, until she was replaced with an all-new 3100 Open model in 1992. Her popularity derives from her large cockpit and good offshore handling along with the realization that she's a well-engineered boat built to high standards. The addition of the optional radar arch, swim platform, and bench seating in the cockpit transforms the 3100 into a conservative but good-looking family sportboat with genuine eye appeal. Although more than half of her L.O.A. is committed to the cockpit, the interior accommodations are plush if somewhat compact. Built on a rugged modified-V hull, standard 454 gas engines will cruise at 22–23 knots and reach a top speed of around 32 knots. GM 8.2 diesels (300-hp) were a popular option (22–23 knots cruise). Note that the Tiara 3100 FB Convertible model is the same boat with a flybridge. ❏

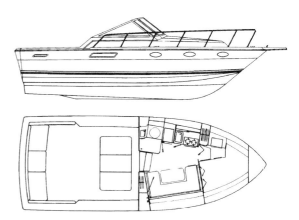

See Page 278 for Pricing Information

219

TIARA 3100 OPEN

SPECIFICATIONS

LOA w/Pulpit	33'10"	Cockpit	NA
Hull Length	31'3"	Water	38 gals.
Beam	12'0"	Fuel	246 gals.
Draft	2'9"	Hull Type	Deep-V
Weight	11,500#	Deadrise Aft	18°
Clearance w/Arch	8'7"	Production	1992–Current

The new Tiara 3100 Open is a complete update of the original 3100 Open model. Her reworked hull features a sharper entry, additional transom deadrise (18° vs. 16°), greater bow flare for a dryer ride, and prop pockets for shallow draft. The 3100 also has a new bi-level cockpit layout which allows for the installation of optional Volvo, Cat, or Cummins diesels in an enlarged engine compartment. Tiara has always been a conservative builder, and it's no surprise that the new 3100 looks a lot like the original—basically a no-glitz express with good-quality construction, systems, and hardware. The slightly enlarged interior of the 3100 has more headroom than before, and there's also a bigger U-shaped dinette. Additional updates include increased fuel, a tilt-away helm console, recessed trim tabs, and an in-deck fish box and livewell in the cockpit. A transom door became standard in 1994. Standard 454-cid gas engines will cruise at 20–21 knots (29 knots top), and 291-hp 3116 Cat diesels will cruise efficiently at 25 knots (30 knots wide open). ❏

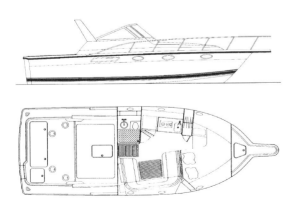

See Page 278 for Pricing Information

TIARA 3100 CONVERTIBLE

SPECIFICATIONS

Length	31'3"	Fuel, Std.	206 gals.
Beam	12'0"	Fuel, Opt.	286 gals.
Draft	2'11"	Cockpit	NA
Weight	13,200#	Hull Type	Modified-V
Clearance	12'2"	Deadrise Aft	16°
Water	36 gals.	Production	1982–92

The Tiara 3100 is an upscale flybridge cruiser with attractive lines and good overall performance. She was originally introduced in 1982 as the 3100 Continental, a designation that lasted through 1986. Built on the same hull used for the original 3100 Open, the Convertible offers the added comforts of a salon and an enclosed lower helm along with the ability to sleep six persons overnight. The stylish interior is an attractive blend of quality fabrics and teak trim with off-white mica cabinets featured in the galley. This is, in fact, one of the more appealing layouts to be found in any 31-foot convertible, and most will find it well-suited to the demands of family cruising. Additional features include a good-size cockpit, wide sidedecks, a molded bow pulpit, and decent engine access. The relatively small flybridge has bench seating forward of the helm console for three guests. Standard 454-cid gas engines will cruise the Tiara 3100 Convertible at 20 knots with a top speed of about 29 knots.❏

See Page 278 for Pricing Information

220

TIARA 3300 FLYBRIDGE

SPECIFICATIONS

Length	32'10"	Fuel	295 gals.
Beam	12'6"	Cockpit	75 sq. ft.
Draft	2'8"	Hull Type	Modified-V
Weight	13,000#	Deadrise Aft	14°
Clearance	11'6"	Designer	L. Slikkers
Water	46 gals.	Production	1986–92

A good-looking boat with a low profile and big cockpit, the Tiara 3300 Flybridge is thirty-three feet of solid construction and good performance. Her rakish profile and glassed-in windshield combine with a practical deck layout to create a capable fishing and diving platform with good cruising accommodations. Note the offset companionway hatch, which allows space in the cockpit for the full-size tackle center. The moderate-deadrise hull is balsa-cored above the waterline, and side exhausts exit just forward of the transom. The ride is dry and comfortable with good lateral stability at trolling speeds. Inside, the upscale cabin is modest in size but well-suited to the needs of a small family. Unlike other Tiaras with their abundant teak woodwork, the interior in the 3300 uses only a modest amount of interior teak trim. A hydraulically operated hatch in the bridge deck provides excellent access to the motors. Standard 454-cid Crusaders will cruise at 20–21 knots, and optional 300-hp GM 8.2 diesels (or 320-hp Cats) cruise around 24–25 knots. ❏

See Page 278 for Pricing Information

TIARA 3300 OPEN

SPECIFICATIONS

LOA w/Pulpit	35'8"	Water	46 gals.
Hull Length	32'10"	Fuel	295 gals.
Beam	12'6"	Cockpit	117 sq. ft.
Draft	2'3"	Hull Type	Modified-V
Weight	11,500#	Deadrise Aft	14°
Clearance	8'8"	Production	1988–Current

Tiara's 3300 Open is a stylish family cruiser whose conservative design and top-quality construction have made her an attractive alternative to the built-in glitz of competitive models in this size range. She's built on a rugged modified-V hull with a shallow skeg and balsa coring in the hullsides. Unlike the Tiara 3100 Open, the 3300 was not designed as a dedicated fisherman. Instead, she's more at home in the family cruiser role where her plush interior and sport-boat profile are most appreciated. Her well-designed interior features overnight berths for six in a cabin of unusual elegance and luxury. The interior is finished with grain-matched teak joinerwork, and the galley features white Formica cabinetry. In spite of her generous interior dimensions, the 3300 still manages to provide an excellent fishing cockpit with a transom door, inwale padding, and cockpit washdown as standard equipment. Standard 454-cid gas engines will cruise the Tiara 3300 Open at 22 knots (32 knots top), and optional 300-hp GM 8.2 diesels will cruise at about 24 knots. ❏

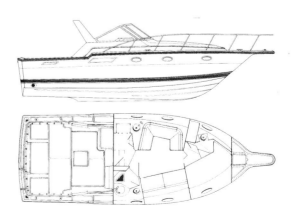

See Page 278 for Pricing Information

TIARA 3600 OPEN

SPECIFICATIONS

Length w/Pulpit	36'8"	Water	85 gals.
Hull Length	36'8"	Fuel	396 gals.
Beam	13'9"	Cockpit	NA
Draft	2'11"	Hull Type	Modified-V
Weight	16,500#	Deadrise Aft	14°
Clearance	9'7"	Production	1985–Current

A hugely popular boat, the 3600 Open is a wide-beamed express-cruiser with conservative lines, top-shelf construction, and very upscale interior accommodations. What sets the 3600 apart from much of the competition is her qualified ability to be transformed from a stylish family cruiser into a tournament-level fisherman. (Indeed, during 1985–86 she was called the Pursuit 3600.) The spacious bi-level cockpit is fitted with an in-deck big fish box on the centerline along with two circulating livewells, rod storage, and a transom door. The interior accommodations are finished with traditional teak cabinetry and designer fabrics throughout. An island berth is forward in the original floorplan, and an alternate layout (new in 1989) has a settee opposite the dinette and overnight berths for six but no stall shower. The bridgedeck has a hydraulic lift for engine access. Standard 454-cid gas engines will cruise at 20 knots and reach about 29 knots top. Optional 375-hp Cats offer cruising speeds at a respectable 26 knots and reach 32+ knots wide open. Note that she can be a wet ride in a chop. ❑

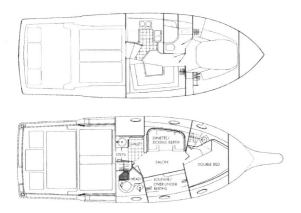

See Page 279 for Pricing Information

TIARA 3600 CONVERTIBLE

SPECIFICATIONS

LOA w/Pulpit	39'8"	Water	85 gals.
Hull Length	36'8"	Fuel	396 gals.
Beam	13'9"	Cockpit	NA
Draft	3'0"	Hull Type	Modified-V
Weight	18,300#	Deadrise Aft	14°
Clearance	12'6"	Production	1987–95

The Tiara 3600 Convertible is a good-looking flybridge sedan with an upscale and comfortable interior to go with her attractive lines. She was built on the same hull used for the 3600 Open, a proven offshore design with cored hullsides and relatively wide beam. The tooling is excellent—typical of the quality you get in a Tiara boat. Inside, a lower helm was optional, and the light-grain interior woodwork and decorator fabrics are impressive. Two floorplans were available: a two-stateroom arrangement, or a single-stateroom floorplan with a dinette. Both have a mid-level galley and include a stall shower in the head. The cockpit is equipped with a transom door and gate, and wide walkaround decks provide safe access to the bow. The cockpit isn't notably roomy and makes no allowance for the addition of tackle centers—a matter of no real consequence to family cruisers but a definite drawback for anglers. Standard 454-cid gas engines cruise the Tiara 3600 at 19–20 knots and reach 28 knots wide open. Optional Cat 375-hp diesels cruise at 25 knots and deliver a top speed of 29–30 knots. ❑

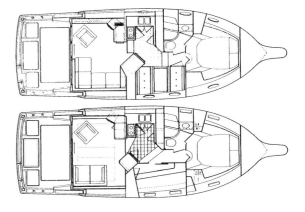

See Page 279 for Pricing Information

TIARA 3700 OPEN

SPECIFICATIONS

Length w/Pulpit..........39'8"	Water ....98 gals.
Hull Length ....37'1"	Waste ....40 gals.
Beam..............................14'2"	Windshield Clearance.......9'9"
Draft ....3'9"	Hull Type ....Deep-V
Weight ....21,000#	Deadrise Aft....................18°
Fuel ....411 gals.	Production 1995–Current

Designed as the replacement boat for the long-running 3600 Open, the Tiara 3700 retains the same conservative profile as her predecessor and for good reason. Like the 3600, this is a true dual-purpose boat with the plush interior accommodations demanded by upscale family cruisers and the hull and cockpit layout of a serious sportfishing machine. She features considerably more beam and deadrise than the 3600, and is a measurably better rough-water performer. The very upscale (plush, actually) interior of the 3700 Open is arranged with a single stateroom forward, a huge U-shaped dinette, a double-entry head with a stall shower, good storage and a surprisingly roomy galley. As usual in a Tiara boat, the joinerwork, appliances, fabrics and hardware are first-rate throughout. Outside, a wraparound lounge is opposite the helm, and the cockpit can easily handle a full-size fighting chair. The entire bridgedeck lifts electrically for complete access to the motors. Twin 422-hp Cat 3208 diesels will cruise the Tiara 3700 at 24–25 knots and reach a top speed of 29 knots.	❏

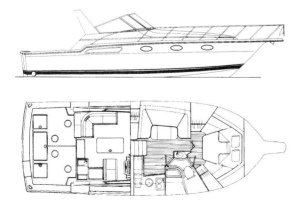

See Page 279 for Pricing Information

TIARA 4300 CONVERTIBLE

SPECIFICATIONS

Length w/Pulpit..........46'7"	Water ....160 gals.
Hull Length ....43'2"	Fuel ....640 gals.
Beam..............................15'2"	Cockpit..................121 sq. ft.
Draft ....4'0"	Hull Type ....Modified-V
Weight ....31,000#	Deadrise Aft ....16°
Clearance ....13'5"	Production 1990–Current

A good sea boat with plenty of eye appeal, the Tiara 4300 Convertible is an upscale sportfisherman with an exceptionally roomy and well-arranged interior. She's built on a beamy modified-V hull with a stepped sheer and balsa-cored hullsides. Two floorplans are offered: the original two-stateroom, two-head layout has the mid-level galley separated from the salon by a breakfast bar. An alternate floorplan introduced in 1992 trades out the guest cabin for a large U-shaped dinette and an enlarged master stateroom. The cockpit is huge and comes with a transom door, in-deck storage boxes, cockpit steps, and (beginning in 1994) direct access to the engine room. Topside, there's plenty of space in the helm console for flush-mounting an array of electronics. Additional features include overhead rod storage in the salon, molded tackle center and pulpit, wide sidedecks, and a choice of teak or oak interior woodwork. No hot rod, the Tiara 4300 will cruise at a respectable 24–25 knots with standard 550-hp 6V92s and reach 28 knots top.	❏

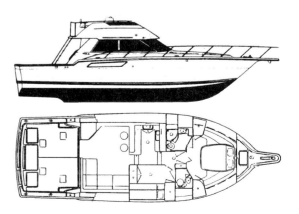

See Page 279 for Pricing Information

TIARA 4300 OPEN

SPECIFICATIONS

Length w/Pulpit	46'7"	Cockpit	167 sq. ft.
Hull Length	43'2"	Water	150 gals.
Beam	15'2"	Fuel	525 gals.
Draft	4'0"	Hull Type	Modified-V
Weight	28,000#	Deadrise Aft	16°
Clearance	10'4"	Production	1991–Current

Conservatively styled (note the absence of an integrated swim platform) and elegantly appointed, the Tiara 4300 Open is one of the larger—and more expensive—production sportboats available in today's market. Built on the same wide-beam hull used in the 4300 Convertible, she's aimed at the market for upscale express cruisers, although she can easily be converted into a serious fishing platform. The belowdeck accommodations are plush, with light ash woodwork, leather upholstery, a teak and holly cabin sole, hydraulically operated dinette, and a spacious master stateroom with a walkaround island berth and built-in TV. Outside, the huge bi-level cockpit—reinforced for a mounted chair—provides seating for ten with in-deck storage compartments, cockpit steps, and a transom door with gate. Additional features include a superb helm console with room for flush-mounting an array of electronics, wide sidedecks, excellent engine room access, and hide-away bench seating at the transom. A surprisingly fast boat with 535-hp 6V92s, she'll cruise around 27 knots and reach 30 knots wide open. ❑

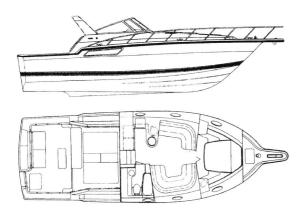

See Page 279 for Pricing Information

TOLLYCRAFT 34 SPORT SEDAN

SPECIFICATIONS

Length	34'0"	Fuel	200/296 gals.
Beam	12'6"	Cockpit	72 sq. ft.
Draft	2'10"	Hull Type	Modified-V
Weight	17,000#	Deadrise Aft	13°
Clearance	13'11"	Designer	Ed Monk
Water	77/116 gals.	Production	1987–93

The Tollycraft 34 Sport Sedan is a versatile and good-looking boat equally at home as a weekend fisherman or family cruiser. Built on an efficient Quadra-Lift hull with solid fiberglass construction and a relatively wide beam, the 34 Sport Sedan features a surprisingly open (and well-appointed) floorplan with two full staterooms—no small achievement in a 34-foot boat. A lower helm was standard, and there's a separate stall shower in the head in addition to a fair amount of storage space. The teak interior woodwork and upscale fabrics are impressive. Outside, an insulated fish box is built into the cockpit sole, and molded steps provide easy access to the wide sidedecks. Two flybridge designs were offered: a helm-aft arrangement with guest seating forward for East Coast buyers, and a helm-forward layout with guest seating aft for the Pacific market. Standard 454-cid gas engines will cruise the Tollycraft 34 Sport Sedan at 20 knots and reach top speeds in the neighborhood of 28–29 knots. Fuel and water were increased in the 1988 models.❑

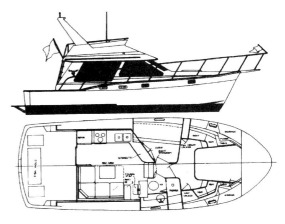

See Page 279 for Pricing Information

SPECIFICATIONS

Length	37'4"	Fuel	300 gals.
Beam	13'2"	Cockpit	89 sq. ft.
Draft	3'0"	Hull Type	Modified-V
Weight	22,000#	Deadrise Aft	NA
Clearance	12'6"	Designer	Ed Monk
Water	140 gals.	Production	1974–85

The Tollycraft 37 Convertible is one of those rare boats whose good reputation has grown over the years. Introduced in 1974, she enjoyed a long production run and remains popular today because of her sturdy construction, practical layout, and low maintenance demands. Showing a distinctive West Coast profile, her relatively heavy displacement and a sharp entry allow the Tollycraft 37 to handle adverse sea conditions with confidence. Two interior layouts were offered with the galley-up floorplan having an extra guest stateroom forward in place of the dinette. Early models were fitted with a wood-grain mica decor; a more appealing full teak interior became standard in 1977. Note that the exterior deck surfaces were given Tollycraft's simulated-teak non-skid treatment. With nearly 90 sq. ft. of space, the cockpit is large enough for a couple of anglers and their gear. Twin 454-cid gas engines will cruise the 37 Convertible at 20–21 knots (about 30 knots top) while optional 210-hp Cat diesels cruise efficiently at 16–17 knots with a top speed of around 21 knots. ❏

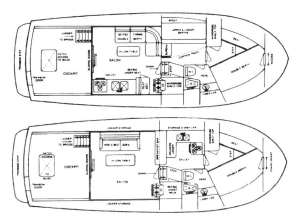

See Page 279 for Pricing Information

TOLLYCRAFT 40 SPORT SEDAN

SPECIFICATIONS

Length	40'2"	Fuel	500 gals.
Beam	14'8"	Cockpit	101 sq. ft.
Draft	3'0"	Hull Type	Modified-V
Weight	26,000#	Deadrise Aft	10°
Clearance	12'4"	Designer	Ed Monk
Water	140 gals.	Production	1987–Current

A good sea boat, the 40 Sport Sedan is the only dedicated sport-fishing design ever offered by Tollycraft. Introduced in 1987 as the Convertible Sportfisherman, she's built using the modified-V hull originally designed for the Tollycraft 40 Sundeck MY. In 1989, Tollycraft slightly revised the deckhouse profile and updated the interior while toning down the emphasis on fishing, renaming her the 40 Sport Sedan. Her slightly reduced cockpit (101 vs. 112 sq. ft.) is still large enough to accommodate a mounted chair and tackle center, and molded steps provide easy access to the wide sidedecks. The original two-stateroom, galley-up floorplan with a lower helm was replaced in 1989 with a pair of more open mid-galley arrangements (and no lower helm), and in 1995 Tollycraft introduced an all-new galley-down floorplan with two staterooms and a lower helm, but without a stall shower in the head. Topside, the helm console can be located aft on the flybridge (for a better view of the cockpit) or forward in the West Coast style. A transom door is standard and wide sidedecks make foredeck access easy and very secure. Caterpillar 375-hp diesels will cruise the Tollycraft 40 at 23 knots (27 top), and the 485-hp 6-71s will cruise around 27 knots and deliver 30 knots wide open. ❏

Original Two-Stateroom Floorplan

Mid-Galley Floorplans (1989–94)

Current Galley-Down, Two-Stateroom Layout

See Page 279 for Pricing Information

TOPAZ 29 SPORTFISHERMAN

SPECIFICATIONS

Length ....29'0"	Fuel ....225 gals.
Beam..............................10'3"	Cockpit...................65 sq. ft.
Draft ....2'6"	Hull Type ....Modified-V
Weight ....8,100#	Deadrise Aft ....NA
Clearance ....NA	Designer ....Topaz
Water ....30 gals.	Production 1983–88

The Topaz 29 proved to be a popular boat over the years due to her rugged construction and single-minded approach to sport-fishing. Like all Topaz models, the bi-cockpit dominates the layout and measures about half of the LOA. The engines are located beneath the raised bridgedeck, and there's room for a full-size marlin chair on the lower level where a large insulated fish box is built into the cockpit sole. A companion seat/tackle center (optional) is to port, and engine access is via a removable centerline hatch. Below, the cabin accommodations are simple and straightforward with upper and lower berths forward that will sleep three plus a mini galley and stand-up head with shower. Recognized as a competent and good-handling offshore fisherman, most Topaz 29s were sold with the factory tower and Volvo diesels. The popular 200-hp TAMD41s cruise at a brisk 26 knots and reach a top speed of around 30 knots. Topaz sold the molds in 1988, and today the boat is in production as the Bimini 29. ❏

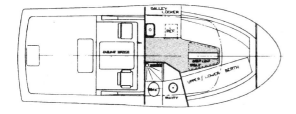

See Page 279 for Pricing Information

TOPAZ 32 SPORTFISHERMAN

SPECIFICATIONS

Length ....32'8"	Fuel ....300 gals.
Beam..............................12'2"	Cockpit...........................NA
Draft ....2'1"	Hull Type ....Deep-V
Weight ....16,500#	Deadrise Aft ....18°
Clearance ....NA	Designer.........Pat Patterson
Water ....40 gals.	Production 1986–91

The Topaz 32 is an attractive open sportfisherman with a large cockpit, stable handling characteristics, and good-quality construction. She was built on a good-running deep-V hull with a relatively wide beam and considerable flare at the bow. The hull is solid fiberglass, and beefy aluminum frames support the engine mounts. Inside, the cabin accommodations are comfortable and extremely well-finished with durable fabrics and superb teak joinerwork throughout. The 32's bi-level cockpit is quite spacious and reinforced to handle a mounted fighting chair. An in-deck removable fish box is just forward of the transom, and two roomy storage bins are also built into the cockpit sole. The raised bridgedeck provides excellent visibility from the helm, and a hatch between the seats offers good access to the diesel engines. (The entire bridgedeck can be raised for major engine work.) The Topaz 32 was available with 306-hp Volvo or 320-hp Cat diesels. She'll cruise around 25 knots with the Cats and reach a top speed of 29 knots. ❏

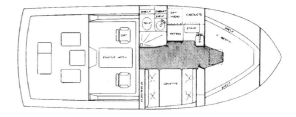

See Page 279 for Pricing Information

TOPAZ 32 ROYALE

SPECIFICATIONS

Length	32'8"	Fuel	350 gals.
Beam	12'2"	Cockpit	NA
Draft	2'1"	Hull Type	Deep-V
Weight	16,500#	Deadrise Aft	18°
Clearance	NA	Designer	Pat Patterson
Water	40 gals.	Production	1990–91

The Topaz 32 Royale incorporates the same dramatic styling and sleek European profile seen in the popular 39 Royale model. Indeed, with her sweeping sheer and curved windshield, the Royale is easily one of the more stylish boats in her class. Designed to meet the needs of sportboat enthusiasts as well as the demands of offshore fishermen, the Royale is built on the proven deep-V hull used for the Topaz 32 SF. She features a bi-level cockpit layout with the engines located below the bridgedeck. Visibility from the raised portside helm position is excellent, and a lounge/dinette opposite provides seating for guests and anglers. The cockpit is large enough for a fighting chair and includes an in-deck fish box and removable floor. Below, the stylish cabin is arranged with a convertible dinette, stand-up head, and a compact galley. No lightweight, 320-hp Cat diesels will cruise the 32 Royale at 21–22 knots. The larger 375-hp Cats cruise at 23 knots and reach a top speed of around 27 knots. ❏

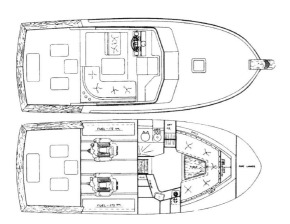

See Page 279 for Pricing Information

TOPAZ 36 SPORTFISHERMAN

SPECIFICATIONS

Length	36'2"	Fuel	300 gals.
Beam	13'0"	Cockpit	NA
Draft	2'5"	Hull Type	Modified-V
Weight	17,800#	Deadrise Aft	NA
Clearance	NA	Designer	Pat Patterson
Water	50 gals.	Production	1980–85

Forerunner of the popular Topaz 37 and a good-selling boat in her own right, the Topaz 36 established the company's name with offshore fishermen in the early 1980s. She was constructed on a solid glass hull with a fairly wide beam and modest transom deadrise. With her low center of gravity, the 36 is a stable boat with a tower, but her relatively flat aftersections can mean a hard ride in a chop. She was designed as a dedicated sportfisherman, and her spacious bi-level cockpit is arranged to meet the requirements of tournament-level anglers. There's room for a full-size tuna chair in the cockpit, and a large in-deck fish box and teak covering boards were standard. The belowdecks accommodations are comfortable and adequate for overnight expeditions with V-berths, convertible dinette, small galley, and a stand-up head compartment with stall shower. The Topaz 36 was available with a variety of diesel engine options from Volvo, GM, and Caterpillar. The popular 355-hp Cats will cruise economically at 23 knots and reach 26–27 knots wide open. ❏

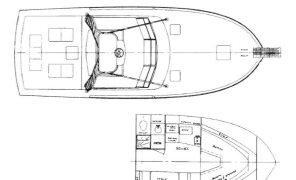

See Page 280 for Pricing Information

TOPAZ 37 SPORTFISHERMAN

SPECIFICATIONS

Length	37'6"	Fuel	350 gals.
Beam	13'0"	Cockpit	81 sq. ft.
Draft	3'4"	Hull Type	Modified-V
Weight	19,800#	Deadrise Aft	NA
Clearance	NA	Designer	Pat Patterson
Water	60 gals.	Production	1986–91

Still a good-selling boat in resale markets, the Topaz 37 SF is a reworked version of the popular Topaz 36 with additional fuel, increased bow flare (for a dryer ride), a larger interior, and improved performance. She was built of solid fiberglass on a modified-V bottom with a relatively wide beam. Offshore, she has a reputation for a solid ride and good handling characteristics. A low center of gravity makes her a stable boat at trolling speeds. The cockpit is a bi-level arrangement with the engines located beneath the raised bridgedeck. (Access to the engines is much improved from the Topaz 36.) The open helm provides good visibility, and there's room on the console for flush-mounting any electronics not fitted in an overhead cabinet. The cabin is set up to sleep four and includes a U-shaped dinette, complete galley, and a separate stall shower in the head. The only engines installed in the Topaz 37 were 375-hp Cat diesels. She'll cruise at 25 knots and reach a top speed of around 28–29 knots. ❏

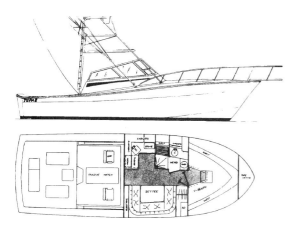

See Page 280 for Pricing Information

TOPAZ 38 FLYBRIDGE SF

SPECIFICATIONS

Length	38'2"	Fuel	430 gals.
Beam	13'0"	Cockpit	125 sq. ft.
Draft	2'7"	Hull Type	Mod. Deep-V
Weight	22,700#	Deadrise Aft	17°
Clearance	11'3"	Designer	Pat Patterson
Water	160 gals.	Production	1985–87

With the distinctive profile of a pure-bred South Florida custom boat, the Topaz 38 Flybridge is a stylish East Coast canyon runner with a practical interior layout and excellent speed to go with her great looks. Aside from her outright sex appeal, serious anglers are attracted to the large and uncluttered fishing cockpit with port and starboard tackle centers, in-deck fish box, transom door, and space for a full-size fighting chair. Unlike most convertibles in this size range, the Topaz 38 was offered with only a single-stateroom floorplan—a fact that limits her aftermarket appeal among those who use their boat for family cruising. In an effort to keep the profile low, the salon settee and dinette are elevated from the salon sole. This—combined with the outboard saddle tanks—makes for a very tight engine room. Additional features include teak covering boards, an offset bridge ladder, and a teak bow pulpit. A fast boat (with a stiff ride), 450-hp 6-71s will cruise the Topaz 38 at 26 knots and deliver about 30 knots top. ❏

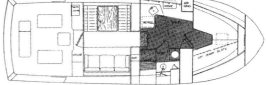

See Page 280 for Pricing Information

TOPAZ 39 ROYALE

SPECIFICATIONS

Length	39'1"	Fuel	400 gals.
Beam	13'0"	Cockpit	NA
Draft	3'1"	Hull Type	Mod. Deep-V
Weight	21,900#	Deadrise Aft	17°
Clearance	NA	Designer	Pat Patterson
Water	60 gals.	Production	1988–91

Before Topaz ceased operations in 1991 the 39 Royale was one of their best-selling boats. Designed to appeal to the upscale end of the family cruiser market as well as the style-conscious sportfisherman, the 39 Royale is an extremely handsome design with an aggressive low-profile appearance and good rough-water performance. She was built on a modified-V hull form with moderate beam and generous flare at the bow—the same hull used in the production of the earlier Topaz 38. Her graceful lines are enhanced by the wraparound windshield and oval portlights in the hullsides. Below, the accommodations are compact but still comfortable with berths for four or five depending on the floorplan. The head is fitted with a stall shower, and the interior is finished with mica counters and teak woodwork. A popular sportboat, the 39 Royale is equally at home as a fisherman and comes equipped with a molded tackle center and a large in-deck fish box. She'll cruise at a fast 30 knots with 485-hp 6-71s and reach 33–34 knots top. ❏

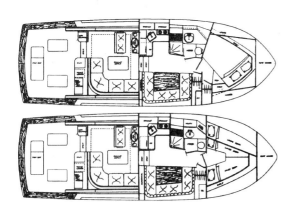

See Page 280 for Pricing Information

TROJAN 36 CONVERTIBLE

SPECIFICATIONS

Length	36'0"	Fuel	250/350 gals.
Beam	13'0"	Cockpit	75 sq. ft.
Draft	2'11"	Hull Type	Modified-V
Weight	16,000#	Deadrise Aft	9°
Clearance	13'0"	Designer	Trojan
Water	80 gals.	Production	1972–89

One of the most popular production boats ever designed, the Trojan 36 Convertible is an affordable blend of traditional styling, comfortable accommodations, and good all-round performance. She was built on an easy-riding modified-V hull with moderate beam, nearly flat aftersections, and solid fiberglass construction. The original two-stateroom floorplan featured a mid-level galley opposite the lower helm. The head compartment was redesigned in 1981, with a separate stall shower, and in 1982 an new single-stateroom dinette layout became available. Outside, the cockpit is big enough for some light-tackle fishing, and the tournament-style flybridge provides seating for up to five. A teak cockpit sole was standard through 1976. Up until the last few years of production the standard fuel capacity was only 250 gallons with an extra 100 gallons optional. A variety of gas and diesel engine options were offered over the years. Among the most popular, twin 350-hp Crusaders will cruise the 36 Convertible at 19 knots and deliver a top speed of around 27–28 knots. ❏

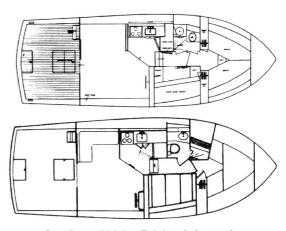

See Page 280 for Pricing Information

TROJAN 12 METER CONVERTIBLE

SPECIFICATIONS

Length ....39'9"	Fuel ....400 gals.
Beam..............................14'3"	Cockpit.................110 sq. ft.
Draft ....3'6"	Hull Type ....Modified-V
Weight ....19,000#	Deadrise Aft....................12°
Clearance ....12'6"	Designer ....H. Schoell
Water ....100 gals.	Production 1986–92

Originally conceived as a sportfishing boat (a market that Trojan had never really tapped with previous models), the 12 Meter Convertible was a little too glitzy for most anglers in spite of her big-boat accommodations and generous cockpit dimensions. Indeed, with over 14 feet of beam, the 12 Meter is a very roomy boat inside—a fact not lost with weekend cruisers seeking a mega-volume interior. Built on a fully cored Delta-Conic hull with wide chine flats and moderate transom deadrise, the 12 Meter's standard two-stateroom floorplan is arranged with the galley down and an island berth in the master stateroom. In 1990, Trojan updated the layout by adding a convertible dinette in the salon. Outside, the cockpit is set up with two in-deck fish boxes, fresh- and salt-water washdowns, a transom door, and molded tackle center. Standard 454-cid gas engines will cruise at 15 knots (24 knots top). Optional 375-hp Cat diesels cruise at 22 knots (25–6 top), and 485-hp Detroit 6-71s cruise at a fast 26 knots (30 knots wide open). ❏

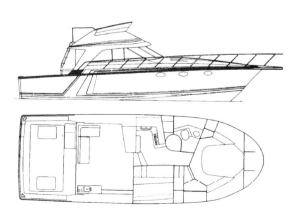

See Page 280 for Pricing Information

UNIFLITE 28 SALTY DOG

SPECIFICATIONS

Length ....28'2"	Water ....30 gals.
Length WL....................24'5"	Fuel................150/210 gals.
Beam...........................10'10"	Cockpit....................90 sq. ft.
Draft ....2'10"	Hull Type ....Modified-V
Weight ....9,000#	Designer..................Uniflite
Clearance ....8'0"	Production 1971–1984

The 28 Salty Dog has long been recognized as a sturdy and well-crafted day fisherman. With nearly 100 sq. ft. of usable cockpit space, she's one of the best fishing platforms in her size range. A molded-in fish well was standard, and the engine access is very good. Although the Salty Dog is rather a plain-Jane boat in her stock form, the addition of a tower and outriggers adds much to her appearance. The cabin accommodations are basic but still comfortable for an occasional offshore weekend. The elevated portside helm is close to the action, and visibility is excellent. The Salty Dog came with several power options including single and twin gas or diesel engines. The standard single Crusader 270-hp gas engine will cruise at 17 knots (25 knots top), and the twin 220s cruise at around 22 knots and reach 30+ wide open. Note that the fuel capacity was increased in 1982. Following Uniflite's demise in 1984, the Salty Dog enjoyed brief resurgence as Chris Craft 282 SF in 1985–86. ❏

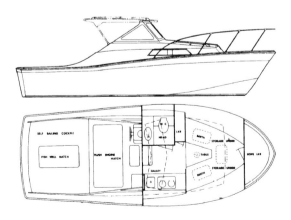

See Page 280 for Pricing Information

231

UNIFLITE 32 SPORT SEDAN

SPECIFICATIONS

Length	31'8"	Fuel	200 gals.
Beam	11'11"	Cockpit	NA
Draft	2'8"	Hull Type	Modified-V
Weight	15,000#	Deadrise Aft	15°
Clearance	11'0"	Designer	Uniflite
Water	75 gals.	Production	1975–84

A popular boat, the Uniflite 32 Sport Sedan was clearly designed with family cruising in mind. She was built on a solid fiberglass hull with a relatively wide beam and moderate transom deadrise. Like all Uniflites, the styling was conservative even by 1975 standards (when she was introduced), and today she looks like a museum piece when compared to her more modern counterparts. Nonetheless, the cabin accommodations are quite expansive for a boat of this size, with both the head and galley conveniently located just inside the companionway door, where they're easily accessed from outside. The cockpit is very spacious with enough room for some light-tackle fishing activities. Topside, the flybridge is arranged with the helm forward and lounge seating aft. Throughout, construction is on the heavy side, and quality is above average. Powered with twin 270-hp Crusaders with V-drives, the Uniflite 32 will cruise around 19 knots and top out at 27–28 knots. Trim tabs are required to keep her running angles down at planing speeds as her tendency is to otherwise run bow-high. ❏

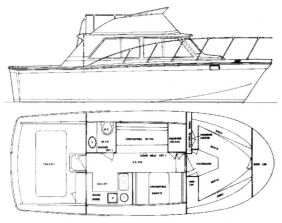

See Page 280 for Pricing Information

UNIFLITE 34 SPORT SEDAN

SPECIFICATIONS

Length	34'2"	Fuel	200 gals.
Beam	11'11"	Cockpit	75 sq. ft.
Draft	2'9"	Hull	Modified-V
Weight	17,000#	Deadrise Aft	15°
Clearance	11'11"	Designer	Uniflite
Water	100 gals.	Production	1974–84

The Uniflite 34 was introduced in 1974 with two model configurations: a Tournament Fisherman model with the helm aft on the bridge (pictured above) and extra fuel capacity (300 gallons); and the Sport Sedan model with the helm console forward on the bridge. She was built on a solid fiberglass modified-V hull with average beam, a well-flared bow, and moderate deadrise at the transom. Inside, the single-stateroom floorplan features a stall shower in the head, a roomy galley area with good counter space, and berths for six when the dinette and salon settee are converted. Teak paneling and cabinetry are used throughout the interior, and an inside helm was a popular option. The cockpit dimensions are generous for a 34-footer, but the flybridge is small by modern standards. In a notable update, the original sliding glass salon doors were replaced in 1977 with a single hinged door. With the 454-cid Crusader gas engines, the Uniflite 34 Sedan will cruise around 20 knots and reach 29–30 knots at full throttle. ❏

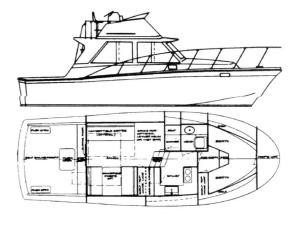

See Page 280 for Pricing Information

Don't Just Fish for the Day,
Fish For The Future.

JOIN THE FOUNDATION.

Billfish are being withdrawn from our oceans faster than they can multiply. Commercial longlines and gillnets pose the greatest threat to these noble pelagics, the ultimate symbols of marine wildlife. For that reason, The Billfish Foundation has spent the last nine years investing member dollars in studying the biology and behavior of the world's billfish species. Now, TBF is the world's leading billfish conservation advocate, delivering the hard scientific facts necessary to rebuild the oceans' billfish populations.

Join The Foundation and participate in an organization that is securing the future of billfish. Your membership dollars will support such programs as the Youth Education Program, Tag & Release Program and No Marlin on the Menu. *To learn more about how you can make a difference, please call today.*

The BILLFISH
F O U N D A T I O N
CONSERVATION THROUGH RESEARCH

The Billfish Foundation · 2419 E. Commercial Blvd., Suite 303 · Ft. Lauderdale, FL 33308
(305) 938-0150 · FAX (305) 938-5311 · TOLL FREE 1-800-438-8247

UNIFLITE 36 SPORT SEDAN

SPECIFICATIONS

Length	36'0"	Fuel, Opt	300 gals.
Beam	12'4"	Cockpit	80 sq. ft.
Draft	3'4"	Hull Type	Modified-V
Weight	20,000#	Deadrise Aft	11°
Water	100 gals.	Designer	A. Nordtvedt
Fuel, Std	216 gals.	Production	1970–84

The Uniflite 36 Sport Sedan is a traditional sedan-style design with a smart profile and a rugged personality. Built on the same solid fiberglass hull as the 36 Double Cabin (a modified-V with single chines and 11° of deadrise at the transom), she was offered with two basic interior layouts during her production years. The two-stateroom version has an in-line galley to port in the salon, while, in the single-stateroom arrangement, the galley replaces the guest stateroom on the lower level, and the salon is considerably enlarged. Outside, the cockpit is large enough for serious fishing, and the wide sidedecks are notable. The flybridge is exceptionally large for a 36-foot boat with the helm console set all the way forward in the West Coast fashion. Standard Crusader 454-cid gas engines will cruise the Uniflite 36 Sport Sedan around 19 knots and reach a top speed of 28–29 knots. The optional 210-hp Caterpillar diesels cruise at 16 knots and reach a top speed of about 18–19 knots. ❏

UNIFLITE 38 CONVERTIBLE

SPECIFICATIONS

Length	38'0"	Fuel	400 gals.
Beam	13'11"	Cockpit	92 sq. ft.
Draft	3'8"	Hull Type	Modified-V
Weight	24,000#	Deadrise Aft	NA
Clearance	12'8"	Designer	Uniflite
Water	100 gals.	Production	1977–84

The 38 Convertible is a comfortable family cruising yacht and a competent offshore sportfisherman. Heavily built, she was available with two basic floorplans: a single-stateroom, galley-down arrangement and the standard two-stateroom, galley-up plan—the latter being somewhat notable for the small galley wedged into the forward corner of the salon. Both layouts had the convenience of a double-entry head, stall shower, and large staterooms. The 38's salon is spacious for a boat of this size. The portside lower helm station was an option, and most were so equipped. As a sportfisherman, the 38 has a large and uncluttered cockpit with a molded-in fish box and wide sidedecks. While the 400-gallon fuel capacity is adequate in the diesel-powered models, those with gas engines carry only 300 gallons—definitely on the light side. Optional 310-hp J&T 6-71Ns will cruise the Uniflite 38 at a steady 19 knots and reach 22 knots at full throttle. Note that in 1985 Chris Craft reintroduced this boat as the 382 Commander. ❏

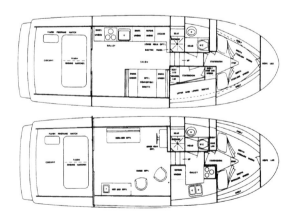

See Page 280 for Pricing Information

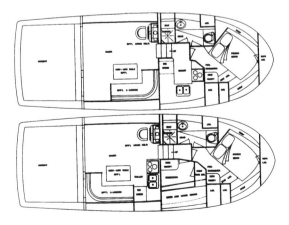

See Page 280 for Pricing Information

234

SPECIFICATIONS

Length	42'0"	Fuel	450/500 gals.
Beam	14'9"	Cockpit	102 sq. ft.
Draft	3'9"	Hull Type	Modified-V
Weight	35,000#	Deadrise Aft	NA
Clearance	12'10"	Designer	A. Nordtvedt
Water	160 gals.	Production	1972–84

The Uniflite 42 is a sturdy West Coast fisherman with a conservative profile masking her rugged construction. She's built on a solid glass hull with a wide beam and moderate transom deadrise. There were two interior layouts offered: The original plan has the galley and dinette at the lower level with a single stateroom forward, and later models have a two-stateroom interior with the galley down (no dinette) and a choice of one or two heads. A lower station is generally found in the salon. Standard 350-hp gas engines cruise at just 17 knots (about 24 knots wide open). Optional 310-hp 6-71s cruise around 18–19 knots, and the more powerful 410-hp 6-71 diesels will cruise the Uniflite 42 Convertible at a solid 24 knots. Note that the standard fuel capacity increased to 500 gallons in 1977. A tournament-style flybridge (with the helm aft rather than forward) was offered for East Coast markets. With the optional 600-gallon fuel capacity, the Uniflite 42 has the ability to range far offshore. ❏

SPECIFICATIONS

Length	48'10"	Fuel	780 gals.
Beam	15'9"	Cockpit	133 sq. ft.
Draft	4'9"	Hull Type	Modified-V
Weight	48,000#	Deadrise Aft	14°
Clearance	13'9"	Designer	A. Nordtvedt
Water	200 gals.	Production	1980–84

The Uniflite 48 Convertible is a handsome and good-running offshore sportfisherman built to compete in tournament-level events. She's constructed on a solid fiberglass modified-V hull design with balsa coring in the hullsides from the waterline up. This was Uniflite's largest (and last) foray into the big-boat sportfishing market. Once considered a relatively fast boat, the Uniflite 48 was one of the early production applications of the then-new 8V92 diesels. Several three-stateroom interior layouts were available, and buyers could choose between having the master stateroom amidships or forward at the bow. Outside, the 48's huge cockpit came with in-deck storage and direct access to the engine room. The flybridge is arranged with the helm console aft on the centerline with bench seating forward. The sidedecks are notably wide. Known for her agile handling, 550-hp 8V92 diesels will cruise the Uniflite 48 Convertible at 24–25 knots and reach 28 knots wide open. Note that these hull molds were later used by Chris Craft in the construction of their 482 Commander. ❏

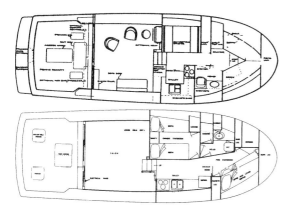

See Page 281 for Pricing Information

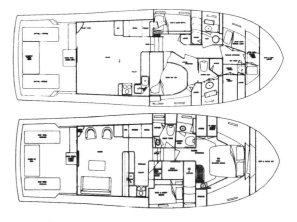

See Page 281 for Pricing Information

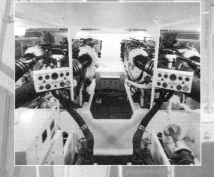

VIKING 35 CONVERTIBLE

1975–84

1985–92

SPECIFICATIONS

Length	35'0"	Fuel	275/300 gals.
Beam	13'1"	Cockpit	80 sq. ft.
Draft	2'5"	Hull Type	Modified-V
Weight	20,000#	Deadrise Aft	15.5°
Clearance	12'4"	Designer	Viking
Water	75 gals.	Production	1975–92

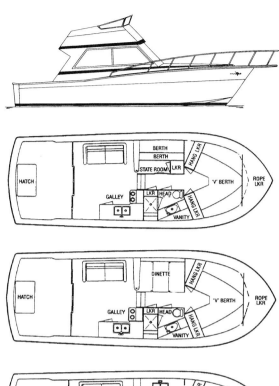

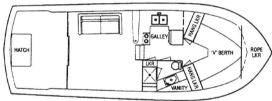

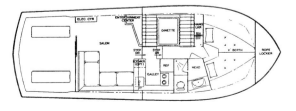

A popular and durable family convertible, the Viking 35 has been recognized as a successful design since her introduction in 1975. She combines the essential elements of modern convertible styling with an attractive interior layout, superior construction, and proven offshore capabilities. Built on a beefed-up modified-V hull with 15.5° of deadrise aft, the hullsides are balsa-cored for weight reduction and strength. She was extensively redesigned and updated in 1985 with a solid front windshield, a completely restyled fly-bridge, and a luxurious teak interior with a choice of one or two staterooms. (The original wood-grain mica interior was replaced with teak in 1980.) Also in 1985, the generator was relocated from beneath the cockpit to the engine room. With her uncluttered cockpit and comfortable interior, the Viking 35 can easily double as a weekend family cruiser. A stiff ride in a chop, 454-cid gas engines will cruise at 18–19 knots with a top speed of nearly 30 knots. Cat 375-hp diesels provide a cruising speed of 24–25 knots and 28 knots top. ❑

See Page 281 for Pricing Information

VIKING 35 SPORTFISHERMAN

SPECIFICATIONS

Length	35'0"	Fuel	300 gals.
Beam	13'1"	Cockpit	NA
Draft	2'5"	Hull Type	Modified-V
Weight	19,000#	Deadrise Aft	15.5°
Clearance	8'6"	Designer	Viking
Water	70 gals.	Production	1984–86

The 35 Sportfisherman was Viking's first entry into the market for open express fishing boats. Designed with a roomy and completely uncluttered cockpit and featuring modest interior comforts, the 35 SF was built on the same proven hull as the Viking 35 Convertible. Her large bi-level cockpit is equipped with two in-deck fish boxes, a built-in tackle cabinet, and full-length lounge seating port and starboard. Engine access, however, is not one of her selling points—working space is at a premium and access is tight. Below, the stylish teak interior provides overnight accommodations for four with a V-berths forward and a convertible dinette. Note that the toilet is fitted in the shower stall compartment to save space (just as in the 35 Convertible). Standard gas engines will cruise the Viking 45 SF around 19 knots with a top speed of 28. The 355-hp Cats cruise at a fast 27 knots and reach over 30 knots wide open. Some thirty-two of these boats were built until production was discontinued in 1986. ❏

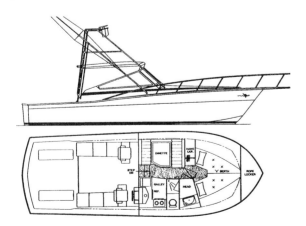

See Page 281 for Pricing Information

VIKING 38 CONVERTIBLE

SPECIFICATIONS

Length	39'4"	Fuel	430 gals.
Beam	14'2"	Cockpit	108 sq. ft.
Draft	4'1"	Hull Type	Modified-V
Weight	32,890#	Deadrise Aft	15.5°
Clearance	11'10"	Designer	B. Wilson
Water	110 gals.	Production	1990–Current

A handsome boat with tremendous eye appeal, the Viking 38 (she's actually over 39 feet) is at the top of the class in today's mid-size convertible market. She's built on a modified-V hull with cored hullsides and better than 14 feet of beam—wide indeed for a 38-footer. Inside, the truly expansive interior of the Viking 38, with its rich teak paneling and upscale fabrics, is the largest to be found in a boat of this size. Two floorplans are offered, and both retain the convenient mid-level galley arrangement and double-entry head. The salon in the dinette layout seems huge—more like a 45-footer. The cockpit has over 100 sq. ft. of uncluttered space and comes with an in-deck fish box, transom door, and molded tackle centers. Topside, the spacious flybridge will seat eight. Crusader gas engines were standard until 1992, when they were replaced with 485-hp 6-71 diesels. A great-running boat, the Viking 38 Convertible will cruise around 26 knots and reach 29+ knots wide open. ❏

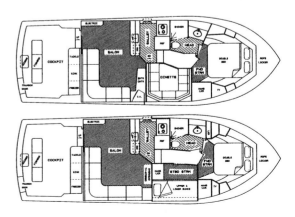

See Page 281 for Pricing Information

VIKING 40 SEDAN

SPECIFICATIONS

Length	40'4"	Fuel	300/350 gals.
Beam	14'6"	Cockpit	100 sq. ft.
Draft	3'6"	Hull Type	Mod. Deep-V
Weight	30,000#	Deadrise Aft	18°
Clearance	11'9"	Designer	B. Wilson
Water	90 gals.	Production	1973–83

A major sales success with over 400 sold, the 40 Sedan contributed mightily to Viking's reputation as a quality East Coast builder. Boasting an aggressive profile and rugged hull construction, the Viking 40's cockpit and spacious interior are big for a 40-footer. Notable, too, are the balsa-cored hullsides—the Viking 40 was one of the early production boats to pioneer this technology. Steel engine mounts were also employed, which have now become a Viking trademark. Three interior layouts were offered with the differences affecting only the lower living area. Early models featured a simulated-wood laminate interior, but in 1982 Viking switched to a more luxurious teak interior. Another update (this one in 1980) moved the generator from under the cockpit to the engine room. Gas power was standard, but most Viking 40 Sedans were equipped with one of several diesel options. The popular 310-hp J&T 6-71Ns and 300-hp Cats will cruise around 20 knots (23–24 knots top), and the larger 410-hp 6-71TIs cruise at 23 knots (26 knots top). ❏

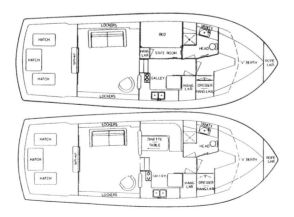

See Page 281 for Pricing Information

VIKING 41 CONVERTIBLE

SPECIFICATIONS

Length	41'2"	Fuel	380/430 gals.
Beam	14'10"	Cockpit	108 sq. ft.
Draft	4'3"	Hull Type	Modified-V
Weight	32,000#	Deadrise Aft	15.5°
Clearance	12'0"	Designer	Viking
Water	125 gals.	Production	1983–89

A popular boat with plenty of eye appeal, the Viking 41 is an upscale tournament-level sportfisherman with classic convertible styling and top-quality construction. She's built on a beamy modified-V hull with a sharp entry, plenty of bow flare, and balsa coring in the hullsides. Several floorplans were offered over the years: The two-stateroom layout sold best, although the single-stateroom arrangement with a full dinette was also quite popular. Indeed, with its wide open dinette and galley, this floorplan gives the interior of the Viking 41 the appearance of a much larger boat. The matched teak woodwork, top-quality hardware, and decorator fabrics are impressive. Outside, the large and unobstructed cockpit is fitted with in-deck fish boxes and a tackle center as standard equipment. The sidedecks are quite wide, and the flybridge will seat six easily. Fast and agile and possessing good seakeeping characteristics, the Viking 41 Convertible will turn an honest 30 knots wide open and cruise at 26 knots with the 485-hp 6-71 diesels. ❑

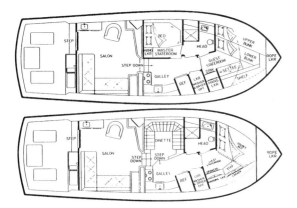

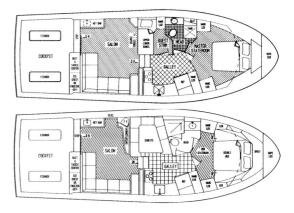

See Page 281 for Pricing Information

VIKING 43 CONVERTIBLE

SPECIFICATIONS

Length	43'0"	Fuel	525 gals.
Beam	15'3"	Cockpit	116 sq. ft.
Draft	4'3"	Hull Type	Modified-V
Weight	38,595#	Deadrise Aft	15.5°
Clearance	12'3"	Designer	B. Wilson
Water	115 gals.	Production	1990–Current

Replacing the popular 41 Convertible in 1990, the Viking 43 has earned a reputation over the past few years as a first-rate tournament fisherman. She has more beam and fuel capacity than the 41, and like her predecessor she offers a choice of a dinette in lieu of a second stateroom. Either way, the mid-level galley is wide open to the salon, and the head compartment and master stateroom are both very spacious. The interior is comprised of rich teak woodwork and cabinetry throughout with quality appliances, excellent detailing, and the latest in designer fabrics—upscale accommodations indeed for a top-level fishing boat. Topside, the flybridge is among the largest in her class and features a particularly well-arranged helm console. The cockpit includes a transom door, molded tackle center, and a big in-deck fish box. Note that a cockpit entry to the engine room became standard in 1995. A good-running sea boat with the original 485-hp 6-71s (24 knots cruise/28 top), now-standard 550-hp 6V-92s will cruise the Viking 43 Convertible at a fast 26 knots and reach 30 knots top. Optional 600-hp MANs became available in 1995. ❑

See Page 281 for Pricing Information

VIKING 43 EXPRESS & OPEN FISHERMAN

43 Express

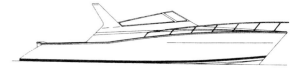

43 Open Sportfish

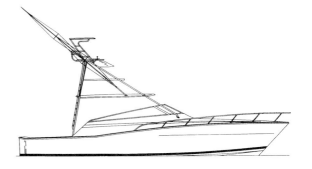

SPECIFICATIONS

Length ....43'0"	Fuel ....525 gals.
Beam..............................15'3"	Cockpit..................116 sq. ft.
Draft ....4'3"	Hull Type ....Modified-V
Weight ....34,500#	Deadrise Aft ....15.5°
Clearance ....8'6"	Designer ....B. Wilson
Water ....115 gals.	Production 1994–Current

Built on the Viking 43 Convertible hull, the 43 Express/Open Fisherman is one of the larger full-production boats of her type on the market. Both versions of this model share the same single-stateroom floorplan (an optional two-stateroom layout is available), and the only notable difference between the two is the bolt-on swim platform and radar arch of the Express. The deck plan is somewhat unusual: the helm is centered on the raised bridgedeck (visability forward is excellent), and the steps leading down to the cockpit are offset to starboard. This permits a full set of in-line tackle centers and a centerline access door to the spacious engine room. A fish box is built into the cockpit sole, and a transom door and transom livewell are standard. Inside, the plush interior features a wide open salon/galley area along with a big stateroom forward and plenty of storage—an excellent day-boat layout. Standard 550-hp 6V92s will cruise at 28 knots with a top speed of 32 knots. Optional 600-hp MANs became available in 1995, and 625-hp 6V92s became optional in 1996. ❏

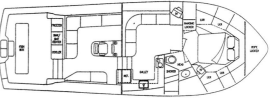

Standard Floorplan

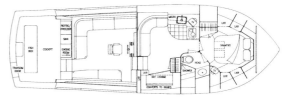

Optional Two-Stateroom Floorplan

See Page 281 for Pricing Information

242

VIKING 45 CONVERTIBLE

SPECIFICATIONS

Length	45'5"	Fuel	600 gals.
Beam	15'0"	Cockpit	120 sq. ft.
Draft	4'0"	Hull Type	Modified-V
Weight	44,400#	Deadrise Aft	15.5°
Clearance	12'5"	Designer	B. Wilson
Water	160 gals.	Production	1987–93

The Viking 45 Convertible is one of those rare cases where the product is so well-matched to the market that her success was assured. (Indeed, 250 were built in six years.) A superb blend of good looks and impressive performance, she's constructed on Viking's standard modified-V hull form with moderate transom deadrise, a wide beam, and balsa coring in the hullsides. Originally offered with two staterooms and two heads, in late 1988 a spacious two-stateroom dinette layout became available at the expense of one of the head compartments. Both floorplans feature a mid-level galley, and the beautiful teak interior woodwork and stylish decor package are most impressive. The cockpit is set up for serious fishing (molded tackle center, transom door, etc.), and the big flybridge will seat eight comfortably. A good performer with standard 485-hp 6-71s, the Viking 45 Convertible will cruise at 24 knots and turn 27 knots on the wall. The 550-hp 6V92s (since 1990) will cruise at a fast 27 knots and reach a top speed of 30 knots. ❏

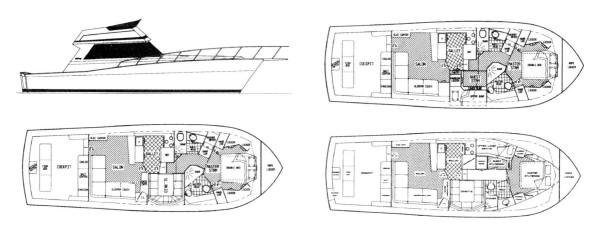

See Page 281 for Pricing Information

VIKING 46 CONVERTIBLE

SPECIFICATIONS

Length	46'6"	Fuel	620/750 gals.
Beam	16'0"	Cockpit	120 sq. ft.
Draft	4'0"	Hull Type	Modified-V
Weight	44,000#	Deadrise Aft	15.5°
Clearance	NA	Designer	B. Wilson
Water	200 gals.	Production	1981–85

The first to display the graceful profile of today's modern Viking yachts, the 46 Convertible is a good-looking canyon runner with plenty of muscle and speed. Built on the standard Viking hull with moderate transom deadrise and reversed chines, the hull bottom is grid-reinforced, and the engines rest on rigid steel beds. The Viking 46 has a reputation for being quite agile, although the ride can be hard in a chop. Her lush two-stateroom, galley-down interior includes an incredibly spacious master stateroom. A triple-stateroom layout—unusual in an under-50-foot convertible—became available in 1982. The interior is finished with traditional teak woodwork and top-quality furnishings, appliances, and hardware. The cockpit can easily handle a full-size chair, and the flybridge will seat six comfortably. The engine room is tight (air intakes are located under the gunnels). Originally offered with 500-hp 6V92s (24 knots cruise/28 top), 675-hp 8V92s became available in 1983 raising the cruising speed to a fast 27–28 knots and the top speed to 31 knots. ❏

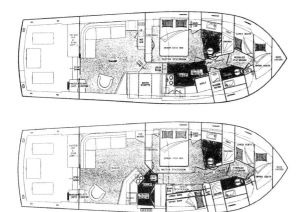

See Page 281 for Pricing Information

VIKING 47 CONVERTIBLE

SPECIFICATIONS

Length	47'2"	Fuel	700 gals.
Beam	15'6"	Cockpit	110 sq. ft.
Draft	4'5"	Hull Type	Modified-V
Weight	46,300#	Deadrise Aft	15.5°
Clearance	12'9"	Designer	Viking
Water	160 gals.	Production	1994–Current

Replacing the popular 45 Convertible in the Viking line-up in 1994, the new Viking 47 is a great-looking boat with tremendous eye appeal and good overall performance. She rides on a new hull design with a deepened forefoot for improved headsea handling and additional flare at the bow for deflecting spray. The hull is solid fiberglass below the waterline and balsa-cored above. Inside, the two-stateroom layout is unusual in that the salon, galley and dinette are on a single level—completely unique in a modern convertible under 50 feet. The master stateroom is huge, and both head compartments have stall showers. Viking interiors are an elegant blend of grain-matched teak cabinetry and designer fabrics, and the 47's accommodations are plush indeed. Note the starboard-side (rather than centerline) salon door. Outside, the cockpit comes with an in-deck fish box in addition to a molded tackle center and direct access to the spacious engine room. Standard 680-hp MAN diesels will cruise the Viking 47 at a fast 28 knots and reach 31 knots top. ❏

See Page 282 for Pricing Information

VIKING 48 CONVERTIBLE

SPECIFICATIONS

Length ....48'7"
Beam..............................16'0"
Draft ....4'7"
Weight ....45,500#
Clearance ....12'5"
Water ....200 gals.

Fuel ....680 gals.
Cockpit..................144 sq. ft.
Hull Type ....Modified-V
Deadrise Aft ....15.5°
Designer ....B. Wilson
Production 1985–90

Built on a lengthened and reworked Viking 46 hull, the popular 48 Convertible used the additional hull length to create a huge 144-sq. ft. fishing cockpit. Unlike the 46 Convertible, the 48 has a solid front windshield and a much-improved engine room. In the original floorplan the galley and dinette are at mid-level. An alternate three-stateroom layout replaced the dinette with a small private cabin, and in 1989 the Plan "C" arrangement offered an L-shaped dinette on the deckhouse level and two very spacious staterooms. The 48's massive cockpit is fitted with two in-deck fish boxes, a tackle center, and a transom door—all standard. The flybridge has seating for eight. Additional features include reasonably wide sidedecks, a molded pulpit, and an optional hardtop. A stiff ride in a chop, the Viking 48 will cruise at 23–24 knots with 550-hp 6V92s (about 26 knots top). With the 735-hp 8V92s (standard in later models), the cruising speed is a blistering 27–28 knots, and the top speed is about 31 knots. ❏

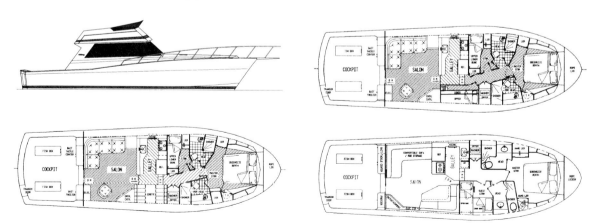

See Page 282 for Pricing Information

VIKING 50 CONVERTIBLE

SPECIFICATIONS

Length	50'7"	Fuel	850 gals.
Beam	16'4"	Cockpit	140 sq. ft.
Draft	4'9"	Hull Type	Modified-V
Weight	58,814#	Deadrise Aft	15.5°
Clearance	13'10"	Designer	B. Wilson
Water	208 gals.	Production	1991–Current

In many respects, the Viking 50 is best described as a scaled-down version of the popular Viking 53 Convertible introduced a few years ago. She's built on a modified-V hull with a wide beam, a well-flared bow, and balsa coring in the hullsides. Inside, her three-stateroom layout is virtually identical to the 53 with only slightly reduced interior dimensions. Note that the salon, galley, and dinette are on the same level. Originally available with two or three staterooms, the current three-stateroom layout has the owner's cabin amidships where the ride is best. Additional features include a stand-up engine room, a huge in-deck fish box, relatively wide sidedecks, direct cockpit engine room access, and a superb bridge layout. At 60,000 lbs., the Viking 50 is no lightweight. Standard power in 1991 was 730-hp 8V92s (27 knots cruise/30 top), however those engines were replaced in 1992 with 820-hp MANs (30/33 knots respectively). Optional 1,100-hp 12-cylinder MANs (available since 1995) will cruise at a fast 34 knots with a top speed of 38 knots making the Viking 50 Convertible one of the fastest (and most popular—over 50 have been built). ❏

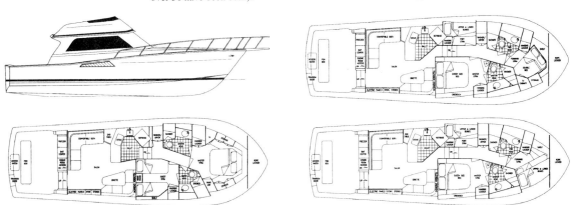

See Page 282 for Pricing Information

VIKING 53 CONVERTIBLE

SPECIFICATIONS

Length	53'7"	Fuel	900/1,100 gals.
Beam	16'7"	Cockpit	148 sq. ft.
Draft	4'10"	Hull Type	Modified-V
Weight	68,600#	Deadrise Aft	15°
Clearance	13'4"	Designer	B. Wilson
Water	200 gals.	Production	1990–Current

A very popular boat with over 60 delivered to date, the Viking 53 is a sleek and well-proportioned sportfisherman with the angular good looks common to all modern Viking designs. She's built on a modified-V hull with cored hullsides, a wide beam and a shallow keel. The original galley-up floorplan has three staterooms and two heads on the lower level with the master stateroom to starboard. In 1992 an offset double bed replaced the V-berths in the forward stateroom, and the current standard layout (available since 1993) has a walkaround queen bed in the forward stateroom. The salon, galley, and dinette are on the same level. With its elegant decor, lush teak woodwork, and clever use of mirrors, the high-style interior is slightly overwhelming for a tournament-level fisherman. The cockpit features a full tackle center, transom door, in-deck fish box, and access to an award-winning engine room. The flybridge is equally large and features a superb helm console. Standard 845-hp MANs will cruise at a fast 27–28 knots (33 knots top), and optional 1,000-hp MANs cruise at 31 knots and deliver 35 knots top. The newest 1,100-hp MANs are a knot or so faster. ❏

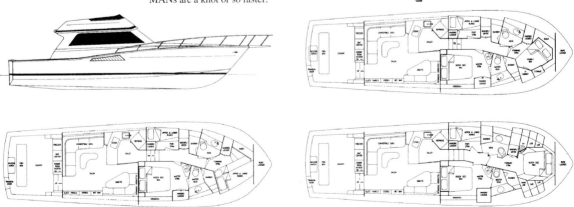

See Page 282 for Pricing Information

VIKING 57 CONVERTIBLE

SPECIFICATIONS

Length	57'2"	Fuel	1,500 gals.
Beam	18'0"	Cockpit	176 sq. ft.
Draft	5'3"	Hull Type	Modified-V
Weight	69,000#	Deadrise Aft	15.5°
Clearance	14'6"	Designer	B. Wilson
Water	250 gals.	Production	1989–91

A good-looking boat with a superb layout to go with her modern styling, the Viking 57 Convertible was built on the standard Viking hull form with a flat keel section, reversed outer chines, and 15.5° of deadrise at the transom. Inside, the three-stateroom interior is arranged with the salon, galley, and dinette all on the same level. Needless to say, the decor is upscale in the extreme—especially the elegant teak woodwork—and each stateroom has a private head. Note that the master stateroom is forward in this layout. The tournament-size fishing cockpit is fitted with molded tackle centers, transom door, teak covering boards, and direct access to the spacious (and well-arranged) stand-up engine room. The only engines ever used in the Viking 57 Convertible were the 1,080-hp 12V92s. A good performer, she'll cruise at 28 knots and reach a top speed of 32 knots. Fast and agile but wet in a headsea, the Viking 57 was replaced in 1992 with the new 58 Convertible. A total of 29 were built. ❏

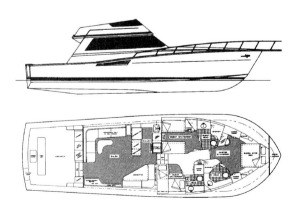

See Page 282 for Pricing Information

VIKING 58 CONVERTIBLE

SPECIFICATIONS

Length	58'11"	Fuel	1,500 gals.
Beam	18'0"	Cockpit	165 sq. ft.
Draft	5'3"	Hull Type	Modified-V
Weight	81,500#	Deadrise Aft	15.5°
Clearance	14'6"	Designer	B. Wilson
Water	260 gals.	Production	1991–Current

The Viking 58 is basically an updated version of the earlier 57 Convertible with a sharper entry, additional bow flare, and a redesigned transom. She's a dryer boat than her predecessor with slightly better headsea and backing-down characteristics. Her modified-V hull retains the same 15.5° of transom deadrise, and the hull-sides are cored with balsa. Inside, the lush interior of the Viking 58 is quite similar to the 57, although the galley has been slightly enlarged by moving the companionway to starboard. The master stateroom is now amidships rather than forward and all three heads have separate stall showers. The spacious cockpit comes standard with a transom door, in-deck fish box, engine room access and a molded tackle center. The 53's meticulously arranged engine room ranks among the best to be found in a boat this size. Note that an enclosed flybridge became optional in 1995. A great-running boat with tremendous eye appeal, the original 1,100-hp MANs cruise at 29 knots. Beginning in 1995, the standard 1,200-hp MANs will cruise at over 30 knots, and 1,450-hp 16V92 Detroits are optional. ❏

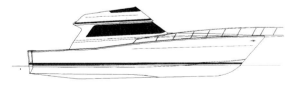

See Page 282 for Pricing Information

Largest volume viking dealer in the world!

During our 15 years of service and dedication to the yachting industry, HMY has become the highest volume Viking Dealer in the world. We offer a full range of New and Quality Pre-Owned Viking Convertibles and MY's, many of which are available at our docks for your private tour and sea trial.

We are fully staffed with trained professionals to answer any questions you may have concerning a New Viking yacht, or to give you an appraisal on the yacht you presently own. Please call for the latest specs on our 38'-68' range. We are open 7 days a week and ready to be of service to you.

HMY

Yacht Sales Inc.

At Harbour Towne Marina
850 N.E. 3rd Street, Suite 213, Dania, FL 33004
(305) 926-0400 · Fax (305) 921-2543
5 Minutes South From Ft. Lauderdale Airport by Land
Just South of Port Everglades Inlet by Water.

The Flagship
68' Convertible
Is Now Available!

VIKING 68 CONVERTIBLE

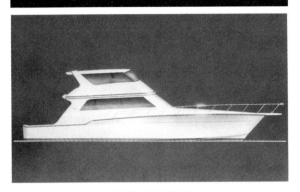

SPECIFICATIONS

Length w/Pulpit..........73'3"	Water ....400 gals.
Hull Length ....68'8"	Cockpit.................175 sq. ft.
Beam.............................19'4"	Clearance ....19'0"
Draft ....5'9"	Hull Type ....Modified-V
Weight ....108,000#	Deadrise Aft................15.5°
Fuel ....2,000 gals.	Production 1995–Current

With her yacht-style accommodations and massive cockpit, the Viking 68 joins the rarified ranks of full production 65-foot-plus convertibles. This is a state-of-the-art boat and, if the past means anything, the new Viking is very likely to exceed the performance standards set by her predecessors. With a beam of over 19 feet, she's a big boat inside and out. The accommodations include four staterooms and four heads (including a main deck day head), with a spectacular full beam master suite. The salon is huge with unusually generous headroom allowing the galley and dinette to be raised two steps above the salon sole. Note the walk-in storage room forward of the galley. The flybridge is available in two configurations: an open layout, or an enclosed bridge arrangement with generous lounge seating, a wet bar, and second helm station overlooking the cockpit. The Viking's full walk-around engine room is a masterpiece of engineering, and her 175-sq. ft. cockpit is an impressive fishing platform with a complete array of built-in fishing features. Twin Detroit 1400-hp 16V92s are standard.. ❏

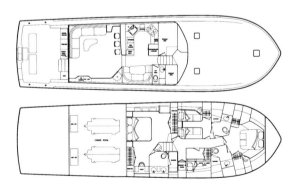

See Page 282 for Pricing Information

WELLCRAFT 2800 COASTAL

SPECIFICATIONS

Length w/Pulpit..........29'8"	Water ....20 gals.
Hull Length ....27'7"	Fuel ....182 gals.
Beam.............................9'11"	Cockpit...................55 sq. ft.
Draft ....2'4"	Hull Type ....Modified-V
Weight ....8,200#	Deadrise Aft...................16°
Clearance ....7'6"	Production 1986–94

The 2800 Coastal is a versatile express boat with a conservative profile and several notable design features. Built on a modified-V hull with moderate beam, she's a capable fisherman able to meet the needs of most weekend anglers. While the Coastal has wide sidedecks and a large cockpit, she still manages to provide a surprisingly spacious interior layout below with good headroom, a small galley area, compact head with shower, and berths for four. For most, however, the chief attraction of the 2800 Coastal is her practical and well-arranged deck plan. The large bi-level cockpit has a fiberglass liner for easy clean up and comes standard with removable in-deck fish boxes and a transom door. The helm seat is mounted on an above-deck livewell, and the companion seat pod contains a tackle center with sink. Updates in 1990 included new deckhouse window styling and upgraded tackle centers, and in 1993 a dinette floorplan became standard. With 350-cid gas engines, the 2800 Coastal will cruise around 20 knots and reach 29–30 knots top. ❏

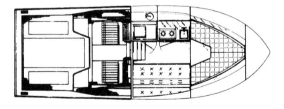

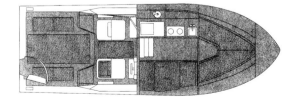

See Page 282 for Pricing Information

WELLCRAFT 2900 SPORT BRIDGE

SPECIFICATIONS

Length............................28'8"	Fuel..........................200 gals.
Beam ....10'8"	Cockpit Area..................NA
Draft................................2'6"	Hull Type.........Modified-V
Weight.......................9,200#	Deadrise Aft ....16°
Clearance........................NA	Designer ....B. Collier
Fresh Water.............45 gals.	Production..............1983–86

The 2900 Sport Bridge is a good-looking flybridge fisherman with a big fishing cockpit and an attractive low-profile appearance. She was built on a conventional modified-V hull form with 16° of deadrise at the transom and generous flare at the bow. The compact cabin layout of the Sport Bridge is straightforward and efficient, with the head conveniently located just inside the cabin door. The small galley is to port across from the convertible dinette, and V-berths are fitted in the forward stateroom. This is a practical layout for a small convertible and one that will suit the needs of family cruisers as well as a couple of overnight anglers. Engines are accessed via hatches in the raised engine deck, and the flybridge will accommodate three with a bench seat. Additional features include rod holders, swim platform, and a well-arranged and unobstructed fishing cockpit. A popular model, the 2900 Sport Bridge will cruise economically around 20 knots and reach 28 knots top with the optional Crusader 270-hp (or Volvo 260-hp) gas engines. ❑

WELLCRAFT 3200 COASTAL

SPECIFICATIONS

Length..........................32'0"	Fuel.......................290 gals.
Beam ....11'6"	Cockpit ....71 sq. ft.
Draft..............................3'0"	Hull Type........Modified-V
Weight....................13,200#	Deadrise Aft...................14°
Clearance......................8'3"	Designer ....B. Collier
Water......................80 gals.	Production.............1984–86

One of the early fishboat designs from Wellcraft, the 3200 Coastal is a good-looking express fisherman with a well-arranged deck plan and a comfortable interior layout. She was built on a solid fiberglass, modified-V hull form and features wide walka-round sidedecks and a molded bow pulpit. No longer in production, 3200 Coastals are popular today because of a solid and dry ride, good all-around handling qualities, and a large, unobstructed fishing cockpit. Below, the roomy teak-paneled cabin will sleep four and includes a full galley and a stand-up head with shower. The Coastal's bi-level cockpit includes a 19-inch transom door (that unfortunately opens into the cockpit rather than out), and rod storage beneath the gunwales. An optional 60 gallons of fuel (or a generator instead) provide a cruising range of close to 300 miles. Twin 350-hp Crusaders will cruise the 3200 Coastal around 22 knots with a top speed of 30 knots. The Wellcraft 3200 Sport Bridge (1985–86) is essentially the same boat with a flybridge and salon. ❑

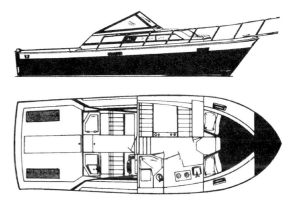

See Page 282 for Pricing Information   **See Page 282 for Pricing Information**

WELLCRAFT 3300 COASTAL

SPECIFICATIONS

LOA w/Pulpit	36'6"	Water	52 gals.
HullLength	33'4"	Fuel	288 gals.
Beam	12'8"	Hull Type	Modified-V
Draft	2'8"	Deadrise Aft	16°
Weight	13,800#	Designer	Wellcraft
Clearance	8'4"	Production	1989–Current

Together with the 3300 Sport Bridge, the 3300 Coastal is the largest model in Wellcraft's fleet of fishing boats. Introduced in 1989, she's constructed on a modified-V hull form with 16° of deadrise aft and prop pockets below (side exhausts were added in 1992). Designed as a dedicated sportfisherman, the 3300 Coastal comes standard with synchronized throttle controls, insulated in-deck fish boxes, bow pulpit, and the same inward-opening transom door found on the earlier 3200 Coastal. A factory marlin or tuna tower is optional. The bi-level cockpit is fitted with under-gunwale storage and padded coaming. Both helm and companion seats are mounted on raised boxes (with built-in livewell and bait prep station) that swing back for engine access. Although she's primarily a fishing boat, the accommodations aboard the 3300 Coastal are suitable for weekend cruising. A popular boat, standard 454-cid gas engines will cruise the 3300 Coastal at 20–21 knots with a top speed of about 30 knots. Optional 375-hp Cat diesels will cruise around 25 knots. ❏

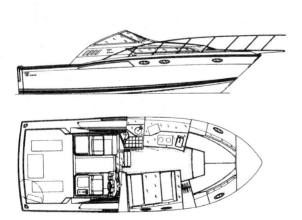

See Page 282 for Pricing Information

WELLCRAFT 3300 SPORT BRIDGE

SPECIFICATIONS

Length	33'4"	Fuel	274 gals.
Beam	12'8"	Cockpit	104 sq. ft.
Draft	2'10"	Hull Type	Modified-V
Weight	15,300#	Deadrise Aft	NA
Clearance	9'9"	Designer	Wellcraft
Water	50 gals.	Production	1991–92

A good-looking boat, the 3300 Sport Bridge is built on the same wide-beam hull used in the production of the 3300 Coastal. Although she's most at home as a fisherman, her upscale interior and wide-open deck layout make her an equally competent family cruiser. The floorplan is arranged with an island berth forward, compact galley, and a stand-up head. The salon is quite roomy, and rod storage is located below the sole. Outside, there's seating for five on the small bridge, and the cockpit includes in-deck fish boxes, tackle center, and an inward-opening transom door (a dubious feature that Wellcraft seems to favor in their fishing boats). Prop pockets in the hull allow the engines to be located aft of the salon bulkhead where they're accessible via flush hatches in the forward part of the cockpit. This design allows for a lower overall deckhouse profile without the use of engine boxes. Standard 454-cid gas engines will cruise the 3300 Sport Bridge at 19 knots and deliver a top speed of around 27 knots. ❏

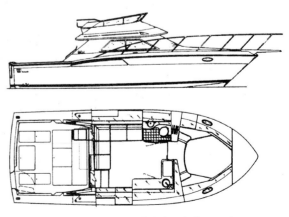

See Page 282 for Pricing Information

About These Prices...

❏ Values contained in the RETAIL HIGH-LOW PRICE GUIDE are intended to provide the reader with *general price estimates only* and are not meant to represent exact market values.

❏ The prices in this book reflect the market conditions projected by our staff to exist for 1996. Do not use these prices after December 31, 1996.

❏ We believe readers will find these prices to closely reflect real-world market conditions. Indeed, if you expect to purchase a boat in excellent condition for less than the published Retail High, you are likely to be very disappointed. In many cases—often depending on location, availability, condition or outfitting—a given model may sell at a price 10–15% *higher* than the published Retail High. On the other hand, a boat in particularly poor condition will almost certainly sell for less than the published Retail Low.

❏ The prices published in this guide apply to boats found on the East Coast, Florida, and the Gulf of Mexico. Prices in other regions must be adjusted as follows:

Great Lakes . . . .+10–15%
Pacific Northwest . . . .+10–15%
Inland Rivers & Lakes . . . . .+5–10%
California . . . .+5–10%

❏ Those wishing to establish a consistent pattern for depreciation based on the prices in this book will be disappointed; we know of no such schedule. Rather, we have evaluated each model on its own merits and assigned values based on our research and experience.

❏ The *Retail High* is the average selling price of a clean, well-equipped and well-maintained boat with low-to-moderate engine hours. Boats with an exceptional equipment list—or those with unusually low hours—will often sell at a figure higher than the published Retail High.

❏ The *Retail Low* is the average selling price of a boat with below-average maintanance, poor equipment, high-time engines or excessive wear. High-time boats in poor condition will usually sell for less than the published Retail Low.

❏ The following abbreviations are used throughout the Price Guide:

S—single engine
T—twin engines
D—diesel engine(s)
G—gas engine(s)
IB—inboard engine(s)
I/O—inboard/outboard engine(s)
VD—V-drive(s)

Retail High-Low Price Guide

IMPORTANT!

Please note the use of asterisks as follows:

*   Outboard models only—Price is for a fully-rigged boat *without* motors

****   Indicates pre-1975 model—Prices are not given for boats built before 1975.

******   Insufficient data— Not enough information to render an estimated value.

> For information on how to apply these prices to boats in different regions, see "About These Prices" on the previous page.

Year	Power	Retail Low	Retail High
Albemarle 30 Express Fisherman			
1995	T/Diesel	******	******
1995	T/Gas	******	******
Albemarle 32 Flybridge			
1995	T/Gas	127,297	142,710
1995	T/Diesel	157,747	176,846
1994	T/Gas	121,895	136,654
1994	T/Diesel	144,525	162,023
1993	T/Gas	110,341	123,700
1993	T/Diesel	131,544	147,470
1992	T/Gas	97,792	109,633
1992	T/Diesel	119,860	134,373
1991	T/Gas	91,734	102,841
1991	T/Diesel	111,639	125,156
1990	T/Gas	85,668	96,040
1990	T/Diesel	103,230	115,728

Year	Power	Retail Low	Retail High
1989	T/Gas	78,386	87,877
1989	T/Diesel	93,378	104,684
1988	T/Gas	74,103	83,075
Albemarle 32 Express			
1995	T/Gas	115,300	129,260
1995	T/Diesel	144,929	162,477
1994	T/Gas	107,721	120,763
1994	T/Diesel	138,926	155,746
1993	T/Gas	99,172	111,179
1993	T/Diesel	126,102	141,370
1992	T/Gas	91,905	103,032
1992	T/Diesel	114,133	127,952
1991	T/Gas	85,920	96,323
1991	T/Diesel	103,019	115,492
1990	T/Gas	81,218	91,052
Albin 28 Tournament			
1995	S/Diesel	70,735	79,299

Year	Power	Retail Low	Retail High
1994	S/Diesel	64,576	72,394
1993	S/Diesel	60,498	67,813
Albin 32 Sportfisher			
1995	S/Diesel	134,030	150,258
1995	T/Diesel	149,331	167,411
1994	S/Diesel	114,011	127,816
1994	T/Diesel	138,977	155,804
1993	S/Diesel	100,280	112,422
1993	T/Diesel	128,159	143,676
1992	S/Diesel	95,287	106,824
1992	T/Diesel	119,421	133,880
1991	S/Diesel	86,133	96,561
1991	T/Diesel	109,434	122,684
1990	S/Diesel	71,429	80,077
1990	T/Diesel	102,283	114,667
1989	S/Diesel	62,976	70,601
1989	T/Diesel	93,830	105,190

Year	Power	Retail Low	Retail High
Atlantic 34 Sportsman			
1992	T/Gas	87,849	98,485
1992	T/Diesel	113,073	126,763
1991	T/Gas	77,411	86,784
1991	T/Diesel	103,505	116,037
1990	T/Gas	68,278	76,545
1990	T/Diesel	95,677	107,261
1989	T/Gas	61,755	69,232
1989	T/Diesel	89,153	99,948
1988	T/Gas	57,406	64,357
1988	T/Diesel	83,500	93,610
Bertram 28 FB Cruiser			
1994	T/Gas	101,621	113,925
1994	T/Diesel	118,693	133,064
1993	T/Gas	93,491	104,811
1993	T/Diesel	108,531	121,672
1992	T/Gas	84,549	94,786
1992	T/Diesel	97,150	108,912
1991	T/Gas	75,606	84,760
1991	T/Diesel	86,581	97,064
1990	T/Gas	67,883	76,102
1989	T/Gas	62,599	70,178
1988	T/Gas	57,314	64,254
1987	T/Gas	53,249	59,697
1986	T/Gas	49,185	55,140
1985	T/Gas	44,307	49,671
1984	T/Gas	42,681	47,848
1983	T/Gas	39,835	44,659
1982	T/Gas	35,364	39,646
1981	T/Gas	32,886	36,868
1980	T/Gas	25,963	29,106
1979	T/Gas	23,532	26,680
1978	T/Gas	21,821	24,740
1977	T/Gas	20,537	23,285
1976	T/Gas	19,681	22,315
1975	T/Gas	18,826	21,344
Bertram 28 SF			
1983	T/Gas	35,364	39,646
1982	T/Gas	32,112	36,000
1981	T/Gas	29,267	32,810
1980	T/Gas	22,763	25,519
1979	T/Gas	21,302	24,152
1978	T/Gas	19,694	22,329
1977	T/Gas	19,483	22,089
1976	T/Gas	18,636	21,129
1975	T/Gas	17,789	20,168
Bertram 28 Bahia Mar			
1992	T/Gas	80,139	89,842
1992	T/Diesel	95,745	107,337
1991	T/Gas	74,234	83,222
1991	T/Diesel	87,309	97,880
1990	T/Gas	67,907	76,129
1989	T/Gas	62,002	69,509
1988	T/Gas	55,253	61,943
1987	T/Gas	51,036	57,215
1986	T/Gas	49,349	55,323
1985	T/Gas	43,865	49,176
Bertram 28 Moppie			
1994	T/Gas	96,507	108,192
1993	T/Gas	89,269	100,078
1992	T/Gas	83,267	93,349
1991	T/Gas	73,825	82,763
1990	T/Gas	66,528	74,583
1989	T/Gas	60,948	68,328
1988	T/Gas	52,364	58,704
1987	T/Gas	41,204	46,193
Bertram 30 FB Cruiser			
1985	T/Gas	59,593	66,809
1985	T/Diesel	75,571	84,721
1984	T/Gas	57,866	64,872
1984	T/Diesel	72,548	81,332
Bertram 30 Moppie			
1995	T/Gas	119,278	133,720
1995	T/Diesel	153,255	171,811
1994	T/Gas	106,620	119,529
1994	T/Diesel	140,638	157,666
Bertram 31 FB Cruiser			
1986	T/Gas	72,922	81,752
1983	T/Gas	51,300	57,511
1983	T/Diesel	66,139	74,147
1982	T/Gas	46,636	52,283
1982	T/Diesel	61,475	68,918
1981	T/Gas	42,821	48,005
1981	T/Diesel	53,844	60,363
1980	T/Gas	39,005	43,728
1980	T/Diesel	45,365	50,857
1979	T/Gas	34,160	38,730
1979	T/Diesel	40,991	46,476
Bertram 31 SF			
1982	T/Gas	45,552	51,067
1982	T/Diesel	58,749	65,862
1981	T/Gas	48,106	53,930
1981	T/Diesel	51,086	57,271
1980	T/Gas	36,186	40,567
1980	T/Diesel	41,720	46,771
1979	T/Gas	34,194	38,769
1979	T/Diesel	38,468	43,615
1978	T/Gas	30,775	34,892
1978	T/Diesel	34,194	38,769
1977	T/Gas	26,500	30,046
1977	T/Diesel	31,630	35,861
1976	T/Gas	23,936	27,138
1976	T/Diesel	28,210	31,984
1975	T/Gas	21,371	24,230
1975	T/Diesel	24,791	28,107
Bertram 31 Bahia Mar			
1981	T/Gas	36,483	40,900
1981	T/Diesel	44,638	50,043
1980	T/Gas	34,337	38,494
1980	T/Diesel	39,488	44,269
1979	T/Gas	31,406	35,607
1979	T/Diesel	35,650	40,419
1978	T/Gas	28,859	32,720
1978	T/Diesel	30,557	34,645
1977	T/Gas	25,888	29,352
1977	T/Diesel	28,010	31,758
1976	T/Gas	22,918	25,984
1976	T/Diesel	25,464	28,871
1975	T/Gas	20,371	23,097
1975	T/Diesel	22,069	25,021
Bertram 33 FB Cruiser			
1992	T/Gas	142,369	159,607
1992	T/Diesel	180,007	201,802
1991	T/Gas	127,193	142,593

Year	Power	Retail Low	Retail High
1991	T/Diesel	162,109	181,736
1990	T/Gas	122,229	137,028
1990	T/Diesel	150,239	168,430
1989	T/Gas	116,287	130,366
1989	T/Diesel	135,809	152,253
1988	T/Gas	104,828	117,520
1988	T/Diesel	127,321	142,737
1987	T/Gas	95,915	107,529
1987	T/Diesel	118,833	133,221
1986	T/Gas	89,549	100,392
1986	T/Diesel	110,345	123,705
1985	T/Gas	81,910	91,827
1985	T/Diesel	101,857	114,190
1984	T/Gas	75,968	85,166
1984	T/Diesel	94,218	105,625
1983	T/Gas	70,027	78,505
1983	T/Diesel	86,579	97,061
1982	T/Gas	64,510	72,320
1982	T/Diesel	78,939	88,497
1981	T/Gas	59,841	67,086
1981	T/Diesel	72,149	80,884
1980	T/Gas	53,475	59,950
1980	T/Diesel	72,998	81,836
1979	T/Gas	46,161	52,337
1979	T/Diesel	62,947	71,368
1978	T/Gas	41,965	47,579
1978	T/Diesel	59,590	67,562
1977	T/Gas	38,608	43,773
1977	T/Diesel	55,393	62,804

Bertram 33 SF

Year	Power	Retail Low	Retail High
1992	T/Gas	135,315	151,699
1992	T/Diesel	176,856	198,269
1991	T/Gas	127,690	143,151
1991	T/Diesel	166,162	186,280
1990	T/Gas	117,484	131,709
1990	T/Diesel	156,932	175,933
1989	T/Gas	108,480	121,615
1989	T/Diesel	141,067	158,147
1988	T/Gas	99,905	112,001
1988	T/Diesel	127,346	142,765
1987	T/Gas	97,332	109,117
1987	T/Diesel	123,059	137,958
1986	T/Gas	85,326	95,657
1986	T/Diesel	107,194	120,172
1985	T/Gas	81,896	91,812

Year	Power	Retail Low	Retail High
1985	T/Diesel	106,765	119,692
1984	T/Gas	75,464	84,601
1984	T/Diesel	96,474	108,155
1983	T/Gas	69,890	78,352
1983	T/Diesel	91,329	102,387
1982	T/Gas	63,693	71,405
1982	T/Diesel	86,096	96,520
1981	T/Gas	58,422	65,496
1981	T/Diesel	78,189	87,656
1980	T/Gas	58,241	65,292
1980	T/Diesel	75,713	84,880
1979	T/Gas	54,044	61,274
1979	T/Diesel	69,992	79,356

Bertram 35 Convertible

Year	Power	Retail Low	Retail High
1986	T/Gas	96,376	108,045
1986	T/Diesel	126,096	141,363
1985	T/Gas	88,958	99,729
1985	T/Diesel	117,459	131,681
1984	T/Gas	85,503	95,856
1984	T/Diesel	111,845	125,387
1983	T/Gas	81,617	91,499
1983	T/Diesel	108,391	121,514
1982	T/Gas	72,116	80,848
1982	T/Diesel	96,731	108,443
1981	T/Gas	73,189	82,050
1981	T/Diesel	88,308	99,000
1980	T/Gas	62,172	69,700
1980	T/Diesel	73,321	82,198
1979	T/Gas	58,084	65,855
1979	T/Diesel	67,835	76,910
1978	T/Gas	52,572	59,606
1978	T/Diesel	63,595	72,104
1977	T/Gas	45,789	51,915
1977	T/Diesel	59,356	67,297
1976	T/Gas	39,853	45,185
1976	T/Diesel	55,116	62,490
1975	T/Gas	36,461	41,339
1975	T/Diesel	50,876	57,683

Bertram 37 Convertible

Year	Power	Retail Low	Retail High
1995	435D	345,935	387,820
1995	485D	364,175	408,268
1994	450D	334,398	374,885
1994	550D	354,664	397,606
1993	375D	257,554	288,737

Year	Power	Retail Low	Retail High
1993	450D	299,776	336,071
1993	550D	324,264	363,525
1992	375D	238,132	266,964
1992	450D	275,287	308,618
1992	550D	297,242	333,231
1991	375D	215,054	241,092
1991	450D	259,101	290,472
1990	375D	198,644	222,695
1990	450D	228,873	256,584
1989	375D	185,689	208,172
1989	450D	207,281	232,378
1988	375D	172,734	193,648
1988	450D	190,007	213,013
1987	375D	164,097	183,966
1987	435D	174,461	195,584
1987	450D	179,870	201,648
1986	375D	160,529	179,965
1986	435D	171,995	192,820

Bertram 38 Convertible

Year	Power	Retail Low	Retail High
1976	T/Diesel	67,411	76,430
1975	T/Diesel	62,234	70,560

Bertram 38 III Convertible

Year	Power	Retail Low	Retail High
1986	T/Diesel	163,356	183,135
1985	T/Diesel	148,150	166,087
1984	T/Diesel	140,330	157,320
1983	T/Diesel	132,573	148,625
1982	T/Diesel	122,641	137,490
1981	T/Diesel	105,325	118,078
1980	T/Diesel	98,245	110,140
1979	T/Diesel	91,892	104,186
1978	T/Diesel	84,043	95,287

Bertram 38 Special

Year	Power	Retail Low	Retail High
1987	375D	155,461	174,283
1987	435D	173,598	194,616
1986	375D	149,481	167,580
1986	435D	163,236	183,000

Bertram 42 Convertible

Year	Power	Retail Low	Retail High
1987	T/Diesel	233,344	261,596
1986	T/Diesel	220,859	247,599
1985	T/Diesel	205,790	230,707
1984	T/Diesel	197,172	221,045
1983	T/Diesel	189,043	211,932
1982	T/Diesel	177,399	198,878
1981	T/Diesel	164,859	184,819

Year	Power	Retail Low	Retail High
1980	T/Diesel	153,210	171,760
1979	T/Diesel	143,570	162,778
1978	T/Diesel	137,295	155,663
1977	T/Diesel	128,262	145,422
1976	T/Diesel	113,987	129,237

Bertram 43 Convertible

Year	Power	Retail Low	Retail High
1995	550 hp DD	468,532	525,260
1995	665 hp MAN	486,435	545,331
1994	550 hp DD	436,545	489,400
1994	665 hp MAN	465,642	522,020
1993	T/Diesel	425,209	476,692
1992	T/Diesel	394,421	442,176
1991	T/Diesel	354,909	397,880
1990	T/Diesel	328,291	368,039
1989	T/Diesel	309,658	347,150
1988	T/Diesel	294,574	330,240

Bertram 43 Moppie

Year	Power	Retail Low	Retail High
1995	550 DD	407,394	456,720
1995	600 MAN	425,725	477,270

Bertram 46 Conv. (Early)

Year	Power	Retail Low	Retail High
1987	T/Diesel	303,329	340,055
1986	T/Diesel	290,348	325,502
1985	T/Diesel	257,895	289,120
1984	T/Diesel	251,404	281,843
1983	T/Diesel	231,067	259,043
1982	T/Diesel	208,133	233,333
1981	T/Diesel	189,959	212,959
1980	T/Diesel	175,970	197,276
1979	T/Diesel	163,150	184,977
1978	T/Diesel	151,434	171,694
1977	T/Diesel	143,000	162,131
1976	T/Diesel	134,062	151,998
1975	T/Diesel	129,593	146,931

Bertram 46 Convertible

Year	Power	Retail Low	Retail High
1995	735 DD	588,170	659,383
1995	820MAN	614,254	688,626

Bertram 46 Moppie

Year	Power	Retail Low	Retail High
1995	T/Diesel	527,911	591,829
1994	T/Diesel	497,790	558,060
1993	T/Diesel	474,366	531,800

Bertram 50 Convertible

Year	Power	Retail Low	Retail High
1995	735D	710,509	796,535
1995	900D	766,775	859,613

Year	Power	Retail Low	Retail High
1994	735D	653,762	732,918
1994	900D	733,057	821,813
1993	735D	607,039	680,536
1992	735D		
	Galley up	572,802	642,155
	Galley dn	555,704	622,986
1991	735D		
	Galley up	548,431	614,832
	Galley dn	531,157	595,468
1991	840D		
	Galley up	582,977	653,562
	Galley dn	565,704	634,197
1990	735D		
	Galley up	502,656	563,516
	Galley dn	489,701	548,992
1990	840D		
	Galley up	535,475	600,309
	Galley dn	522,520	585,785
1989	735D		
	Galley up	471,574	528,671
	Galley dn	458,475	513,986
1989	840D		
	Galley up	506,506	567,832
	Galley dn	493,406	553,146
1988	735D		
	Galley up	444,790	498,644
	Galley dn	431,835	484,120
1987	735D	428,338	480,200

Bertram 54 Convertible

Year	Power	Retail Low	Retail High
1995	1100D	936,596	1,049,996
1995	1250D	967,705	1,084,871
1993	T/Diesel	876,625	982,764
1992	T/Diesel	847,350	949,943
1991	T/Diesel	807,963	905,789
1990	T/Diesel	725,483	813,322
1989	T/Diesel	647,753	726,180
1988	T/Diesel	561,386	629,356
1987	T/Diesel	518,202	580,944
1986	T/Diesel	457,745	513,167
1985	T/Diesel	421,471	472,501
1984	T/Diesel	397,288	445,390
1983	T/Diesel	384,333	430,867
1982	T/Diesel	360,582	404,240
1981	T/Diesel	345,036	386,812

Bertram 58 Convertible

Year	Power	Retail Low	Retail High
1983	T/Diesel	462,063	518,008
1982	T/Diesel	435,290	487,993
1981	T/Diesel	405,493	454,589
1980	T/Diesel	365,574	409,836
1979	T/Diesel	337,230	382,347
1978	T/Diesel	325,259	368,774
1977	T/Diesel	311,515	353,192

Bertram 60 Convertible

Year	Power	Retail Low	Retail High
1995	1250 Cat	1,217,657	1,365,086
1995	1400 DD	1,277,882	1,432,603
1994	T/Dsl	1,245,678	1,396,500
1993	T/Dsl	1,196,900	1,341,816
1992	T/Dsl	1,131,408	1,268,394
1991	T/Dsl	1,051,518	1,178,832
1990	T/Dsl	924,127	1,036,017

Bertram 72 Convertible

Year	Power	Retail Low	Retail High
1994	T/Diesel		******
1993	T/Diesel		******
1992	T/Diesel		******
1991	T/Diesel		******
1990	T/Diesel		******

Bimini 29 SF

Year	Power	Retail Low	Retail High
1993	T/Gas	72,548	81,332
1993	T/Diesel	84,208	94,403
1992	T/Gas	66,071	74,070
1992	T/Diesel	76,435	85,689
1991	T/Gas	60,457	67,777
1991	T/Diesel	67,366	75,523
1990	T/Gas	56,570	63,420
1990	T/Diesel	63,048	70,682
1989	T/Gas	53,116	59,547
1989	T/Diesel	59,161	66,324

Black Watch 30 SF

Year	Power	Retail Low	Retail High
1994	T/Gas	101,913	114,252
1994	T/Diesel	123,073	137,974
1993	T/Gas	90,685	101,665
1993	T/Diesel	112,277	125,871
1992	T/Gas	80,321	90,046
1992	T/Diesel	101,049	113,284
1991	T/Gas	69,957	78,427
1991	T/Diesel	93,708	105,054
1990	T/Gas	65,639	73,586
1990	T/Diesel	84,640	94,888

Year	Power	Retail Low	Retail High
1989	T/Gas	57,118	64,033
1989	T/Diesel	70,964	79,556
1988	T/Gas	48,463	54,331
1988	T/Diesel	64,041	71,795
1987	T/Gas	42,406	47,540
1987	T/Diesel	59,714	66,944
1986	T/Gas	38,944	43,659
1986	T/Diesel	50,194	56,272

Black Watch 30 Flybridge

Year	Power	Retail Low	Retail High
1994	T/Gas	127,823	143,300
1994	T/Diesel	152,870	171,378
1993	T/Gas	114,004	127,808
1993	T/Diesel	141,210	158,307
1992	T/Gas	99,322	111,348
1992	T/Diesel	111,845	125,387
1991	T/Gas	86,799	97,308
1991	T/Diesel	105,800	118,609
1990	T/Gas	79,458	89,078
1990	T/Diesel	97,595	109,411
1989	T/Gas	69,957	78,427
1989	T/Diesel	82,480	92,467

Black Watch 36 Flybridge

Year	Power	Retail Low	Retail High
1994	T/Gas	145,097	162,664
1994	T/Diesel	181,371	203,330
1993	T/Gas	137,755	154,434
1993	T/Diesel	168,848	189,291
1992	T/Gas	126,096	141,363
1992	T/Diesel	151,142	169,442
1991	T/Gas	116,595	130,712
1991	T/Diesel	144,665	162,180

Blackfin 29 Combi

Year	Power	Retail Low	Retail High
1995	T/OB*	76,044	85,251
1995	T/Gas	92,144	103,300
1995	T/Diesel	113,956	127,753
1994	T/Gas	90,004	100,901
1994	T/Diesel	109,879	123,183
1993	T/Gas	81,644	91,529
1993	T/Diesel	99,778	111,859
1992	T/Gas	73,221	82,087
1992	T/Diesel	89,914	100,801
1991	T/Gas	74,707	83,753
1991	T/Diesel	91,981	103,118
1990	T/Gas	69,525	77,943
1990	T/Diesel	81,185	91,015

Year	Power	Retail Low	Retail High
1989	T/Gas	58,254	65,307
1989	T/Diesel	72,818	81,634
1988	T/Gas	51,829	58,104
1988	T/Diesel	64,679	72,510
1987	T/Gas	48,797	54,706
1987	T/Diesel	60,457	67,777
1986	T/Gas	45,638	51,164
1986	T/Diesel	56,609	63,463
1985	T/Gas	41,689	46,736
1985	T/Diesel	53,098	59,527
1984	T/Gas	37,739	42,309
1984	T/Diesel	49,588	55,591
1983	T/Gas	35,545	39,849
1983	T/Diesel	46,516	52,148

Blackfin 29 Flybridge SF

Year	Power	Retail Low	Retail High
1995	T/Gas	115,086	129,020
1995	T/Diesel	130,856	146,700
1994	T/Gas	107,298	120,289
1994	T/Diesel	124,008	139,023
1993	T/Gas	100,475	112,640
1993	T/Diesel	119,436	133,896
1992	T/Gas	93,519	104,841
1992	T/Diesel	107,880	120,942
1991	T/Gas	84,037	94,212
1991	T/Diesel	100,004	112,112
1990	T/Gas	74,959	84,035
1990	T/Diesel	93,806	105,164
1989	T/Gas	66,392	74,431
1989	T/Diesel	83,098	93,159
1988	T/Gas	60,396	67,708
1988	T/Diesel	75,388	84,515
1987	T/Gas	56,112	62,906
1987	T/Diesel	70,676	79,233
1986	T/Gas	47,546	53,302
1986	T/Diesel	63,394	71,070

Blackfin 31 Combi

Year	Power	Retail Low	Retail High
1995	T/Gas	131,392	147,300
1995	T/Diesel	166,280	186,412
1994	T/Gas	119,235	133,672
1994	T/Diesel	160,391	179,810
1993	T/Gas	113,143	126,841
1993	T/Diesel	144,621	162,131

Blackfin 32 SF

Year	Power	Retail Low	Retail High
1991	T/Gas	104,504	117,157
1991	300D	135,596	152,014
1991	375D	154,597	173,315
1990	T/Gas	95,004	106,506
1990	300D	121,777	136,522
1990	375D	140,778	157,823
1989	T/Gas	87,231	97,792
1989	300D	109,686	122,966
1989	375D	130,414	146,204
1988	T/Gas	79,458	89,078
1988	300D	105,800	118,609
1988	375D	119,186	133,617
1987	T/Gas	73,844	82,785
1987	300D	99,322	111,348
1987	375D	111,413	124,903
1986	T/Gas	67,747	75,950
1986	300D	93,535	104,860
1986	375D	103,151	115,640
1985	T/Gas	64,251	72,030
1985	300D	87,416	98,000
1985	355D	97,032	108,780
1984	T/Gas	55,072	61,740
1984	300D	72,992	81,830
1984	355D	86,542	97,020
1983	T/Gas	51,138	57,330
1983	300D	70,807	79,380
1983	355D	77,800	87,220
1982	T/Gas	45,920	51,479
1982	300D	64,378	72,172
1981	T/Gas	43,218	48,451
1981	300D	62,127	69,649
1980	T/Gas	39,381	44,149
1980	T/Diesel	52,817	59,212

Blackfin 32 Combi

Year	Power	Retail Low	Retail High
1992	T/Gas	110,850	124,271
1992	T/Diesel	143,933	161,359
1991	T/Gas	99,679	111,747
1991	T/Diesel	129,754	145,464
1990	T/Gas	86,789	97,297
1990	T/Diesel	116,865	131,014
1989	T/Gas	79,485	89,109
1989	T/Diesel	106,123	118,972
1988	T/Gas	76,478	85,737
1988	T/Diesel	102,257	114,637

Year	Power	Retail Low	Retail High
Blackfin 33 SF			
1984	O/B*	27,274	30,576
1984	T/Gas	42,379	47,510
1984	T/Diesel	53,289	59,741
1983	O/B*	25,176	28,224
1983	T/Gas	39,023	43,747
1983	T/Diesel	48,673	54,566
1982	O/B*	22,239	24,931
1982	T/Gas	36,925	41,395
1982	T/Diesel	45,316	50,803
1981	O/B*	20,141	22,579
1981	T/Gas	33,987	38,102
1981	T/Diesel	42,379	47,510
1980	O/B*	19,301	21,638
1980	T/Gas	31,889	35,750
1980	T/Diesel	40,701	45,629
1979	O/B*	17,011	19,286
1979	T/Gas	29,042	32,928
1979	T/Diesel	36,096	40,925
1978	O/B*	15,766	17,875
1978	T/Gas	27,798	31,517
1978	T/Diesel	34,436	39,043
Blackfin 33 Flybridge			
1995	T/Gas	184,020	206,301
1995	375D	218,531	244,990
1994	T/Gas	150,842	169,105
1994	320D	205,151	229,990
1994	425D	222,316	249,234
1993	T/Gas	132,724	148,793
1993	320D	180,336	202,170
1993	425D	206,459	231,456
1992	T/Gas	122,190	136,984
1992	320D	166,431	186,582
1992	425D	185,813	208,311
1991	T/Gas	109,686	122,966
1991	320D	153,301	171,863
1991	425D	170,143	190,743
1990	T/Gas	91,549	102,633
1990	T/Diesel	136,028	152,498
Blackfin 33 Combi			
1995	T/Gas	167,324	187,583
1995	T/Diesel	216,468	242,677
1994	T/Gas	141,920	159,103
1994	T/Diesel	204,409	229,158

Year	Power	Retail Low	Retail High
Blackfin 38 Combi			
1995	485D	362,769	406,692
1995	550D	383,082	429,464
1994	485D	332,399	372,645
1994	550D	357,298	400,558
1993	485D	308,089	345,391
1993	550D	318,474	357,034
1992	485D	277,367	310,949
1992	550D	288,184	323,077
1991	485D	249,240	279,418
1991	550D	262,222	293,971
1990	485D	210,729	236,244
1990	550D	223,278	250,312
1989	485D	193,854	217,325
1989	550D	204,239	228,967
Blackfin 38 Convertible			
1995	485D	383,851	430,326
1995	550D	410,049	459,696
1994	485D	343,918	385,558
1994	550D	363,843	407,896
1993	485D	322,261	361,279
1993	550D	333,523	373,904
1992	485D	291,941	327,288
1992	550D	303,202	339,913
1991	485D	265,086	297,181
1991	550D	274,182	307,378
1990	485D	226,102	253,478
1990	550D	238,664	267,560
1989	485D	196,215	219,972
1989	550D	201,846	226,285
Boston Whaler 31 SF			
1992	T/Gas	118,342	132,670
1992	T/Diesel	137,068	153,664
1991	T/Gas	141,181	158,275
1991	T/Diesel	121,679	136,411
1990	T/Gas	86,489	96,961
1990	T/Diesel	103,448	115,973
1989	T/Gas	71,227	79,850
1989	T/Diesel	90,729	101,714
1988	T/Gas	63,171	70,820
1988	T/Diesel	81,402	91,258
Brenden 28 SF			
1995	T/Gas	95,811	107,411
1994	T/Gas	88,605	99,333

Year	Power	Retail Low	Retail High
1993	T/Gas	79,053	88,624
1992	T/Gas	69,523	77,941
1991	T/Gas	60,170	67,455
1990	T/Gas	52,067	58,371
1989	T/Gas	45,697	51,230
1988	T/Gas	44,250	49,608
Cabo 31 Express			
1995	350 hp D.	173,351	194,340
Cabo 35 Flybridge SF			
1995	375 hp D.	251,859	282,353
1994	375 hp D.	240,359	269,461
1993	375 hp D.	231,956	260,040
1992	375 hp D.	225,932	253,287
Cabo 35 Express SF			
1995	375 hp D.	251,325	281,755
1994	375 hp D.	238,373	267,234
1993	375 hp D.	227,781	255,360
Californian 35 Convertible			
1987	T/Diesel	78,523	88,031
1986	T/Diesel	69,799	78,250
1985	T/Diesel	62,819	70,425
Californian 38 Convertible			
1987	T/Diesel	123,020	137,915
1986	T/Diesel	110,805	124,221
1985	T/Diesel	101,208	113,462
1984	T/Diesel	88,121	98,790
Californian 42 Convertible			
1989	T/375D	200,116	224,345
1989	T/485D	215,709	241,826
1988	T/375D	183,656	205,892
1988	T/485D	196,650	220,460
1987	T/375D	170,661	191,324
1987	T/485D	181,923	203,950
1986	T/375D	159,399	178,699
1986	T/450D	168,062	188,411
Californian 48 Convertible			
1989	T/Diesel	256,741	287,826
1988	T/Diesel	239,625	268,638
1987	T/Diesel	216,518	242,733
1986	T/Diesel	202,870	227,433
Carolina Classic 28			
1995	T/Gas	77,015	86,340
1995	T/Diesel	102,857	115,311

Year	Power	Retail Low	Retail High
1994	T/Gas	72,509	81,288
1994	T/Diesel	98,666	110,613

Chase 38 SF

Year	Power	Retail Low	Retail High
1992	T/Diesel	215,132	241,179
1991	T/Diesel	201,184	225,543
1990	T/Diesel	188,082	210,854
1989	T/Diesel	174,557	195,692
1988	T/Diesel	165,259	185,268

Cheoy Lee 48 Sport Yacht

Year	Power	Retail Low	Retail High
1986	T/Diesel	223,624	250,700
1985	T/Diesel	212,612	238,355
1984	T/Diesel	204,142	228,858
1983	T/Diesel	195,248	218,887
1982	T/Diesel	180,848	202,744
1981	T/Diesel	172,800	193,722
1980	T/Diesel	164,753	184,701

Cheoy Lee 50 Sport Yacht

Year	Power	Retail Low	Retail High
1995	T/Diesel	******	******
1994	T/Diesel	******	******
1993	T/Diesel	******	******
1992	T/Diesel	******	******
1991	T/Diesel	416,289	466,692
1990	T/Diesel	392,106	439,581
1989	T/Diesel	366,196	410,534
1988	T/Diesel	343,309	384,875
1987	T/Diesel	328,195	367,931
1984	T/Diesel	558,389	625,997
1983	T/Diesel	525,235	588,828

Cheoy Lee 58 Sport Yacht

Year	Power	Retail Low	Retail High
******		******	******

Cheoy Lee 66 Sport Yacht

Year	Power	Retail Low	Retail High
1997		******	******
1998		******	******
1985		******	******
1984		******	******

Cheoy Lee 70 SF

Year	Power	Retail Low	Retail High
1995	T/Diesel	******	******
1994	T/Diesel	******	******
1993	T/Diesel	******	******
1992	T/Diesel	******	******

Chris Craft 30 Tournament SF

Year	Power	Retail Low	Retail High
1977	T/Gas	14,861	16,660
1976	T/Gas	13,549	15,190
1975	T/Gas	12,238	13,720

Chris Craft 315 Sport Sedan

Year	Power	Retail Low	Retail High
1990	T/Gas	53,846	60,366
1990	T/Diesel	65,951	73,936
1989	T/Gas	48,420	54,282
1989	T/Diesel	61,777	69,257
1988	T/Gas	45,080	50,539
1988	T/Diesel	58,020	65,045
1987	T/Gas	45,172	50,642
1987	T/Diesel	57,105	64,018
1986	T/Gas	42,615	47,775
1986	T/Diesel	56,252	63,063
1985	T/Gas	40,485	45,386
1985	T/Diesel	51,565	57,808
1984	T/Gas	37,501	42,042
1984	T/Diesel	48,155	53,986
1983	T/Gas	34,518	38,698
1983	T/Diesel	44,320	49,686

Chris Craft 360 Sport Sedan

Year	Power	Retail Low	Retail High
1986	T/Gas	76,400	85,650
1986	T/Diesel	99,577	111,634
1985	T/Gas	70,391	78,914
1985	T/Diesel	91,851	102,973
1984	T/Gas	66,957	75,064
1984	T/Diesel	87,989	98,642
1983	T/Gas	62,665	70,252
1983	T/Diesel	82,409	92,387
1982	T/Gas	57,085	63,997
1982	T/Diesel	78,975	88,537
1981	T/Gas	55,368	62,072
1981	T/Diesel	70,820	79,395
1980	T/Gas	50,647	56,779
1980	T/Diesel	64,811	72,658
1979	T/Gas	46,684	52,930
1979	T/Diesel	59,841	67,846
1978	T/Gas	41,591	47,156
1978	T/Diesel	52,626	59,666
1977	T/Gas	38,196	43,306
1977	T/Diesel	49,230	55,817
1976	T/Gas	34,376	38,976
1976	T/Diesel	42,864	48,599
1975	T/Gas	30,981	35,126
1975	T/Diesel	38,196	43,306

Chris 382/392 Commander SS

Year	Power	Retail Low	Retail High
1990	T/Gas	117,891	132,165
1990	T/Diesel	148,119	166,053
1989	T/Gas	106,231	119,094
1989	T/Diesel	135,596	152,014
1988	T/Gas	97,595	109,411
1988	T/Diesel	124,368	139,427
1987	T/Gas	92,413	103,602
1987	T/Diesel	113,141	126,839
1986	T/Gas	88,958	99,729
1986	T/Diesel	107,527	120,546
1985	T/Gas	81,617	91,499
1985	T/Diesel	101,913	114,252

Chris Craft 422 Sport Sedan

Year	Power	Retail Low	Retail High
1990	T/Diesel	212,779	238,542
1989	T/Diesel	192,080	215,336
1988	T/Diesel	170,400	191,031
1987	T/Diesel	158,481	177,669
1986	T/Diesel	150,976	169,256
1985	T/Diesel	145,237	162,822
1984	T/Diesel	140,381	157,378
1983	T/Diesel	135,967	152,429
1982	T/Diesel	126,696	142,036
1981	T/Diesel	116,543	130,654
1980	T/Diesel	108,597	121,745
1979	T/Diesel	100,326	113,749
1978	T/Diesel	89,712	101,714
1977	T/Diesel	85,088	96,471
1976	T/Diesel	80,463	91,228
1975	T/Diesel	73,989	83,888

Chris 45 Commander SF

Year	Power	Retail Low	Retail High
1981	T/Diesel	141,642	158,791
1980	T/Diesel	126,960	142,331
1979	T/Diesel	112,299	127,324
1978	T/Diesel	105,040	119,094
1977	T/Diesel	97,782	110,863
1976	T/Diesel	91,377	103,602
1975	T/Diesel	84,972	96,340

Chris Craft 482 Convertible

Year	Power	Retail Low	Retail High
1988	T/Diesel	255,811	286,783
1987	T/Diesel	242,934	272,348
1986	T/Diesel	230,487	258,394
1985	T/Diesel	214,177	240,109

Year	Power	Retail Low	Retail High
Contender 35			
1995	O/B*	76,914	86,226
1995	T/Diesel	144,197	161,656
1994	O/B*	64,972	72,838
1994	T/Diesel	114,664	128,547
1993	O/B*	60,640	67,983
1993	T/Diesel	103,955	116,542
1992	O/B*	56,309	63,127
1992	T/Diesel	95,292	106,830
1991	O/B*	52,844	59,242
1991	T/Diesel	86,629	97,118
1990	O/B*	49,379	55,357
1990	T/Diesel	80,565	90,320
1989	O/B*	46,780	52,444
1989	T/Diesel	73,635	82,550
Cruisers 3210 Sea Devil			
1990	T/Gas	51,388	57,610
1989	T/Gas	45,343	50,833
1988	T/Gas	38,001	42,603
Davis 44 SF			
1993	T/Diesel	******	******
1992	T/Diesel	******	******
1991	T/Diesel	******	******
Davis 44 Express SF			
1995	T/Diesel	******	******
1993	T/Diesel	309,496	346,969
1992	T/Diesel	293,847	329,425
Davis 47 Flybridge SF			
1993	T/Diesel	419,772	470,596
1992	T/Diesel	402,638	451,388
1991	T/Diesel	391,501	438,903
1990	T/Diesel	365,801	410,091
1989	T/Diesel	335,817	376,477
1988	T/Diesel	318,255	356,789
1987	T/Diesel	295,125	330,858
1986	T/Diesel	278,313	312,010
Davis 61 Flybridge SF			
1993	T/Diesel	900,035	1,009,008
1992	T/Diesel	865,418	970,200
1991	T/Diesel	813,493	911,988
1990	T/Diesel	761,568	853,776
1989	T/Diesel	718,297	805,266
1988	T/Diesel	679,353	761,607

Year	Power	Retail Low	Retail High
1987	T/Diesel	640,410	717,948
Dawson 33 Express			
1995	T/300 D		164,285
Dawson 38 Convertible SF			
1994	T/Diesel	301,477	337,979
1993	T/Diesel	259,101	290,472
1992	T/Diesel	228,873	256,584
1991	T/Diesel	198,644	222,695
1990	T/Diesel	183,962	206,235
1989	T/Diesel	168,416	188,807
1988	T/Diesel	153,733	172,347
1987	T/Diesel	146,060	163,744
Delta 36 SFX			
1995	T/Diesel	219,755	246,362
1994	T/Diesel	194,377	217,912
1993	T/Diesel	183,343	205,541
1992	T/Diesel	161,274	180,800
1991	T/Diesel	149,062	167,110
1990	T/Diesel	131,928	147,902
1989	T/Diesel	118,221	132,535
1988	T/Diesel	108,853	122,032
1987	T/Diesel	100,627	112,811
Delta 38 SF			
1995	T/Diesel	196,007	219,739
1994	T/Diesel	159,238	178,518
1993	T/Diesel	151,083	169,375
1992	T/Diesel	142,069	159,271
1991	T/Diesel	131,768	147,722
1990	T/Diesel	120,180	134,730
1989	T/Diesel	112,024	125,588
1988	T/Diesel	103,869	116,446
1987	T/Diesel	94,427	105,860
1986	T/Diesel	84,984	95,274
1985	T/Diesel	76,400	85,650
1984	T/Diesel	70,820	79,395
Donzi F-33			
1992	T/OB*	40,850	45,796
1991	T/OB*	36,492	40,910
1990	T/OB*	32,151	36,044
1989	T/OB*	28,499	31,949
1988	T/OB*	25,465	28,548
1987	T/OB*	21,732	24,363

Year	Power	Retail Low	Retail High
Donzi 65 SF			
1994	T/Diesel	1,491,781	1,672,400
1993	T/Diesel	1,422,105	1,594,288
1992	T/Diesel	1,324,942	1,485,362
1991	T/Diesel	1,245,446	1,396,240
1990	T/Diesel	1,157,116	1,297,216
1989	T/Diesel	1,068,787	1,198,192
1988	T/Diesel	967,208	1,084,314
1987	T/Diesel	874,462	980,339
Dorado 30			
1995	O/B*	49,033	54,970
1995	S/IO Dsl	63,655	71,362
1995	S/Diesel	64,757	72,598
1994	O/B*	45,194	50,666
1994	S/IO Dsl	62,048	69,560
1994	S/Diesel	62,843	70,452
1993	O/B*	42,572	47,726
1993	S/IO Dsl	56,195	62,998
1993	S/Diesel	60,452	67,771
1992	O/B*	40,869	45,817
1992	S/IO Dsl	54,492	61,089
1992	S/Diesel	56,195	62,998
1991	O/B*	39,166	43,908
1991	S/IO Dsl	52,789	59,180
1991	S/Diesel	52,789	59,180
1990	O/B*	36,612	41,044
1990	S/IO Dsl	49,383	55,362
1990	S/Diesel	49,383	55,362
1989	O/B*	33,206	37,226
1989	S/IO Dsl	45,977	51,544
1989	S/Diesel	45,977	51,544
1988	O/B*	29,800	33,408
1988	S/IO Dsl	43,423	48,681
1988	S/Diesel	43,423	48,681
Duffy 35 Sport Cruiser			
1995	S/Diesel	218,329	244,764
1994	S/Diesel	198,640	222,691
1993	S/Diesel	187,413	210,104
1992	S/Diesel	167,549	187,835
1991	S/Diesel	152,866	171,375
1990	S/Diesel	138,184	154,915
1989	S/Diesel	128,684	144,265
1988	S/Diesel	120,048	134,583
1987	S/Diesel	111,411	124,900

Year	Power	Retail Low	Retail High
1986	S/Diesel	103,638	116,186
1985	S/Diesel	95,002	106,504
1984	S/Diesel	88,299	98,990
1983	S/Diesel	79,380	88,991

Duffy 42 FB Cruiser

Year	Power	Retail Low	Retail High
1995	S/375D	350,130	392,522
1994	S/375D	320,805	359,647
1993	S/375D	289,784	324,870
1992	S/375D	264,140	296,121
1991	S/375D	238,495	267,371
1990	S/375D	221,399	248,205
1989	S/375D	205,157	229,997
1988	S/375D	192,335	215,622
1987	S/375D	180,367	202,206
1986	S/375D	171,007	191,712
1985	S/375D	157,919	177,040

Dyer 29

Year	Power	Retail Low	Retail High
1995	S/Gas	84,725	94,983
1994	S/Gas	75,213	84,319
1993	S/Gas	65,695	73,649
1992	S/Gas	58,869	65,997
1991	S/Gas	52,044	58,345
1990	S/Gas	47,778	53,563
1989	S/Gas	41,806	46,868
1988	S/Gas	37,540	42,085
1987	S/Gas	35,518	39,818
1986	S/Gas	32,053	35,934
1985	S/Gas	28,588	32,049
1984	S/Gas	25,122	28,164
1983	S/Gas	21,657	24,280
1982	S/Gas	20,791	23,308
1981	S/Gas	19,925	22,337
1980	S/Gas	19,058	21,366
1979	S/Gas	17,988	20,395
1978	S/Gas	17,132	19,424
1977	S/Gas	16,587	18,806
1976	S/Gas	15,714	17,816
1975	S/Gas	14,841	16,827

Egg Harbor 33 Sedan

Year	Power	Retail Low	Retail High
1981	T/Gas	46,206	51,801
1981	T/Diesel	60,889	68,261
1980	T/Gas	44,047	49,380
1980	T/Diesel	51,388	57,610
1979	T/Gas	40,564	45,991

Year	Power	Retail Low	Retail High
1979	T/Diesel	47,396	53,737
1978	T/Gas	36,721	41,634
1978	T/Diesel	47,823	54,221
1977	T/Gas	34,587	39,214
1977	T/Diesel	43,980	49,864
1976	T/Gas	31,171	35,341
1976	T/Diesel	40,137	45,507
1975	T/Gas	28,182	31,952
1975	T/Diesel	37,575	42,603

Egg Harbor 33 Convertible

Year	Power	Retail Low	Retail High
1989	T/Gas	91,758	102,868
1989	T/Diesel	116,627	130,748
1988	T/Gas	85,326	95,657
1988	T/Diesel	108,909	122,095
1987	T/Gas	78,895	88,447
1987	T/Diesel	97,332	109,117
1986	T/Gas	74,178	83,159
1986	T/Diesel	90,472	101,426
1985	T/Gas	69,462	77,872
1985	T/Diesel	85,326	95,657
1984	T/Gas	65,562	73,500
1984	T/Diesel	81,734	91,630
1983	T/Gas	59,880	67,130
1983	T/Diesel	76,926	86,240
1982	T/Gas	55,509	62,230
1982	T/Diesel	71,681	80,360

Egg Harbor 34/35 Golden Egg

Year	Power	Retail Low	Retail High
1995	T/Gas	170,318	190,940
1995	T/Diesel	199,907	224,111
1994	T/Gas	137,462	154,105
1994	T/Diesel	171,335	192,080
1993	T/Gas	122,601	137,445
1993	T/Diesel	151,405	169,736
1992	T/Gas	******	******
1992	T/Diesel	******	******
1991	T/Gas	******	******
1991	T/Diesel	******	******
1990	T/Gas	107,959	121,030
1990	T/Diesel	138,187	154,918

Egg Harbor 36 Sedan

Year	Power	Retail Low	Retail High
1985	T/Gas	91,384	102,448
1985	T/Diesel	111,454	124,949
1984	T/Gas	76,438	85,693

Year	Power	Retail Low	Retail High
1984	T/Diesel	98,216	110,108
1983	T/Gas	71,741	80,427
1983	T/Diesel	90,957	101,969
1982	T/Gas	64,908	72,767
1982	T/Diesel	83,270	93,352
1981	T/Gas	59,784	67,022
1981	T/Diesel	75,157	84,256
1980	T/Gas	55,941	62,714
1980	T/Diesel	67,897	76,118
1979	T/Gas	52,358	59,363
1979	T/Diesel	63,336	71,810
1978	T/Gas	46,446	52,660
1978	T/Diesel	59,536	67,501
1977	T/Gas	39,691	45,001
1977	T/Diesel	49,402	56,011
1976	T/Gas	36,313	41,171
1976	T/Diesel	46,869	53,139

Egg Harbor 37 Convertible

Year	Power	Retail Low	Retail High
1989	T/Gas	122,951	137,837
1989	T/Diesel	167,043	187,268
1988	T/Gas	131,430	147,343
1988	T/Diesel	153,052	171,583
1987	T/Gas	110,232	123,578
1987	T/Diesel	137,789	154,472
1986	T/Gas	103,448	115,973
1986	T/Diesel	128,462	144,016
1985	T/Gas	97,513	109,319
1985	T/Diesel	121,679	136,411

Egg Harbor 38 Golden Egg

Year	Power	Retail Low	Retail High
1995	T/Diesel	303,317	340,042
1994	T/Diesel	251,845	282,338
1993	T/Gas	177,420	198,901
1993	T/Diesel	215,008	241,041
1992	T/Gas	******	******
1992	T/Diesel	******	******
1991	T/Gas	******	******
1991	T/Diesel	******	******
1990	T/Gas	144,896	162,439
1990	T/Diesel	170,723	191,394

Egg Harbor 40 Sedan

Year	Power	Retail Low	Retail High
1986	T/Gas	125,328	140,503
1986	T/Diesel	158,041	177,176
1985	T/Gas	117,681	131,930
1985	T/Diesel	147,845	165,745

Year	Power	Retail Low	Retail High
1984	T/Gas	102,812	115,260
1984	T/Diesel	134,250	150,504
1983	T/Gas	97,163	108,927
1983	T/Diesel	127,391	142,815
1982	T/Gas	84,208	94,403
1982	T/Diesel	113,573	127,324
1981	T/Gas	77,768	87,184
1981	T/Diesel	104,270	116,894
1980	T/Gas	73,423	82,313
1980	T/Diesel	97,753	109,588
1979	T/Gas	67,445	76,468
1979	T/Diesel	85,917	97,412
1978	T/Gas	60,142	68,188
1978	T/Diesel	76,466	86,697
1977	T/Gas	51,980	58,934
1977	T/Diesel	65,727	74,520
1976	T/Gas	49,832	56,499
1976	T/Diesel	61,861	70,137
1975	T/Gas	47,684	54,064
1975	T/Diesel	58,424	66,240

Egg Harbor 41 SF

Year	Power	Retail Low	Retail High
1989	375D	190,007	213,013
1989	485D	206,417	231,409
1988	375D	181,371	203,330
1988	485D	195,189	218,822
1987	375D	166,688	186,870
1987	485D	177,916	199,457
1986	355D	154,165	172,831
1986	450D	167,552	187,839
1985	355D	145,960	163,633
1985	450D	159,347	178,640
1984	355D	126,960	142,331
1984	450D	135,164	151,530

Egg Harbor 42 Golden Egg

Year	Power	Retail Low	Retail High
1995	485D	382,510	428,823
1994	435D	305,606	342,608
1994	485D	321,691	360,640
1993	425D	281,077	315,109
1993	485D	301,585	338,100
1992	425D	******	******
1992	485D	******	******
1991	425D	******	******
1991	485D	******	******
1990	375D	232,527	260,680
1990	485D	245,814	275,576

Egg Harbor 43 SF

Year	Power	Retail Low	Retail High
1989	375D	213,036	238,829
1989	485D	229,554	257,347
1988	375D	199,483	223,636
1988	485D	212,612	238,355
1987	355D	182,965	205,118
1987	485D	196,095	219,837
1986	355D	177,036	198,471
1986	485D	185,930	208,442

Egg Harbor 46 Sedan

Year	Power	Retail Low	Retail High
1983	T/Diesel	179,042	200,720
1982	T/Diesel	160,755	180,219
1981	T/Diesel	156,077	174,975
1980	T/Diesel	148,848	166,870
1979	T/Diesel	137,087	155,427
1978	T/Diesel	122,789	139,217
1977	T/Diesel	105,128	119,192
1976	T/Diesel	95,456	108,227
1975	T/Diesel	92,120	104,445

Egg Harbor 48 SF

Year	Power	Retail Low	Retail High
1986	540D	237,667	266,442
1986	675D	256,340	287,377
1985	500D	210,929	236,468
1985	675D	230,452	258,354
1984	500D	192,393	215,687
1984	675D	216,022	242,177
1983	T/Diesel	186,117	208,651
1982	T/Diesel	172,384	193,256
1981	T/Diesel	162,041	181,661
1980	T/Diesel	152,560	171,032
1979	T/Diesel	146,805	166,446
1978	T/Diesel	138,463	156,988

Egg Harbor 54 Golden Egg

Year	Power	Retail Low	Retail High
1995	760D	******	******
1995	900D	******	******
1994	735D	******	******
1994	900D	******	******
1993	735D	******	******
1993	900D	******	******
1992	735D	******	******
1992	900D	******	******
1991	735D	******	******
1991	900D	******	******
1990	735D	528,143	592,088

Year	Power	Retail Low	Retail High
1990	900D	573,460	642,893
1989	735D	445,299	499,214
1988	735D	420,330	471,222

Egg Harbor 58 Golden Egg

Year	Power	Retail Low	Retail High
1995	900 DD		1,044,244
1995	1110 DD		1,101,443
1995	1250 Cat		1,134,209
1994	900D	******	******
1994	1080D	******	******
1993	900D	******	******
1993	1080D	******	******
1992	900D	******	******
1992	1080D	******	******
1991	900D	******	******
1991	1080D	******	******
1990	900D	636,122	713,141
1990	1080D	659,921	739,822

Egg Harbor 60 Convertible

Year	Power	Retail Low	Retail High
1989	900D	592,814	664,590
1989	1080D	627,941	703,970
1988	900D	564,397	632,732
1988	1080D	590,051	661,493
1987	870D	524,374	587,863
1987	1000D	558,606	626,240
1986	870D	481,194	539,456
1986	1000D	505,702	566,930

Fountain 27/29 Center Console

Year	Power	Retail Low	Retail High
1995	T/200 OB	54,061	60,607
1994	T/200 OB	47,829	53,621
1993	T/200 OB	42,536	47,687

Fountain 27/29 SF Cruiser

Year	Power	Retail Low	Retail High
1995	O/B*	59,888	67,214
1995	S/350hp IO	54,037	65,648
1994	O/B*	53,786	60,366
1994	S/350hp IO	48,997	58,991
1993	O/B*	48,348	54,263
1993	S/350hp IO	43,258	52,550

Fountain 8.8M/31 Center Console

Year	Power	Retail Low	Retail High
1995	O/B*	71,703	80,385
1994	O/B*	65,708	73,664
1993	O/B*	60,903	68,278
1992	O/B*	56,178	62,980

Year	Power	Retail Low	Retail High
1991	O/B*	52,328	58,661
1990	O/B*	46,665	52,317
1989	O/B*	41,032	46,000
1988	O/B*	38,155	42,775
1987	O/B*	35,630	39,944
1986	O/B*	33,469	37,522
1985	O/B*	31,816	35,669

Fountain 31/32 SF Cruiser

Year	Power	Retail Low	Retail High
1995	O/B*	80,980	90,785
1995	T/385hp IO	90,160	101,077
1994	O/B*	70,005	78,482
1994	T/385hp IO	76,098	85,312
1993	O/B*	60,102	67,380
1993	T/385hp IO	65,908	73,888

Gamefisherman 34

Year	Power	Retail Low	Retail High
1995	T/Diesel	251,949	282,454
1994	T/Diesel	238,788	267,700
1993	T/Diesel	224,060	251,188
1992	T/Diesel	216,155	242,326

Gamefisherman 40

Year	Power	Retail Low	Retail High
1995	T/Diesel	374,696	420,063
1994	T/Diesel	349,786	392,137
1993	T/Diesel	342,146	383,572
1992	T/Diesel	324,139	363,384
1991	T/Diesel	310,633	348,243
1990	T/Diesel	297,127	333,102
1989	T/Diesel	289,128	324,135
1988	T/Diesel	285,850	320,460
1987	T/Diesel	271,558	304,437
1986	T/Diesel	261,986	293,706

Garlington 44

Year	Power	Retail Low	Retail High
1995	T/Diesel	508,279	569,820
1994	T/Diesel	474,844	532,336
1993	T/Diesel	453,427	508,326
1992	T/Diesel	445,822	499,800
1991	T/Diesel	405,173	454,230
1990	T/Diesel	393,809	441,490

Grady-White 280/300 Marlin

Year	Power	Retail Low	Retail High
1995	O/B*	70,525	79,064
1994	O/B*	62,165	69,692
1993	O/B*	54,212	60,776
1992	O/B*	48,366	54,221
1991	O/B*	43,615	48,896
1990	O/B*	39,297	44,055

Year	Power	Retail Low	Retail High
1989	O/B*	35,842	40,182

Hatteras 32 FB & SF

Year	Power	Retail Low	Retail High
1986	T/Gas	75,571	84,721
1986	T/Diesel	109,686	122,966
1985	T/Gas	71,685	80,364
1985	T/Diesel	107,095	120,062
1984	T/Gas	68,662	76,975
1984	T/Diesel	96,731	108,443
1983	T/Gas	65,639	73,586
1983	T/Diesel	91,981	103,118
1982	T/Gas	60,457	67,777
1982	T/Diesel	88,094	98,760

Hatteras 36 Conv. (Early)

Year	Power	Retail Low	Retail High
1977	T/Gas	49,701	56,350
1977	T/Diesel	60,937	69,090
1976	T/Gas	44,515	50,470
1976	T/Diesel	55,751	63,210
1975	T/Gas	41,489	47,040
1975	T/Diesel	51,429	58,310

Hatteras 36 Convertible

Year	Power	Retail Low	Retail High
1987	T/Gas	113,141	126,839
1987	T/Diesel	148,424	166,395
1986	T/Gas	101,687	113,998
1986	T/Diesel	136,303	152,806
1985	T/Gas	98,658	110,603
1985	T/Diesel	126,351	141,649
1984	T/Gas	95,353	106,898
1984	T/Diesel	120,075	134,613
1983	T/Gas	90,939	101,949
1983	T/Diesel	114,777	128,674

Hatteras 36 SF

Year	Power	Retail Low	Retail High
1986	T/Gas	99,754	111,832
1986	T/Diesel	127,823	143,300
1985	T/Gas	91,981	103,118
1985	T/Diesel	120,914	135,554
1984	T/Gas	86,367	96,824
1984	T/Diesel	112,709	126,355
1983	T/Gas	82,480	92,467
1983	T/Diesel	103,640	116,189

Hatteras 36 Sedan Cruiser

Year	Power	Retail Low	Retail High
1987	T/Gas	105,570	118,353
1987	T/Diesel	143,087	160,412
1986	T/Gas	96,846	108,571
1986	T/Diesel	130,872	146,718

Hatteras 37 Convertible

Year	Power	Retail Low	Retail High
1983	T/Diesel	127,557	143,002
1982	T/Diesel	117,907	132,182
1981	T/Diesel	105,738	118,541
1980	T/Diesel	96,507	108,192
1979	T/Diesel	88,787	100,666
1978	T/Diesel	84,638	95,962
1977	T/Diesel	80,904	91,728

Hatteras 38 Convertible

Year	Power	Retail Low	Retail High
1993	T/Diesel	289,891	324,990
1992	T/Diesel	267,158	299,505
1991	T/Diesel	252,618	283,204
1990	T/Diesel	234,918	263,361
1989	T/Diesel	216,349	242,544
1988	T/Diesel	204,690	229,473

Hatteras 39 Convertible

Year	Power	Retail Low	Retail High
1995	465D	329,888	369,830
1994	465D	310,420	348,005

Hatteras 39 Sport Express

Year	Power	Retail Low	Retail High
1995	465D	315,131	353,286

Hatteras 41 Convertible

Year	Power	Retail Low	Retail High
1991	535D	305,987	343,034
1990	465D	261,847	293,550
1990	535D	277,484	311,080
1989	465D	231,886	259,962
1989	535D	246,466	276,307
1988	465D	207,672	232,816
1988	535D	221,626	248,459
1987	465D	197,424	221,328
1986	450D	186,553	209,140

Hatteras 42 Convertible

Year	Power	Retail Low	Retail High
1978	T/Diesel	109,310	123,935
1977	T/Diesel	99,490	112,800
1976	T/Diesel	89,032	100,944
1975	T/Diesel	80,152	90,875

Hatteras 43 Conv. (Early)

Year	Power	Retail Low	Retail High
1984	T/Diesel	191,735	214,949
1983	T/Diesel	180,075	201,878
1982	T/Diesel	166,593	186,764
1981	T/Diesel	157,156	176,184
1980	T/Diesel	150,978	169,258
1979	T/Diesel	143,540	162,744

Year	Power	Retail Low	Retail High

Hatteras 43 Convertible

Year	Power	Retail Low	Retail High
1995	T/Diesel	467,572	524,184
1994	T/Diesel	408,477	457,934
1993	T/Diesel	381,330	427,500
1992	T/Diesel	349,802	392,155
1991	T/Diesel	322,924	362,023

Hatteras 45 Conv. (Early)****

Hatteras 45 Convertible

Year	Power	Retail Low	Retail High
1991	T/Diesel	366,764	411,171
1990	T/Diesel	330,857	370,916
1989	T/Diesel	290,248	325,390
1988	T/Diesel	260,753	292,324
1987	T/Diesel	241,517	270,759
1986	T/Diesel	225,701	253,028
1985	T/Diesel	211,167	236,735
1984	T/Diesel	198,771	222,837

Hatteras 46 Conv. (Early)

Year	Power	Retail Low	Retail High
1985	650D	235,236	263,718
1984	650D	229,270	257,030
1983	650D	218,190	244,608
1982	650D	199,440	223,587
1981	435D	170,461	191,100
1980	435D	161,938	181,545
1979	435D	154,102	174,719
1978	435D	144,737	164,101
1977	435D	140,961	159,820
1976	435D	134,908	152,956
1975	435D	129,719	147,074

Hatteras 46 Convertible

Year	Power	Retail Low	Retail High
1995	720D	587,688	658,843
1995	780D	626,397	702,239
1994	720D	607,620	681,188
	780D	632,611	709,205
1993	T/Diesel	544,976	610,959
1992	T/Diesel	493,900	553,700

Hatteras 48 Convertible

Year	Power	Retail Low	Retail High
1991	T/Diesel	441,363	494,802
1990	T/Diesel	433,575	486,070
1989	T/Diesel	402,852	451,628
1988	T/Diesel	370,399	415,246
1987	T/Diesel	347,916	390,040

Hatteras 50 Conv. (1980-83)

Year	Power	Retail Low	Retail High
1983	T/Diesel	276,003	309,420
1982	T/Diesel	256,597	287,664
1981	T/Diesel	229,336	257,103
1980	T/Diesel	216,005	242,158

Hatteras 50 Conv. (Current)

Year	Power	Retail Low	Retail High
1995	780D	695,475	779,680
1995	870D	770,191	863,443
1994	780D	685,368	768,349
1994	870D	744,234	834,343
1993	780D	645,843	724,040
1993	870D	689,572	773,063
1992	780D	588,659	659,932
1992	870D	620,615	695,757
1991	780D	549,976	616,565
1991	870D	579,409	649,562

Hatteras 52 Convertible

Year	Power	Retail Low	Retail High
1991	T/Diesel	510,859	572,712
1990	T/Diesel	479,615	537,685
1989	T/Diesel	457,745	513,167
1988	T/Diesel	423,198	474,438
1987	T/Diesel	371,810	416,827
1986	T/Diesel	345,468	387,296
1985	T/Diesel	319,558	358,249
1984	T/Diesel	302,285	338,884

Hatteras 53 Convertible

Year	Power	Retail Low	Retail High
1980	T/Diesel	231,032	259,004
1979	T/Diesel	215,632	244,481
1978	T/Diesel	203,676	230,925
1977	T/Diesel	185,315	210,108
1976	T/Diesel	164,820	186,870
1975	T/Diesel	144,672	164,028

Hatteras 54 Convertible

Year	Power	Retail Low	Retail High
1995	1040D	945,964	1,060,498
1995	1206D	978,357	1,096,813
1994	870D	880,943	987,605
1994	1040D	932,764	1,045,699
1993	870D	837,760	939,193
1993	1040D	880,943	987,605
1992	870D	761,757	853,988
1992	1040D	818,759	917,892
1991	870D	734,120	823,004
1991	1040D	777,303	871,416

Hatteras 55 Convertible

Year	Power	Retail Low	Retail High
1989	T/Diesel	623,398	698,877
1988	T/Diesel	559,681	627,445

Year	Power	Retail Low	Retail High
1987	T/Diesel	523,947	587,385
1986	T/Diesel	453,453	508,356
1985	T/Diesel	427,510	479,271
1984	T/Diesel	400,387	448,864
1983	T/Diesel	378,000	423,767
1982	T/Diesel	355,182	398,186
1981	T/Diesel	295,339	331,098
1980	T/Diesel	303,328	340,054

Hatteras 58 Convertible

Year	Power	Retail Low	Retail High
1994	1040D	1,145,893	1,284,633
1994	1350D	1,294,434	1,451,160
1993	1040D	1,039,791	1,165,686
1993	1350D	1,188,333	1,332,212
1992	1040D	933,690	1,046,738
1992	1350D	1,061,012	1,189,475
1991	1040D	819,101	918,275
1991	1350D	933,690	1,046,738
1990	1040D	739,664	829,220
1990	1350D	843,783	945,945

Hatteras 60 Convertible

Year	Power	Retail Low	Retail High
1986	840D	560,522	628,388
1985	650D	492,292	551,897
1985	840D	527,702	591,595
1984	650D	456,450	511,715
1984	840D	494,019	553,833
1983	650D	438,744	491,866
1983	840D	472,428	529,627
1982	650D	414,130	464,271
1982	840D	435,722	488,477
1981	650D	371,369	416,333
1980	650D	350,416	392,843
1979	650D	330,618	374,850
1978	650D	320,082	362,905
1977	650D	315,227	357,400

Hatteras 65 Convertible

Year	Power	Retail Low	Retail High
1995	1040D	1,355,028	1,519,090
1995	1350D	1,513,849	1,697,140
1994	1035D	1,286,326	1,442,070
1994	1350D	1,492,139	1,672,801
1993	1035D	1,305,621	1,463,701
1993	1350D	1,393,520	1,562,242
1992	1035D	1,192,425	1,336,799
1992	1350D	1,301,762	1,459,375
1991	1035D	1,111,386	1,245,948

Year	Power	Retail Low	Retail High
1991	1235D	1,204,430	1,350,258
1990	1035D	956,169	1,071,939
1990	1235D	1,045,355	1,171,922
1989	1035D	871,272	976,762
1989	1235D	961,743	1,078,188
1988	1035D	794,521	890,719
1988	1235D	888,852	996,470
1987	1035D	739,209	828,710
1987	1235D	819,390	918,599

Hatteras 82 Convertible
Year	Power	Retail Low	Retail High
1995	T/D	******	******
1994	T/D	******	******
1993	T/D	******	******
1992	T/D	******	******

Henriques 28 Express
Year	Power	Retail Low	Retail High
1995	T/Diesel	90,280	101,211
1994	T/Diesel	84,051	94,228

Henriques 35 Maine Coaster
Year	Power	Retail Low	Retail High
1995	T/Diesel	150,350	168,554
1994	T/Diesel	138,467	155,232
1993	T/Diesel	127,047	142,429
1992	T/Diesel	115,887	129,919
1991	T/Diesel	111,595	125,107
1990	T/Diesel	103,869	116,446
1989	T/Diesel	98,719	110,671
1988	T/Diesel	90,135	101,048
1987	T/Diesel	80,692	90,462
1986	T/Diesel	72,108	80,838
1985	T/Diesel	64,382	72,177
1984	T/Diesel	57,514	64,478
1983	T/Diesel	55,798	62,553
1982	T/Diesel	54,081	60,629
1981	T/Diesel	51,506	57,742
1980	T/Diesel	49,789	55,817
1979	T/Diesel	46,684	52,930
1978	T/Diesel	43,642	49,480
1977	T/Diesel	41,930	47,540

Henriques 38 SF
Year	Power	Retail Low	Retail High
1995	T/Diesel	237,629	266,400
1994	T/Diesel	213,994	239,904
1993	T/Diesel	197,438	221,343
1992	T/Diesel	184,561	206,907
1991	T/Diesel	175,977	197,284
1990	T/Diesel	163,101	182,848
1989	T/Diesel	154,517	173,225
1988	T/Diesel	145,932	163,601

Henriques 38 El Bravo
Year	Power	Retail Low	Retail High
1995	T/Diesel	240,850	270,011
1994	T/Diesel	217,115	243,403
1993	T/Diesel	200,086	224,312
1992	T/Diesel	187,315	209,994
1991	T/Diesel	177,699	199,214

Henriques 44 SF
Year	Power	Retail Low	Retail High
1995	T/Diesel	327,560	367,220
1994	T/Diesel	302,258	338,855
1993	T/Diesel	278,420	312,130
1992	T/Diesel	261,286	292,922
1991	T/Diesel	231,303	259,308
1990	T/Diesel	215,883	242,021
1989	T/Diesel	205,602	230,496
1988	T/Diesel	184,186	206,486
1987	T/Diesel	158,485	177,674
1986	T/Diesel	141,352	158,466
1985	T/Diesel	128,502	144,060
1984	T/Diesel	121,036	135,691
1983	T/Diesel	112,391	125,999

Hydra-Sports 2800 SF
Year	Power	Retail Low	Retail High
1995	O/B*	77,071	86,402
1994	O/B*	72,149	80,884
1993	O/B*	64,510	72,320
1992	O/B*	57,719	64,707
1991	O/B*	50,080	56,143

Hydra-Sports 3300 SF
Year	Power	Retail Low	Retail High
1992	O/B*	64,310	72,097
1991	O/B*	56,695	63,559
1990	O/B*	50,348	56,444
1989	O/B*	45,271	50,752

Innovater 31
Year	Power	Retail Low	Retail High
1991	T/Gas	******	******
1991	T/Diesel	******	******
1990	T/Gas	******	******
1990	T/Diesel	******	******
1989	T/Gas	******	******
1989	T/Diesel	******	******
1988	T/Gas	******	******
1988	T/Diesel	******	******

Intrepid 30
Year	Power	Retail Low	Retail High
1995	O/B*	40,024	44,870
1994	O/B*	35,160	39,417
1993	O/B*	30,903	34,645
1992	O/B*	27,470	30,796
1991	O/B*	24,894	27,908

Intrepid 31 Walkaround
Year	Power	Retail Low	Retail High
1995	O/B*	59,877	67,127

Intrepid 33 Cuddy
Year	Power	Retail Low	Retail High
1995	O/B*	70,727	79,290
1994	O/B*	66,086	74,088
1993	O/B*	60,929	68,306

Intrepid 38 Evolution
Year	Power	Retail Low	Retail High
1993	T/Diesel	******	******
1992	T/Diesel	******	******
1991	T/Diesel	******	******

Island Gypsy 32 Fisherman
Year	Power	Retail Low	Retail High
1995	S/Diesel	134,051	150,281
1995	T/Diesel	151,831	170,214
1994	S/Diesel	120,180	134,730
1994	T/Diesel	138,206	154,940
1993	S/Diesel	107,910	120,975
1993	T/Diesel	125,328	140,503
1992	S/Diesel	98,138	110,021
1992	T/Diesel	118,531	132,882
1991	S/Diesel	90,491	101,448
1991	T/Diesel	111,309	124,785
1990	S/Diesel	82,419	92,398
1990	T/Diesel	99,838	111,926
1989	S/Diesel	73,498	82,396
1989	T/Diesel	91,341	102,400
1988	S/Diesel	61,602	69,061
1988	T/Diesel	75,197	84,302
1987	S/Diesel	53,105	59,535
1987	T/Diesel	61,602	69,061

Jefferson FS35 Center Console
Year	Power	Retail Low	Retail High
1995	T/200 O/B	70,342	78,859
1994	T/200 O/B	63,459	71,142

Jersey 36 Convertible SF
Year	Power	Retail Low	Retail High
1992	T/Gas	139,765	156,687
1992	T/Diesel	165,177	185,176

Year	Power	Retail Low	Retail High
1991	T/Gas	127,059	142,443
1991	T/Diesel	152,471	170,932
1990	T/Gas	114,353	128,199
1990	T/Diesel	139,765	156,687
1989	T/Gas	105,883	118,702
1989	T/Diesel	127,059	142,443
1988	T/Gas	97,412	109,206
1988	T/Diesel	118,589	132,947
1987	T/Gas	90,135	101,048
1987	T/Diesel	111,595	125,107
1986	T/Gas	81,550	91,424
1986	T/Diesel	103,011	115,483

Jersey 40 Dawn Convertible

Year	Power	Retail Low	Retail High
1988	T/Diesel	157,849	176,961
1987	T/Diesel	140,054	157,011
1986	T/Diesel	130,717	146,543
1985	T/Diesel	116,287	130,366
1984	T/Diesel	106,101	118,948
1983	T/Diesel	98,037	109,907
1982	T/Diesel	90,135	101,048
1981	T/Diesel	83,267	93,349
1980	T/Diesel	76,400	85,650
1979	T/Diesel	69,602	78,914
1978	T/Diesel	64,509	73,139
1977	T/Diesel	59,416	67,365
1976	T/Diesel	55,936	63,420
1975	T/Diesel	53,010	60,102

Jersey Devil 44 SF

Year	Power	Retail Low	Retail High
1985	T/Diesel	143,334	160,689
1984	T/Diesel	135,229	151,602
1983	T/Diesel	123,184	138,099
1982	T/Diesel	115,887	129,919
1981	T/Diesel	103,440	115,964
1980	T/Diesel	93,613	104,948

Jersey 44 Convertible SF

Year	Power	Retail Low	Retail High
1992	T/Diesel	290,728	325,928
1991	T/Diesel	270,404	303,143
1990	T/Diesel	240,359	269,461
1989	T/Diesel	214,606	240,590

Jersey 47 Convertible

Year	Power	Retail Low	Retail High
1992	T/Diesel	300,479	336,859
1991	T/Diesel	286,401	321,077
1990	T/Diesel	272,178	305,133
1898	T/Diesel	259,420	290,830
1988	T/Diesel	244,961	274,620
1987	T/Diesel	221,145	247,920

Jupiter 31

Year	Power	Retail Low	Retail High
1995	T/200 O/B	80,695	90,465
1994	T/200 O/B	74,536	83,560
1993	T/200 O/B	66,965	75,073
1992	T/200 O/B	62,395	69,948
1991	T/200 O/B	59,924	67,179
1990	T/200 O/B	57,295	64,232
1989	T/200 O/B	53,464	59,937

Luhrs 290 (Early)

Year	Power	Retail Low	Retail High
1988	T/Gas	35,195	39,457
1987	T/Gas	33,908	38,013
1986	T/Gas	30,045	33,683

Luhrs 290

Year	Power	Retail Low	Retail High
1991	T/Gas	40,785	45,723
1990	T/Gas	37,811	42,389
1989	T/Gas	34,837	39,055

Luhrs 290 Open

Year	Power	Retail Low	Retail High
1995	T/Gas	85,819	96,210
1995	T/Diesel	105,867	118,685
1994	T/Gas	74,741	83,790
1994	T/Diesel	91,350	102,410
1993	T/Gas	67,625	75,813
1993	T/Diesel	84,531	94,766
1992	T/Gas	59,172	66,336
1992	T/Diesel	76,078	85,289

Luhrs Alura 30

Year	Power	Retail Low	Retail High
1990	S/Gas	31,697	35,535
1989	S/Gas	27,842	31,213
1988	S/Gas	25,272	28,332
1987	S/Gas	21,417	24,010

Luhrs 300 SF

Year	Power	Retail Low	Retail High
1995	T/Gas	80,182	89,890
1995	T/Diesel	104,737	117,418
1994	T/Gas	74,531	83,555
1994	T/Diesel	94,234	105,644
1993	T/Gas	69,819	78,273

Year	Power	Retail Low	Retail High
1993	T/Diesel	88,238	98,921
1992	T/Gas	63,822	71,550
1992	T/Diesel	80,528	90,278
1991	T/Gas	47,974	53,782
1991	T/Diesel	59,539	66,748

Luhrs 320 Convertible

Year	Power	Retail Low	Retail High
1995	T/Gas	112,491	126,111
1995	T/Diesel	144,800	162,332
1994	T/Gas	92,425	103,615
1994	T/Diesel	129,683	145,385
1993	T/Gas	81,905	91,822
1993	T/Diesel	113,900	127,690
1992	T/Gas	73,800	82,736
1992	T/Diesel	98,969	110,952
1991	T/Gas	66,548	74,605
1991	T/Diesel	85,318	95,648
1990	T/Gas	57,170	64,092
1990	T/Diesel	79,085	88,661
1989	T/Gas	52,406	58,751
1989	T/Diesel	68,604	76,910
1988	T/Gas	46,212	51,808
1988	T/Diesel	60,505	67,831

Luhrs 320 Open

Year	Power	Retail Low	Retail High
1995	T/Gas	113,657	127,418
1995	T/Diesel	157,864	176,978
1994	T/Gas	96,144	107,784
1994	T/Diesel	138,926	155,746

Luhrs 340

Year	Power	Retail Low	Retail High
1987	T/Gas	52,358	58,697
1987	T/Diesel	62,310	69,854
1986	T/Gas	47,165	52,876
1986	T/Diesel	56,252	63,063
1985	T/Gas	44,569	49,965
1985	T/Diesel	51,925	58,212
1984	T/Gas	41,973	47,055
1984	T/Diesel	48,463	54,331
1983	T/Gas	36,348	40,748
1983	T/Diesel	45,002	50,450

Luhrs 342

Year	Power	Retail Low	Retail High
1989	T/Gas	61,523	68,972
1989	T/Diesel	74,452	83,467
1988	T/Gas	58,403	65,474
1988	T/Diesel	69,548	77,969
1987	T/Gas	53,499	59,976

Year	Power	Retail Low	Retail High
1987	T/Diesel	65,090	72,971
1986	T/Gas	48,595	54,478
1986	T/Diesel	56,174	62,975

Luhrs Alura 35

Year	Power	Retail Low	Retail High
1989	T/Gas	54,492	61,089
1989	T/Diesel	68,115	76,362
1988	T/Gas	51,191	57,389
1988	T/Diesel	62,282	69,823

Luhrs 350

Year	Power	Retail Low	Retail High
1995	T/Gas	136,413	152,929
1995	T/Diesel	179,572	201,314
1994	T/Gas	121,725	136,463
1994	T/Diesel	158,564	177,762
1993	T/Gas	107,355	120,353
1993	T/Diesel	146,662	164,419
1992	T/Gas	98,969	110,952
1992	T/Diesel	132,243	148,254
1991	T/Gas	90,864	101,865
1991	T/Diesel	120,725	135,342
1990	T/Gas	81,052	90,866
1990	T/Diesel	110,060	123,386

Luhrs 380 Convertible

Year	Power	Retail Low	Retail High
1995	T/Diesel	269,763	302,425
1994	T/Diesel	239,826	268,863
1993	T/Diesel	226,213	253,602
1992	T/Diesel	203,074	227,662
1991	T/Diesel	183,956	206,229
1990	T/Diesel	166,963	187,178
1989	T/Diesel	154,202	172,872

Luhrs 380 Open

Year	Power	Retail Low	Retail High
1995	T/Diesel	276,131	309,564
1994	T/Diesel	245,499	275,223
1993	T/Diesel	228,565	256,239
1992	T/Diesel	205,393	230,261
1991	T/Diesel	185,200	207,623

Luhrs 400

Year	Power	Retail Low	Retail High
1990	T/Gas	125,202	140,361
1990	T/Diesel	150,071	168,242
1989	T/Gas	109,338	122,576
1989	T/Diesel	138,066	154,782
1988	T/Gas	100,436	112,506
1988	T/Diesel	128,764	144,354
1987	T/Gas	93,998	105,378
1987	T/Diesel	120,609	135,212

Mako 282 CC

Year	Power	Retail Low	Retail High
1995	T/OB*	35,778	40,245

Mako 286 Inboard

Year	Power	Retail Low	Retail High
1995	T/Gas	85,115	95,420
1994	T/Gas	77,045	86,373
1993	T/Gas	71,941	80,651
1992	T/Gas	62,941	70,562
1991	T/Gas	54,436	61,027
1990	T/Gas	45,930	51,491
1989	T/Gas	42,103	47,200
1988	T/Gas	38,700	43,386
1987	T/Gas	34,873	39,095
1986	T/Gas	31,620	35,448
1985	T/Gas	28,757	32,239

Mako 263/293 Walkaround

Year	Power	Retail Low	Retail High
1995	O/B	45,822	51,370
1994	O/B	40,150	45,011
1993	O/B	36,277	40,669

Mako 295 Dual Console

Year	Power	Retail Low	Retail High
1995	O/B*	53,499	59,977
1994	O/B*	47,386	53,124
1993	O/B*	42,309	47,432

Marlin 350 Sportfish

Year	Power	Retail Low	Retail High
1995	T/200 O/B	71,397	80,042
1994	T/200 O/B	66,954	75,060
1993	T/200 O/B	60,518	67,845
1992	T/200 O/B	58,003	65,026
1991	T/200 O/B	56,169	62,970

Mediterranean 38 Convertible

Year	Power	Retail Low	Retail High
1995	T/Diesel	231,902	259,980
1994	T/Diesel	209,624	235,004
1993	T/Diesel	189,212	212,121
1992	T/Diesel	177,568	199,067
1991	T/Diesel	164,469	184,382
1990	T/Diesel	150,399	168,609
1989	T/Diesel	139,241	156,099
1988	T/Diesel	132,448	148,485
1987	T/Diesel	124,686	139,782
1986	T/Diesel	120,512	135,103
1985	T/Diesel	117,592	131,830

Mediterranean 54 Convertible

Year	Power	Retail Low	Retail High
1995	DD 6V92	576,660	646,480
1995	DD 8V92	648,508	727,027

Mikelson 48 Sedan & 50 SF

Year	Power	Retail Low	Retail High
1995	T/Diesel	516,768	579,336
1994	T/Diesel	465,199	521,524
1993	T/Diesel	439,084	492,247
1992	T/Diesel	407,752	457,121
1991	T/Diesel	357,963	401,304
1990	T/Diesel	331,781	371,952

Mikelson 60 Sportfisher

Year	Power	Retail Low	Retail High
1995	T/Diesel	723,788	811,421
1994	T/Diesel	654,088	733,283
1993	T/Diesel	600,898	673,652
1992	T/Diesel	518,254	581,003

Mikelson 72 SF

Year	Power	Retail Low	Retail High
1995	T/Diesel	******	******
1994	T/Diesel	******	******

Nauset 35 Sport Cruiser

Year	Power	Retail Low	Retail High
1994	S/Diesel	150,124	168,300
1989	S/Diesel	85,659	96,030
1984	S/Diesel	57,400	64,350

North Coast 31 SF

Year	Power	Retail Low	Retail High
1990	T/Gas	59,478	66,679
1990	T/Diesel	98,988	110,973
1989	T/Gas	55,229	61,916
1989	T/Diesel	91,766	102,876
1988	T/Gas	51,506	57,742
1988	T/Diesel	80,720	90,493

Ocean 29 Super Sport

Year	Power	Retail Low	Retail High
1992	T/Gas	94,837	106,320
1992	T/Diesel	109,297	122,530
1991	T/Gas	83,355	93,447
1991	T/Diesel	97,836	109,681
1990	T/Gas	75,606	84,760
1990	T/Diesel	85,906	96,308

Ocean 32 Super Sport

Year	Power	Retail Low	Retail High
1992	T/Gas	108,186	121,285
1992	T/Diesel	131,582	147,514
1991	T/Gas	98,303	110,205
1991	T/Diesel	118,889	133,284
1990	T/Gas	91,377	102,440

Year	Power	Retail Low	Retail High
1990	T/Diesel	107,889	120,952
1989	T/Gas	83,080	93,139
1989	T/Diesel	96,465	108,145

Ocean 35 Super Sport

Year	Power	Retail Low	Retail High
1994	T/Diesel	187,048	209,696
1993	T/Diesel	167,839	188,160
1992	T/Gas	131,732	147,682
1992	T/Diesel	154,954	173,716
1991	T/Gas	119,066	133,482
1991	T/Diesel	142,288	159,516
1990	T/Gas	108,933	122,122
1990	T/Diesel	127,932	143,422
1989	T/Gas	101,333	113,602
1989	T/Diesel	118,644	133,009
1988	T/Gas	94,999	106,502
1988	T/Diesel	112,733	126,382

Ocean 35 Sport Cruiser/SF

Year	Power	Retail Low	Retail High
1993	T/Diesel	149,843	167,986
1992	T/Gas	118,880	133,273
1992	T/Diesel	138,201	154,934
1991	T/Gas	102,387	114,783
1991	T/Diesel	123,875	138,874
1990	T/Gas	96,909	108,643
1990	T/Diesel	117,977	132,261

Ocean 38 SS (Early)

Year	Power	Retail Low	Retail High
1991	T/Diesel	165,688	185,749
1990	T/Gas	122,354	137,169
1990	T/Diesel	157,191	176,224
1989	T/Gas	115,132	129,072
1989	T/Diesel	146,146	163,840
1988	T/Gas	107,060	120,023
1988	T/Diesel	137,649	154,315
1987	T/Gas	100,263	112,402
1987	T/Diesel	130,851	146,694
1986	T/Gas	92,562	103,769
1986	T/Diesel	117,498	131,725
1985	T/Gas	84,531	94,766
1985	T/Diesel	112,427	126,039
1984	T/Gas	76,078	85,289
1984	T/Diesel	103,128	115,615

Ocean 38 Super Sport

Year	Power	Retail Low	Retail High
1995	T/Diesel	292,313	327,705
1994	T/Diesel	262,318	294,078
1993	T/Diesel	241,310	270,527

Year	Power	Retail Low	Retail High
1992	T/Diesel	218,190	244,608

Ocean 40 Super Sport

Year	Power	Retail Low	Retail High
1980	T/Diesel	90,226	101,151
1979	T/Diesel	80,720	90,493
1978	T/Diesel	75,197	84,302
1977	T/Diesel	67,975	76,205

Ocean 42 SS (Early)

Year	Power	Retail Low	Retail High
1983	T/Diesel	124,872	139,991
1982	T/Diesel	116,634	130,756
1981	T/Diesel	107,414	120,419
1980	T/Diesel	100,428	112,587

Ocean 42 Super Sport

Year	Power	Retail Low	Retail High
1995	485D	338,603	379,600
1994	435D	294,024	329,623
1994	485D	310,825	348,459
1993	425D	277,222	310,787
1993	485D	290,663	325,856
1992	425D	263,153	295,014
1992	485D	274,369	307,589
1991	425D	239,288	268,260
1991	485D	258,577	289,884

Ocean 44 Super Sport

Year	Power	Retail Low	Retail High
1991	T/Diesel	249,883	280,138
1990	T/Diesel	239,718	268,742
1989	T/Diesel	221,083	247,851
1988	T/Diesel	207,748	232,901
1987	T/Diesel	195,779	219,483
1986	T/Diesel	182,527	204,627
1985	T/Diesel	169,110	189,585

Ocean 46 Super Sport

Year	Power	Retail Low	Retail High
1985	T/Diesel	172,501	193,387
1984	T/Diesel	163,108	182,856
1983	T/Diesel	155,533	174,365

Ocean 48 SS (1986-90)

Year	Power	Retail Low	Retail High
1990	T/Diesel	281,549	315,638
1989	T/Diesel	260,220	291,726
1988	T/Diesel	242,303	271,640
1987	T/Diesel	221,827	248,685
1986	T/Diesel	200,497	224,773

Ocean 48 SS (1991-94)

Year	Power	Retail Low	Retail High
1994	550D	402,393	451,114
1994	735D	427,543	479,308
1993	T/Diesel	369,123	413,815

Year	Power	Retail Low	Retail High
1992	T/Diesel	331,352	371,471
1991	T/Diesel	301,000	337,444

Ocean 48 Super Sport

Year	Power	Retail Low	Retail High
1995	620D	446,234	500,262
1995	760D	506,674	568,020

Ocean 50 Super Sport

Year	Power	Retail Low	Retail High
1985	T/Diesel	222,317	249,235
1984	T/Diesel	202,875	227,438
1983	T/Diesel	185,969	208,485
1982	T/Diesel	170,986	191,688

Ocean 53 Super Sport

Year	Power	Retail Low	Retail High
1995	760D	603,200	676,233
1995	820D	621,802	697,087
1994	760D	572,802	642,155
1994	820D	589,901	661,324
1993	760D	525,781	589,441
1993	820D	542,880	608,609
1992	735D	483,462	541,998
1992	820D	497,996	558,291
1991	735D	440,288	493,597
1991	820D	453,112	507,973

Ocean 55 Super Sport

Year	Power	Retail Low	Retail High
1990	T/Diesel	408,670	458,150
1989	T/Diesel	374,997	420,400
1988	T/Diesel	328,649	368,441
1987	T/Diesel	303,368	340,099
1986	T/Diesel	296,561	332,467
1985	T/Diesel	279,116	312,910
1984	T/Diesel	258,354	289,634
1983	T/Diesel	245,648	275,390
1982	T/Diesel	234,636	263,045
1981	T/Diesel	220,236	246,901

Ocean 58 Super Sport

Year	Power	Retail Low	Retail High
1995	1110 DD	******	******
1995	1200 MAN	******	******
1994	1080 DD	706,671	792,232
1994	1100 MAN	743,036	833,000
1993	1080 DD	620,479	695,604
1993	1100 MAN	645,130	723,240
1992	1050 MAN	616,021	690,606
1992	1080 DD	577,995	647,976
1991	1050 MAN	597,925	670,320
1991	1080 DD	562,522	630,630
1990	1050 MAN	526,244	589,960

Year	Power	Retail Low	Retail High
1990	1080 DD	511,209	573,104

Ocean 63 Super Sport

Year	Power	Retail Low	Retail High
1991	1050DD	731,781	820,382
1991	1050MAN	756,039	847,578
1990	1050DD	705,884	791,350
1990	1050MAN	730,798	819,280
1989	1050DD	671,329	752,611
1989	1050MAN	696,662	781,011
1988	1050DD	613,888	688,215
1987	1050DD	563,986	632,272
1986	1050DD	521,874	585,060

Ocean 66 Super Sport

Year	Power	Retail Low	Retail High
1995	1110 DD	1,090,924	1,223,009
1995	1200 MAN	1,146,091	1,284,855
1994	1080DD	1,044,036	1,170,443
1994	1100MAN	1,094,964	1,227,538
1993	1040DD	975,615	1,093,739
1993	1100MAN	1,026,963	1,151,304

Ocean Master 31 CC

Year	Power	Retail Low	Retail High
1995	T/200 OB	76,411	85,662
1994	T/200 OB	71,602	80,271
1993	T/200 OB	64,640	72,466
1992	T/200 OB	61,637	69,100
1991	T/200 OB	59,980	67,242
1990	T/200 OB	57,098	64,011
1989	T/200 OB	52,027	58,326
1988	T/200 OB	48,775	54,680
1987	T/200 OB	44,199	49,550
1986	T/200 OB	41,673	46,719
1985	T/200 OB	39,560	44,350
1984	T/200 OB	38,066	42,675
1983	T/200 OB	37,840	42,421
1982	T/200 OB	37,176	41,677
1981	T/200 OB	36,761	41,212
1980	T/200 OB	36,365	40,768
1979	T/200 OB	34,231	38,811
1978	T/200 OB	33,155	37,591
1977	T/200 OB	31,830	36,088
1976	T/200 OB	30,316	34,372
1975	T/200 OB	29,424	33,360

Orca 36

Year	Power	Retail Low	Retail High
1995	T/Diesel	******	******
1994	T/Diesel	******	******
1993	T/Diesel	******	******
1992	T/Diesel	******	******
1991	T/Diesel	******	******
1990	T/Diesel	******	******

Pace 36 SF

Year	Power	Retail Low	Retail High
1992	T/Gas	110,004	123,323
1992	T/Diesel	126,928	142,296
1991	T/Gas	101,542	113,837
1991	T/Diesel	118,466	132,810
1990	T/Gas	93,927	105,299
1990	T/Diesel	111,697	125,220
1989	T/Gas	85,056	95,354
1989	T/Diesel	103,768	116,332
1988	T/Gas	76,550	85,819
1988	T/Diesel	96,113	107,750

Pace 40 SF

Year	Power	Retail Low	Retail High
1992	T/Diesel	162,971	182,703
1991	T/Diesel	152,786	171,284
1990	T/Diesel	143,449	160,817
1989	T/Diesel	135,809	152,253
1988	T/Diesel	127,321	142,737

Pace 48 SF

Year	Power	Retail Low	Retail High
1992	T/Diesel	267,829	300,256
1991	T/Diesel	248,943	279,084
1990	T/Diesel	225,766	253,101
1989	T/Diesel	208,749	234,024
1988	T/Diesel	195,121	218,746
1987	T/Diesel	177,376	198,852

Pacemaker 30 SF

Year	Power	Retail Low	Retail High
1980	T/Gas	25,324	28,390
1979	T/Gas	21,220	24,059
1978	T/Gas	19,098	21,653
1977	T/Gas	17,970	20,374
1976	T/Gas	16,686	18,919
1975	T/Gas	15,403	17,464

Pacemaker 34 Convertible

Year	Power	Retail Low	Retail High
1992	T/Gas	108,186	121,285
1992	T/Diesel	131,732	147,682
1991	T/Gas	96,266	107,922
1991	T/Diesel	115,688	129,695
1990	T/Gas	87,656	98,270
1990	T/Diesel	101,857	114,190
1989	T/Gas	80,637	90,400
1989	T/Diesel	95,745	107,337

Year	Power	Retail Low	Retail High
1988	T/Gas	71,300	79,933
1988	T/Diesel	89,125	99,916

Pacemaker 36 SF

Year	Power	Retail Low	Retail High
1980	T/Gas	51,768	58,036
1980	T/Diesel	58,670	65,774
1979	T/Gas	46,069	52,232
1979	T/Diesel	53,747	60,937
1978	T/Gas	40,950	46,428
1977	T/Gas	34,765	39,417
1976	T/Gas	29,678	33,648
1975	T/Gas	26,527	30,076

Pacemaker 37 SF

Year	Power	Retail Low	Retail High
1992	T/Gas	134,551	150,842
1992	T/Diesel	178,700	200,336
1991	T/Gas	120,675	135,286
1991	T/Diesel	148,847	166,869
1990	T/Gas	109,322	122,559
1990	T/Diesel	135,392	151,784

Pacemaker 38 SF

Year	Power	Retail Low	Retail High
1980	T/Gas	61,873	69,365
1980	T/Diesel	78,289	87,768
1979	T/Gas	54,937	62,287
1979	T/Diesel	70,752	80,218

Pacemaker 40 SF

Year	Power	Retail Low	Retail High
1979	T/Gas	62,404	70,753
1979	T/Diesel	76,082	86,261
1978	T/Gas	53,001	60,092
1978	T/Diesel	64,969	73,661
1977	T/Gas	44,452	50,399
1977	T/Diesel	53,856	61,061
1976	T/Gas	34,920	39,592
1976	T/Diesel	46,269	52,459
1975	T/Gas	31,428	35,633
1975	T/Diesel	38,412	43,551

Pacemaker 48 SF

Year	Power	Retail Low	Retail High
1980	T/Diesel	140,189	157,163
1979	T/Diesel	129,844	147,216
1978	T/Diesel	120,194	136,274
1977	T/Diesel	109,666	124,338
1976	T/Diesel	92,996	105,438
1975	T/Diesel	77,205	87,534

Pacifica 36 SF

Year	Power	Retail Low	Retail High
1992	300D	182,776	204,906

Year	Power	Retail Low	Retail High
1992	375D	192,931	216,290
1991	300D	170,507	191,151
1991	375D	184,469	206,804
1990	300D	154,429	173,127
1990	375D	167,122	187,356
1989	300D	145,503	163,120
1989	375D	159,667	178,999
1988	300D	89,705	100,567
1988	375D	142,928	160,233
1987	300D	122,755	137,617
1987	375D	132,627	148,685
1986	300D	112,454	126,069
1986	355D	121,467	136,174
1985	300D	104,299	116,927
1985	355D	113,741	127,513
1984	T/Diesel	100,436	112,596
1983	T/Diesel	90,993	102,010
1982	T/Diesel	84,984	95,274
1981	T/Diesel	79,404	89,018
1980	T/Diesel	69,103	77,470
1979	T/Diesel	63,236	71,696
1978	T/Diesel	58,143	65,922
1977	T/Diesel	55,172	62,553
1976	T/Diesel	52,201	59,185
1975	T/Diesel	49,655	56,298

Pacifica 44 SF

Year	Power	Retail Low	Retail High
1995		******	******
1992	485D	345,726	387,585
1992	550D	354,057	396,924
1991	485D	317,401	355,831
1991	550D	324,066	363,303
1990	485D	287,411	322,209
1990	550D	295,741	331,549
1989	485D	268,250	300,729
1989	550D	280,746	314,738
1988	485D	251,588	282,050
1988	550D	265,751	297,927
1987	485D	237,010	265,706
1987	550D	251,588	282,050
1986	450D	228,341	255,988
1986	535D	242,076	271,386
1985	450D	214,177	240,109
1985	535D	224,907	252,138
1984	450D	200,013	224,230
1984	535D	210,314	235,778

Year	Power	Retail Low	Retail High
1983	450D	185,420	207,870
1983	535D	193,146	216,531
1982	T/Diesel	177,265	198,727
1981	T/Diesel	165,676	185,735
1980	T/Diesel	149,796	167,933
1979	T/Diesel	138,859	157,437
1978	T/Diesel	132,247	149,940
1977	T/Diesel	126,750	143,707
1976	T/Diesel	121,857	138,160
1975	T/Diesel	121,702	137,984

Phoenix 29 Convertible

Year	Power	Retail Low	Retail High
1987	T/Gas	44,209	49,562
1987	T/Diesel	56,656	63,516
1986	T/Gas	42,063	47,156
1986	T/Diesel	51,506	57,742
1985	T/Gas	39,488	44,269
1985	T/Diesel	47,643	53,411
1984	T/Gas	37,965	42,561
1984	T/Diesel	46,352	51,964
1983	T/Gas	34,433	38,602
1983	T/Diesel	41,496	46,521
1982	T/Gas	30,902	34,643
1982	T/Diesel	38,406	43,056
1981	T/Gas	28,694	32,168
1981	T/Diesel	35,316	39,592
1980	T/Gas	25,753	28,871
1980	T/Diesel	31,762	35,607
1979	T/Gas	24,038	27,254
1979	T/Diesel	30,270	34,320
1978	T/Gas	22,257	25,235
1978	T/Diesel	28,934	32,806
1977	T/Gas	20,477	23,216
1977	T/Diesel	26,709	30,282

Phoenix 29 SF Convertible

Year	Power	Retail Low	Retail High
1995	T/Gas	88,531	99,250
1995	T/Diesel	113,626	127,383
1994	T/Gas	101,070	113,308
1994	T/Diesel	101,796	114,121
1993	T/Gas	83,001	93,051
1993	T/Diesel	96,376	108,045
1992	T/Gas	78,792	88,331
1992	T/Diesel	92,696	103,919
1991	T/Gas	66,994	75,105
1991	T/Diesel	83,426	93,527
1990	T/Gas	58,567	65,658

Year	Power	Retail Low	Retail High
1990	T/Diesel	75,842	85,025
1989	T/Gas	52,859	59,259
1989	T/Diesel	68,258	76,522
1988	T/Gas	46,348	51,960
1988	T/Diesel	57,983	65,003

Phoenix 33/34 Convertible

Year	Power	Retail Low	Retail High
1995	T/Gas	158,099	177,241
1995	T/Diesel	232,143	260,250
1994	T/Gas	161,877	181,476
1994	T/Diesel	206,249	231,221
1993	T/Gas	151,195	169,501
1993	T/Diesel	194,335	217,864
1992	T/Gas	132,551	148,599
1992	T/Diesel	180,133	201,943
1991	T/Gas	118,956	133,358
1991	T/Diesel	162,290	181,939
1990	T/Gas	110,034	123,357
1990	T/Diesel	154,642	173,366
1989	T/Gas	93,560	104,887
1989	T/Diesel	131,676	147,619
1988	T/Gas	82,731	92,748
1988	T/Diesel	118,682	133,052
1987	T/Gas	76,234	85,464
1987	T/Diesel	108,287	121,398

Phoenix 33/34 Tournament

Year	Power	Retail Low	Retail High
1995	T/Gas	147,157	164,974
1995	T/Diesel	217,937	244,324
1994	T/Gas	143,738	161,141
1994	T/Diesel	196,485	220,275
1993	T/Gas	137,462	154,105
1993	T/Diesel	186,144	208,681
1992	T/Gas	123,715	138,694
1992	T/Diesel	169,150	189,630
1991	T/Gas	113,312	127,032
1991	T/Diesel	163,101	182,848
1990	T/Gas	103,869	116,446
1990	T/Diesel	151,941	170,338

Phoenix 37/38 Convertible

Year	Power	Retail Low	Retail High
1995	375D	307,028	344,202
1995	485D	330,235	370,219
1994	375D	290,242	325,384
1994	485D	308,858	346,254
1993	375D	266,549	298,822
1993	485D	285,165	319,692

Year	Power	Retail Low	Retail High
1992	375D	242,934	272,348
1992	485D	260,961	292,557
1991	375D	216,323	242,515
1991	485D	229,554	257,348
1990	375D	193,575	217,012
1990	485D	214,177	240,109
1989	375D	165,247	185,254
1989	485D	176,836	198,246

Phoenix 38 Convertible

Year	Power	Retail Low	Retail High
1988	375D	145,503	163,120
1988	485D	157,950	177,074
1987	375D	137,348	153,978
1987	450D	147,649	165,526
1986	375D	131,339	147,241
1986	450D	135,202	151,572
1985	355D	123,184	138,099
1985	410D	127,047	142,429
1984	355D	111,595	125,107
1984	410D	120,180	134,730
1983	300D	106,445	119,333
1983	410D	114,171	127,994
1982	300D	96,144	107,784
1982	410D	109,020	122,220

Post 42 SF

Year	Power	Retail Low	Retail High
1983	310D	127,047	142,429
1983	450D	148,508	166,488
1982	310D	124,472	139,542
1982	450D	142,499	159,752
1981	310D	124,472	139,542
1981	410D	134,773	151,091
1980	310D	114,171	127,994
1980	410D	126,188	141,467
1979	T/Diesel	108,647	123,182
1978	T/Diesel	101,856	115,483
1977	T/Diesel	94,985	107,692
1976	T/Diesel	85,729	97,198
1975	T/Diesel	81,485	92,387

Post 43 SF (Early)

Year	Power	Retail Low	Retail High
1989	T/Diesel	239,963	269,017
1988	T/Diesel	216,573	242,795
1987	T/Diesel	205,311	230,170
1986	T/Diesel	186,253	208,804
1985	T/Diesel	171,995	192,820
1984	T/Diesel	163,175	182,932

Post 43 SF

Year	Power	Retail Low	Retail High
1995	550D	412,389	462,320

Post 44 SF

Year	Power	Retail Low	Retail High
1994	T/Diesel	375,120	420,538
1993	T/Diesel	326,119	365,604
1992	T/Diesel	300,449	336,826
1991	T/Diesel	274,696	307,995
1990	T/Diesel	258,235	288,896

Post 46 SF

Year	Power	Retail Low	Retail High
1995	T/Diesel	475,108	532,632
1994	T/Diesel	422,219	473,340
1993	T/Diesel	370,784	415,677
1992	T/Diesel	334,786	375,320
1991	T/Diesel	313,325	351,261
1990	T/Diesel	291,006	326,240
1989	T/Diesel	267,829	300,256
1988	T/Diesel	248,085	278,122
1987	T/Diesel	218,898	245,402
1986	T/Diesel	194,004	217,493
1985	T/Diesel	187,137	209,794
1984	T/Diesel	180,269	202,096
1983	T/Diesel	173,402	194,397
1982	T/Diesel	165,676	185,735
1981	T/Diesel	157,092	176,112
1980	T/Diesel	148,508	166,488
1979	T/Diesel	136,657	154,940
1978	T/Diesel	127,320	144,354

Post 50 SF

Year	Power	Retail Low	Retail High
1995	T/Diesel	615,664	690,206
1994	T/Diesel	544,637	610,579
1993	T/Diesel	505,090	566,244
1992	T/Diesel	465,884	522,291
1991	T/Diesel	433,505	485,992
1990	T/Diesel	394,876	442,686
1989	T/Diesel	359,149	402,633

Precision 2800

Year	Power	Retail Low	Retail High
1994	T/Diesel	84,269	94,472
1993	T/Diesel	77,321	86,683
1992	T/Diesel	68,824	77,157

Pro-Line 2950 Walkaround

Year	Power	Retail Low	Retail High
1995	O/B*	42,597	47,754
1995	I/O Gas	62,656	70,242
1994	O/B*	39,242	43,993

Year	Power	Retail Low	Retail High
1994	T I/O Gas	61,366	68,796
1993	O/B*	35,882	40,226
1993	T I/O Gas	54,939	61,591
1992	O/B*	33,343	37,380
1992	T I/O Gas	45,497	51,005

Pursuit 2800 Open

Year	Power	Retail Low	Retail High
1992	O/B*	35,195	39,457
1991	O/B*	30,903	34,645
1990	O/B*	27,470	30,796
1989	O/B*	24,354	27,303

Pursuit 2855 Express

Year	Power	Retail Low	Retail High
1995	O/B*	56,080	62,870
1994	O/B*	52,589	58,957
1993	O/B*	47,435	53,179

Pursuit 3000 Express

Year	Power	Retail Low	Retail High
1995	T/Gas	101,876	114,211
1995	T/Diesel	126,503	141,819

Pursuit 3250

Year	Power	Retail Low	Retail High
1993	T/Gas	109,835	123,133
1993	T/Diesel	138,783	155,587
1992	T/Gas	103,023	115,497
1992	T/Diesel	122,606	137,451
1991	T/Gas	91,851	102,973
1991	T/Diesel	111,595	125,107
1990	T/Gas	82,409	92,387
1990	T/Diesel	103,011	115,483

Radovich 34 SF

Year	Power	Retail Low	Retail High
1994	T/Gas	******	******
1994	T/Diesel	******	******
1993	T/Gas	******	******
1993	T/Diesel	******	******
1992	T/Gas	******	******
1992	T/Diesel	******	******
1991	T/Gas	******	******
1991	T/Diesel	******	******
1990	T/Gas	******	******
1990	T/Diesel	******	******
1989	T/Gas	******	******
1989	T/Diesel	******	******
1988	T/Gas	******	******
1988	T/Diesel	******	******

Rampage 28 Sportsman

Year	Power	Retail Low	Retail High
1995	T/Gas	90,128	101,040

Year	Power	Retail Low	Retail High
1995	T/Diesel	112,956	126,632
1994	T/Gas	78,753	88,288
1994	T/Diesel	99,776	111,856
1993	T/Gas	69,653	78,086
1993	T/Diesel	86,437	96,902
1992	T/Gas	62,195	69,725
1992	T/Diesel	77,849	87,275
1991	T/Gas	58,254	65,307
1991	T/Diesel	71,961	80,674
1990	T/Gas	49,687	55,703
1990	T/Diesel	61,252	68,669
1989	T/Gas	47,117	52,822
1988	T/Gas	41,549	46,579
1987	T/Gas	39,407	44,178
1986	T/Gas	35,980	40,337

Rampage 31 SF

Year	Power	Retail Low	Retail High
1995	T/Gas	117,499	131,725
1995	T/Diesel	151,310	169,630
1994	T/Gas	105,486	118,258
1994	T/Diesel	134,558	150,850
1993	T/Gas	94,121	105,517
1993	T/Diesel	119,983	134,510
1992	T/Gas	85,641	96,011
1992	T/Diesel	105,568	118,350
1991	T/Gas	81,550	91,424
1991	T/Diesel	97,860	109,709
1990	T/Gas	69,532	77,951
1990	T/Diesel	90,135	101,048
1989	T/Gas	59,355	66,542
1989	T/Diesel	84,126	94,311
1988	T/Gas	48,930	54,855
1988	T/Diesel	79,404	89,018
1987	T/Gas	45,497	51,005
1987	T/Diesel	65,670	73,621
1986	T/Gas	43,350	48,599
1986	T/Diesel	59,661	66,884
1985	T/Gas	41,634	46,674
1985	T/Diesel	52,364	58,704

Rampage 33 SF

Year	Power	Retail Low	Retail High
1995	T/Gas	149,336	167,417
1995	T/Diesel	180,689	202,566
1994	T/Gas	125,871	141,111
1994	T/Diesel	163,423	183,210
1993	T/Gas	117,620	131,861
1993	T/Diesel	144,892	162,435

Year	Power	Retail Low	Retail High
1992	T/Gas	109,581	122,849
1992	T/Diesel	132,920	149,014
1991	T/Gas	105,157	117,889
1991	T/Diesel	124,901	140,023
1990	T/Gas	100,007	112,115
1990	T/Diesel	118,892	133,287

Rampage 36 SF

Year	Power	Retail Low	Retail High
1995	T/Diesel	251,214	281,630
1994	T/Diesel	222,659	249,618
1993	T/Diesel	201,168	225,524
1992	T/Diesel	186,278	208,832
1991	T/Diesel	169,968	190,547
1990	T/Diesel	159,559	178,877
1989	T/Diesel	152,720	171,211

Rampage 40 SF

Year	Power	Retail Low	Retail High
1990	T/Diesel	213,103	238,904
1989	T/Diesel	188,137	210,916
1988	T/Diesel	166,790	186,984

Riviera 33 Conv.

Year	Power	Retail Low	Retail High
1995	T/210 D	126,236	141,520
1994	T/210 D	122,086	136,868
1993	T/210 D	111,757	125,288
1992	T/210 D	102,241	114,620

Riviera 36 Conv.

Year	Power	Retail Low	Retail High
1995	T/315 D	175,921	197,221
1994	T/300 D	167,189	187,432
1993	T/300 D	158,508	177,700

Riviera 39 Conv.

Year	Power	Retail Low	Retail High
1995	T/ 375 D	242,927	272,340
1994	T/ 375 D	230,039	257,891
1993	T/ 375 D	219,760	246,368

Riviera 42 Conv.

Year	Power	Retail Low	Retail High
1995	T/ 375 D	283,140	317,422
1994	T/ 375 D	263,688	295,614
1993	T/ 375 D	248,090	278,128
1992	T/ 375 D	235,026	263,482

Riviera 48 Conv.

Year	Power	Retail Low	Retail High
1995	T/600 D	******	******
1994	T/ 550 D	******	******
1993	T/ 550 D	******	******

Ronin 38 Convertible

Year	Power	Retail Low	Retail High
1992	T/Diesel	184,815	207,192
1991	T/Diesel	176,414	197,774

Year	Power	Retail Low	Retail High
1990	T/Diesel	165,493	185,531
1989	T/Diesel	157,933	177,055
1988	T/Diesel	142,812	160,103
1987	T/Diesel	134,411	150,685
1986	T/Diesel	125,170	140,325

Ronin 48 Convertible

Year	Power	Retail Low	Retail High
1992	T/Diesel	315,493	353,692
1991	T/Diesel	301,152	337,615
1990	T/Diesel	288,079	322,959
1989	T/Diesel	272,738	305,760
1988	T/Diesel	252,283	282,828
1987	T/Diesel	225,861	253,208

Rybo Runner 30 CC

Year	Power	Retail Low	Retail High
1989	Seadrive	42,921	48,118
1989	T/Gas	60,885	68,257
1988	Seadrive	41,750	46,805
1988	T/Gas	56,536	63,382
1987	Seadrive	40,010	44,855
1987	T/Gas	53,057	59,481
1986	Seadrive	36,966	41,442
1986	T/Gas	46,534	52,168
1985	Seadrive	33,922	38,029
1985	T/Gas	42,620	47,780
1984	Seadrive	30,443	34,128
1984	T/Gas	39,141	43,880
1983	Seadrive	26,963	30,228
1983	T/Gas	36,531	40,954

Sea Ray 310 Amberjack/Laguna 31

Year	Power	Retail Low	Retail High
1994	T/Gas	79,225	88,817
1994	T/Diesel	117,571	131,806
1993	T/Gas	74,221	83,208
1993	T/Diesel	106,962	119,913
1992	T/Gas	66,299	74,326
1992	T/Diesel	94,504	105,946
1991	T/Gas	59,210	66,379
1991	T/Diesel	86,731	97,232

Sea Ray 310 Sport Bridge

Year	Power	Retail Low	Retail High
1993	T/Gas	81,332	91,179
1993	T/Diesel	104,468	117,117
1992	T/Gas	72,404	81,170
1992	T/Diesel	96,432	108,108

Sea Ray 390 Sedan SF

Year	Power	Retail Low	Retail High
1986	T/Gas	78,695	88,224

Year	Power	Retail Low	Retail High
1986	T/Diesel	101,542	113,837
1985	T/Gas	75,311	84,429
1985	T/Diesel	97,311	109,094
1984	T/Gas	71,080	79,686
1984	T/Diesel	84,619	94,864
1983	T/Gas	66,003	73,994
1983	T/Diesel	80,649	90,414

Sea Ray 440 Convertible

Year	Power	Retail Low	Retail High
1991	T/Diesel	200,856	225,175
1990	T/Diesel	182,517	204,615
1989	T/Diesel	160,685	180,140
1988	T/Diesel	153,065	171,598

Shamrock 31 Grand Slam

Year	Power	Retail Low	Retail High
1994	T/Gas	93,640	104,978
1994	T/Diesel	121,552	136,269
1993	T/Gas	88,238	98,921
1993	T/Diesel	112,548	126,175
1992	T/Gas	85,537	95,893
1992	T/Diesel	99,042	111,034
1991	T/Gas	77,433	86,808
1991	T/Diesel	90,939	101,949
1990	T/Gas	72,031	80,752
1990	T/Diesel	84,636	94,884
1989	T/Gas	65,670	73,621
1989	T/Diesel	76,829	86,131
1988	T/Gas	61,807	69,290
1988	T/Diesel	73,128	81,982
1987	T/Gas	57,514	64,478
1987	T/Diesel	69,330	77,724

Silverton 37 Convertible

Year	Power	Retail Low	Retail High
1995	T/Gas	139,043	155,878
1995	T/Diesel	175,114	196,316
1994	T/Gas	129,682	145,383
1994	T/Diesel	164,263	184,152
1993	T/Gas	124,494	139,568
1993	T/Diesel	155,618	174,460
1992	T/Gas	114,120	127,937
1992	T/Diesel	145,243	162,829
1991	T/Gas	97,693	109,522
1991	T/Diesel	131,843	147,806
1990	T/Gas	88,184	98,860

Silverton 41 Convertible

Year	Power	Retail Low	Retail High
1995	T/Gas	179,894	201,675
1995	T/Diesel	225,563	252,873
1994	T/Gas	168,188	188,552
1994	T/Diesel	208,554	233,803
1993	T/Gas	158,809	178,037
1993	T/Diesel	199,046	223,146
1992	T/Gas	145,074	162,639
1992	T/Diesel	183,469	205,682
1991	T/Gas	133,056	149,166
1991	T/Diesel	163,101	182,848

Southern Cross 44 SF

Year	Power	Retail Low	Retail High
1990	T/Diesel	240,359	269,461
1989	T/Diesel	231,775	259,837
1988	T/Diesel	223,191	250,214
1987	T/Diesel	206,022	230,966

Southern Cross 52 SF

Year	Power	Retail Low	Retail High
1990	T/Diesel	356,246	399,379
1989	T/Diesel	334,786	375,320
1988	T/Diesel	313,325	351,261
1987	T/Diesel	296,157	332,014
1986	T/Diesel	278,988	312,767

Stamas 288 Liberty

Year	Power	Retail Low	Retail High
1994	I/O Gas	63,523	71,215
1993	O/B*	45,497	51,005
1993	I/O Gas	55,798	62,553
1992	O/B*	39,488	44,269
1992	I/O Gas	49,359	55,336
1991	O/B*	36,054	40,419
1991	I/O Gas	45,926	51,486
1990	O/B*	32,620	36,570
1990	I/O Gas	42,492	47,637
1989	O/B*	31,762	35,607
1989	I/O Gas	39,917	44,750
1988	O/B*	29,186	32,720
1988	I/O Gas	37,341	41,863
1987	O/B*	25,412	28,489
1987	I/O Gas	35,625	39,938

Stamas 290 Express

Year	Power	Retail Low	Retail High
1995	O/B*	57,523	64,488
1994	O/B*	53,468	59,942
1993	O/B*	47,289	53,014
1992	O/B*	39,771	44,586

Stamas 290 Tarpon

Year	Power	Retail Low	Retail High
1995	T 200 O/B	61,915	69,411

Stamas 310 Express

Year	Power	Retail Low	Retail High
1995	O/B*	70,655	79,210
1995	T/Gas	85,646	96,016
1994	O/B*	66,894	74,994
1994	T/Gas	74,033	82,996
1993	O/B*	60,523	67,851
1993	T/Gas	66,629	74,697

Stamas 32 Sport Sedan/SF

Year	Power	Retail Low	Retail High
1987	T/Gas	57,514	64,478
1986	T/Gas	54,081	60,629
1985	T/Gas	48,501	54,373
1984	T/Gas	47,213	52,930
1983	T/Gas	43,350	48,599
1982	T/Gas	40,346	45,231
1981	T/Gas	36,912	41,381
1980	T/Gas	31,762	35,607
1979	T/Gas	27,586	31,277
1978	T/Gas	25,888	29,352
1977	T/Gas	22,069	25,021

Stamas 360 Express

Year	Power	Retail Low	Retail High
1995	T/Gas	160,811	180,281
1995	T/Diesel	201,964	226,417
1994	T/Gas	138,034	154,747
1994	T/Diesel	164,805	184,758
1993	T/Gas	120,466	135,052
1993	T/Diesel	146,400	164,126
1992	T/Gas	102,898	115,357
1992	T/Diesel	132,178	148,182

Stratos 3300 CC

Year	Power	Retail Low	Retail High
1995	T/OB*	49,172	55,125
1994	T/OB*	42,870	48,061
1993	T/OB*	38,573	43,243
1992	T/OB*	36,394	40,679

Strike 29 SF

Year	Power	Retail Low	Retail High
1995	T/Gas	98,315	110,219
1995	T/Diesel	117,397	131,611

Year	Power	Retail Low	Retail High
1989	T/Gas	55,798	62,553
1989	T/Diesel	66,873	74,970
1988	T/Gas	51,506	57,742
1988	T/Diesel	61,226	68,639
1987	T/Gas	48,930	54,855
1987	T/Diesel	57,625	64,602
1986	T/Gas	42,921	48,118
1986	T/Diesel	52,222	58,545
1985	T/Gas	36,054	40,419
1985	T/Diesel	45,920	51,479

Striker 34 Canyon Runner

Year	Power	Retail Low	Retail High
1975	T/Diesel	42,488	74,269

Striker 37 Canyon Runner

Year	Power	Retail Low	Retail High
1990	T/Diesel	206,022	230,966
1989	T/Diesel	193,416	216,531
1988	T/Diesel	175,977	197,284

Striker 41 SF

Year	Power	Retail Low	Retail High
1983	T/Diesel	164,959	221,202
1982	T/Diesel	159,959	215,202
1981	T/Diesel	153,959	210,202

Striker 44 SF

Year	Power	Retail Low	Retail High
1975	T/Diesel	140,344	210,456

Striker 50 SF

Year	Power	Retail Low	Retail High
1989	T/Diesel	472,134	529,298
1988	T/Diesel	436,080	488,879
1987	T/Diesel	407,752	457,121

Striker 54 SF

Year	Power	Retail Low	Retail High
1975	T/Diesel	199,712	363,710

Striker 58/60 SF

Year	Power	Retail Low	Retail High
1995	T/Diesel	******	******
1990	T/Diesel	772,583	866,124
1989	T/Diesel	708,201	793,947
1988	T/Diesel	652,403	731,394

Striker 62 SF

Year	Power	Retail Low	Retail High
1995	T/Diesel	******	******
1990	T/Diesel	1,030,110	1,154,832
1989	T/Diesel	965,728	1,082,655
1988	T/Diesel	897,054	1,005,666
1987	T/Diesel	828,380	928,677
1986	T/Diesel	816,202	912,477

Striker 70 SF

Year	Power	Retail Low	Retail High
1995	T/Diesel	******	******
1989	T/Diesel	1,420,694	1,592,706
1988	T/Diesel	1,339,143	1,501,282
1987	T/Diesel	1,258,451	1,410,820
1986	T/Diesel	1,188,919	1,332,869
1985	T/Diesel	1,107,368	1,241,444
1984	T/Diesel	1,030,110	1,154,832
1983	T/Diesel	961,436	1,077,843

Tiara 2900 Open

Year	Power	Retail Low	Retail High
1995	T/Gas	91,013	102,032
1994	T/Gas	79,474	89,097
1993	T/Gas	73,542	82,446

Tiara 3100 Open (Early)

Year	Power	Retail Low	Retail High
1992	T/Gas	88,847	99,604
1992	T/Diesel	113,357	127,081
1991	T/Gas	77,258	86,612
1991	T/Diesel	106,473	119,364
1990	T/Gas	71,678	80,357
1990	T/Diesel	97,242	109,015
1989	T/Gas	66,099	74,102
1989	T/Diesel	86,524	97,000
1988	T/Gas	60,519	67,846
1988	T/Diesel	77,254	86,608
1987	T/Gas	59,231	66,403
1987	T/Diesel	69,532	77,951
1986	T/Gas	53,652	60,148
1986	T/Diesel	64,382	72,177
1985	T/Gas	50,194	56,272
1985	T/Diesel	59,661	66,884
1984	T/Gas	48,072	53,892
1984	T/Diesel	51,506	57,742
1983	T/Gas	37,771	42,344
1983	T/Diesel	42,921	48,118
1982	T/Gas	35,195	39,457
1981	T/Gas	31,333	35,126
1980	T/Gas	28,253	31,674
1979	T/Gas	26,190	29,694

Tiara 3100 Open

Year	Power	Retail Low	Retail High
1995	T/Gas	126,165	140,230
1995	T/Diesel	161,167	179,470
1994	T/Gas	117,307	130,299
1994	T/Diesel	147,841	164,530
1993	T/Gas	96,965	117,584

Year	Power	Retail Low	Retail High
1993	T/Diesel	142,556	159,816
1992	T/Gas	96,369	106,826
1992	T/Diesel	134,806	151,128

Tiara 3100 Convertible

Year	Power	Retail Low	Retail High
1992	T/Gas	95,285	106,822
1991	T/Gas	87,130	97,680
1990	T/Gas	81,550	91,424
1989	T/Gas	73,825	82,763
1988	T/Gas	70,391	78,914
1987	T/Gas	67,816	76,026
1986	T/Gas	61,377	68,809
1985	T/Gas	58,802	65,922
1984	T/Gas	54,939	61,591
1983	T/Gas	51,076	57,260
1982	T/Gas	46,784	52,449

Tiara 3300 Flybridge

Year	Power	Retail Low	Retail High
1992	T/Gas	111,027	124,470
1992	T/Diesel	128,108	143,619
1991	T/Gas	100,351	112,502
1991	T/Diesel	119,568	134,044
1990	T/Gas	86,259	96,703
1990	T/Diesel	110,600	123,991
1989	T/Gas	80,281	90,001
1989	T/Diesel	104,195	116,810
1988	T/Gas	73,599	82,510
1988	T/Diesel	97,134	108,894
1987	T/Gas	70,604	79,152
1987	T/Diesel	93,282	104,577
1986	T/Gas	67,181	75,314
1986	T/Diesel	89,003	99,780

Tiara 3300 Open

Year	Power	Retail Low	Retail High
1995	T/Gas	128,133	143,647
1995	T/Diesel	164,316	184,211
1994	T/Gas	115,887	129,919
1994	T/Diesel	151,083	169,375
1993	T/Gas	107,732	120,776
1993	T/Diesel	139,923	156,865
1992	T/Gas	105,436	117,596
1992	T/Diesel	126,188	141,467
1991	T/Gas	91,422	102,491
1991	T/Diesel	115,029	128,956
1990	T/Gas	84,555	94,792
1990	T/Diesel	107,303	120,295
1989	T/Gas	78,546	88,056

Year	Power	Retail Low	Retail High
1989	T/Diesel	100,007	112,115
1988	T/Gas	72,262	81,012
1988	T/Diesel	89,138	99,931

Tiara 3600 Open

Year	Power	Retail Low	Retail High
1995	T/Gas	196,964	220,812
1995	T/Diesel	244,463	274,062
1994	T/Gas	174,134	195,218
1994	T/Diesel	232,701	260,875
1993	T/Gas	173,436	194,435
1993	T/Diesel	220,063	246,708
1992	T/Gas	148,597	166,589
1992	T/Diesel	193,481	216,907
1991	T/Gas	135,088	151,444
1991	T/Diesel	176,922	198,343
1990	T/Gas	122,755	137,617
1990	T/Diesel	161,813	181,405
1989	T/Gas	113,312	127,032
1989	T/Diesel	151,083	169,375
1988	T/Gas	99,864	111,9
1988	T/Diesel	132,855	148,940
1987	T/Gas	93,623	104,958
1987	T/Diesel	117,950	132,231
1986	T/Gas	86,966	97,495
1986	T/Diesel	115,660	129,664
1985	T/Gas	81,668	91,556
1985	T/Diesel	105,948	118,776

Tiara 3600 Convertible

Year	Power	Retail Low	Retail High
1995	T/Gas	196,964	220,812
1995	T/Diesel	233,759	262,062
1994	T/Gas	174,134	195,218
1994	T/Diesel	225,698	253,025
1993	T/Gas	168,217	188,584
1993	T/Diesel	213,441	239,284
1992	T/Gas	146,361	164,082
1992	T/Diesel	190,570	213,644
1991	T/Gas	133,056	149,166
1991	T/Diesel	174,260	195,359
1990	T/Gas	122,755	137,617
1990	T/Diesel	161,813	181,405
1989	T/Gas	113,312	127,032
1989	T/Diesel	151,083	169,375
1988	T/Gas	105,972	119,070
1988	T/Diesel	140,424	157,780
1987	T/Gas	100,303	112,700
1987	T/Diesel	133,447	149,940

Tiara 3700 Open

Year	Power	Retail Low	Retail High
1995	T/Diesel	273,108	303,511

Tiara 4300 Convertible

Year	Power	Retail Low	Retail High
1995	T/Diesel	451,004	505,610
1994	T/Diesel	407,009	456,288
1993	T/Diesel	363,371	407,366
1992	T/Diesel	323,090	362,208
1991	T/Diesel	292,039	327,398
1990	T/Diesel	272,738	305,760

Tiara 4300 Open

Year	Power	Retail Low	Retail High
1995	T/Diesel	376,745	422,360
1994	T/Diesel	343,370	384,944
1993	T/Diesel	327,918	367,622
1992	T/Diesel	311,513	349,230
1991	T/Diesel	292,723	328,165

Tollycraft 34 Sport Sedan

Year	Power	Retail Low	Retail High
1993	T/Gas	137,478	154,123
1992	T/Gas	127,167	142,564
1991	T/Gas	116,856	131,005
1990	T/Gas	107,405	120,409
1989	T/Gas	99,671	111,739
1988	T/Gas	94,619	106,076
1987	T/Gas	90,083	100,990

Tollycraft 37 Convertible

Year	Power	Retail Low	Retail High
1985	T/Gas	91,454	102,526
1985	T/Diesel	113,886	127,674
1984	T/Gas	84,551	94,789
1984	T/Diesel	105,258	118,002
1983	T/Gas	79,375	88,985
1983	T/Diesel	97,493	109,297
1982	T/Gas	75,061	84,149
1982	T/Diesel	89,728	100,592
1981	T/Gas	70,747	79,313
1981	T/Diesel	82,826	92,854
1980	T/Gas	66,433	74,477
1980	T/Diesel	78,512	88,018
1979	T/Gas	61,257	68,673
1979	T/Diesel	73,335	82,215
1978	T/Gas	56,080	62,870
1978	T/Diesel	66,433	74,477
1977	T/Gas	49,178	55,132
1977	T/Diesel	59,531	66,739
1976	T/Gas	45,727	51,263
1976	T/Diesel	56,080	62,870
1975	T/Gas	42,276	47,394
1975	T/Diesel	52,629	59,001

Tollycraft 40 Sport Sedan

Year	Power	Retail Low	Retail High
1995	T/Diesel	319,514	358,200
1994	T/Diesel	282,099	316,255
1993	T/Gas	220,236	246,901
1993	T/Diesel	260,048	291,533
1992	T/Gas	205,412	230,283
1992	T/Diesel	240,235	269,322
1991	T/Gas	175,260	196,480
1991	T/Diesel	213,305	239,131
1990	T/Gas	164,146	184,020
1990	T/Diesel	202,191	226,671
1989	T/Gas	151,322	169,644
1989	T/Diesel	186,374	208,940
1988	T/Gas	129,622	145,316
1988	T/Diesel	165,676	185,735
1987	T/Gas	123,184	138,099
1987	T/Diesel	154,517	173,225

Topaz 29 SF

Year	Power	Retail Low	Retail High
1988	T/Gas	45,675	51,205
1988	T/Diesel	55,723	62,470
1987	T/Gas	42,934	48,133
1987	T/Diesel	50,699	56,838
1986	T/Gas	41,107	46,084
1986	T/Diesel	47,959	53,765
1985	T/Gas	36,997	41,476
1985	T/Diesel	43,848	49,157
1984	T/Gas	33,799	37,892
1984	T/Diesel	41,564	46,597
1983	T/Gas	32,278	36,186
1983	T/Diesel	40,117	44,975

Topaz 32 SF

Year	Power	Retail Low	Retail High
1991	T/Diesel	124,181	139,217
1990	T/Diesel	112,699	126,344
1989	T/Diesel	106,320	119,192
1988	T/Diesel	97,814	109,657
1987	T/Diesel	90,584	101,552
1986	T/Diesel	86,524	97,000

Topaz 32 Royale

Year	Power	Retail Low	Retail High
1991	T/Diesel	129,622	145,316
1990	T/Diesel	115,217	129,167

Topaz 36 SF

Year	Power	Retail Low	Retail High
1985	T/Diesel	91,827	102,945
1984	T/Diesel	87,496	98,089
1983	T/Diesel	82,298	92,262
1982	T/Diesel	75,367	84,493
1981	T/Diesel	66,637	74,705
1980	T/Diesel	59,714	66,944

Topaz 37 SF

Year	Power	Retail Low	Retail High
1991	T/Diesel	168,421	188,813
1990	T/Diesel	159,872	179,228
1989	T/Diesel	150,467	168,685
1988	T/Diesel	141,918	159,101
1987	T/Diesel	132,514	148,558
1986	T/Diesel	124,218	139,258

Topaz 38 FB

Year	Power	Retail Low	Retail High
1987	T/Diesel	141,640	158,789
1986	T/Diesel	134,773	151,091
1985	T/Diesel	124,472	139,542

Topaz 39 Royale

Year	Power	Retail Low	Retail High
1991	T/Diesel	200,985	225,320
1990	T/Diesel	182,845	204,983
1989	T/Diesel	173,402	194,397
1988	T/Diesel	163,101	182,848

Trojan 36 Convertible

Year	Power	Retail Low	Retail High
1989	T/Gas	92,789	104,023
1988	T/Gas	86,718	97,218
1987	T/Gas	81,515	91,385
1986	T/Gas	77,179	86,524
1985	T/Gas	72,844	81,663
1984	T/Gas	69,375	77,774
1983	T/Gas	66,773	74,858
1982	T/Gas	63,304	70,969
1981	T/Gas	59,836	67,080
1980	T/Gas	54,633	61,247
1979	T/Gas	48,875	55,414
1978	T/Diesel	43,731	49,581
1977	T/Gas	39,443	44,720
1976	T/Gas	37,246	42,229
1975	T/Gas	34,927	39,600

Trojan 12 Meter Convertible

Year	Power	Retail Low	Retail High
1992	T/Gas	172,035	192,864
1992	T/Diesel	209,798	235,200
1991	T/Gas	156,545	175,498

Year	Power	Retail Low	Retail High
1991	T/Diesel	199,700	223,879
1990	T/Gas	149,775	167,909
1990	T/Diesel	186,161	208,701
1989	T/Gas	135,390	151,782
1989	T/Diesel	166,276	186,408
1988	T/Gas	128,620	144,193
1988	T/Diesel	154,852	173,601
1987	T/Gas	117,197	131,387
1987	T/Diesel	142,582	159,846
1986	T/Gas	107,889	120,952
1986	T/Diesel	130,313	146,091

Uniflite 28 Salty Dog

Year	Power	Retail Low	Retail High
1984	T/Gas	31,470	35,280
1983	T/Gas	29,721	33,320
1982	T/Gas	26,225	29,400
1981	S/Gas	20,106	22,540
1981	T/Gas	24,914	27,930
1980	S/Gas	17,920	20,090
1980	T/Gas	21,417	24,010
1979	S/Gas	15,558	17,640
1979	T/Gas	18,584	21,070
1978	S/Gas	13,830	15,680
1978	T/Gas	17,287	19,600
1977	S/Gas	12,965	14,700
1977	T/Gas	15,991	18,130
1976	S/Gas	12,101	13,720
1976	T/Gas	14,694	16,660
1975	S/Gas	11,237	12,740
1975	T/Gas	13,398	15,190

Uniflite 32 Sport Sedan

Year	Power	Retail Low	Retail High
1984	T/Gas	51,819	58,093
1983	T/Gas	46,637	52,284
1982	T/Gas	43,183	48,411
1981	T/Gas	40,592	45,506
1980	T/Gas	38,001	42,602
1979	T/Gas	35,013	39,697
1978	T/Gas	32,451	36,792
1977	T/Gas	30,743	34,856
1976	T/Gas	29,035	32,919
1975	T/Gas	27,327	30,983

Uniflite 34 Sport Sedan

Year	Power	Retail Low	Retail High
1984	T/Gas	60,948	68,328
1984	T/Diesel	74,164	83,143
1983	T/Gas	56,227	63,035

Year	Power	Retail Low	Retail High
1983	T/Diesel	70,391	78,914
1982	T/Gas	54,081	60,629
1982	T/Diesel	66,528	74,583
1981	T/Gas	51,138	57,330
1981	T/Diesel	61,628	69,090
1980	T/Gas	47,677	53,449
1980	T/Diesel	56,506	63,347
1979	T/Gas	40,158	45,531
1979	T/Diesel	51,507	58,398
1978	T/Gas	35,793	40,582
1978	T/Diesel	47,142	53,449
1977	T/Gas	32,301	36,623
1977	T/Diesel	41,904	47,510
1976	T/Gas	30,555	34,643
1976	T/Diesel	38,412	43,551
1975	T/Gas	27,500	31,179
1975	T/Diesel	35,793	40,582

Uniflite 36 Sport Sedan

Year	Power	Retail Low	Retail High
1984	T/Gas	71,249	79,876
1984	T/Diesel	84,126	94,311
1983	T/Gas	67,386	75,545
1983	T/Diesel	80,692	90,462
1982	T/Gas	64,382	72,177
1982	T/Diesel	75,541	84,688
1981	T/Gas	59,880	67,130
1981	T/Diesel	72,992	81,830
1980	T/Gas	55,181	61,862
1980	T/Diesel	64,452	72,255
1979	T/Gas	47,142	53,449
1979	T/Diesel	56,745	64,337
1978	T/Gas	44,523	50,480
1978	T/Diesel	51,944	58,893
1977	T/Gas	40,595	46,026
1977	T/Diesel	47,142	53,449
1976	T/Gas	35,793	40,582
1976	T/Diesel	42,777	48,500
1975	T/Gas	36,230	41,077
1975	T/Diesel	39,285	44,541

Uniflite 38 Convertible

Year	Power	Retail Low	Retail High
1984	T/Diesel	118,463	132,806
1983	T/Diesel	109,449	122,701
1982	T/Diesel	102,153	114,521
1981	T/Diesel	96,573	108,266
1980	T/Diesel	89,276	100,085
1979	T/Diesel	80,212	90,943

Year	Power	Retail Low	Retail High
1978	T/Diesel	77,014	87,318
1977	T/Diesel	71,024	80,527

Uniflite 42 Convertible

Year	Power	Retail Low	Retail High
1984	T/Diesel	145,932	163,601
1983	T/Diesel	136,919	153,496
1982	T/Diesel	130,051	145,798
1981	T/Diesel	119,321	133,768
1980	T/Diesel	106,016	118,851
1979	T/Diesel	98,105	111,230
1978	T/Diesel	91,691	103,958
1977	T/Diesel	86,401	97,961
1976	T/Diesel	81,112	91,963
1975	T/Diesel	75,822	85,966

Uniflite 48 Convertible

Year	Power	Retail Low	Retail High
1984	T/Diesel	212,028	237,699
1983	T/Diesel	203,373	227,997
1982	T/Diesel	190,392	213,444
1981	T/Diesel	179,142	200,831
1980	T/Diesel	170,487	191,129

Viking 35 Convertible

Year	Power	Retail Low	Retail High
1992	T/Gas	140,782	157,827
1992	T/Diesel	169,110	189,585
1991	T/Gas	121,896	136,655
1991	T/Diesel	156,233	175,150
1990	T/Gas	111,595	125,107
1990	T/Diesel	144,215	161,676
1989	T/Gas	102,582	115,002
1989	T/Diesel	131,768	147,722
1988	T/Gas	97,002	108,747
1988	T/Diesel	123,184	138,099
1987	T/Gas	92,710	103,935
1987	T/Diesel	118,463	132,806
1986	T/Gas	91,851	102,973
1986	T/Diesel	112,454	126,069
1985	T/Gas	88,418	99,123
1985	T/Diesel	108,162	121,257
1984	T/Gas	78,975	88,537
1984	T/Diesel	94,427	105,860
1983	T/Gas	75,541	84,688
1983	T/Diesel	85,843	96,236
1982	T/Gas	69,532	77,951
1982	T/Diesel	79,834	89,499
1981	T/Gas	63,953	71,696
1981	T/Diesel	76,400	85,650

Year	Power	Retail Low	Retail High
1980	T/Gas	60,519	67,846
1980	T/Diesel	72,108	80,838
1979	T/Gas	57,294	64,959
1979	T/Diesel	67,055	76,026
1978	T/Gas	54,323	61,591
1978	T/Diesel	62,811	71,215
1977	T/Gas	52,626	59,666
1977	T/Diesel	59,416	67,365
1976	T/Gas	49,655	56,298
1976	T/Diesel	56,021	63,516
1975	T/Gas	47,957	54,373
1975	T/Diesel	53,474	60,629

Viking 35 SF

Year	Power	Retail Low	Retail High
1986	T/Gas	79,243	88,837
1986	T/Diesel	102,153	114,521
1985	T/Gas	72,966	81,801
1985	T/Diesel	93,139	104,416
1984	T/Gas	66,099	74,102
1984	T/Diesel	84,126	94,311

Viking 38 Convertible

Year	Power	Retail Low	Retail High
1995	T/Diesel	346,553	388,512
1994	T/Diesel	322,909	362,006
1993	T/Diesel	299,630	335,908
1992	T/Diesel	273,408	306,512
1991	T/Diesel	242,934	272,348
1990	T/Diesel	230,936	258,896

Viking 40 Sedan

Year	Power	Retail Low	Retail High
1983	T/Gas	119,321	133,768
1983	T/Diesel	133,056	149,166
1982	T/Gas	103,869	116,446
1982	T/Diesel	124,472	139,542
1981	T/Gas	97,860	109,709
1981	T/Diesel	117,604	131,843
1980	T/Gas	91,851	102,973
1980	T/Diesel	106,445	119,333
1979	T/Gas	84,880	96,236
1979	T/Diesel	95,066	107,784
1978	T/Gas	78,090	88,537
1978	T/Diesel	85,729	97,198
1977	T/Gas	70,026	79,395
1977	T/Diesel	81,061	91,905
1976	T/Gas	63,660	72,177
1976	T/Diesel	75,543	85,650
1975	T/Gas	57,307	64,974

Year	Power	Retail Low	Retail High
1975	T/Diesel	71,299	80,838

Viking 41 Convertible

Year	Power	Retail Low	Retail High
1989	T/Gas	171,685	192,472
1989	T/Diesel	225,766	253,101
1988	T/Gas	161,384	180,924
1988	T/Diesel	206,880	231,929
1987	T/Gas	152,800	171,300
1987	T/Diesel	189,583	212,537
1986	T/Gas	139,065	155,902
1986	T/Diesel	172,114	192,953
1985	T/Gas	130,051	145,798
1985	T/Diesel	161,384	180,924
1984	T/Gas	122,755	137,617
1984	T/Diesel	151,941	170,338
1983	T/Gas	115,458	129,437
1983	T/Diesel	144,215	161,676

Viking 43 Convertible

Year	Power	Retail Low	Retail High
1995	550hp DD	436,974	489,881
1995	600hp MAN	456,989	512,320
1994	T/Diesel	396,912	444,969
1993	T/Diesel	359,511	403,040
1992	T/Diesel	321,909	360,885
1991	T/Diesel	294,837	330,534
1990	T/Diesel	282,529	316,736

Viking 43 Express Yacht/SF

Year	Power	Retail Low	Retail High
1995	550hp DD	383,259	429,663
1995	600hp MAN	408,670	458,150
1994	T/Diesel	369,123	413,815

Viking 45 Convertible

Year	Power	Retail Low	Retail High
1993	T/Diesel	377,707	423,438
1992	T/Diesel	347,662	389,756
1991	T/Diesel	323,439	362,600
1990	T/Diesel	305,323	342,290
1990	T/Diesel	287,406	322,204
1989	T/Diesel	266,112	298,332
1988	T/Diesel	246,368	276,197
1987	T/Diesel	231,775	259,837

Viking 46 Convertible

Year	Power	Retail Low	Retail High
1985	T/Diesel	230,487	258,394
1984	T/Diesel	212,460	238,184
1983	T/Diesel	202,588	227,117
1982	T/Diesel	191,858	215,087
1981	T/Diesel	181,986	204,020

Year	Power	Retail Low	Retail High

Viking 47 Convertible

Year	Power	Retail Low	Retail High
1995	T/diesel	578,178	648,182
1994	T/Diesel	540,808	606,287

Viking 48 Convertible

Year	Power	Retail Low	Retail High
1990	T/Diesel	362,133	405,979
1989	T/Diesel	342,349	383,799
1988	T/Diesel	318,264	356,798
1987	T/Diesel	289,018	324,012
1986	T/Diesel	267,944	300,386
1985	T/Diesel	253,235	283,896

Viking 50 Convertible

Year	Power	Retail Low	Retail High
1995	820D	686,617	769,750
1994	820D	660,987	741,017
1993	735D	579,437	649,593
1993	820D	622,358	697,711
1992	735D	546,350	612,500
1992	820D	579,437	649,593
1991	735D	519,181	582,042

Viking 53 Convertible

Year	Power	Retail Low	Retail High
1995	T/Diesel	812,677	911,073
1994	T/Diesel	769,436	862,596
1993	T/Diesel	701,041	785,921
1992	T/Diesel	652,403	731,394
1991	T/Diesel	583,729	654,405
1990	T/Diesel	532,363	596,820

Viking 57 Convertible

Year	Power	Retail Low	Retail High
1991	T/Diesel	698,707	783,304
1990	T/Diesel	655,106	734,424
1989	T/Diesel	623,101	698,544

Viking 58 Convertible

Year	Power	Retail Low	Retail High
1995	1200MAN	1,064,235	1,193,089
1994	1100MAN	944,268	1,058,596
1993	1100MAN	875,594	981,607
1992	1100MAN	858,425	962,360
1991	1100MAN	815,504	914,242

Viking 68 Conv

Year	Power	Retail Low	Retail High
1995	T/Diesel	******	******

Wellcraft 2800 Coastal

Year	Power	Retail Low	Retail High
1994	T/Gas	57,348	64,292
1993	T/Gas	48,463	54,331
1992	T/Gas	44,829	50,256
1991	T/Gas	41,194	46,182
1990	T/Gas	36,348	40,748
1989	T/Gas	33,521	37,579
1988	T/Gas	31,097	34,863
1987	T/Gas	29,078	32,599
1986	T/Gas	27,463	30,788

Wellcraft 2900 Sport Bridge

Year	Power	Retail Low	Retail High
1986	T/Gas	34,337	38,494
1985	T/Gas	32,620	36,570
1984	T/Gas	30,045	33,683
1983	T/Gas	27,470	30,796

Wellcraft 3200 Coastal

Year	Power	Retail Low	Retail High
1986	T/Gas	43,180	48,408
1985	T/Gas	39,377	44,144
1984	T/Gas	35,788	40,121

Wellcraft 3300 Coastal

Year	Power	Retail Low	Retail High
1995	T/Gas	95,727	107,317
1994	T/Gas	88,397	99,100
1993	T/Gas	80,657	90,423
1992	T/Gas	73,732	82,659
1991	T/Gas	69,251	77,636
1990	T/Gas	61,104	68,502
1989	T/Gas	54,586	61,195

Wellcraft 3300 Sport Bridge

Year	Power	Retail Low	Retail High
1992	T/Gas	81,791	91,694
1991	T/Gas	72,839	81,658

Notes

Notes

Notes

Notes

Notes

Notes